T5-CRZ-207

Developing Cultures

WITHDRAWN

Also Available:
Developing Cultures: Case Studies
edited by Lawrence E. Harrison and Peter L. Berger

Culture Matters Research Project Advisory Board

Morris Altman
University of Saskatchewan

Tamar Jacoby
Manhattan Institute

Stephen Bosworth
The Fletcher School, Tufts University

Timur Kuran
University of Southern California

Harold Caballeros
El Shaddai Church, Guatemala

Roderick MacFarquhar
Harvard University

Houchang Chehabi
Boston University

Harvey Nelsen
University of South Florida

Kent R. Hill
U.S. Agency for International Development

Lucian Pye
Massachusetts Institute of Technology

Robert Hodam
International Center for Economic Growth

Robert Rotberg
Harvard University

Ronald Inglehart
University of Michigan

John Sanbrailo
Pan-American Development Foundation

MONTGOMERY COLLEGE
ROCKVILLE CAMPUS LIBRARY
ROCKVILLE, MARYLAND

Developing Cultures

Essays on Cultural Change

Edited by

Lawrence E. Harrison
and Jerome Kagan

Routledge
Taylor & Francis Group
New York London

346680

NOV 2 0 2006

Published in 2006 by
Routledge
Taylor & Francis Group
270 Madison Avenue
New York, NY 10016

Published in Great Britain by
Routledge
Taylor & Francis Group
2 Park Square
Milton Park, Abingdon
Oxon OX14 4RN

© 2006 by Lawrence E. Harrison and Jerome Kagan.
Routledge is an imprint of Taylor & Francis Group

Printed in the United States of America on acid-free paper
10 9 8 7 6 5 4 3 2 1

International Standard Book Number-10: 0-415-95281-6 (Hardcover) 0-415-95282-4 (Softcover)
International Standard Book Number-13: 978-0-415-95281-1 (Hardcover) 978-0-415-95282-8 (Softcover)
Library of Congress Card Number 2005013571

No part of this book may be reprinted, reproduced, transmitted, or utilized in any form by any electronic, mechanical, or other means, now known or hereafter invented, including photocopying, microfilming, and recording, or in any information storage or retrieval system, without written permission from the publishers.

Trademark Notice: Product or corporate names may be trademarks or registered trademarks, and are used only for identification and explanation without intent to infringe.

Library of Congress Cataloging-in-Publication Data

Developing cultures : essays on cultural change / edited by Lawrence Harrison and Jerome Kagan.
    p. cm.
  Includes bibliographical references and index.
  ISBN 0-415-95281-6 (hb : alk. paper) -- ISBN 0-415-95282-4 (pb : alk. paper)
  1. Progress. 2. Social values. 3. Social change. 4. Culture. I. Harrison, Lawrence E. II. Kagan, Jerome.

HM891.D48 2005
306'.09172'4--dc22   2005013571

Taylor & Francis Group
is the Academic Division of Informa plc.

Visit the Taylor & Francis Web site at
http://www.taylorandfrancis.com

and the Routledge Web site at
http://www.routledge-ny.com

Contents

Part III Religion

Part IV The Media

Acknowledgments

We wish to express our profound gratitude to the Fletcher School at Tufts University, and particularly to its dean, Stephen Bosworth, for providing the Culture Matters Research Project (CMRP), on which this book is based, with an ideal home. The CMRP was made possible by the generous financial support of the Smith Richard Foundation, the John Templeton Foundation, the Donner Foundation, and the Sidney A. Swensrud Foundation.

We are especially indebted to Lupita Ervin, who managed the administration of the CMRP, including two major conferences, with skill and diligence, also to Fran Parisi for her help with financial administration.

The book has been the beneficiary of the skillful and sure hands of editors George Scialabba and Helen Snively in Cambridge, Massachusetts, and Lynn Goeller at EvS Communications.

Finally, our thanks to Rob Tempio at Routledge for his unflagging interest and support.

Introduction

LAWRENCE E. HARRISON

In April 1999, a group of scholars, journalists, politicians, and development practitioners met in Cambridge, Massachusetts, to discuss the relationship between cultural values and human progress. What motivated the organizing of the symposium—and what has motivated my work on culture over the past quarter century—was the conviction that values, beliefs, and attitudes are a key but neglected component of development and that the neglect of cultural factors may go a long way toward explaining the agonizingly slow progress toward democratic governance, prosperity, and social justice in so many countries in Africa, Latin America, the Islamic world, and elsewhere. Understanding how culture influences the behavior of individuals and societies, and which forces shape cultural change, can, I believe, accelerate the pace of progress.[1]

In the 1999 symposium, sponsored by the Academy for International and Area Studies of Harvard University, a wide range of views was presented. Many thought that cultural values were influential in the political, economic, and social evolution of societies; but others disagreed. Economist Jeffrey Sachs argued that cultural values played an insignificant role and that other factors, particularly geography, were far more influential. Anthropologist Richard Shweder argued that the fundamental thesis of the symposium was invalid because the idea of "progress," and indeed the UN Universal Declaration of Human Rights, which offers a widely accepted definition of progress, is a Western imposition on the rest of the world.

One year later, in the spring of 2000, the papers prepared for the symposium were published in the book *Culture Matters*[2] along with commentary by its coeditors, Samuel Huntington, then Chairman of the Harvard Academy, and me. The book received favorable critical attention in *The New York Times, The Washington Post, The Wall Street Journal, The Boston Globe, Foreign Affairs,* and *Time,* among other newspapers and magazines. Eight foreign-language editions have been published: two in Chinese (Beijing and Taipei), and one each in Estonian, German, Korean, Polish, Portuguese, and Spanish. A ninth, in Arabic, was contracted in 2005. Not least important and gratifying, *Culture Matters* was for several years a best-seller at the World Bank bookstore.

During the final session of the 1999 symposium, we tried to focus attention on the malleability of culture and what might be done to strengthen the values and attitudes that nurture progress. No one at the symposium believed that culture is genetically determined. Everyone believed that culture is acquired—transmitted from generation to generation through the family, the church, the school, and other socializing instruments.[3] But it was clear in that final session that the collective wisdom, substantial though it was, was not prepared to address cultural change and what promotes or impedes it. We did not have a satisfactory disaggregation of the word *culture* into components that would allow a better understanding of *how* culture influences the behaviors that promote progress. The participants in the symposium agreed that culture changes, but many were uncomfortable discussing measures to encourage or facilitate cultural change. Thus, my introduction to *Culture Matters* called for a comprehensive research program aimed at better understanding culture, cultural transmission, and cultural change, and particularly the factors that drive change.

By the spring of 2002, two years after the publication of *Culture Matters*, we had raised the money necessary to make that research program possible. Since then, more than sixty professionals from around the world, mostly scholars but also journalists, development practitioners, politicians, and businesspeople, have participated in the Culture Matters Research Project (CMRP) administered by the Fletcher School at Tufts University. The goal of the CMRP is to produce guidelines for strengthening the values and attitudes that nurture human progress as defined by the UN Universal Declaration of Human Rights:

- The right to life, liberty, and security of person
- Equality before the law
- Freedom of thought, conscience, and religion
- The right to take part in...government...directly or through chosen representatives
- [The right to assure that] the will of the people [is] the basis of the authority of government
- The right to an [adequate] standard of living
- [The right to] adequate medical care and necessary social services
- The right to education

As I mentioned at the outset, anthropologist Richard Shweder views the UN Declaration as anything but "universal." He sees it as an imposition of Western values on the rest of the world, as did the American Anthropological Association when they opposed the Declaration. Allegations of Western bias notwithstanding, I believe that the large majority of the world's people would today agree with the following affirmations, which are essentially a restatement of the UN Declaration:

Life is better than death.
Health is better than sickness.
Liberty is better than slavery.
Prosperity is better than poverty.
Education is better than ignorance.
Justice is better than injustice.

I want to stress as forcefully as I can that the CMRP guidelines will only prove useful when political, intellectual, and other leaders *within* a society conclude that some traditional values and attitudes are obstacles to bringing about the kind of society to which they aspire. Any efforts to impose the guidelines from outside, whether by governments or development assistance institutions, are almost certain to fail.

To produce the guidelines, the CMRP sought to address three tasks:

Task 1. What are the values, beliefs, and attitudes that influence the political, economic, and social evolution of societies?

Task 2. What are the instruments and institutions that transmit cultural values, beliefs, and attitudes, and how amenable are they to application or modification for the purpose of promoting progressive values?

Task 3. What can we learn about the role of culture and cultural change from case studies, including studies of societies that have experienced political, economic, and social transformations?

With respect to the values and attitudes that matter (Task 1), the CMRP has produced a typology of cultural values that derives principally from the work of the Argentine journalist and scholar Mariano Grondona, who is a professor of political science at the National University of Buenos Aires and has been a visiting professor at Harvard. The typology consists of twenty-five factors that are viewed very differently in cultures conducive to progress and cultures that resist progress. By disaggregating "culture," the typology offers specific value, belief, and attitude targets for change. The typology is presented in the CMRP overview book *The Central Liberal Truth* by Lawrence Harrison, published by Oxford University Press. That title derives from Daniel Patrick Moynihan's aphorism, "The central conservative truth is that it is culture, not politics, that determines the success of a society. The central liberal truth is that politics can change a culture and save it from itself."

The instruments and institutions of cultural transmission and change (Task 2) are the focus of this book, including child-rearing practices, several aspects of education, religion, the media, political leadership, and development projects. The Task 3 case studies make up the companion volume *Developing Cultures: Case Studies*.

The *Central Liberal Truth* makes clear our appreciation that numerous factors other than culture influence the evolution of societies, prominent among them geography, including climate and the environment; the vagaries of history, including conquests and colonization; and leaders with a transforming vision. The CMRP attempts to trace one thread—culture—in a highly complex tapestry of cause and effect. But we believe it may be a crucial thread, one that has not been accorded the attention it merits.

Child rearing, education, religion, and the media are the principal means of transmitting cultural values from generation to generation, and modifications or reforms of these instruments or institutions are central to the process of cultural change, strengthening the values and attitudes that nurture human progress.

Political leadership with a vision of a better society has been the driving force behind many of the transformations the world has witnessed in the past 150 years, among them Japan's rapid modernization under the Meiji leadership starting in 1868; Mustafa Kemal's cultural revolution in Turkey starting in 1923; Seretse Khama's visionary democratic leadership of Botswana following its independence in 1966; Lee Kuan Yew's leadership of Singapore's economic and social transformation; and King Juan Carlos's democratic vision for Spain.

Since the 1950s, "development," initially focused on accelerating economic growth but subsequently embracing social and political dimensions, has been the dominant priority of the poor, mostly authoritarian and unjust, countries. The rich, mostly democratic countries have attached varying priorities—high in the Scandinavian countries, lower in the United States—to helping the poor countries, bilaterally and through multilateral institutions such as the World Bank, the UN Development Program, and regional development banks, as well as through their support of nongovernmental organizations such as CARE and Catholic Relief Services.

Fifty years later the results have, with a few exceptions, been disappointing, even disillusioning, above all in Africa, but also in Latin America and the Islamic countries. Fifty years ago, many development experts expected poverty and injustice to be eliminated from the world by the end of the twentieth century. That so much poverty and injustice is still with us importantly reflects, I believe, a failure to appreciate the power of culture to thwart or facilitate progress.

For most development institutions, cultural change is a taboo. This attitude is driven by cultural relativism, the idea that no culture is better or worse than any other. This idea was initially propagated by anthropologists and now is largely accepted throughout the development and academic communities. As a result, cultural analysis has largely been limited to adapting projects to the existing culture.

Most of the contributors to *Culture Matters* rejected this conventional wisdom, concluding that we have failed to confront culture and cultural change at great cost. The Culture Matters Research Project both confronts culture and presents guidelines for cultural change grounded in the lessons of experience. The essays in this volume address the principal tools available to promote progressive cultural change.

Notes

1. I appreciate that the word *progress* implies a value judgment with which some people may be uncomfortable. I use it in this book as shorthand for the goals of democratic governance, an end to poverty, and social justice articulated in the UN Universal Declaration of Human Rights.
2. Lawrence Harrison and Samuel Huntington, eds., *Culture Matters* (New York: Basic Books, 2000).
3. In its 3 June 2005 edition, the *New York Times* reports on a study by three researchers at the University of Utah that presents evidence that higher-than-average IQs of Ashkenazic Jews are the result of a centuries-long process of genetic selection ("Researchers Say Intelligence and Disease May Be Linked in Ashkenazic Genes," p. A21). But one wonders how the comparably high IQs of East Asians would then be explained.

Part I
Child Rearing

1

Culture, Values, and the Family

JEROME KAGAN

The "Culture Matters" project celebrates the values of political democracy, social justice, and economic prosperity, societal features that parents can enhance by promoting ethical attitudes with their children. To analyze how families can advance or retard democracy, social justice, and prosperity, I examine a hierarchy of ethical values, then consider their origin in biology and nurturance, and suggest how families can change the hierarchy.

Factors Influencing Value Hierarchies

Many things shape a person's hierarchy of ethical values, among the most important of which are family values and practices, the values of the child's role models, the social class, religion, and ethnicity of the child's family, and the historical context.

Family Influences

The first influences on the development of values come from the family in the form of the behaviors that are rewarded and punished, as well as the behaviors parents display as role models for their children. Most children regard what parents do as more relevant than what they say. One important value has to do with fulfilling role assignments. In his essay in this volume, Luis Herrera notes that Costa Rican children are frequently allowed to avoid responsibility for assigned tasks. Costa Rican parents tell children complaining of a headache or stomach ache that they do not have to go to school that day. Children often avoid accountability for mistakes. For example, if a child is confronted with something he broke, and he resists confessing, his parents will often not insist. Among adults, absenteeism is high: teachers in Costa Rica take many paid sick days, and disability payments to public employees are four times larger than in comparable societies. Furthermore, Costa Ricans, like many Latin Americans, are prone to ignore legal requirements or to treat laws as nonbinding. Children are told that, while they should obey the rules, it is chiefly important not to be caught disobeying them.

Identification

Young children are biologically prepared to seek and detect similarities among a number of objects or events. For example, most two-year-olds presented with a random array of four red cubes and four yellow spheres will touch successively all of the objects with the same color and shape. Most five-year-old girls believe that they share more features with their mothers than with their fathers. Therefore, a five-year-old girl who sees her mother frightened by a thunderstorm infers that a fear of storms might be one of her personal characteristics. On the other hand, a girl who perceives her mother to be bold and forceful with her father and popular with neighbors will assume that she, too, possesses these qualities.

A child's identification with her gender can be symbolically creative. The categories "male" and "female" are associated in the minds of both children and adults with concepts that seem unrelated to gender. By eight years of age, the concept "female" is linked, unconsciously, to the concept "natural" because all cultures regard giving birth and caring for infants as prototypically natural events. Therefore, the concept "female" is semantically closer to the concept "nature" than is the concept "male." This claim was affirmed in a study of seven-year-old American children. In ancient times, the Pythagoreans regarded the number two as female and the number three as male in the belief that natural events occur more often in pairs than in trios.

Humans award salience to categories defined by less frequent, or uncommon, features. The more distinctive the features shared between child and parent, the more strongly the child identifies with the parent. A father who is tall and thin, with red hair and freckles, would engender a stronger identification in a son with these features than in a son who is short, chubby, brown-haired, and without freckles. Members of minority groups in a society are more strongly identified with that group than with the majority. The distinctive facial features, food prohibitions, and religious rituals of Jews in Central Europe during the Middle Ages contributed to a strong identification with that social category.

Children learn the behavioral properties of the categories to which they belong and seek consistency. A Vietnamese child whose family has immigrated to Montana will believe she should behave in ways that accord with her understanding of the stereotype for children in Vietnam, not Montana. If she failed to do so, she would violate the principle of consistency and risk uncertainty.

Young adults who decide that their childhood identification is a source of shame or anxiety may try to change their category membership. However, attempts to dilute a childhood identification may generate guilt if the person believes that the original category is the true one. An attempt to alter one's identification is an act of disloyalty to other members of the category and can have some of the same emotional consequences that would follow abandoning one's family. John McWhorter argues that many African Americans who identify strongly with their ethnic category believe that whites are morally tainted because of their prejudice, greed, and hypocrisy and, therefore, are not desirable role models. One sad consequence of this belief is an unwillingness to work diligently at school because these distrusted middle-class whites want them to master academic tasks, attend college, and become professionals. In this case, blacks' strong ethnic identification thwarts actions likely to benefit them.

Increasing ethnic diversity in the United States has made the category "American" more fuzzy than it was a century ago and identification with a national category more difficult. Many Mexican immigrants who have lived in America for a decade believe they are here temporarily and will eventually return to their native country. Many Dominicans living in America say, "One foot here, one foot there."

Social Class

The features that define social class, as distinct from ethnicity, are less salient and less stable, since those that define class are apparently more malleable. The signs children use for class include the quality of residence, neighborhood, and material possessions. Most seven-year-olds can distinguish between drawings of homes belonging to poor and to wealthy families, even though few parents remind their children of their social class and our society has no rituals linked to class membership. Thus, a child's discovery of his social class is conceptually difficult and more diffuse, and probably does not form before age six or seven.

Marx wanted to make class a more important psychological category than ethnicity or religion, but the nonviolent collapse of Communism in the Soviet Union, compared with the violent conflicts in Bosnia, Northern Ireland, and the Middle East, proves how difficult it is to do this. Because many Americans believe that only hard work and intelligence are needed to gain wealth, class has a greater potential for shame in America than in many other parts of the world. Youth who identify with their poor families are vulnerable to feelings of shame or impotence if they wonder whether the reason for their status is that their parents are lazy or incompetent. The emphasis on material wealth as a primary goal makes it theoretically possible for all American citizens, no matter what their ethnic, national, or religious origin, to believe that they can attain a higher status. The price of this change in social accounting is increased narcissism, selfishness, disloyalty, and, for those who remain poor, a readiness for shame that is hard to rationalize.

Of course, identification with a less advantaged social class may also provide some protection from shame or guilt over a family's class position. Protective beliefs of this kind include the notion that the rich are corrupt and morally flawed, that secure jobs in a competitive society are scarce, that employers are prejudiced against the poor, or that the middle class is inherently more talented. Each of these rationalizations permits adolescents who identify with a disadvantaged family to mute the intensity of their feelings of shame. These protections are becoming more difficult to exploit as American society tries to eliminate prejudice and provide more opportunities for the poor. As such psychological protection is torn away, adolescents from poor families confront their status without a healing rationalization. It is possible that today, for the first time in American history, adults who grew up poor regard this personal feature as a serious stigma.

Parents' social class affects their preferred practices for socializing their children. Working- and middle-class parents participating in a study conducted in 1980 heard a tape recording of a brief essay that compared the relative value of restrictive and permissive strategies of socialization. Each parent was told that he or she would have to remember as much of the essay as possible as soon as the reading was over. American working-class mothers recalled more of the essay emphasizing that excessive restrictiveness was bad for children because it made them excessively fearful. Middle-class mothers remembered more sentences claiming that permissiveness would place their child at risk for delinquency and poor school grades. How can we explain this difference?

Working-class American mothers, anxious over their less secure economic position, do not want their children to be afraid of risk, for that trait might put them at an economic disadvantage. As a result, they favor a more permissive regimen. Middle-class mothers have become apprehensive about their children not performing well in school, or being tempted by asocial friends; hence, they have favored a more restrictive regimen since World War II.

Finally, family myths aid a child's identification. Children are emotionally moved by stories of heroic family members who displayed qualities symbolic of strength, bravery, compassion, or intelligence. Jewish parents oppressed during the Spanish Inquisition probably told their children that, although their lives were harsh, they could trace their religious identity to the patriarchs celebrated in the Bible. In *Angela's Ashes,* Frank McCourt's chronically unemployed father reminded him that, as a son of Ireland, he possessed the courage of those who came before him. These family myths help children cope with anxiety and shame.

Environment

Another set of influences includes the values of friends and teachers. The values promoted in the school are usually those promoted by the majority in the society. Hence, children from the majority group find support for what they were taught at home, while those from a minority group, whether ethnic or religious, may be exposed to a different set of values. They can either resist or change their childhood beliefs. In Mao's postrevolutionary society, Chinese adolescents who were born in the early 1930s had to suppress the values they were taught by their mothers and grandmothers in order to fit in.

A final set of influences involves conditions in the immediate environment, especially social demands necessary to maintain social harmony, civility, and productivity. Each person tries continually to gain qualities that will increase her self-respect, while simultaneously trying to avoid acquiring features that diminish it. Most individuals are risk-averse; faced with the slim possibility of gaining an important goal following effort, and the relatively certain expectation of experiencing shame and guilt following failure to attain that goal, they favor the latter, avoidant strategy.

Childhood experiences usually generate one or two serious sources of doubt or uncertainty that exert a strong influence on life choices. The doubts usually center on one or more of the following properties: talent, acceptability to others, physical attractiveness, social status, economic position, sexual potency, and moral character. Obviously, these qualities are not independent. Wealth is usually, but not always, correlated with higher social status and greater ability at the skills the society values.

The intensity and timing of each source of uncertainty are influenced by the importance the community places on that quality. For example, contemporary American society places a higher value on sexual potency than on piety; the reverse was true three hundred years ago in Puritan New England. Eighteenth-century Chinese society placed a higher value on talent and status than did the People's Republic of China in the mid-twentieth century; contemporary Chinese resemble modern Americans.

Democracy, Social Justice, and Prosperity: Are They Biologically Prepared Motives?

Some psychological characteristics are relatively easy to acquire—language is the obvious example—while others, like learning to read and to manipulate numbers in an equation, are more difficult. It is useful to ask, therefore, whether children find it easy or difficult to understand, and eventually to favor, the concepts of democracy, social justice, and prosperity.

Most students of human nature agree that chronic uncertainty over meeting survival needs and maintaining status with group members generates a universal motive to mute this undesirable feeling. Hence, it is easy for families to promote a desire for economic security and the accumulation of wealth. However, the case for democracy or social justice is less obvious, because these values pit an early childhood assumption about people against a moral imperative acquired later.

Anthropologists suspect that most early humans were communitarian, concerned with the opinions of their neighbors, empathic toward those in need of help, and loyal to the ethical requirements of the social categories to which they belonged. Humans were neither democratic nor egalitarian during the first eighty to ninety millennia of our existence. This fact suggests that some of the values promoted by the Culture Matters project, including political democracy and competitive capitalism, do not have an obvious priority in human biology.

Democracy

The deep assumption behind a preference for a democratic society is that all persons should have equal power to select the community's representatives; no one should have more voice and no one less than another. This belief does not strike children as having obvious validity. Most families are not democratic, not even those headed by politically liberal parents with doctorates in sociology. Children's experiences lead them to conclude that some individuals are rightfully entitled to more power to decide what will be done. When parents are, in addition, nurturing, just, and affectionate, children assume that an authoritarian arrangement does not violate natural law. Indeed, children want parents and some legitimate authority figures to protect them from yielding to temptations they suspect will be psychologically harmful. When, many years ago, I asked my twenty-year-old daughter what mistakes my wife and I had made during her childhood years, she replied that we gave her too much freedom during early adolescence, having assumed, incorrectly, that she could handle those challenges easily and wisely.

The first human foraging groups, consisting of thirty to fifty individuals, were not democratic. Nor were the ancient civilizations that matured after agriculture was invented around ten thousand years ago. Although Western schools and colleges teach students about the creative intuition that led to Athenian democracy, most teachers and professors do not dwell on the fact that the slave residents of Athens had no political power.

The task, then, is to teach children that, despite obvious differences in experience, abilities, character, and wisdom, members of a community should have an equal voice in deciding political matters. In order to promote this democratic ethic, parents must encourage a sense of personal agency in their children by providing experiences that allow them to feel they have some power to affect family life. Put simply, consulting the child, asking her opinions, and, when appropriate, taking the child's preferences into account, should strengthen the child's sense of agency. Psychologists call parents who adopt these practices authoritatively democratic. Research indicates that such families are more common in Europe and North America in homes where parents have attended college. This last fact does not mean that parents who have less education cannot promote this standard, only that it is a bit more difficult for such parents, many of whom feel less agency themselves, to believe that children should have a deep faith in their own potency.

The assumption that all legitimate members of a community should have equal power to decide on the future of the community is harder to promote than a sense of agency, because this premise requires the child to understand the difference between economic gain and symbolic signs of status, on the one hand, and political privilege, on the other. Students who are more talented in mathematics should have preference in admission to schools of engineering; those who are more adept with their hands should be given preference in surgical residencies; and those who have acquired a firmer conscience should be awarded prized judicial positions. The exception to the principle that variation in privilege should be a function of personal qualities is the belief that the power to decide who should govern belongs equally to all.

One important reason why children resist the notion that all have equal political influence derives from the human moral sense. One psychological consequence of the large frontal lobe that evolved in our species between 100,000 and 200,000 years ago is the conviction that people can be sorted into categorical bins labeled "ideal," "good," "bad," and "evil." This evaluation is based on the degree to which an individual's characteristics are or are not in accord with community mores. Since political power belongs in the "good" bin, it can be difficult to persuade youth that people categorized as bad because of their personal qualities should have an equal vote with good ones. This lesson requires adolescents to understand John Donne's message that the vitality of the larger community should, on occasion, take precedence over a person's sentiments. That is why a Boston judge several decades ago ordered busing of African-American and Caucasian children to schools miles from their homes, and why the American Civil Liberties Union defended the right of neo-Nazis to march in an Illinois city.

Unlike a sense of agency, which can emerge before age seven, this more abstract idea has to wait until the years before puberty, when the maturing cognitive abilities make it possible for youth to understand that the vitality of the community should, on some occasions, have priority over the desires of the individual. Promotion of this goal requires discussion between parents and children and is accomplished less easily through parental rewards and punishments. Parents have to be clever, sensing when it is appropriate to teach this lesson.

One class of opportunities occurs when a member of the extended family who lives some distance away is ill or lonely. By insisting that the visit include the child, even though he may have had a different plan for the day, families teach the child that the psychological state of the larger family unit can take precedence over personal wishes. By emphasizing the social categories to which the child belongs—family, clan, ethnicity, and religion—and explaining why the requirements of these groups deserve priority, parents prepare youth to award a similar allegiance to the political community

Social Justice

The task of persuading children that impoverished or disenfranchised members of the society deserve empathy confronts the same difficulties that accompanied teaching them that all should have an equal political voice. Families have an ally as they try to meet this assignment. Nature has endowed nearly all children with the ability to empathize with those in physical or psychic distress. An empathic concern over a whining puppy or a crying infant comes easily to all children. This sentiment, which Hume assumed was the foundation of human morality, is part of what makes the teaching of social justice possible.

Reminding children regularly of the deprivation experienced by disenfranchised citizens should, by adolescence, create a concern for strangers in need. It helps, of course, if parents not only promote this ethic in conversation but also display it in their behavior. We noted earlier that because most children identify with their parents, they are more likely to believe in the validity of an attitude if they see it practiced by their role models. Words alone, without support in the daily behavior of role models, are often too weak to maintain a strong empathic concern for the less privileged.

Promotion of social justice requires concern for the vitality of the community. A comparison of European with East Asian cultures in the eighteenth century, before the West began to influence the latter, reveals that the individual was the primary social entity in European society. Each person was to attain salvation, wealth, status, and happiness on his or her own. Community praise for success and blame for failure were assigned to the individual, not to his family or the actions of others. For East Asian youth and adults, in contrast, the imperative was to seek harmony with, and become part of, a group: first family and later peers and community. In these societies, each person's pride or shame rested on the success or failure of the groups of which he was a member, and not only on the individual's talent or perseverance. Both an individualistic and a communal ethic are possible human properties, but once one of these values is practiced for a while it becomes a bit difficult to adopt the other.

The Western concern with social justice is revealed in the degree of dignity and power awarded women over the last few centuries. Most husbands in contemporary Western nations cede wives greater autonomy than in Islamic or Asian societies. Nikolas Gvosdev, in his contribution to this volume, notes that in Byzantine society, especially among the less well-educated in rural areas, women were regarded as less pure than men and were not entitled to serve in the ministry. Some clerics removed all references to women in books of canon law. Bassam Tibi describes a similar inequality in Islamic states.

These facts are relevant to economic development because, for most of human history, women only attained respect through the status and accomplishments of their husbands and grown sons. Hence, husbands and sons who wished to please their wives and mothers worked at accumulating wealth and prestige, thus enhancing the family's social status.

Economic Prosperity

The attainment of economic prosperity requires an ethic that celebrates individual achievement and associates work with virtue. Many have noted that this view, inherent in Luther's sermons, is one basis for the economic prosperity of Protestant societies. The belief that economic gain requires a work ethic has, as a corollary, the conclusion that those who are poor failed to learn or to practice a work ethic. If they had done so, they would not be economically distressed. Hence, empathy for their state is not a moral imperative, because their condition is their fault. As with the abstract idea of the priority of the community, parents must explain to children that some citizens are unable to improve their position because of structural conditions in the society rather than because of individual moral failure.

Changing Value Hierarchies

I have argued here that the values communicated to the child in the home during the first decade of life will greatly influence its moral standards as an adult and therefore the economic and political development of the society. In order to change behavior one must alter the family's value hierarchy. Sharon Kagan remarks that this goal has been achieved to some degree through more than fifty thousand parent-education programs that serve millions of American parents.[1] Unfortunately, these programs are small efforts with limited budgets. Most programs try to alter parental behavior, rather than parental values, not only because the latter is difficult but also because some regard changing parental values as an inappropriate incursion into family privacy. However, it is probably impossible to change parental behaviors with children without changing the adult values first.

Richard Niemi, Steven Finkel, and Thomas Lickona believe that schools can affect value systems. Lickona argues that contemporary American society will condone arranging school environments to promote the values of hard work, perseverance, honesty, respect for authority, compassion for others, and humility. He believes that these goals can be attained if the principals and teachers construct the school environment with sufficient skill and care. However, Niemi and Finkel remind us that contemporary high school and college students have become disengaged from their society and its politics and, for that reason, believes that courses in civic education could play a benevolent role.

Who is the Beneficiary?

To promote one value over another we must first analyze the different interests of three distinct constituencies: the community, the family, and the individual. Although all three influence each other reciprocally, under optimal conditions what benefits one should benefit the other. This ideal is rarely attained.

Most communities wish individuals to conform to their laws and play their assigned roles efficiently. The efficient production of needed goods and services represents one important role assignment. The family is interested in a different set of goals; it wants loyalty and affection from its members. Neither intention presupposes conformity to community laws or a work ethic.

The individual, the central agent in Western views of human society, desires a select set of feelings: sensory delight and freedom from pain, fear, and intimidation. But each agent also wants symbolic affirmation that it is good, meaning a judgment that its character or personality is in accord with, and not seriously discrepant from, the ideal acquired during childhood and adolescence. This judgment defines a sense of virtue. When one fails to match the ideal, dissatisfaction, anxiety, shame, guilt, or sadness results.

In a perfect world, the interests of all three beneficiaries, like the complicated pieces of a puzzle, form a coherent pattern. The individual would work hard, obey laws, show loyalty and affection to the family, and, through these actions, experience sensory delights and a feeling of virtue. Unfortunately, this smooth meshing of interests is uncommon because few communities agree sufficiently on the features that define virtue. Finding a balance among the three constituencies is like walking on top of a picket fence: one is always off balance.

Consider the three goals of political democracy, social justice, and economic prosperity. Western nations contain many citizens who regard the freedom of the individual as more important than the needs of the society and an equal number who believe that the community has precedence. Social justice is a less pressing ideal among those who favor the individual. This conflict is captured in Garrett Hardin's essay, "The Tragedy of the Commons."[2]

I do not believe that the facts of human biology can help very much as we try to decide which balance of interests best accords with our genetic predispositions. Humans are equally capable of subduing self-interest in the service of a larger group and ignoring the group to serve only the self. Humans want to belong to groups that award the self a definition, status, protection, and affirmation of acceptability, but they also want to be free of group restraints. The popular song "It Is a Hard Time for Lovers" captures the tension in couples who want loyalty, love, and personal freedom at the same time.

Although most of us would like to believe that humans can arrange more ideal conditions, the controlling agency, hiding behind a curtain, is historical change, which brings new machines, new wars, new forms of contraception, new medicines, new forms of transportation, and new modes of communication. If cars, trains, planes, and the contraceptive pill had not been invented, the contemporary world would be very different. These changes hastened the celebration of personal agency and made democracy a desirable political form and concern for genetically unrelated strangers in distress a moral imperative. Neither ethic is in closer accord with our biology, however, than its opposite.

When asked what they want in life for themselves and their children, most Americans and Europeans answer, "to be happy." Usually, however, humans decide that they are happy when their life conditions and personal characteristics are not seriously discrepant from what they have come to believe is proper, good, and moral. The vicissitudes of history, like the changing cloud patterns on a blustery March afternoon, dictate what life conditions will frame that judgment. It is not obvious that a thirty-year-old American who commutes forty miles each way on a crowded highway to a factory assembly line, insurance office, or hotel kitchen experiences more sensory delight and feels more virtuous throughout the year than a laborer who worked on one of Pharoah's pyramids, a monk or nun in a medieval village, or George Bernard Shaw's nineteenth-century London flower girl heroine in *Pygmalion*.

At the moment, personal freedom to perfect oneself, free of restraint from the community or family, is a central feature of that judgment. For this reason, the promotion of democracy has become an ethical ideal. It is assumed that promotion of this ideal will be followed by social justice and economic prosperity for as long as history will allow.

What Should Be Done?

The explicit goal of the Culture Matters Research Project is to persuade nations that do not now enjoy political democracy, concern for the disadvantaged, and economic prosperity to implement changes that will allow them to command these goals if they choose. A society can possess any one feature of this trio without the others. Many Latin American and African nations have some of the defining features of political democracy without social justice or prosperity. The People's Republic of China during Mao's reign was concerned with the plight of peasants but was a totalitarian form of government. Attainment of all three features requires those with political power, whether a dictator or an elected assembly, to acknowledge the will of the majority and to allocate resources and legal protections to the less advantaged.

Permanent social change, however, requires a change in the values of the community. Adoption of an ethic that combines democracy, social justice, and economic prosperity requires that youth be socialized by family, school, and media to believe in four propositions:

1. It is possible for every person to improve his or her economic and social position through education and the conscientious application of individual talents. Many people in less developed societies hold a fatalistic belief that they are passive victims of social forces they cannot change. As a result, improving one's talents in order to work toward a goal is unlikely to result in a better life. This attitude might be called the "helplessness ideology."

2. The political and judicial system is generally fair and just; conformity to the law is expected and violations are punished.

3. Individuals who are members of a social category that has experienced prejudice are entitled to dignity, freedom from bigotry, and an opportunity to improve their lives. The belief that members of some social categories are inherently less talented or less virtuous than the majority because of their historical origins or presumed biology is a formidable obstacle to progress. That is why, in part, Rwanda, Guatemala, Nigeria, and Russia are less prosperous than Botswana, Costa Rica, Chile, and France.

   Furthermore, people must identify with their nation more strongly than with their tribe, clan, or region. America's advantage, as Tocqueville appreciated almost two hundred years ago, is that most Americans believe they are members of the same national category; hence they are receptive to the notion that all citizens have equal dignity and are entitled to equal opportunity and equal legal protection.

4. The accumulation of wealth, which usually brings status, is a virtue and does not imply that a person has violated an ethical standard simply because he is more advantaged than a neighbor.

Persuading a majority to believe in and to adopt these ideas requires the cooperation of family, educational institutions, and the mass media. The family's responsibility is to praise perseverance, academic achievement, and autonomy in children and to chastise the avoidance of responsibility, school failure, excessive dependence, and passivity. Parents, who are role models for their children, must display these desirable behaviors in their daily activities.

The school has a similar task and, in addition, must believe that children from disadvantaged or minority groups are sufficiently talented to profit from pedagogy. Teachers must communicate the idea that improvement in status can be a result of hard work, is a virtue, and is not a basis either for guilt or worry because some have attained a goal that others have not.

The media's responsibility is to celebrate the values of education, talent, and perseverance, and to praise heroes and heroines who conquer childhood disadvantages. The Abraham Lincoln story, among many others, is effective. These values are more difficult to promote in less developed societies, where individuals worry about the silent criticism they might provoke by attempts to improve their position. Australians use the phrase "lop off the tall poppies," implying that anyone who tries to attain a status higher than his neighbor is a legitimate target of criticism. Many youth in less developed nations persuade themselves that the few who are well educated or wealthy are morally compromised. George Comstock, the antihero of Orwell's novel, *Keep the Aspidistra Flying*, held this assumption. Contemporary Islamic societies denigrate America's conspicuous consumption. Hence, it may be difficult to persuade Islamic adolescents to adopt Western views, for if they do, they will become the "hated ones." This dynamic is an effective obstacle to attaining goals the individual may want but be unable to work toward, because these goals were

categorized as bad during childhood. All three sources of influence—
family, schools, and media—must disseminate the same values. If any
one source promotes a different ethic, it dilutes the moral power of
the message.

Citizens within regions in America and Europe with a great deal of
ethnic diversity are less certain than earlier generations about what is
sinful and what is sacred. One benevolent consequence of this doubt
is greater tolerance of minority values. But humans still want to believe in sins and sacraments in order to make a host of daily decisions
after they have provided for food and shelter.

The balance between individual and community interests shifts
with history as a result of inventions, migrations, wars, and national
catastrophes. The West has enjoyed extraordinary gains in material
comfort, health, literacy, and personal liberties over the past thousand years because each individual pursued a philosophy of self-
interest. Millions living in remote areas know about, and compare
themselves with, affluent citizens in North America and Europe. This
comparison, which was impossible two hundred years ago, engenders
a combination of envy, anger, and shame rather than awe or respect.
This novel state of affairs makes it reasonable to consider whether
advantaged societies should share more of their resources and technical expertise with the poorer nations, as America did with Germany
and Japan at the end of World War II, while not insisting, at least
initially, that these societies mimic all the features of the democratic
West. The hope is that as the citizens of these nations become educated and their lives improve, they will feel empowered and demand
democratic institutions and social justice.

In sum, the achievement of democracy, justice, and economic
growth requires parents to reward educational achievement, perseverance, and perfection of self; teachers to believe in the potential
success of all children; media to celebrate those who develop special
talents and have compassion for those with a compromised status;
and political leaders to legislate a concern for those with educational
and material shortfalls and to enforce laws without prejudice. The
state's critical responsibility is to guarantee a just judicial system, so
that a majority believe that violations of the law will be punished in
a fair manner. Because the United States has done this, when the Supreme Court decided that school segregation was unconstitutional,
many citizens living in Southern states began to obey that judgment
without starting a second Civil War.

Although nations with rich natural resources have a clear advantage, these resources are no guarantee of economic prosperity or democracy. Nigeria, despite its petroleum wealth, has less democracy and prosperity than Costa Rica. Attainment of the three ideals, like the creation of a perfect storm, requires many independent factors to converge in the proper temporal sequence. The first phase of this sequence for many contemporary societies is a change in the values that families, schools, and the media promote.

The extraordinary economic gains attained by Americans and Europeans over the past few centuries are correlated with political democracy, high levels of public education, a spirit of entrepreneurship, and individual liberty. As a result, many scholars have assumed that these four features must be necessary for economic progress. But it may not be true. Since the mid-1970s, the People's Republic of China has enjoyed greater economic growth than more democratic India. Although democracy and personal liberty did contribute to the West's rapid economic and political development, the inevitability of changing relations among social phenomena is a historical fact. The contemporary world represents a new constellation of features, and it remains possible that a new combination of factors will facilitate economic development in the next two centuries. Culture always matters, but the relations among values, political structures, and forms of economic activity are always changing.

Notes

1. Sharon Kagan and Amy Lowenstein, chapter 3 this volume.
2. Garrett Hardin, "The Tragedy of the Commons," *Science* 162 (1968): 1243–48.

2

Parenting Practices and Governance in Latin America

The Case of Costa Rica

LUIS DIEGO HERRERA AMIGHETTI

Parenting styles and practices[1] and child development have rarely been included in discussions of economic development and social progress. The usual assumption is that progress is determined by such powerful and related factors as natural resources, political organization, and economic policies. Parenting does not seem, at first glance, to play any role. The implicit belief seems to be that values and attitudes affect the private lives of individuals and groups but not their way of wielding power, doing business, and managing public institutions.

Children of all cultures are genetically programmed, or "wired," to acquire the categories "good" and "bad." By the end of their second year, children are cognitively mature enough to understand some actions as moral violations.[2] Soon afterwards, they pay attention to parents' voices, nonverbal language, and other behaviors and can make mental representations and categorize events, even those they have not yet experienced, as good or bad.[3]

In a variety of ways, parents transmit their approval or disapproval and help children internalize standards. This process is not always apparent. Communication of what is desirable as a personal attribute, an attitude, or a behavior takes many subtle but powerful forms that are interwoven with the myriad daily interactions between parents and children.

Behaviors directed toward children create in their minds a set of internal representations that guide their attitudes and behaviors in an often automatic, unconscious way. These adult behaviors are the result of informal social emphasis on the community's prevalent values, an essential part of its cultural landscape. Some parenting practices are more effective than others in enabling children to internalize these values.

However, it is possible to hold certain ideas, explicitly assume some moral standards, and meanwhile leave unchanged the behaviors that contradict them. Many people in Latin American societies, as elsewhere, pay mere lip service to some moral ideas or beliefs. For example, in Costa Rica, family planning methods are widely used by people who consider themselves committed Catholics, although the Costa Rican Catholic Church forbids such practices.

The evidence suggests that a major determinant of children's behavior is what parents actually do, regardless of what they say. Systematic studies have shown an insignificant correlation between children's behavior and what parents say they believe in.[4] One focus in this chapter is on such inconsistencies and double standards among Latin American elites. I am interested in the mechanisms by which children develop values and moral rules—in other words, how character and commitment are formed, which is the true test of a moral life.[5] I believe that parenting practices play a major role in determining to what extent an individual's declared principles and values actually influence how he or she makes use of power and manages business or public office.

The examples of child rearing patterns addressed in this chapter are mostly drawn from Latin American elites, though I believe they are widespread across Latin American societies. Because most countries in Latin America are heterogeneous in their cultural, ethnic, and social composition, the national identity of a given group is less informative than its social position. For example, from a sociocultural point of view, a Mayan group in Guatemala may be more akin to an Araucanian group in Chile than to the other social sectors in Guatemala. Within this analysis, it is appropriate to talk about cultural groups as a universe of implicit shared meanings and common practices, and to emphasize how groups behave rather than the ways they see themselves.

No one group, of course, is solely responsible for Latin America's generally disappointing rate of economic and social progress. But the ruling elites must bear paramount responsibility. As Carlos Alberto Montaner has written: "Those who occupy leading positions in public and private organizations and institutions are the ones chiefly responsible for perpetuating poverty."[6]

The World Bank defines governance as the way "power is exercised in the management of a country's economic and social resources for development."[7] The international financing institutions view good governance as respect for the rule of law, integrity, transparency (less corruption), and accountability. Good governance reflects social norms: beliefs grounded in the prevailing values of a community, which designates behaviors as "desirable or legitimate in the shared view of societal members"; their violation "elicits at least informal disapproval."[8] Clearly, these social norms also apply to the private domain. Parenting practices, in particular, can be seen as both a source and a reflection of social norms.

I suggest that several socialization and parenting practices are unfavorable to good governance. These include: a culture of somatization[9] and lack of accountability; a confusing dichotomy between honesty and cleverness; overprotection and diminished autonomy; meandering styles of communication and fear of assertiveness; authoritarian and inconsistent parenting leading to impaired moral reasoning skills; and deficient future awareness associated with diminished capacity for delayed gratification. The progress-resistant values that result from these may constitute an obstacle to political, social, and economic development.

Somatization, Accountability, and Cleverness

In Costa Rica, among all classes and age groups, individuals commonly use physical complaints, illnesses, and vague symptoms and maladies to explain why they do not feel well at work, school, or home. This culture of somatization validates not doing homework, coming late or not showing up for work, procrastinating, and getting extra attention from those around the complainer. A prominent physician once remarked that Costa Ricans can be divided into two categories: those who are tired and those who have a headache.

This is not really funny. Data from *Latinobarómetro*,[10] a public opinion survey conducted annually in many Latin American nations, show that Costa Rica has the highest proportion of people who admit to feigning an illness to justify not showing up to work. Recently, there has been a public debate about the near bankruptcy of the Costa Rican social security system, which provides medical care nationwide. A significant cause is the abuse of disability pay for public employees, which is almost four times what it should be. It is also noteworthy that among all public sector employees, teachers have the highest rate of paid sick days.[11]

From birth, Costa Rican parents pay immediate and abundant attention to their children's physical complaints. Any headache or stomach ache is a good enough reason to skip school or not do homework. Parents who react differently may be perceived—even by themselves—as insensitive or negligent. Costa Ricans are socialized from early childhood in a culture where physical complaints are a way of rendering oneself unaccountable.

Accountability is, in fact, something new in Latin American culture. The word has no exact translation in Spanish. It is often translated as *responsibilidad*, or more recently, as *rendición de cuentas*. But *responsabilidad* is inaccurate, precisely because it lacks sufficient emphasis on the external element. The need to position oneself as unaccountable permeates everyday language. In Costa Rican Spanish, if one breaks, loses, or damages something or makes a mistake, this is expressed in a passive, impersonal form: "it was broken," "it got lost," "it got damaged," instead of "I lost it" or "I broke it." A child who is confronted with something that he or she broke will sometimes resist quite a while before saying "I did it." Very often parents do not insist, and their children's misbehavior or mistakes are ignored or quickly forgotten.

The rule of law in Latin America is a rare phenomenon. Children are taught many contradictory standards of behavior: they are supposed to abide by the rules, but if they break them, the important thing is to get away with it. Not being caught is an achievement. Parents often comment with pride on how their small children were able to take a shortcut, lie cleverly, or cheat successfully. This sends a powerful message that being shrewd is better than being truthful.

When adolescents from elite families break the law, they are almost always bailed out, either through political influence or through intimidation or bribery. The whole incident is often trivialized, glossed over as the natural result of growing pains. Often I hear parents sharing anecdotes of how their child accomplished something cleverly but unethically. Parents—including those who explicitly teach honesty and truthfulness—delight in this supposedly astute behavior, even when it implies lying to them. They feel proud of being outsmarted by their children, choosing not to notice the moral inconsistency.

A set of very popular children's bedtime stories features the character Tío Conejo, whose core message to children is that being sly and cunning is a better way to get what you want than being honest and truthful. This, too, reinforces cultural attitudes that, in Costa Rica and other Latin American countries, all too frequently become sociopathic behaviors.

Overprotection and Diminished Autonomy

Licht, Chanan, and Schwartz, using Schwartz's model of cultural values, describe the bipolar dimension of Embeddedness/Autonomy, arguing that in many countries, diminished autonomy correlates strongly with poor norms of governance.[12] Mariano Grondona, referring to progress-resistant traits in Latin American and other poor regions, also argues that lack of self-confidence and autonomy undermine economic development.[13]

In affluent and middle-class families, many of whom send their children to private schools, parents, particularly mothers, are very involved in their children's activities and responsibilities. All parents want to believe that their children are competent to cope with increasingly difficult school requirements. Since this is not always the case,[14] many parents end up sitting with their children and assuming most of the responsibility for homework. Children get used to this scheme and depend on it. To outsiders, and even the school, it appears that the child is succeeding; privately, the parents know this is not true and often quarrel with their children about it. This dynamic teaches the child dishonesty, damages his sense of competence and productivity, and weakens his potential to trust his abilities to cope with external demands.

This kind of overprotection is not limited to schoolwork; it extends to other areas of children's functioning, such as choosing friends and learning from failures. Even if it does not damage self-esteem, it can harm children by fostering false confidence, an undue sense of being exceptionally gifted or accomplished, based not on actual interaction with the environment but instead on their parent's overinvolvement. Entitlement follows as a consequence.

The result may well be an important segment of young adults who feel entitled to privilege. If their parents continue to support this feeling in adulthood, the children may never come to terms with reality. This dynamic obviously interferes with the child's internalizing an ethic of effort and reward and a sense of responsibility.

Ambiguous Communication and Fear of Assertiveness

Grusec and Goodnow[15] have made an interesting contribution to the topic of styles of discipline. They conclude that two factors determine how well values are transmitted. First, the child must accurately perceive messages involving values; here, parents' clarity, frequency, and consistency in expressing values are critical. Second, those messages must be accepted; here, what matters is the parents' fairness and persuasiveness, and the appropriateness of the message to the child's temperament and developmental level. Parental empathy and warmth are also very important.

Unfortunately, one salient aspect of parent–child communication in Latin America is a meandering, verbose style. Direct communication is avoided, and many kinds of circumlocution are employed to evade commitment, clear-cut answers, interlocutor disappointment, or potential confrontations. This trait is particularly evident when dealing with contentious or emotional issues. Very early, children receive the message that there is something wrong about being straightforward, claiming what you believe is just, or requesting compensation for wrongdoing. It is suggested that confrontation is impolite or rude, or that the other person may become angry, resentful, or vindictive. There is even an unrealistic, almost catastrophic, perception of the consequences of confrontation, as if there were only two options: acquiescence or violent confrontation. In Costa Rica, several colloquial expressions describe this oblique communication style: *paños tibios, plato de babas, enaguas meadas.*

This linguistic pattern interferes with the way demands and censure are transmitted to children. Children perceive this as ambivalence about the importance of certain values, which lends itself to a superficial internalization of norms. The indirect communication style is intimately related to the fear of straightforwardness or assertiveness in Latin countries; although assertiveness is included in the official Spanish dictionary (*asertivo*), the thing itself is unknown to most people. When I explain to parents the concept and its relevance, they often seem perplexed, as if they have discovered a previously unknown dimension of human nature. They do not know how to be assertive and cannot model it for their children.

When we add to this oblique communication style and fear of assertiveness a weak emphasis on accountability and an informal encouragement of short cuts and getting away with bad behavior, the stage is set for children to resort to "illicit" strategies to affirm themselves and accomplish what is expected of them. These illicit strategies may well mold children's character and commitment and pave the way for corrupt behavior and disrespect for the rule of law during adult life.

Authoritarian and Inconsistent Parenting Styles

Several researchers have discussed how values are internalized and transmitted. Sears, Maccoby, and Levin found that mothers who used praise, affect withdrawal, isolation, and reasoning as a disciplinary style were more effective in developing their children's moral conscience (defined as the internalization of maternal values).[16] Martin Hoffman made a distinction among three different approaches to discipline: power assertion, love withdrawal, and appeals to children's sense of pride and need to be good.[17] In general, these theories of how children internalize values support the idea that power-assertive discipline, by itself, is detrimental to children's moral development, while love withdrawal, reasoning, and warmth all had more positive effects. However, it is important to consider the role that class, and particularly educational level, plays in mediating the relations between the form of socialization and children's development.

According to these views, mere power assertion inhibits the development of moral reasoning, while a persuasive discussion allows children to entertain psychological scenarios different from their own and thus fosters the development of empathy and respect for others. Diana Baumrind, however, has found a considerable difference between an authoritative and a merely authoritarian parenting style. Authoritative parents use a democratic style of communication, which at the same time conveys high expectations, consistent limits, and firm rules.[18] In Baumrind's studies, children of authoritative parents displayed more adaptive behaviors, were more in charge, and showed more social competence and responsibility.

In working with parents on developing effective discipline styles, I use an exercise in which they have to situate themselves on a matrix consisting of expectations and demands versus sensitivity and empathy. Most parents in Costa Rica position themselves either in the authoritarian zone or in the permissive zone. This bipolar aggregation of parents may confuse children and weaken their internalization of a balanced, fair, and rational conception of authority. In short, the authoritarian style, by denying children the opportunity to negotiate rules and values, undermines their capacity for moral reasoning.[19]

In one family meeting with me, while attempting to negotiate an adolescent child's limits, the father said, "I am willing to talk about her curfew, allowance, and other rules; however, she has to understand that in every relationship there is someone who dominates and, in this case, that person is me." To which the fourteen-year-old replied, in a style typical of the interaction, "It is not that I want you to allow me to do what I please.... I just want to do what I want!"

When moral reasoning is insufficiently developed, children are less competent to make decisions based upon adherence to principles and rules and are more likely to opt for self-centered and impulsively chosen alternatives, disregarding future consequences to themselves as well as thoughts of the common good.

Within the Latin American culture of child rearing, caregivers commonly give in to children's wishes as long as they are not actually inconvenienced by them. Even then, when children are very young, parents feel uneasy about frustrating them. Parents show an extraordinary inclination to please and satisfy their children until they are close to school age; indeed, foreigners comment that our society seems very child oriented and child friendly. However, as children begin to manifest distinct selves and parents increase their level of expectations, this permissive style gives way to an authoritarian, arbitrary style. If children do not comply with parental rules, parents may give in until they run out of patience, then resort to coercive interactions. The resulting pattern resembles what Patterson and Bank have described, when discussing defiant and antisocial children, as negative reinforcement.[20] As children become more difficult to manage, parents resort to a confusing strategy: they establish some ill-defined rules and simultaneously use their power to apply them in an arbitrary, discretionary way. Of course, not all parents show this pattern but it is widespread.

It is, of course, hardly unique to Latin America. But here this pattern, in concert with other parenting styles described above, seems to produce characteristic results: low perseverance, lack of responsibility for one's actions, and great difficulty in postponing satisfaction.

Deficient Future Awareness and Diminished Capacity for Delayed Gratification

For historical reasons beyond the scope of this paper, but clearly manifested in our persistent inability to produce social and economic development, Latin American culture suffers from time myopia. Like the Buendías in *One Hundred Years of Solitude* by Gabriel García Márquez, we seem unable to learn from our errors; previous political experiences, even disastrous ones, do not seem to exert the influence they should. (The current political crises in Colombia and Venezuela are cases in point.) As in Garcia Marquez's novel, we repeat nonprogressive attitudes and values because we do not develop in the next generation a critical understanding of the mistakes of the previous ones. The inability of parents and children to openly debate and negotiate without falling into an authoritarian mode is related to the repetition of traditional strategies that do not foster the development of independent, analytical minds among our citizens. Thus, we repeat our mistakes endlessly.

In Costa Rica, the ways that children are socialized do not introduce them early to the notions of planning, anticipating alternative outcomes, and preparing for difficult times. Developmentally, this is related to intolerance for delayed gratification. It is interesting that in Costa Rica the population has been remarkably eager to embrace the diagnosis of Attention Deficit Disorder (ADHD) in children. In some private schools, up to a third of the students are taking medications for ADHD, a diagnosis that is certainly valid for a small proportion of school-age children. Although this social and medical trend is certainly common elsewhere too, it was manifested here earlier and more strongly. I suspect this diagnosis is often used as a rationalization, an excuse to avoid perseverance and justify the culturally induced intolerance of frustration.

One likely outcome of the cultural trait of limited future awareness is an indisposition to save and to develop well thought-out strategies for allocating limited resources. Costa Ricans are notorious for conspicuous consumption.[21] Members of the middle and upper-middle classes commonly get into debt through loans and credit-card spending on consumption rather than investing in housing, small businesses, and education. A dangerously high number of citizens work mainly to pay for their cars, vacations, or electronic gadgets.

Procrastination is widespread in our culture, maybe more than in other Western cultures. Children learn that if they have not planned their tasks and done their homework or chores, they may give perfunctory excuses, or simply do nothing, and the system will not consistently respond with negative consequences. I emphasize consistency because, in some situations, depending on parental personality and mood, or the degree of professionalism in the schools and other settings where children are socialized (soccer teams, clubs, etc.), children get a range of responses in situations where they are not made accountable. All this weakens the habit of seeing one's behavior in relation to prospective outcomes—in other words, future awareness.

What Can Be Done?

What can be done to change this syndrome? Thomas Lickona, in his landmark book *Educating for Character*, states that "the long-term success of the new values education depends on forces outside the school—on the extent to which families and communities join schools in a common effort to meet the needs of children and foster their healthy development."[22] I see at least three potentially fruitful approaches, involving three different sectors of the society.

1. The preschool and school must develop curricula centered on values. A parent–school partnership is needed: parents must participate actively in identifying the values their children will be learning in the classroom. Moreover, children must work with their parents on projects or homework requiring active discussion of values.

2. From the health-system perspective, private and public-sector physicians, nurses, and social workers should combine their health education and health-promoting activities with training

parents to set limits, teaching children how to tolerate frustration, and teaching both parents and teachers to employ effective, noncoercive discipline techniques.

3. The mass media need to be involved. As Canada has done in the case of adolescent violence, the media should be encouraged to promote an agenda of social responsibility that portrays corruption, disrespect for the rule of law, and lack of accountability as public and private problems relevant to all citizens.

None of the above can be accomplished without governmental support and pressure from opinion leaders and from the enlightened sectors of the ruling elites. There are hopeful signs. Recently I consulted at an elite private school in Costa Rica, where the board of directors approved an initiative, informed by the work of Thomas Lickona, Sheldon Berman, and others, to develop a curriculum to promote character and social responsibility within the school. Some years ago at the National Children's Hospital in Costa Rica, we developed a program requiring that parents of children with behavioral problems participate in a thirty-hour workshop on effective, nonaggressive discipline techniques. It should be possible to develop similar programs on a wider scale that will promote parenting practices favorable to social progress.

In his 1950 work *El Laberinto de la Soledad*, Octavio Paz, thinking of Mexican immigrants to the United States, wrote that the Mexican "feels suspended between the earth and the sky and oscillates between powers and forces in conflict....The world that surrounds us exists by itself, has a life of its own and has not been created, as in the United States, by man."[23] I believe this applies to all Latin Americans. More than fifty years later, the Journal of World Business published the results of the GLOBE survey of leaderships and cultures in productive organizations. According to Enrique Ogliastri, one contributor to the GLOBE study, the Latin American cluster is characterized by "an acceptance of life as it comes to us," and people attribute "the results of work...to external, unpredictable factors." Further, "in the Latin American countries we are more focused on the present than the future...and we are not concerned with a job well done because, due to the...elitist structure, outstanding performance does not predict success."[24]

The literary perspective of Octavio Paz coincides remarkably well with the contemporary research of the GLOBE survey. Both support the view that in our Latin American culture, "things" befall us. We do not feel like protagonists, because our sense of agency has not developed. This attitude, I suggest, is connected with the traits I have discussed: little sense of ownership over one's actions, a deficient sense of future awareness, and an inability to delay gratification. I contend that, in good part, these reflect poor parenting practices in Latin American countries.

Notes

1. N. Darling and L. Steinberg. "Parenting Style as Context: An Integrative Model." *Psychological Bulletin*, 113 (1993): 487–96. Darling and Steinberg distinguish between parenting practices and parenting style. Practices are parental strategies to help children attain their socialization goals; styles are independent of the specific content being transmitted and concern parental behavior such as the timbre of the parent's voice, emotional tone, and body language that contribute indirectly, through emotional arousal, to the child's internalization of values.
2. Jerome Kagan, *The Nature of the Child* (New York: Basic Books, 1984).
3. Jerome Kagan, *Three Seductive Ideas* (Cambridge, MA: Harvard University Press, 1998).
4. I. E. Sigel. "Reflections On the Belief-Behavior Connection: Lessons Learned From a Research Program on Parent Belief Systems and Teaching Strategies," in *Thinking About the Family: Views of Parents and Children*, ed. R. D. Ashmore and D. M. Brudzinski. (Hillsdale, NJ: Erlbaum, 1986), 35–65.
5. W. Damon. *Nurturing Children's Moral Growth* (New York: Free Press, 1990).
6. C. A. Montaner. "Culture and the Behavior of Elites in Latin America," in *Culture Matters*, ed. L. E. Harrison and S. P. Huntington (New York: Basic Books, 1990), 58.
7. The World Bank. *Governance and Development* (Washington, D.C.: World Bank. 1992).
8. Amir N. Licht, Chanan Goldschmidt, and Shalom H. Schwartz, *Culture Rules: The Foundations of the Rule of Law and Other Norms of Governance*, 2002. Available at http://papers.ssrn.com/sol3/papers.cfm?abstract_id=314559
9. Converting stress and anxiety into physical symptoms.
10. http://www.latinobarometro.org/English/inibiblio-i.htm
11. *La Nación*, Sunday January 12, 2003.
12. Licht et al., 2002..
13. M. Grondona, M. (2000). "A Cultural Typology of Economic Development," in Harrison and Huntington, *Culture Matters*. 44–55, at. 47.
14. Kagan, 1984.
15. J. Grusec and J. Goodnow, "Impact of Parental Discipline Methods on Child's Internalization of Values: A Reconceptualization of Current Points of View." *Developmental Psychology*, 30 (1994): 4–19.
16. R. R. Sears, E. E. Maccoby, and H. Levin, *Patterns of Child-Rearing* (New York: Row-Peterson, 1957).

17. M. L. Hoffman. "Affective and Cognitive Processes in Moral Internalization," in *Social Cognition and Social Development: A Socio-Cultural Perspective*, ed. E.T. Higgins, D. Ruble, and W. Hartup (Cambridge, UK: Cambridge University Press, 1983), 236–74.

18. D. Baumrind, "Current Patterns of Parental Authority." *Developmental Psychology Monograph*, 4, no. 1, Pt. 2 (1971):

19. C. Gilligan, *In a Different Voice* (Cambridge, MA: Harvard University Press, 1982).

20. G. R. Patterson and L. Bank, "Some Amplifying Mechanisms for Pathological Processes in Families," in *The Minnesota Symposium on Child Psychology: Systems and Development*, ed. M. R. Gunnar & E. Thelen (Hillsdale, NJ: Erlbaum, 1989), 169–209.

21. *La Nación*, February 19, 2003.

22. Thomas Lickona, *Educating for Character: How Our Schools Can Teach Respect and Responsibility* (New York: Bantam Books, 1991), 395.

23. Octavio Paz, *El Laberinto de la Soledad* (México: Fondo de Cultura Económica, 1950),18.

24. Summa, Edición # 105 February 2003. Editorial San Jose, S.A. 56.

Part II
Education

3

Cultural Values and Parenting Education

SHARON L. KAGAN
AMY E. LOWENSTEIN

Despite the increasingly vast literature on *parenting* across cultures, comparatively little attention has been accorded the cultural dimensions of formal *parenting education*. First, formal parenting education is absent from the practice of many cultures that rely on the informal transmission of cultural values, norms, and beliefs and is primarily a characteristic of literate societies. Second, because many scholars regard parenting education as a comparatively underdeveloped phenomenon shrouded in ambiguity, they do not consider it worthy of serious study. Third, the interaction of parenting and culture is so complex that scholars have avoided it.

This inattention is unwise. The cultural roots of, and biases inherent in, parenting education should command attention because there is growing global interest in parenting education as a workable intervention to enhance parenting capacities and skills, and increase children's life chances. Moreover, given the increasing cultural pluralism that characterizes even heretofore culturally homogeneous nations, attention to culture, in all its manifestations, should be accorded priority. Finally, because cultural inculcation occurs early in life, an intense focus on the early years, and the practices attendant to them, should be a priority for scholarly inquiry and government policy.

The purpose of this chapter is to address the void at the intersection of parenting education and culture, focusing on parenting education programs that serve the families of young children. This chapter begins by placing parenting education in three contexts: the definitional context, the historical context, and the contemporary context. Our review suggests that more attention has been accorded its strategic intentions than its cultural intentions. The chapter considers analytic work on the relationship between parenting and culture. It examines key theories of cultural parenting and suggests which of them have salience. The chapter concludes with suggestions for advancing culturally sound parenting education.

Section I—Parenting Education in Context: Diverse Definitions and Assumptions

Parenting education is both similar to, and different from, parenting. Both share a commitment to fostering the well-being of children by parents or other nurturing adults. But parenting and parenting education part company in their strategies, degrees of formality, and goals. Parenting refers to the usual efforts carried out by nurturing adults that advance their children's well-being and development. Parenting education, on the other hand, provides a means of supporting parents as they carry out these functions. Parenting education typically involves materials and/or another adult who supports, teaches, mentors, or coaches the parent. In most parenting education efforts, the primary focus of the interaction is between the parent and the supporting adult. While parenting is informal and continuous, parenting education is formal and intermittent and is often accompanied by a formal curriculum and a process of transmitting information to parents so it can be replicated.

Parenting and parenting education also differ in their orientations. Parenting is private, inculcates values, and acculturates children to familial and social norms. Parenting education is less private, and while it inculcates values, it focuses more on changing behaviors. Parenting education involves a range of educational and supportive activities that help parents and prospective parents understand their social, emotional, psychological, and physical needs, as well as those of their children, with the goal of enhancing the relationships between them and within the family unit and the community.

Parenting education usually has three distinct objectives: normative, preventive, and remedial. Each is linked to goals, programs, and strategies. The normative objective states that parenting education is something all parents need in order to carry out their parenting role. There is no stigma attached to parenting education; rather, it is an evolving necessity, emerging as a result of the demands of an increasingly mobile and complex society. From this perspective, parenting education is regarded as a social necessity, akin to the education that adults need to perform the responsibilities of daily living. Parenting education is regarded as essential, just as driver education is for driving an automobile.

Slightly less normative and more didactic, preventive parenting education is the ongoing transmission of information that helps parents prepare themselves and their children for the world. Inherent in this approach is the belief that parenting can be improved with regular supports or interventions. Such interventions might occur over a span of years or might be used to meet a transitional need in the family. In other words, parenting education can support families through the exigencies of daily living and also can assist in crisis prevention.

Finally, parenting education with remedial objectives can be seen as "the purposive learning activity of parents who are attempting to change their method of interaction with their children for the purpose of encouraging positive behavior in their children" (Croake and Glover 1977, 151). Parenting education may be regarded as an antidote to negative conditions, sometimes situational, and often enduring. The goal of this type of parenting education is to alter behavior or interaction patterns between parents and children, often with participation by governmental agencies.

Irrespective of which of the three types of parenting education is being considered, we contend that parenting education, like parenting, influences and reflects culture in ways that are deep-seated and not well understood. To begin to clarify the relationship between parenting education and culture, we turn to a brief history of parenting education.

Section II—Parenting Education In Historical Context

Within the West, writings about parenting and child rearing date to fifteenth-century Europe, when children were exalted and considered crucial to the future of the state. Later, the Protestant church had a significant influence on child-rearing; it claimed that parents were too indulgent with their children, thereby jeopardizing the future order of the church and state. Consequently, parents were encouraged to train their children in good habits at an early age.

A fundamental shift in beliefs occurred in the eighteenth century, when childhood was seen not merely as a preparation for adulthood or heaven, but as a stage of life with value in its own right. Rather than innately evil, children were considered angelic messengers from God. Proper child rearing involved giving children freedom to grow. John Locke's argument that a child was a *tabula rasa*, a blank slate, with respect to ideas (not abilities or temperament) was influential and carried with it profound implications for child rearing and education.

Under the influence of Romanticism, childhood came to be considered the best part of life, and a large body of imaginative children's literature emerged. Mothers, who had been reestablished as children's primary caregivers, worried not simply about their children's behavior but also about their health and whether they would live. The primary emphasis in child rearing during this time was on hygiene and routine.

Although many assumed that raising a child was instinctive, many women felt the need to inform themselves about parenting. Some turned to relatives, extended families, friends, and community groups for advice. But mothers also wanted to hear from and share their experiences with other mothers. It isn't surprising, then, that in the early nineteenth century parenting education in the United States took the form of informal mother support groups, often called mothers' or child study groups. Early on, and in clear contrast to later efforts, the groups focused mainly on the religious and moral improvement of children—the inculcation of mainstream values.

The first formalization of these efforts occurred near the turn of the twentieth century, when hundreds of these small groups joined together to form the National Congress of Mothers (which became the National Parent-Teacher Association). As these small groups converged to create a formal women's organization, the goals shifted dramatically to embrace more action-oriented political intentions. The organization became the vehicle for reinforcing collective and individual female identities, for disseminating recent child-rearing information to all classes, and for changing society.

As the focus of parenting education switched from a focus on personal values to a social change orientation, the stage was set for federal support for parenting education which took hold in the twentieth century. High infant mortality rates, coupled with a decline in confidence in the ability of the poor to raise children properly, led to the identification of childhood as an arena for necessary intervention by the state (Brim 1959; Cunningham, 1995). In 1918 the United States Public Health Service began support of parenting education programs, placing special emphasis on improving children's physical conditions—the hygienic, health, and nutritional aspects of parenting. Little Mothers' Leagues were created for girls aged twelve and up who had immigrant parents, so they could teach parents about hygiene. In Europe and the United States, nurses began to make visits to working-class homes to enforce proper hygiene (Cunningham 1995). Parenting education became a vehicle for social reform.

Parenting education reached a critical juncture in the twentieth century. Upper- and middle-class women saw the importance of providing parenting education to the poor, indigent, and working classes. Yet with this alteration came important operational shifts. When parenting education served upper- and middle-class families, there was a focus on non-hierarchical group sharing and collective learning. As parenting education changed its focus to serve the lower classes, it became more hierarchical, didactic, and prescriptive in orientation.

So, parenting education came of age with somewhat divided orientations—the normative, preventive, and remedial—that are manifest to this day. Early on, the tensions in parenting education made it, on the one hand, the purview of mothers as the guardians of private morality and, on the other hand, a tool of social mobility and progress for the poor.

The post-World War II era brought major societal changes that mirrored the prior evolution of parenting education. As the sense of shared responsibility for child rearing eroded, informal supports for parents returned, this time in a new form. Increasingly, middle-class parents looked to "experts," like Dr. Spock, Selma Fraiberg, Thomas Gordon, Erik Erikson, and John Bowlby, to guide their parenting. In the 1960s, as the nation became more concerned about its poor, grassroots, community-based parenting programs emerged, and the nation turned to education of young children and their parents as a way to break the cycle of poverty.

Best known and most pervasive among these efforts was the national Head Start program, which had a two-fold perspective on parenting education. First, the Head Start program engaged parents in pedagogical and policy aspects of the program. In addition, parents were seen to be in need of more education and opportunity, so parenting education—along with literacy education and job training—emerged as an important component of Head Start.

Perhaps influenced by the parent empowerment component of Head Start and as a result of a growing self-help movement in the United States, parenting education programs continued to emerge in communities. They were driven sometimes by specific social concerns, such as school readiness and child abuse prevention, and sometimes simply by parents' desires to offer the best to their children (Carter 1996). Gradually, the programs began to be replicated and, as they grew, they developed statewide technical-assistance and training arms. Parenting education surpassed its first surge to evolve into a full-fledged movement in the United States and in many other western nations.

This brief review points to several key facts. First, not once, but twice, parenting education evolved as a middle-class effort that was modified to accommodate the needs of mostly poor populations. What mattered most was not the inculcation of values but providing support to needy parents. Somewhat lost in the zeal to do good was the reality that such programs were important mechanisms for acculturation.

Second, we see that parenting education is multifaceted. On the one hand, it is an inculcator and reflector of values; on the other hand, it is a potent means of behavior modification and an instrument of social action and social improvement.

Third, despite remarkable growth in the United States parenting education movement, parenting education has remained on the fringe of public policy—a desirable policy adornment if funds were available. But, parenting education has never had a rich empirical research base, a codified social strategy, or robust public support.

Section III—Parenting Education in the Contemporary Context

To better understand parenting education in the contemporary context, let us first look at the numbers and the penetration levels.

Today there are more than 50,000 parenting education programs in the United States serving millions of parents and caregivers. For the most part, the programs are small, community-based efforts with budgets under $25,000, but there are also state-funded and federally funded multimillion-dollar programs, nonprofit programs with hundreds of sites, and a growing number of for-profit parenting education businesses. In most cases, the larger programs, including Parents as Teachers (PAT) and the Minnesota Early Learning Design (MELD), now the national MELD program, have been designed by practitioners. The Home Instruction for Parents of Preschool Youngsters (HIPPY) model was developed originally in Israel and is now in use throughout the United States and in countries around the world. Another particularly noteworthy parenting education effort is the Avance Parent-Child Education Program, developed in Texas, designed to accommodate the needs of low-income Mexican-American mothers in the Southwest.

A second way of understanding the contemporary American parenting education context has been proffered by Carter (1996). Reflecting both the breadth and the highly idiosyncratic nature of parenting education programs, he has classified efforts by the focus area of their activity. The areas are: education, multiple and complex needs, health care, normative, special needs, advocacy, and work.

A third way to understand the nature of contemporary parenting education is to examine the didactic strategies used by the programs. In some, the programs are highly structured, aiming to impart a standard body of information in a prescribed manner, with the goal of changing aspects of parenting style or behaviors. In the middle of the spectrum are programs that teach more general parenting skills, with the goal of enhancing the parent-child relationship as well as improving academic performance of children. The final group of programs functions to empower parents to be wise decision-makers for themselves and their children.

What is of central interest for this paper is that in contemporary theories and visions of parenting education, there is virtually no mention of culture. Indeed, culture is often regarded as the silent elephant in the room. It is there, so huge and omnipresent that no one knows quite what to do with it. As such, it is important to examine the relationship between parenting and culture to uncover its properties and nuances.

Section IV—Parenting and Culture

Understanding the relationship between parenting and culture is gaining some currency. Perhaps this is due to globalization and the ability of scholars to travel; perhaps it is due to the growing knowledge base that has emerged from the blending of cultural anthropology and social and developmental psychology; or perhaps it is simply due to the fact that so many countries on the planet are becoming more culturally diverse.

Clearly, the caring, rearing and apprenticing of children into their culture are the concerns of parents in every society. The task of parenting is for parents to create the conditions in which children can develop to their fullest capacity both inside and outside the family. Inherent in these definitions are several assumptions: first, parenting is directed toward socializing children into the culture in which they will live, with the mother often playing the dominant role. Second, parents are the driving force in the child-parent relationship, and as the experience of parenting unfolds over time, conceptions of parenting become richer and more refined. Third, more recently, parenting refers to the functions executed by a caring adult irrespective of blood relationship.

With regard to the role of parents as agents of acculturation, there are a number of studies and theories. One body of parenting work focuses on the role of the parent as a socializing agent. Early on, for example, the Whitings (Whiting and Whiting 1975) noted that the level of cultural complexity affected how parents fashioned their children's social roles and behavior, with children in less complex societies being acculturated toward more cooperative behavior and children in more complex societies being socialized toward more competitive behavior.

This perspective of parents as socializing agents represents a subtle departure from the literature that focuses on more intimate and emotional dimensions of parent-child interactions. In this body of literature, parents are regarded as the force that drives the parent-child interactions. Darling and Steinberg (1993) have noted that this emerges in two primary domains. *Parenting style* refers to the emotional climate in which parenting behaviors are manifest and *parenting practices* refer to observed interaction approaches used by parents.

Baumrind (1972) has classified parenting styles as authoritarian, authoritative, and permissive. Parents who are controlling, cold, and unresponsive are characterized as authoritarian; parents who are warm and responsive, provide structure for their children's learning, and set behavioral limits and explicit standards for competent behavior, are characterized as authoritative; and parents who are warm and responsive but exert little control are characterized as permissive. Over the years, this thinking has been expanded to include disengaged parents.

Two predominant assumptions frame the research. In one conception, the assumption is that the adult is the controlling force in the relationship and has the power to influence child behaviors. In this model, one that is very difficult to examine empirically, a direct and linear relationship between the parents' behavior and child outcomes is assumed. The flaw in this line of inquiry, however, is that it does not take into consideration the responses of the child and the impact that such responses evoke, in turn, on the parents. More recently, in the second conception, parenting is regarded as an interactive relationship with the parent influencing the child and the child influencing the parent.

The treatment of culture in this literature varies and is somewhat controversial, as well. Some of this literature has attributed cultural variation to differences in the way the individual relates to his/her social context. In one version, the individual functions quite individually and quite independently of his setting; in the other, the individual is enmeshed in, and dependent upon, the collective. Scholars note that, in cultures that emphasize individualism, the developmental goal is independence, with socialization patterns directed at producing autonomous, self-fulfilled individuals who engage in relationships out of choice. In collectivist cultures, the developmental goal is interdependence, with individuals existing in a network of relationships often prescribed by others.

Despite (or perhaps because of) the popularity of the independence-dependence frame, criticisms of it abound. Most germane to parenting education is the concern that the simplification masks the intensity and depth of cultural variation. The framework is criticized because it falsely polarizes cultures. In so doing, it tends to overgeneralize cultural hegemony and depreciates within-culture variation. Criticisms of the dependence-independence frame also emerge because of the close (and some suggest questionable) links that have been made between economic development and cultural predispositions (Harkness and Super 2002). Kagitçibasi (1996) notes, for example, that as a rule more rural/agrarian societies are collective in orientation because the model supports the extended family as an economic necessity. In industrial, technological societies, where the unit of employment is the individual, independence and self-reliance are more valued. However accurate, it is still true that most contemporary societies, even those that are primarily agrarian, are moving toward industrial complexity.

Finally, criticisms exist because the dependence-independence frame does not allow for the nuanced and idiosyncratic behavior of parents. For example, Chao (1994) noted that Chinese immigrants to the United States practiced combinations of behavior labeled separately in the literature as authoritarian and authoritative. Whereas these parenting styles may be considered contradictory in some cultures, amongst this population they were complementary. In other cases, immigrant parents may rely on their native culture and incorporate patterns from the mainstream culture as well to affect a unique parenting style not subject to clear categorization (LeVine et al. 1994; Reese, Balzano, Gallimore, and Goldenberg 1995).

Despite the fact that the individual-collective cultural framework is not foolproof, its wide use argues that we must examine its implications for parenting education. Specifically, we now turn to a discussion of the assumptions about young children that the framework evokes, discerning how this does and should impact parenting education programs and practices.

Section V—Parenting Education and Culture

As noted earlier, parenting education tends to alter parenting behaviors rather than parents' values. To alter values is considered by many an inappropriate incursion on family privacy; to alter behaviors so that they conform to operative cultural norms is, however, acceptable, if not desirable. The transmission of culture, therefore, is both an implicit influencer of, and an explicit goal of, parenting education. The role of culture in parenting education is manifest in two ways. The first relates to conceptions of dependence and independence, and the second relates to socio-economic status and its social correlate, race.

The Dependence-Independence Frame

The independence-oriented perspective views children starting life as naturally dependent on their parents, but as they grow, they are socialized to independence. Family and generational ties, while important, do not hold the same value as in the more dependence-oriented or collective approach. In the collective approach, children start life as highly individualized and somewhat asocial creatures who gradually become socialized to the collective as they mature. Being part of the collective is the goal.

Operationally, for those who value individuality and independence, children are encouraged to express themselves, to speak out, and to be individualistic in their responses. In the collective approach, young children are indulged and coddled. As they mature, they are socialized to follow directions, conform, develop familial loyalty, and internalize elders' commands (Kagitçibasi 1996). Such different values are manifest in various dimensions of parenting education efforts, in the goals of the program, in the way the program is carried out, and in its curriculum. Each will be explored from the dependence-independence perspective.

Explicit mention of the dependence-independence framework is rare. It is clear, however, that this framework implicitly guides the goals of parenting education programs and, in some cases, even determines their activities. In considering the development and application of parenting education programs, parents' preferred values regarding the dependence-independence dichotomy must be considered.

The dependence-independence framework influences aspects of pedagogical strategy. In teaching and learning, the role of reinforcement is critical. In highly individualistic and competitive settings, reinforcement for correct responses is expected. Praise for correct responses is part of a teaching strategy. For more collectively oriented parents, however, such reinforcement is less necessary. Reinforcement that praises an individual respondent calls attention to his or her difference from the group. Moreover, in highly collective groups, people are expected to fulfill their roles; the use of praise and reinforcement is not necessary and can be considered insulting.

Patterns and amounts of communication are also influenced by the dependence-independence paradigm, both for parents in the parenting education setting and for parents in the parent-child relationship. Parents in all cultures use a variety of communication styles, but parent-child (and teacher-parent) styles vary by culture. With regard to parent-child communication, Azuma (1994) notes that Japanese mothers rely more on empathy and non-verbal communication than do mothers in the United States. Verbalization is less necessary when there is close physical and psychological proximity between mother and child. Other studies have shown that this deep connection "permits" mothers in collective cultures to "enter their children's reality" and to speak on their behalf (Choi 1992).

Mothers in individualistic cultures withdraw so that the children can speak on their own, thereby encouraging self-expression and autonomy in the child. The use of questions and responses is also more frequently observed in individually oriented cultures, even when the questioner knows the answer to the question being posed. This style elicits dialogue and confirms the knowledge of those being questioned.

The Socio-Economic Status/Race Frame

As influential as the dependence-independence frame is in the United States, the salience of a socio-economic status (SES)/race frame can not be overlooked. As noted in the historical review presented earlier, parenting education emerged from two tracks early in its history: normative parenting education for the middle- and upper-classes, and preventive/remedial parenting education for the poor. The reality of public funding in the United States has meant, however, that many of the parenting education programs are designed to prevent problems in at-risk populations, populations over-represented amongst the poor.

Parenting goals vary by socio-economic class, with parents of lower economic and educational status valuing conformity to authority and more authoritarian parenting practices when compared to parents of higher educational and economic status, who value self-direction and authoritative parenting (Hoff-Ginsburg and Tardiff 1995; Kohn 1990). Data also reveal that parents of low SES are less likely to enroll in, participate in, and complete parenting education programs than their higher-SES peers (Fine 1989; McMahon, Forehand, Griest, and Wells 1981).

One can certainly associate differences in goals and participation rates with SES, but SES alone does not reveal the entire picture. Additionally, racial and ethnic differences must be examined in any discussion of parenting education. Slaughter (1988) has noted that, typically, racial and ethnic diversity was deemphasized in family intervention efforts. Nowhere is that more true than in parenting education. Heretofore, typical models of parenting education have been based on euro-centric philosophies that may not reflect the values or intents of non-whites. As Dunst and Paget (1991) have indicated, many of the commercially available parenting education materials are not culturally sensitive. Alvy (1994), for example, noted that in two popular programs (Parent Effectiveness Training [PET] and Systematic Training for Effective Parenting [STEP]), modal families are two-parent families with adequate financial resources.

Cultural sensitivity "implies not only an understanding of a group's unique values, beliefs and customs, but an appreciation of these differences as well" (Gorman and Balter 1997, 4). Cultural sensitivity acknowledges different ways of being, with differences being accepted as strengths, not weaknesses. In parenting education, such diversity manifests itself in the acceptance of non-traditional childrearing practices.

Less apparent is the degree to which such cultural sensitivity is invoked in parenting education programs. It is clear that attempts are being made in three distinct ways (Gorman and Balter, 1997). First, many parenting education programs have been translated into the language of the population being served. Second, some parenting education programs have been culturally adapted. A culturally adapted program, one according to Alvy (1994) that has been "transcultured," incorporates the values and cultural predispositions of the served group. Third, culturally specific programs are designed precisely to facilitate successful parenting within a specific culture. They are not adaptations of existing programs but begin with the cultural values and expectations of participating populations. Within the United States, these programs are far less prevalent than the transliterated or transcultured programs that exist for African American parents (Effective Black Parenting Program), for Hispanic parents (Los Niños Bien Educados and the Houston Parent-Child Development Program), and for Native American parents (Positive Indian Parenting).

Evaluations of the handful of culturally sensitive parenting education programs show weak support for their overall efficacy (Gorman and Balter 1997). Results suggest that programs are more effective in producing greater behavioral change in parents than in children. The weak findings may be attributable to the fact that the majority of the culturally sensitive programs are either translated or culturally adapted versions of traditional parenting education programs; that is, they are not culturally specific. Although they represent attempts at creating programs for parents outside the mainstream American culture, these efforts remain essentially variations on a euro-centric theme.

It is important to place this research within the context of research conducted on parenting education programs in general. Such reviews also yield quite mixed results. Parenting education research focuses either on program content (e.g., PAT, HIPPY) or means of delivery (e.g., home visiting). First-line effects are often found in the parents, in their parenting practices, and/or in the home environment, and the effects tend to be more pronounced for lower-SES populations (Powell 1989).

Given the caveats discussed earlier, available data suggest that parenting education programs do not need to be culturally sensitive to achieve results. They also suggest that positive results on non-culturally sensitive tests are best achieved through non-culturally sensitive interventions. These findings, however, do not support an acultural stance; they merely reflect the status of the pedagogical and evaluation enterprises. The key questions are: what do we really want out of parenting education programs; for whom; and how do we best achieve it?

Section VI—Moving Beyond Current Parenting Education Paradigms: Strategies for Consideration

In addressing these critical questions, we suggest that, first, a conceptual shift must take place, and second, that it must be accompanied by strategic and practical changes. As this paper has suggested, parenting education is inherently a critical instrument of cultural inculcation, and therefore a value-laden enterprise. In practice, however, too little consideration has been given to the values being inculcated, both in the vision of the programs and in the strategies used to carry them out. Parenting education programs have been largely oriented to changing parenting behaviors, with modest attention paid to values inculcation. Parenting education programs must become more overt about the values they espouse and ensure that the behavior changes they advocate align with those values.

Reconceptualizing Parenting Education to Embrace Values

A first step, then, is to consider the values that parenting education should incorporate. The United Nations Universal Declaration of Human Rights and the Culture Matters Research Project are relevant here. The global goals of both are to produce societies that are socially just, that assure citizens economic prosperity, and that are governed by democratic principles and mechanisms. If one believes that such goals are culturally influenced and that parenting education is a useful mechanism of cultural transmission, then parenting education should incorporate reinforcement of the values linked to these goals.

By embracing the United Nations Human Rights goals as legitimate ends of parenting education, we do two important things. First, we enlarge the frame of parenting education and set it in a broader context. Second, we elevate the ends of parenting education to acknowledge its potency not merely as a means for behavioral change but as a vehicle for value change. Parenting education could become a means for inculcating values essential to human rights and to an improved human condition. Furthermore, the promotion of the United Nations Human Rights goals could open the door to more culturally sensitive societies, ones that might be more receptive to advancing parenting education programs. Bringing values to the forefront of parenting education is not inconsistent with its early goals. But, given today's interpretation of the function of parenting education (as largely behavioral change), its inability to deliver on that fully, and the controversy likely to surround integration of values into parenting education, a transformation of this scope depends on a broad consensus that culture matters and that parenting education can play an important role in cultural change.

Parenting education is a good candidate, given the reforms already afoot and its inherent orientation toward promoting behavioral changes. Recent efforts to reform parenting education so that it is more "culturally relevant" are not inconsistent with such a reconceptualization. Those espousing this orientation want a voice and want the values they favor expressed in parenting education programs. Such values are manifest in racial or linguistic sensitivity; however, the intentions behind them are congruent with precisely the goals of social justice, democratic representation, and prosperity.

The purposes of parenting education need to be re-examined with an eye toward its potency as an accelerator and inculcator of values, not only as a device for altering behaviors. The United Nations Human Rights agenda, with its broad goals and emphasis on social justice, is a good place to start. Consideration could be given to adopting social justice, democratic governance, and prosperity as ultimate goals. Interim goals that are correlated in the literature with these ultimate goals could be specified. For example, goals of trust and tolerance have been linked to social justice, democratic governance, and prosperity. Benjamin Franklin's thirteen virtues (temperance, silence, order, resolution, frugality, industry, sincerity, justice, moderation, cleanliness, tranquility, chastity, and humility) could be individually examined for their relevance to a contemporary vision for parenting education.

Strategic and Practice Changes

In addition to broad reconceptualizations, we need to address strategic and practice changes in the content, pedagogy, and infrastructure of parenting education efforts. With regard to the content, we return to the issue of culturally translated, culturally adapted, and culturally specific programs. To date, neither culturally specific nor culturally universal parenting education efforts has been given sufficient attention from programmatic or evaluative perspectives. When this occurs, data from evaluations should be used to guide the design of a new values-driven conceptualization of parenting education. For example, if a goal of values-driven parenting education is the promotion of social justice, then the values of tolerance and trust would need to be emphasized in a revamped parenting education curriculum. Parenting education should make a clear commitment to a values orientation, with the understanding that cultural values transcend behaviors. In other words, culture trumps content.

With regard to the pedagogy of parenting education, the more remedial the objective, the more prescriptive and didactic the program. At the other extreme, parenting education efforts that are more normative in intention might use strategies that elicit divergent reactions from parents and use instructional technologies that are more varied. Parenting efforts that are in the middle—those designed to be preventive—would incorporate elements from each. Whatever the intention, the instructional strategies employed need to reflect the cultural orientations of the participants.

Finally, attention must also be accorded the infrastructure of parenting education. By infrastructure we mean the essential supports that influence the delivery of parenting education, including professional development, regulation and quality control, funding, and governance. Parenting educators need to have experience with the curriculum to be taught and the pedagogies to be used. Moreover, professional staff will need to be familiar with the program content. Attention to professional development of parent educators is a critical quality safeguard. To date, most parenting education programs are not regulated and have limited quality standards. Guidelines for program monitoring and program quality should be established.

Funding for parenting education has remained highly irregular and uncertain with the exception of several states and countries. Reliable funding is indispensable. How parenting education programs are governed is another serious issue that is likely to influence their nature and financing. Policymakers should carefully examine alternative governance possibilities before consigning parenting education to any single governance apparatus.

Parenting education with value content should become a matter of priority for ministers of education and human services agencies worldwide. In summary, it is necessary to:

- Distinguish between efforts that explicitly promote behaviors only and those that explicitly promote behaviors and values;
- Delineate through an inclusive process the values to be promoted;
- Assure that the content of parenting education reflects the desired values;
- Align instructional strategies and pedagogy with the values;
- Establish a delivery system/systems that effectively promote values; and
- Develop the infrastructure to support parenting education adequately.

References

Alvy, K. T., *Parent Training Today: A Social Necessity*. Studio City, CA: Center for Improvement of Child Caring, 1994.

Azuma, H., "Two Nodes of Cognitive Socialization in Japan and the United States," in *Cross-Cultural Roots of Minority Child Development*, ed. P. M. Greenfield and R. R. Cocking (Hillsdale, NJ: Erlbaum, 1994), 275–284.

Baumrind, D., "An Exploratory Study of Socialization Effects on Black Children: Some Black-White Comparisons," *Child Development* 43 (1972): 262–267.

Brim, O. G., *Education for Child Rearing*. New York: Russell Sage Foundation, 1959.

Carter, N., *See how we grow: A report on the status of parenting education in the U.S.* (Philadelphia, PA: The Pew Charitable Trusts), retrieved January 23, 2003, from http://www.pewtrust.com (December 1996).

Chao, R., "Beyond Parental Control and Authoritarian Parenting Style: Understanding Chinese Parenting through the Cultural Notion of Training," *Child Development* 65 (1994): 1111–1119.

Choi, S. H., (1992). "Communicative Socialization Processes: Korea and Canada," in *Innovations in Cross-Cultural Psychology*, ed. S. Iwawaki, Y. Kashima, and K. Leung (Lisse, The Netherlands: Swets & Zeitlinger, 1992), 103–121 .

Croake, J. W. and K. E. Glover, "A History and Evaluation of Parent Education," *The Family Coordinator* 26 (1977): 151–158.

Cunningham, H., *Children and Childhood in Western Society since 1500*. London: Longman Group, 1995.

Darling, N. and L. Steinberg, "Parenting Style as Context: An Integrative Model," *Psychological Bulletin* 113 (1993): 487–496.

Dunst, C. J. and K. Paget, "Parent-Professional Partnerships and Family Empowerment," in *Collaboration with Parents of Exceptional Children*, ed. M. Fine (Brandon, VT: Clinical Psychology Publishing, 1991), 25–44.

Fine, M. J., *The Second Handbook on Parent Education: Contemporary Perspectives*. New York: Academic Press, 1989.

Gorman, J. C. and L. Balter, "Culturally Sensitive Parent Education: A Critical Review of Quantitative Tesearch," *Review of Educational Research* 67, no. 3 (1997): 339–369.

Harkness, S. and C. M. Super, "Culture and Parenting," in *Handbook of parenting: Vol. 2. Biology and ecology of parenting*, 2nd ed. (Mahwah, NJ: Erlbaum, 2002), 253–280.

HIPPY USA, *The HIPPY model*, retrieved March 3, 2003, from http://www.hippyusa.org/Model/model.html (2003).

Hoff-Ginsburg, E. and T. Tardiff, (1995). "Socioeconomic Status and Parenting," in *Handbook of parenting: Vol. 2. Biology and ecology of parenting*, ed. M. Bornstein (Mahwah, NJ: Erlbaum, 1995), 161–188).

Kagitçibasi, Ç., *Family and Human Development Across Cultures: A View from the Other Side*. Mahwah, NJ: Erlbaum, 1996.

Kohn, M., "Position in the Class Structure and Psychological Functioning in the United States, Japan, and Poland," *American Journal of Sociology* 94 (1990): 964–1008.

LeVine, R. A., S. Dixon, S. LeVine, A. Richman, P. Leiderman, C. Keefer, et al., *Child Care and Culture: Lessons from Africa*. Cambridge: Cambridge University Press, 1994.

McMahon, R. J., R. Forehand, D. L. Griest, and K. C. Wells, "Who drops out of treatment during parent behavioral training?" *Behavioral Counseling Quarterly* 1 (1981): 79–85.

National Black Child Development Institute, *The Spirit of Excellence: Parent Empowerment Project (PEP). NBCDI Parent Education Curriculum*. Washington, DC: Author, n.d.

Olds, D. L. and H. Kitzman, "Review of Research on Home Visiting for Pregnant Women and Parents of Young Children," *Future of Children* 3 (1993): 53–92.

Parents as Teachers, *What is PAT?* Retrieved January 24, 2003 from http://www.patnc.org. (2003).

Powell, D. R. *Families and Early Childhood Programs*, Washington, DC: National Association for the Education of Young Children, 1989.

Reese, L., S. Balzano, R. Gallimore, and C. Goldenberg, "The concept of *educación*: Latino family values and American schooling," *International Journal of Educational Research* 23, no. 1 (1995): 57–81.

Slaughter, D. T., "Programs for Racially and Ethnically Diverse American Families: Some Critical Issues," in *Evaluating Family Programs,* ed. H. B. Weiss and F. H. Jacobs (New York: Aldine de Gruyter, 1988), 461–476.

Whiting, B. B. and J. W. M. Whiting, *The Children of Six Cultures: A Psychocultural Analysis*. Cambridge, MA: Harvard University Press, 1975.

4

Character Education

Restoring Virtue to the Mission of Schools

THOMAS LICKONA

Character matters. Societies need character not only to survive but also to progress toward the dignity and development of all their members. Progressive cultural change requires the widespread internalization of values such as democracy, social and economic justice, honesty, and individual initiative and responsibility. Such values must become virtues, habits of mind, heart, and conduct, in the character of many citizens. Just as character enables a culture to flourish, it also enables a person to lead a fulfilling life.

As we begin a new millennium, there is a renewed concern for character. It springs in part from a sense that in recent decades character has eroded. James Q. Wilson notes that throughout much of the industrialized West we find "high and rising levels of property crime, high and rising levels of out-of-wedlock births, and high levels of both divorce and drug abuse."[1] In these societies many adults worry that young people are put off by hard work and drawn to the easy pleasures of sex, drugs, drinking, and endless absorption in the electronic media. Young people, for their part, could point out that many adults are so preoccupied with their jobs and personal pursuits that they neglect their children's needs for love, discipline, and moral teaching. Many social commentators point to the pervasiveness of a hedonistic media culture, steadily declining levels of participation in civic organizations, and a general atrophy of common life. These concerns are not limited to the West.

Such trends pose special dangers for democracies. As the authors of *The Federalist Papers* emphasized, democracy is government by the people; the people themselves are responsible for ensuring a free and just society. That means the people, or at least a critical mass of citizens, must in some basic sense be good. They must understand, and be committed to, the moral foundations of democracy: respect for the rights of individuals, voluntary compliance with the law, participation in public life, and concern for the common good. These democratic virtues, the Founders maintained, must be instilled at an early age.

The History of Character Education

Throughout most of American history, cultivating the virtues that make for good citizenship and a productive life has been a primary purpose of schooling. Horace Mann, considered the father of the common school, argued that character was the highest goal of education.[2] Modeling good character was considered the first responsibility of teachers. Within the school curriculum, books like the *McGuffey Readers* gave pupils a daily diet of inspiring tales about honesty, hard work, thrift, kindness, patriotism, and courage. Instruction in virtue through discipline, edifying stories, and the teacher's good example remained a major mission of public schools until around the middle of the twentieth century. At that point, several forces converged to reshape the Zeitgeist and weaken support for teaching character. Prominent among these was the philosophy of logical positivism, which argued that value statements such as "Stealing is bad" and "Kindness is good" could not be proven in the way that scientific claims could be proven; therefore moral statements had no status as objective truth. As a result of positivism, morality was made to seem entirely a matter of subjective and variable opinion, not a matter for public transmission through the schools.

The 1960s saw a worldwide surge of "personalism." This philosophical movement celebrated the worth, autonomy, and subjectivity of the individual person. It emphasized individual rights and freedom over responsibility. It rightly protested societal oppression and injustice such as racism and sexism, and it advanced human rights. But it also undermined moral authority, further eroded belief in objective moral standards, led people to become preoccupied with self-fulfillment (weakening social commitments such as marriage and parenting), and fueled the socially destabilizing sexual revolution.

At the same time, the rapidly intensifying pluralism of American society raised the vexing question, "*Whose* values should we teach in the school?" Finally, the increasing secularization of the public arena, notably Supreme Court rulings against promoting religion in public schools, caused people to worry that if schools became involved in moral education, they would also become involved in religion and thus violate the First Amendment.

For most educators, a significant shift had occurred: from having students learn and practice virtuous behavior to having them discuss values and "options"; from "making the right decision" to "making your own decision."

Since 1990, there has been a return to the virtue-centered philosophy of character education. The resurgence of character education is evident in a spate of books and curricular materials, federal funding for character education, character education mandates in more than two-thirds of states, the emergence of national advocacy groups such as the Character Education Partnership and the Character Counts! Coalition, the appearance of university-based centers for character education (we operate one on our campus at SUNY Cortland), a *Journal of Research on Character Education*, a *National Schools of Character* awards competition, national reports on how to prepare future teachers to be character educators, and an explosion of grassroots character-education initiatives.

Although the current character education movement is in part a reaction against educational approaches perceived as having failed, it does not advocate simply dusting off the *McGuffey Readers*. Even a quick survey reveals an effort to integrate modern techniques—moral reflection, cooperative learning, classroom problem-solving meetings, conflict resolution, service learning, and participatory student government—into a comprehensive approach that blends the best of the old and the new.

Broadly defined, character education is the deliberate effort to cultivate virtue, and it permeates every phase of school life: the example of adults, relationships among peers, the handling of rules and discipline, the content of the curriculum, the rigor of academic standards, the conduct of extracurricular activities, and the involvement of parents. Understood this way, *everything* in the moral and intellectual life of the school is character education, because everything affects the developing values and character of students.

A core theoretical principle guiding character education is that of Aristotle: virtues are not mere thoughts but habits we develop by performing virtuous actions. Acting on that principle, character educators seek to help students perform virtuous acts repeatedly—until it becomes easy for them to do so and unnatural for them to do the opposite.

The Content of Character

Is it possible in postmodern, increasingly multicultural, and frequently fractious societies to agree on the content of character? Character education answers confidently that the content of character is virtue and that virtues are objectively good human qualities—good for us whether we know it or not. Because they are intrinsically good, virtues have a claim on our conscience. Virtues transcend time and culture (although their cultural expression and emphasis varies); justice, generosity, and honesty will always and everywhere be virtues, regardless of how many people exhibit them.

We can claim that virtues are objectively good, and not simply subjective preferences like taste in music and clothes, because they meet certain ethical criteria. They affirm our inherent human dignity. They promote the happiness and well-being of the individual. They serve the common good, making it possible for us to live and work in community. They define our rights and duties as citizens. They meet the classical ethical tests of reversibility ("Would you like to be treated this way?") and universalizability ("Would you want all persons to act this way in a similar situation?")

Of the many human virtues we could try to foster, which ones should schools promote? The virtues chosen will vary with the developmental level of the students and the culture of a school and its community. But reaching community consensus on desirable virtues is not as difficult as might be imagined. Hundreds of communities, for example, have adopted the "Six Pillars of Character": Trustworthiness, Respect, Responsibility, Fairness, Caring, and Citizenship, advanced by the California-based Character Counts! Coalition.

Our character education center at the State University of New York at Cortland promotes "ten essential virtues" that are affirmed by nearly all philosophical, religious, and cultural traditions: wisdom, justice, fortitude, self-mastery, love, positive attitude, hard work, integrity, gratitude, and humility.[3] The ancient Greeks considered *wisdom* the master virtue, the one that steers the others. Wisdom, or good judgment, tells us how to put the other virtues into practice. It tells us when to act, how to act, and how to integrate competing virtues (e.g., being truthful and yet charitable).

Justice is the virtue of treating others as they deserve to be treated. Character education programs often focus on justice because it covers so many of the interpersonal virtues: civility, courtesy, honesty, respect, responsibility, and tolerance (correctly defined not as "acceptance" of other people's beliefs or behaviors but as respect for their freedom of conscience as long as they do not violate the rights of others). Justice also includes social justice, working to create a world that respects the rights of all persons.

Fortitude is the virtue that enables us to do what is right in the face of life's difficulties. As the educator James Stenson points out, it is the inner toughness that enables us to overcome or withstand hardships, defeats, inconvenience, and pain.[4] Patience, perseverance, courage, resilience, and endurance are all aspects of fortitude.

Self-control, which the Greeks called "temperance," is the ability to govern ourselves. It enables us to control our temper, regulate our appetites and impulses, and pursue even legitimate pleasures in moderation. It is the power to say no, resist temptation, and delay gratification in the service of higher and distant goals. An old saying recognizes the importance of self-mastery: "Either we rule our desires, or our desires rule us." Reckless and criminal behavior flourishes in the absence of self-control.

Love is the virtue that enables us to sacrifice for the sake of another. It goes beyond justice, giving more than fairness requires. A whole cluster of important human traits—empathy, compassion, kindness, generosity, service, loyalty, patriotism (love of what is noble in one's country), and forgiveness—make up the virtue of love.

A *positive attitude* is a sixth essential virtue. If we have a negative attitude in life, we are a burden to ourselves and others. The character strengths of hope, enthusiasm, flexibility, resilience, and a sense of humor are all part of a positive attitude. Lincoln observed: "Most people are about as happy as they make up their minds to be."

Hard work is the way we develop our gifts and talents and use them to contribute to the lives of others. The virtue of work includes initiative, diligence, goal-setting, and resourcefulness.

Integrity is the virtue of adhering to moral principle, being faithful to moral conscience, and standing up for what we believe. It means being "whole," so that what we say and do in different situations is consistent rather than contradictory. Integrity is different from honesty, which tells the truth to others; integrity, as one sage said, is telling the truth to oneself.

Gratitude has been described as the secret of a happy life. It moves us to count our blessings and be aware that we all drink from wells we did not dig. "A thankful heart," Cicero said, "is the parent of all virtues."

The tenth essential virtue is *humility*, the virtue of striving for virtue. "Humility," writes the educator David Isaacs, "is recognizing our own inadequacies and abilities and pressing them into service without attracting attention or expecting applause."[5] T.S. Eliot pointed out how much harm is done because of "people who want to feel important." Without humility, observes a philosopher, we keep all our defects; they are only crusted over with pride, which conceals them from ourselves. Humility enables us to admit our mistakes, apologize for them, and make amends.

Besides a concept of the virtues comprising good character, schools need a psychology of character, which must be conceived to encompass the cognitive, affective, and behavioral aspects of virtue. Each virtue, and character as a whole, requires knowing the good, desiring the good, and doing the good. To function morally, we must be able to *judge* what is right, *care about* what is right, and then *do* what is right, even in the face of pressure from without and temptation from within.

To possess the virtue of justice, for example, I must first understand justice: know what it demands of me in any situation (the cognitive side of character). Second, I must care about justice: want to be a just person, admire fairness in others, feel constructive guilt when I fall short of that standard, and have the capacity for moral indignation in the face of injustice (the emotional side of character). Third, I must practice justice: behave justly in my personal relationships and try to contribute as a citizen to building a more just society and world (the behavioral side of character).

A Comprehensive Approach to Character Development

In order to develop human character in its cognitive, emotional, and behavior dimensions we need a comprehensive approach to character education. Such an approach requires that we identify the character development opportunities present in every phase of classroom and school life, and use those opportunities to foster character development.

Our character education center defines a comprehensive approach in terms of twelve mutually supportive strategies. These include nine classroom strategies: (1) the teacher as a caregiver, model, and ethical mentor; (2) creating a caring classroom community; (3) moral discipline that develops moral understanding and self-discipline rather than mere compliance; (4) a democratic classroom environment that involves students in rule setting, problem solving, and generally sharing responsibility for making the classroom the best that it can be; (5) teaching virtues through the content of the curriculum; (6) cooperative learning; (7) fostering the "conscience of craft," the feeling of obligation to do one's work well; (8) moral reflection, including setting goals to improve one's own character; and (9) learning and practicing the skills of conflict resolution. This comprehensive approach also includes three schoolwide strategies: (1) caring beyond the classroom (e.g., service in the school and community); (2) developing a positive moral culture throughout the school; and (3) recruiting parents and the wider community as full partners in character education.

Teaching Character through the Curriculum

Consider just one of the above twelve strategies: mining the academic curriculum for its character-building potential. This requires that teachers look at their academic disciplines and ask: "What are the ethical questions and character lessons embedded in the subjects I teach? How can I draw those out and engage my students in considering them?"

For example, a science teacher can design a lesson on the need for precise and truthful reporting of data and how scientific fraud undercuts the scientific enterprise. A social studies teacher can examine questions of social justice, actual moral dilemmas faced by historical figures, and current opportunities for civic action to improve one's community or country. A literature teacher can have students analyze the moral decisions and moral strengths and weaknesses of characters in novels, plays, and short stories. A mathematics teacher can ask students to consider the virtues (such as perseverance) needed to succeed in math, use cooperative learning to promote peer helpfulness, and have students research and plot morally significant societal trends (e.g., violent crime, teen pregnancy, homelessness, children living in poverty). In all subjects, teachers can engage students in learning about men and women of achievement and in discussing the strengths of character that enabled them to make the contributions they did.

Teaching character through the curriculum also includes making thoughtful use of published character education curricula. For example, Facing History and Ourselves, initially developed for eighth graders and later adapted to high school and college levels, uses history, film, and guest speakers to study the Nazi Holocaust and asks students to look within themselves to probe the universal human tendency toward prejudice and scapegoating.[6]

Schoolwide Character Education

At bottom, character education is about transforming the school culture so that it becomes a school of character. The school must become a place where people speak a common ethical language and where a shared commitment to creating a culture of character is the animating spirit.

In our center's work with schools across the country we have identified twenty recurring components of successful character education programs:

1. Administrative leadership and support.
2. Strong staff involvement.
3. Strong student involvement.
4. Strong parent involvement.
5. A mission and motto that highlight character.
6. A creed or code of behavior that defines "the way" of the school—how people are expected to act, the ideals they are called to honor—and repeated references to this "way" in the school's routines and rituals, assemblies, extracurricular activities, student handbook, report card, public relations, and communications with parents.[7]
7. An agreed-upon set of target virtues, encompassing both work-related and interpersonal virtues, to be modeled, taught, upheld, celebrated, and continually practiced.
8. A schoolwide plan for promoting and teaching the school's target virtues in classrooms and throughout the school environment

9. Behavioral examples, generated by staff and students, of what these virtues "look like" and "sound like."
10. An emphasis on the responsibility of *all* staff and students to model these virtues.
11. Ongoing integration of these virtues into instruction across the curriculum
12. The use, where appropriate, of high-quality published character education curricula.
13. An approach to discipline that seeks not only to control behavior but also to develop the character strengths, such as good judgment and self-control, whose absence typically underlies behavior problems.
14. A schoolwide effort to build a caring community and prevent peer cruelty.
15. A character-rich visual environment (e.g., signs, posters, and quotes)
16. Hiring staff who are persons of good character committed to modeling and teaching character.
17. Staff development in the skills and strategies of character education and accountability for using them (Are they part of lesson plans? Do the principal's observations take note of them? Do staff regularly report what they are doing to promote character development?).
18. Scheduled time for staff planning, sharing, and reflection on the character effort and character-related issues in the school's moral and intellectual culture.
19. At least modest financial support: character education rarely requires a big budget, but some funds are needed for professional development, release time for program development, and a resource library of books and materials.
20. A plan for ongoing assessment of program impact.

We have also found that the most effective way to convey school-wide character education is to provide examples of excellence. We draw them from our own work and from the Character Education Partnership's *National Schools of Character* competition, which over the past six years has recognized sixty elementary, middle, and high schools (ten each year) judged by site visitors and a panel of experts to be exemplary in implementing "eleven principles of effective character education." What follows, as just one example, is the story of Kennedy Middle School (Eugene, Oregon), the only middle school to win a National School of Character award in the 1999 competition.

A substitute teacher says: "When you walk into Kennedy, there's a definite difference: It's a warm and caring place." Just a few years ago, *warm* and *caring* were not words used to describe Kennedy Middle School. Finding parents to help monitor lunch was difficult because they felt uncomfortable and threatened around several groups of students. Here is how Kennedy, through its character education initiative, turned that around:

1. *It tied character education to school improvement.* In the fall of 1995, Kennedy teachers who were unhappy with disrespectful student behavior met with the school's Site Council, which included parents, community members, support staff, and students. Together they came up with three school improvement goals, one of which dealt with school climate and character.

2. *It adopted a character education curriculum: Second Step.* Says Kay Mehas, then principal of Kennedy: "Second Step is a schoolwide curriculum that teaches skills such as how to communicate, problem-solve, and work together in a community. It actually changes students' behavior."

3. *It trained the staff.* Mehas and a Kennedy counselor attended a "train the trainer" institute to learn how to train the other staff to teach the *Second Step* curriculum. Before the new school year began, Kennedy held a training day for all staff. The staff decided to devote every Tuesday morning from 9:45 to 10:25 to teaching Second Step lessons.

4. *It involved support staff in teaching the curriculum.* Kennedy invited every member of the staff—including secretaries, custodians, cafeteria workers, and playground aides—to take part in teaching the *Second Step* lessons. A secretary would be paired with an eighth-grade math teacher, a custodian with an eighth-grade science teacher, and so on. This would show students that the entire school was committed to character development.

5. *It made a more effective use of the curriculum in year 2.* Mehas says that after their year of *Second Step*, "some students still weren't coming to school with common expectations about classroom behavior. We wanted to say to them right at the start of the school year, 'This is how we treat each other at Kennedy Middle School.'" So instead of spreading out the *Second Step* lessons—one a week over the whole year—Kennedy

decided to concentrate them: a lesson a day for the first three weeks of school. Says Mehas: "We're now able to spend more time teaching the academic curriculum because we have fewer behavior problems."

6. *It provided multiple opportunities for student leadership.* These included five student groups. The Respect Committee meets every day and has the mission of trying to ensure that all students feel comfortable and respected at the school. For example, it organizes assemblies at which students from different backgrounds share their cultural heritages. The Leadership Club meets weekly to discuss ways to improve the school. One year club members worked with a landscape architect to create a design and then plant trees to enhance school grounds. Teens and Tots, a service learning class, involves Kennedy students in working at Relief Nursery, a child care and support facility for abused children and their families. Jump Start Tutors are Kennedy students who work with their at-risk peers, teaching them study skills and helping with assignments in the different subject areas. Finally, Student Conveners are elected representatives from each class who function as Kennedy's student government.

7. *Students developed a system for recognizing positive behavior.* Kennedy's Student Conveners created a schoolwide system, PRIDE (Personal Responsibility in Daily Efforts), to recognize students on a daily basis for "doing the right thing." Every six weeks, Kennedy students who have all their assignments in on time, no more than one absence, no more than one unexcused tardiness, and no behavioral referrals, become members of PRIDE. For each PRIDE celebration, qualifying students participate in special activities such as ice skating, skiing, movies, and swimming. Every six weeks students have a fresh start, so they have many chances to make PRIDE.

8. *It took steps to create closer teacher–student relationships.* In its seventh and eighth grades, Kennedy implemented the practice of "looping": students remain with the same teachers for more than one year. This allows faculty to develop closer relationships with both students and their parents.

9. *It increased parent involvement.* Kennedy has had so many parent volunteers that one parent now serves almost full-time as the volunteer coordinator. Parent volunteers cover the office

and other essential staff functions while the regular staff are teaching the Second Step lessons during the first three weeks of school. Parent volunteers also run the school library and help with the many clubs.

10. *It evaluated impact.* Kennedy looked at academic and behavioral indicators to assess its character education efforts. In 1997, only 59 percent of Kennedy's students met Oregon's state academic standards, and discipline referrals averaged one hundred a month. In 1998, 74 percent of Kennedy's students met state academic standards, and discipline referrals were down to a thirty-five a month.

Participatory Schoolwide Democracy

If a society wishes to build democratic institutions that work and endure, it must develop democratic character in its young and teach them to learn the value of democratic participation by experiencing it firsthand in their formative years. This crucial part of character education is often neglected. Students can experience democratic participation through participatory student government, in which they share responsibility (much as they do in democratic classroom meetings) for solving real-life problems in the school environment.

This kind of student government gives students training in democratic citizenship, and helps schools deal with common student behavior problems such as academic dishonesty, vandalism, peer cruelty, sexual harassment, racial tensions, bad language, and poor sportsmanship. Because such problems are located in the peer culture, they are difficult or impossible to solve by adults acting on their own. Peers are in the best position to shape the norms that influence student behavior.

Unfortunately, student government as practiced in most schools does not govern anything. It is typically an isolated group with no constituency. Members do not represent anyone but themselves; they do not seek input from, or report back to, other students. Schools have a much better chance of solving problems in the school environment if they design a student government in which student delegates serve as representatives of their classrooms (or homerooms) and report back to them.

Experimental Research on Comprehensive Character Education

Case studies of schoolwide character education are often persuasive to educators and the public, but they are not scientifically rigorous in that they lack a control group. Several studies of comprehensive character education have employed an experimental design, and allow us to compare the performance of students in program schools with that of students in equivalent comparison schools that did not implement the character program. Berkowitz and Bier conducted a literature review of such studies.[8] In one example from their review, over a three-year period, California's Developmental Studies Center compared twelve elementary schools implementing *The Child Development Project*, a comprehensive character education program with twelve matched schools not implementing the program. Students in program schools were significantly superior in classroom behavior, achievement motivation, and reading comprehension. Moreover, when program students went on to middle school (when the character program was no longer in effect), they continued to show superiority on character measures such as conflict resolution and academic achievement as measured by grade-point averages and standardized test performance.

Research on Sense of Community

Because a central goal of character education is creating a caring school community, several researchers have examined the correlates of this particular school characteristic. Schaps, Watson, and Lewis report studies that have measured the degree to which a school has a caring community by asking students and staff to indicate their agreement or disagreement with Likert-scale items such as: "People in this school care about each other"; "Students in this school help each other, even if they are not friends"; "I feel I can talk to the teachers in this school about the things that are bothering me"; and "My school is like a family." Parallel items (e.g., "My classroom is like a family") measure each student's experience of the classroom as a caring community.[9]

In their study of six school districts across the United States, Schaps and colleagues found that the stronger a school's sense of community, the more likely its students are to show positive outcomes, among them increased liking for school, empathy toward others' feelings, and motivation to be kind and helpful. Students have higher academic self-esteem, and stronger feelings of social competence, along with more sophisticated conflict resolution skills. They report more frequent acts of altruistic behavior, and fewer delinquent acts, along with less use of tobacco, alcohol, and marijuana, and less feeling of loneliness in school.

Communitywide Character Education

Popenoe points out that as the child moves into the adult world, the moral lessons taught by parents must be sustained by others.[10] He cites a ten-year study of ten communities across America which found that a community consensus on values was a strong predictor of healthy adolescent adjustment. In fact, it was a far stronger predictor than other variables such as affluence or ethnicity.[11]

Efforts to create a community of character are underway in growing numbers of cities, towns, and villages. For example, the book *A Gift of Character: The Chattanooga Story*, describes in detail the efforts of Chattanooga, Tennessee (population 156,000) to implement character-building programs throughout the community. Chattanooga's initiative has included not only implementing character education in all its schools but also taking steps to support and strengthen families.

Research indicates that these communitywide efforts are superior to character education that does not go beyond the school. Pentz reports a study of twenty thousand students in sixth and seventh grades that compared a state-of-the-art school-based drug education curriculum with a program that combined the school curriculum with family involvement (students interviewed their parents and role-played refusal skills at home) and community involvement (extensive media support and participation of community leaders and groups).[12] The more comprehensive, community-wide approach was significantly superior in slowing early adolescent use of marijuana, cigarettes, and alcohol.

Sex and Character

Most citizens of modern societies would likely applaud the fact that people in general, including parents and children, are more comfortable talking about sex than they were in generations past. Couples having sexual problems in their marriages are more likely to try to do something about it. But along with this greater openness have come a sexualizing of popular culture and a sexualizing of children that is disturbing to parents and others across a wide section of the ideological spectrum.

For example, a *New York Times* article titled "The Face of Teenage Sex Grows Younger," quoted psychotherapists counseling children, usually girls, who were emotional wrecks because of early sexual involvement.[13] Dr. Allen Waltzman, a Brooklyn psychiatrist, commented, "I see girls, 7th- and 8th-graders, even 6th-graders who tell me they're virgins...but they've had oral sex 50 or 60 times." Some boys are reportedly demanding oral sex from their girl friends the way they used to expect a good-night kiss.

The breakdown of sexual morality has spawned a plague of problems: promiscuity, sexual addictions, infidelity, unwed pregnancies, fatherless children (one in three U.S. children is now born out of wedlock), STDs (sexually transmitted diseases), abortions, sexual harassment, the sexual abuse of children, children acting out sexually, an ever more eroticized media, a huge pornography industry (next to gambling, the most lucrative Internet business), and the damage that many of these problems do to marriages and families. To a large extent, we are still in cultural denial about the cost of sex without social controls.

Around the world, people bemoan the corruption of their young by American media. In Japan, traditional sexual morality is fast crumbling as teens adopt the latest fashion of their Western peers—"friends with (sexual) privileges" instead of emotional attachments to boyfriends or girl friends. In Latin America, educators complain of the same trend. Much is written about the AIDS epidemic now ravaging southern Africa—the number of AIDS orphans is predicted to reach 40 million in the next ten years—but far less about the moral roots of the crisis. In Uganda, where an emphasis on abstinence and marital fidelity is the new national policy, significant progress has been made in fighting the AIDS epidemic.

How does character education approach a potentially divisive issue such as sex education? Despite continuing battles about it, some common ground is emerging. Abstinence is now regarded as the wisest choice for many reasons. More than a half-million unmarried teens become pregnant each year—taking the surest route to poverty for themselves and their children. One in three sexually active singles gets an STD by age twenty-four. Until the mid-1970s, only two STDs—syphilis and gonorrhea—were common; now more than twenty are. Condom use over the past twenty years has increased most among teens, but teens show the greatest increase of STDs during that same period. According to a National Institutes of Health report, data are insufficient to claim that condoms offer any proven protection against six of the leading eight STDs.[14]

Recognition is also growing that sexual behavior is subject to ethical evaluation because it affects the welfare of self and others. Ethical sexuality, acting with respect for self and others, is part of good character. Sex education must therefore be character education. It must teach students "to see sexuality as an area of their lives that calls for the presence of virtues."[15]

Although a highly sexualized media culture beckons the young toward early sexual involvement, there is a countertrend toward greater sexual restraint. A December 2002 *Newsweek* cover story titled "The New Virginity" reported the latest data from the Centers for Disease Control: high school students who have *not* had sexual intercourse are now in a majority (52%) for the first time in twenty-five years. Moreover, only one-third of students say they are "currently sexually active." Most of this change is accounted for by an increase in the virginity rate among high school boys: up more than 10 percent in the 1990s.

Research reveals that religion operates as a force for sexual self-control. Wallace and Williams report three factors that "relate significantly to lower levels of sexual involvement"; these are "attendance at religious services, self-rated importance of religion, and denominational affiliation."[16]

In an area like sex education, it is especially important to mobilize the peer culture on the side of virtue. How to do that against challenging odds is illustrated by one of the country's most successful public school abstinence programs, Best Friends, developed by Elayne Bennett.[17] Unlike most abstinence programs, which target both sexes, Best Friends was developed for girls in fifth to ninth grade; it was piloted in inner-city schools in Washington, D.C. Girls in the program pledge to stay away from sex, drugs, and drinking through their school years. A program evaluation reported a 1 percent pregnancy rate among Best Friends students in grades 9 through 12, compared to 26 percent of high school-aged African-American girls in Washington, and a 22 percent sexual activity rate for Best Friends high school students, compared to a 73 percent rate for nonparticipants.[18] This suggests that it is possible, with the right intervention, to create strong peer norms that support a young person's healthy development and avoidance of self-injurious behavior.

Lessons Learned

What are the important lessons to be learned from the contemporary character education movement, lessons that can offer practical guidance to communities and countries embarking on systematic character development efforts? Here are seven:

1. *Begin with an adequate concept of character.* Character should be defined to encompass the full range of human virtues, including those needed for achievement (such as self-discipline, goal-setting, and hard work) as well as those needed for positive relationships and responsible citizenship (such as respect for persons and the rule of law, honesty, love, and democratic participation in public life).

2. *Understand how character develops.* Character is both learned (through example) and taught (through explanation and exhortation). It also requires direct experiences. Students must actively contribute to their classrooms, schools, and communities. They must have many and varied opportunities for real-life moral action. To develop the skills and attitudes needed for democratic citizenship, action opportunities must include participation in democratic problem-solving.

3. *Use evidence-based intervention strategies.* Not all methods work equally well to develop character. Schools should make use of programs and practices with proven effectiveness, drawing on available research.[19] Practices such as adult modeling, cooperative learning, conflict resolution, service learning, and democratic student government have been shown to be effective at different ages and in varied settings. In our Center's 2005 study of "Smart & Good High Schools" (www.cortland. edu/character/highschool), we describe many high school character education practices that have research support.

4. *Involve staff, students, and parents.* All three of these groups are essential partners in planning and carrying out a character education initiative. If even one of these three partners is only

weakly involved, a character development program will fall far short of its potential.[20]

5. *Provide adequate staff development.* Adult development is essential to becoming a school of character. We cannot foster students' moral growth without developing the ethical capacities of adults. Adults cannot give what they do not have.

6. *Assess the program.* There are three important reasons to assess a character education initiative. First, what gets measured matters; staff motivation and accountability for implementing a character education effort will be much greater if an effort is made to assess results. Assessment also tells a school how much difference its character education program is actually making. Finally, assessment data can be used to guide decision making about how to increase program effectiveness. Our center's website, http://www.cortland.edu/character, provides a list of instruments for assessing character education.

7. *Don't reinvent the wheel.* Although every school will put its own distinctive stamp on its character education effort, the best way to begin is to study best practice. For example, the award-winning schools described in the Character Education Partnership's annual *National Schools of Character* publication (http://www.character.org) are a gold mine of practices that other schools can adopt or adapt.

When schools return to their historical mission of teaching character, they are often pleasantly surprised by the fruit of their efforts. The Hilltop Elementary School in Lynnwood, Washington, undertook character education in the early 1990s because of its students' increasingly rude and disrespectful behavior, and went on to become a 1999 National School of Character. A Hilltop teacher who was initially skeptical about character education commented on her school's turnaround. Initially "opposed to doing character education," she said, "'We have too much to teach already. This is the job of the home.'" But then, she said, "I saw the change in the kids. I saw the change in how staff related to each other. We're a different school now. I look forward to coming to work."

Educating for character is essential for creating safe and effective schools, for renewing a society's moral culture, and for bringing about progressive and lasting cultural development. It is not possible to build a virtuous society unless virtue exists in the hearts, minds, and souls of individual human beings.

Notes

1. J. Q. Wilson, "Liberalism, Modernism, and the Good Life," in *Seedbeds of Virtue,* ed. M. A. Glendon and D. Blankenhorn (Lanham, MD: Madison Books, 1995).
2. B. E. McClelland, *Schools and the Shaping of Character: Moral Education in America, 1607–Present* (Bloomington, IN: ERIC Clearinghouse for Social Studies, 1992).
3. T. Lickona, *Character Matters: How to Help Our Children Develop Good Judgment, Integrity, and Other Essential Virtues* (New York: Simon & Schuster, 2004).
4. J. Stenson, *Upbringing: A Handbook for Parents of Young Children,* 2000, http://www.Parentleadership.com
5. D. Isaacs, *Character-Building: A Guide for Parents and Teachers* (Dublin, Ireland: Four Courts Press, 1976).
6. Facing History and Ourselves National Foundation. *Facing History and Ourselves: The Holocaust and Human Behavior* (Brookline, MA: Author, 1994).
7. Thanks for this point to Charles Elbot, David Fulton, and Barbara Evans, authors of *Educating for Character in the Denver Public Schools* (Denver, CO: Denver Public Schools, 2003).
8. M. Berkowitz and M. Bier, *What Works in Character Education* (Washington, D.C.: Character Education Partnership, 2003).
9. E. Schaps, M. Watson, and C. Lewis, "A Sense of Community Is Key to Effectiveness in Fostering Character Education," *Journal of Staff Development.* 17, no. 2 (1996): 42–46.
10. D. Popenoe, "The Roots of Declining Social Virtue: Family, Community, and the Need for a 'Natural Communities Policy,'" in *Seedbeds of Virtue,* ed. M. A. Glendon and D. Blankenhorn, 1995.
11. F. A. Ianni, *The Search for Structure: A Report on American Youth Today* (New York: Free Press, 1989).
12. M. A. Pentz, "A Multi-Community Trial for Primary Prevention of Adolescent Drug Abuse," *JAMA* 261 (1989):3259–266.
13. A. Jarrell, "The Face of Teenage Sex Grows Younger," *The New York Times* (April 2, 2000).
14. National Institutes of Health. "Scientific Evidence on Condom Effectiveness for Sexually Transmitted Disease Prevention," 2001, http://www.niaid.nih.gov/dmid/stds/condomreport.pdf. See also *Sex, Condoms, and STDs: What We Now Know,* 2002, http://www.medinstitute.org
15. Character Education Partnership,*Character-Based Sex Education* (Washington, D.C.: Character Education Partnership, 1996).
16. J. M. Wallace and D. R. Williams, "Religion and Adolescent Health-Compromising Behavior," in *Health Risks and Developmental Transitions During Adolescence,* ed. J. Schulenberg et al. (New York: Cambridge University Press, 1997).
17. *Directory of Abstinence Resources, Best Friends* (Sioux Falls, SD: National Abstinence Clearinghouse, 1999).
18. D. Rowberry, "An Evaluation of the Washington, D.C., Best Friends Program." Abstract in Dissertation Abstracts International, publ. no. 57, 0636.

19. E.g., Berkowitz and Beir.
20. See Lickona, 2004, for strategies for developing an effective school–parent part-
    nership and for involving students in creating a school of character.

5

Civic Education and the Development of Civic Knowledge and Attitudes

RICHARD G. NIEMI
STEVEN E. FINKEL

In 1991 Samuel Huntington hailed a "third wave" of democratization, which saw an expansion of democracy in southern Europe, Latin America, and Asia, along with a sudden and dramatic growth in Eastern Europe after the fall of the Soviet Union. Only a few years later, Robert Putnam, in *Bowling Alone*, decried the decline of civil society in the United States, and others noted a pervasive loss of confidence in governmental institutions and a decline in civic and political engagement.[1]

Evidence collected in the past few years has complicated this picture, pointing out that young people as well as old are heavily involved in community service. Nonetheless, trust in government and politics, though rebounding since the mid-1990s (and temporarily spiking immediately after September 11, 2001), remains low. Voter turnout in U.S. presidential elections is generally 50 to 55 percent, with even the heightened turnout in 2004 lower than in most other democracies, both new and established. Confidence in major institutions continues to be low.

Concerns are heightened by the fact that young adults and high school students are especially distrustful, disengaged, and uninterested.

Nationwide surveys, tests (including the most recent national civics assessment), reports from college freshmen, and other prominent data show that students and young adults pay much less attention to politics than previous generations, demonstrate limited knowledge of government and politics, and have an understanding of citizenship that emphasizes rights to the exclusion of responsibilities. They often claim not to know how to vote, and their turnout rates, always lower than among older adults, have dropped further behind.

These observations—especially the generational component, with its suggestion of still lower levels of interest and engagement in the future—have generated national concerns. Among a variety of responses, the National Endowment for the Humanities (NEH) launched an initiative "to encourage the teaching, studying and understanding of American history and culture."[2]

The most frequent call is for increased and improved civic education. It is easy to understand why. Elementary and secondary schools, in particular, reach the target population; schools are the institution designated for training in all subjects, including citizenship; and citizenship education needs improvement after three decades of relative neglect. But can schools effectively teach the knowledge, attitudes, and behavior associated with good citizenship? What is the state of civic education today? How many students do civics courses reach? How can they be most effective? What is the role of community service in civic education?

We address these questions here. First we review the history of civic education in the United States, noting the decline of civics courses in the 1960s and the growth in government courses in recent years. We discuss recent evidence about the effects of formal course work and school "climate." Next, we turn to community service, the effects of which, we suggest, are understudied and perhaps overestimated. Finally, we review civic education efforts abroad, especially in the developing world, and note some recommendations for expanding and strengthening civic education.

From Boom to Bust to Partial Recovery

The goal of training for citizenship has been integral to school curricula practically since the U.S. public school system began. Indeed, the ambitious goal of making all Americans active and informed citizens was one of Horace Mann's critical selling points in his campaign for universal mandatory public education. His arguments focused on the need for basic literacy, so that citizens would be able to receive information about politics and express their wishes. The content of political knowledge that was taught was typically left for the local jurisdiction to establish, in order to protect children from indoctrination.

The content of the "social studies" curriculum developed in the early 1900s. While history had been commonly taught, instruction in social studies for high school students only began to be considered in 1916, after the report of the Social Studies Committee of the Commission on the Reorganization of Secondary Education. Many high schools needed to "Americanize" the many adolescents coming from other countries, and include the American teenagers who were now kept out of the labor market by child labor laws. In response, the Commission report argued for courses in civics, government, and problems of democracy. Also in 1916, the American Political Science Association issued a report declaring its commitment to "education for citizenship and public service."[3] These two reports helped establish a pattern that persisted for more than four decades, of civics courses, usually in eighth or ninth grade, and government courses, usually in twelfth grade.

The turmoil in education that began in the 1960s greatly reshaped the curriculum, including civics. Three major developments occurred: enrollment in civics classes declined precipitously; civics courses, with their focus on the responsibilities of citizens, were transformed into government courses, with a more analytical and "objective" approach; and enrollment in government courses rose steadily after 1990.

In the 1960s, civics classes went into a sharp decline; by the early 1980s, so was any sort of teaching about American government and politics. There was a substantial erosion in the proportion of students taking American government as a stand-alone course. The length of many government classes declined, from a full year to one semester. It is also likely that attention to social studies in the elementary grades dropped precipitously over the same period.

Since the 1980s, this decline has been reversed. The "New Social Studies" that had dominated the 1960s and 1970s began to fade. And, while civics classes per se continued to decline and economics classes and other nongovernment classes continued to increase, enrollments in American government classes quickly rebounded. By 1998, about four out of five graduating seniors had taken an American government course.

Changes since the mid-1980s, however, have not restored the pre-1970s situation. About a fifth of recent graduates have no stand-alone course in government and politics in their four-year high school career. Even fewer (about 50%) have such a course in their senior year. Moreover, a recent survey of state statutes revealed that many states have no requirements at all for civic education, and of those that do, most simply specify that civics topics be taught at some time during the high school years; it is likely that constitutional history, taught in some amount in virtually every American history class, meets the requirements. Despite the move toward high-stakes testing, only five states in the late 1990s had statutes that required some form of testing/assessment in civics.[4]

As important as the changes in the numbers of students taking civic education courses is the content of those courses. Though harder to quantify, it seems clear that the movement from "Civics" to "U.S. Government" has been accompanied by significant changes in emphasis. Some of the change probably occurred because of ambivalence resulting from the civil rights movement and the Vietnam war. Another stimulus was changes in the associated professional disciplines. In the 1950s and 1960s, social science researchers increasingly saw themselves as part of scientific disciplines, with no responsibility for teaching good citizenship.

Nonetheless, some of the new social studies initiatives did include discussion of and teaching about values in American politics. Dealing with controversial issues in contemporary politics is difficult in the best of circumstances; in recent years, the increasing diversity of American students and concerns about political correctness, multiculturalism, and rigorous nonpartisanship have made it particularly difficult for teachers to deal with such topics. The resulting reluctance to deal with such issues has no doubt led to some of the concerns over the supposed blandness of civics and government classes.

A concrete indicator of this shift can be noted in the National Assessment of Educational Progress (NAEP). In the late 1960s, the initial "civics" NAEP was titled "citizenship." In the 1970s, the title was expanded to include "social studies." In 1988, a completely new test was created, this time called "U.S. Government and Politics." Moreover, while the earlier tests included attitudinal questions, the

1988 test included only factual items, and NAEP is now explicitly precluded from asking about student attitudes.

Questions within recent NAEP assessments are indicative of current topical coverage. Student reports indicate that course content leans heavily on the structure of U.S. government: the Constitution, Bill of Rights, the three branches, and generally how laws are made. There is little progression across topics between earlier and later courses. In 1988, the test itself contained little about topics such as the international system and the skills that citizens need to participate effectively in a democratic society.

We cannot return to the type of courses that were taught before the 1960s. Yet the need for revisions—especially some attention to the attitudes and behaviors that underlie responsible citizenship—is driving suggestions to expand and reform the civics curriculum.[5]

Effects of Civic Education

Whether students take government classes in high school or have civics lessons in earlier grades matters only if those classes and lessons have some effect. High school graduates have routinely been shown to know more about all manner of political (and nonpolitical) subjects than those with less education, with college graduates knowing still more. Educational effects are also widely apparent with respect to various forms of political behavior. Greater education has long been associated with higher voter turnout and with participation in more demanding kinds of political behavior and many forms of political attentiveness. Likewise, attitudes such as political tolerance and efficacy have a strong relationship with education levels.

But only recently has persuasive evidence shown that civics courses have an effect on students' knowledge. The most systematic results are the NAEP civics (and history) assessments. In a book based on the 1988 civics NAEP, Niemi and Junn showed that exposure to the civics curriculum was related to greater student knowledge.[6] In fact, course impacts and the effects of individual achievement varied by subject matter. These two factors had the greatest effect on topics that students are least likely to encounter outside the classroom, such as details of constitutional provisions. They had less impact on knowledge of topics that students know relatively well, presumably because they encounter this material in their daily lives as well as in the classroom.

Having perhaps convinced skeptics that civics (and history) courses have a genuine effect, recent work has begun to shift the focus to
what kinds of courses are most effective, what kinds of teaching have
the greatest effect, and so on. Major efforts are underway to improve
civics course work. The development of the voluntary National Standards for Civics and Government in 1994 was an important step,
in part because it was the basis for the most recent NAEP civics assessment, which has served as a starting point for revisions of state
standards.

Community Service: The New Wave of Youth Participation

Though the young usually lack interest in politics and government,
they are often heavily involved in community service. In schools at
all levels, voluntary service—often in the form of so-called service
learning—has surged dramatically. Efforts are increasingly well-co-
ordinated; in 1997, for example, a wide-ranging group of nonprofit
organizations, universities, schools, and government organizations
established the Partnering Initiative on Education and Civil Society
to help build service learning opportunities into elementary, secondary, and postsecondary classroom curricula.[7] "Voluntary" service is
also increasingly required. School systems at both state and local
levels have established service components in courses or encouraged
voluntary service.

Still, concerns remain about the extent of and kind of participation. The push for voluntarism has quickly outstripped evaluation of
its effects. Here, after laying out the theoretical context for student
voluntarism, we discuss the extent and kinds of participation that
have been observed, and finally review the more limited work on the
effects of participation.

Theoretical Context

Theorists have long suggested linking school and community in civic education to develop shared or common democratic values and
fundamental citizen participatory skills. Since the early 1900s, the
United States has heard from many advocates for applied civics and
seen many experiments based on the assumption that service in the

community will strengthen one's intellectual appreciation of democracy and practical skills for participation. Since the mid-1990s, service learning has resurfaced as a widely proposed means to renew political engagement. Advocates say it is an essential part of civic education that can arouse interest, increase knowledge, and generate positive participatory and civil attitudes.

Practice

Some community service education programs aim to develop the skills needed to influence public affairs; others bolster civic "charity" or service as an alternative to government or public programs. Currently, community service for secondary students is found in two general formats. *Service learning* generally refers to community service that is incorporated into school courses. The service interval in the community is typically preceded by preparatory sessions that provide an informational and conceptual framework. Postservice activities include written reflections and classroom discussion. *Community service* generally refers to voluntary work in the community that is not linked to the school curriculum, although the school may encourage or even arrange it. Proponents of student service tend to favor more systematic and substantial service learning programs. In practice, however, more students are involved in community service that is not assimilated into school courses, is not debriefed, and is likely to be for short periods of time.

Extent of and Kinds of Participation

Rates of community service among high school students are high by almost any yardstick. Overall rates are at levels associated with voting turnout in closely fought presidential elections, and they are higher than comparable adult rates. In the 1996 and 1999 National Household Education Surveys (NHES), for example, just over half of students in grades nine to twelve claimed to have participated in "community service activity or volunteer work at your school or in your community" during the present school year.[8]

On the other hand, participation at least once, which is what is denoted by most of the rates cited, is not the same as sustained

participation. In the 1996 NHES survey, many students only participated once or twice or a few hours altogether. If one excludes these,
the rate of participation drops from just over half to below 30 percent. If one sets the bar relatively high (at least 35 hours), the figure
drops to just 14 percent. This puts quite a different face on participation rates.

The kinds of activities students engage in suggest additional qualifications. According to the Independent Sector survey, the most
frequent type of work is baby-sitting (13 percent of all teenagers),
followed by cleaning or janitorial work (9 percent).[9] Such services are
unlikely to enhance students' understanding of civic organizations or
of adult social and political concerns. Less than 1 percent of reported
activities take place in explicitly political organizations.

As with all kinds of "public" participation, youthful community
service varies across types of individuals. Differences occur along the
same lines as those found in adult political participation although
sometimes with a twist; for example, females typically outperform
males. Differences also echo variations in family background, including both family status and degree of parental involvement. A variety
of school-related factors, such as grades earned by the student and
district policies toward service, are also important.

Importantly, analysis of the 1996 NHES data revealed that African
Americans and Hispanics participate in community service at rates
similar to those for non-Hispanic whites. This pattern is similar to
that found for African Americans over the years with respect to many
kinds of political participation. Rather more surprising are possible
school effects. In one study, when a school encouraged students to
participate by helping arrange for their service, the probability of a
student participating increased considerably; when a school required
such service, there was no statistically significant effect.[10]

Participation also varies across types of schools and communities.
It is greatest in church-related schools and least prevalent in public
schools; in 1999, the difference recorded in NHES was quite large,
with over 70 percent of the students in church-related schools having
participated, just under 70 percent of those in other private schools,
and 50 percent of those in public schools. Participation also depends
to some extent on the wealth of the community; in the 1996 NHES,
54 percent of all students participated when poverty rates were very
low (less than 5 percent in the given zip code living below the poverty level), while it declined steadily to 42 percent when poverty rates

were high —more than 20 percent below the poverty level. Overall, then, a relatively large percentage of students participate in community service; sustained participation is less frequent. Many standard variables associated with skills, resources, and enhanced opportunities are correlated with regular participation, though surprisingly, service seems to be encouraged most when schools facilitate but do not require it. And wealthier and church-related schools foster higher rates of participation.

Effects of Participation

Despite the high frequency of volunteer work, research on the effects of community service is still inadequate. Very few have rigorously examined whether community service contributes specifically to gains in civic knowledge. But some positive results have been reported. In the 1996 NHES study, regular, sustained participation in community service (over 35 hours) was associated with a substantial difference in political knowledge. For example, it had a larger effect than did participation in school government and about the same as participation in one to two in-school or out-of-school activities. The relationship between community service and knowledge was also comparable to the difference made by moving up two grades in school. Involvement in community service was unrelated to self-reported ability to "write a letter to a government office," perhaps because this is a frequent assignment in high school civics courses, and a very high proportion of students claimed the ability. Involvement was, however, related to self-reported ability to "make a statement at a public meeting."

Research on attitudinal effects has been more mixed. Studies in the 1980s raised considerable doubt about whether service learning programs could improve political efficacy and, therefore, whether they would have any lasting effect on participation. With hindsight, it seems likely that the intensely activist programs designed in the 1970s, when tested in the 1980s, confronted an increasingly conservative climate in both school and community. Still, in the 1996 NHES study, as in others, the findings were only weakly supportive of service effects on specifically political attitudes.

Overall, community service holds considerable potential for involving young people in the broader social world. Indeed, given young people's disdain for many forms of political behavior, it may be the primary means of societal involvement for them today. We would, however, offer two cautionary observations. First, much current participation is decidedly nonpolitical. Second, more research is needed about what kinds of activities students participate in and what effects that participation has. As noted above, participation often seems to consist of infrequent and low-level tasks, hardly the kind of thing proponents tout when they promote community service/ service learning.

International Civic Education

The increased attention given to civic education and its effects has by no means been limited to the United States and other advanced industrialized democracies.[11] Since the early 1990s, there has been an explosion of civic education programs in the newly emerging countries of Eastern Europe, Africa, and Latin America, many of which had little or no prior experience with democratic political systems. Much activity is occurring in the formal school system, with a variety of specialized civic education programs, often funded by the United States or other international donors and philanthropic organizations, attempting to inculcate the knowledge, values, skills, and participatory orientations that are thought to develop a supportive democratic political culture. At the same time, in the immediate aftermath of many countries' democratic transitions, it was widely recognized that vast numbers of adults also lacked the basic knowledge, skills, and supportive values that would facilitate their effective participation in democratic politics. Hence donors have also funded an extensive array of programs aimed at adults to foster the more immediate consolidation of these often-fragile democracies.

It is difficult to determine the exact numbers internationally of school-age children who are exposed to civic education. Studies along the lines of NAEP or the Department of Education's Transcript Studies simply do not exist outside the United States or Europe. Still, there is evidence that within the school system, children are increasingly exposed to civic education topics. In a comprehensive study of civic education teachers, curricula, textbooks, and national standards across some twenty-four advanced and new democracies in 1999, Torney-Purta and her colleagues found courses in virtually every country that covered such areas as the importance of elections, individual rights and obligations, and the role of political parties, civil society, and the media.[12] Though the topics were often not discussed in a separate civics course, by age fourteen the majority of students in these countries would likely have some exposure to the subject matter of democracy.

Importantly, many specialized programs have been instituted for younger students in emerging democracies, some even at the preschool level. For example, the Step by Step program run by Children's Resource International has trained over 500,000 students in some thirty Eastern European countries since 1994. The program promotes a "child-centered" approach to teaching children as young as three in ways designed to counter the often rigid, rote-oriented teaching and learning culture of previous authoritarian regimes. The program focuses on developing critical thinking, communication and interpersonal skills, and cooperative learning patterns among children, and in involving parents, teachers, and the wider community.

At the middle school level and beyond, programs are also increasingly emphasizing more active, participatory forms of democracy education. Patrick, for example, identifies the "active learning of civic knowledge, skills and virtue" as one of the key "global trends" in recent democracy education.[13] Examples of this approach in specialized programs in developing democracies are legion, ranging from the Democracy for All program run by Street Law, where high school students in postapartheid South Africa engage in mock elections, trials, and simulated human rights cases, to the Project Citizen program run by the U.S.-based Center for Civic Education and currently in operation in approximately fifteen developing democracies (as well as many U.S. states). Project Citizen students work as a group to identify community or national problems, participate in simulated legislative hearings on the topic, and then have the opportunity to engage in public presentations to educators, government officials, and journalists.

Programs directed at developing the civic capacity of adults are even more numerous. These efforts, implemented in developing democracies by thousands of nongovernmental organizations, vary widely. For example, they provide instruction about women's social and political rights, educate voters, organize to solve neighborhood problems, and encourage public participation in constitutional and political reform processes. We have little data on the rates of exposure to these kinds of democracy training activities, though the

2001 to 2002 Kenya National Civic Education Program, an election awareness and constitutional reform program consisting of some fifty thousand discrete workshops, lectures, drama and puppet shows, and community meetings conducted by nearly eighty different NGOs, appears to have reached nearly 18 percent of the adult Kenyan population.[14]

The Effects of Civic Education in Developing Democracies

Despite the proliferation of civic education programs in new democracies, relatively little research has been conducted on the effectiveness of these programs in changing democratic orientations among students or adults. Still, a small but growing body of work focuses on the effects of civic education in international contexts, with the results both replicating and extending the findings reported earlier in the United States.

Research on school-age students in developing contexts consistently echoes the long-standing finding that civic education has the strongest effects on students' levels of civic knowledge as opposed to such attitudes and values as political efficacy, tolerance, and trust in government. Finkel and Ernst, for example, found that high-school students who received civics instruction on at least a weekly basis were far more likely to identify correctly the names of key South African political leaders and possess basic knowledge of the South African constitutional structure than students who received civics instruction less often or not at all.[15] The differences between these groups on political knowledge was over 10 percent, roughly double the effect that Niemi and Junn attributed solely to exposure to civic education in the United States.[16] These findings, along with those reported in several other studies of developing democracies, suggest that civic education has much potential to increase students' store of basic political knowledge, perhaps more so than in advanced settings, where civics instruction may be redundant to other sources of political information.

Although the effects of civic education on attitudes, values, and orientations toward political participation are typically more modest, even these orientations appear open to change under certain conditions related to the classroom and instructional environment. For example, Torney-Purta and colleagues reported a positive effect in more than 80 percent of countries studied of an "open classroom" environment, that is, one where controversial political issues are discussed frequently and freely.[17] Finkel and Ernst find stronger effects of two other variables: the perceived credibility and likability of the civics teacher, and the degree to which active, participatory teaching methodologies were used in the classroom.[18] Importantly, the pedagogical methods that had the greatest impact involved students directly in interactive democratic behaviors such as participation in mock elections, trials, or role-playing activities. Students appeared to learn democratic values and skills by practicing and engaging in democratic participation in venues made available to them inside and outside the classroom.

Among adult populations, the largest effects of civic education are often found on political participation, especially at the local level, rather than on democratic attitudes and values. In nine programs among adults in the Dominican Republic, Poland, and South Africa, for example, individuals who were exposed to civic education were often nearly twice as participatory as individuals in control groups, with the largest effects being seen in community problem-solving participation and attendance at local municipal meetings.[19] Evidently, adult civic education conducted through NGOs and other civil society organizations has beneficial synergies: because civics training encourages participation in politics, it seems to be amplified by the "normal" mobilization processes already taking place within these groups. Democratic attitudes and values were the most difficult to change, though significant effects were found on the values of efficacy, political tolerance, and institutional trust.[20]

Equally important, the Finkel study found consistent evidence that the effects of civic education vary dramatically, depending on the nature and frequency of the individual's experience with democracy training. Specifically, three conditions seem to make adult civic education more effective: (1) attendance at three or more training sessions; less frequent exposure to civic education often has no impact whatsoever; (2) when training sessions were conducted with more participatory methodologies, such as role playing, simulations, mock elections, and the like; (3) by trainers whom the participants see as knowledgeable, inspiring, and interesting. It is not enough, then, for individuals simply to be exposed to civic education; what matters is its frequency, participatory orientation, and overall quality.

A Reminder About Family Effects

With all the emphasis given to the role of schools in civic education, we must remember the abiding importance of the family in imparting knowledge, attitudes, beliefs, and norms to the next generation. Family characteristics are included in many of the analyses noted above, and they routinely prove to be statistically and substantively significant. Relevant family characteristics include the frequency of family discussions, the extent to which resources such as books are found in the home, the nature of family decision making, and parental educational level.

Conclusion

For a generation or more, civic education has been considered old-fashioned, ineffective, even unnecessary. Now, however, in light of widespread disengagement and distrust among the young, we have begun to turn our attention back to the topic of citizenship for democracy. Our study has reinforced some long-standing conclusions and yielded new ones:

> Education is a major factor underlying civic and political participation *and the attitudes that support it.*
> Education is a strong correlate of interest in politics.
> Education promotes both following politics (passive participation) and active participation.
> Education generally increases political tolerance.
> Education encourages personal responsibility in the political life of the community and nation and the feeling that one can participate effectively (political efficacy).
> Civic education per se is an important component of education for democracy.
> Civic education should begin early, and continue through the end of secondary schooling.
>> The way in which the school and classroom ("classroom climate") are run is also an important component of civic education.
>> Students should be encouraged to follow and discuss current events, to discuss controversial social and political issues free-

ly and openly, and to think about school problems and ways of solving them.

Student councils are an excellent way of involving students in understanding how problems can be solved and in actually solving school problems.

Teachers and principals need protection from excessive criticism when raising controversial issues as long as they do it in a responsible, nonpartisan manner.

Community service may be a significant way for young people to become involved in civic engagement.

Sustained, long-term engagement has greater effects than episodic, short-term involvement.

Service should involve projects that meet real needs rather than projects created simply to fulfill some minimum level of involvement.

More uncertain is whether community service should be required; encouraging and facilitating participation seems to stimulate high levels of involvement.

Whether and how such service should be integrated into the curriculum is the subject of continued experimentation and evaluation research.

The family remains a major contributor to all aspects of social and political development.

Attitudes of young people are strongly influenced by their parents' attitudes, especially if parents have strong opinions and express them clearly.

Adult voluntary and political participation is strongly influenced by parental behavior patterns.

Parents are important indirectly as well, because they support good civic education.

Civic education is increasingly prevalent in the new democracies of Eastern Europe, Latin America, Asia, and Africa.

Civics programs funded by U.S. and other international donors are being widely implemented, not only in the formal school system, but also in many community-based programs for adults.

The effects of these programs on democratic orientations can be even greater than those found in the United States, provided that individuals are trained frequently with active participatory methods and in open classroom environments.

Civic education conducted for adults by community-based organizations can have particularly powerful effects on political
participation.

The way civic education is delivered differs from one country to
another, but the goals of an informed, active, and thoughtful
citizenry are widely shared, and many of the same principles
govern instruction of new generations across a wide range of
democratic settings.

Notes

1. Samuel P. Huntington, *The Third Wave: Democratization in the Late Twentieth Century* (Norman, OK: University of Oklahoma Press, 1919); Robert Putnum, *Bowling Alone: The Collapse and Revival of American Community* (New York: Simon & Shuster, 2000).
2. http://www.neh.gov/news/archive/20020917.html
3. American Political Science Association Committee of Seven, *The Teaching of Government* (New York: Macmillan, 1916), 2.
4. Kenneth Tolo, *The Civic Education of American Youth: From State Policies to School District Practices* (Austin, TX: Lyndon B. Johnson School of Public Affairs, 1999).
5. See, for example, Victor Davis Hanson, "The Civic Education America Needs," *City Journal.* 12, no. 3 (2002): 32–42; "The Civic Mission of the Schools," CIR-CLE and Carnegie Corporation of New York, 2003. For more on CIRCLE see http://www.civicyouth.org/
6. Richard G. Niemi and Jane Junn, *Civic Education: What Makes Students Learn* (New Haven, CT: Yale University Press, 1998).
7. http://www.aasa.org/issues_and_insights/outlook/05-97.htm; http://www.foet.org/CivilSociety.htm
8. Brian Kleiner and Chris Chapman, *Service Learning and Community Service among 6th Through 12th Grade Students in the United States: 1996 and 1999.* NCES 2000028 (Washington, D.C.: U.S. Department of Education, National Center for Education Statistics, 2000).
9. Virginia A. Hodgkinson and Murray S. Weitzman, *Giving and Volunteering in the U.S.* (Washington, D.C.: Independent Sector,1996);Virginia A. Hodgkinson and Murray S. Weitzman, *Volunteering and Giving among Teenagers 12 to 17 Years of Age* (Washington, D.C.: Independent Sector, 1997).
10. Richard G. Niemi, Mary A. Hepburn, and Chris Chapman, "Community Service by High School Students: A Cure for Civic Ills?" *Political Behavior* 22 (2000):45–69.
11. See, e.g., Bernard Crick, *Education for Citizenship and the Teaching of Democracy in Schools: Final Report of the Advisory Group on Citizenship* (London: Qualifications and Curriculum Authority, 1998); David Denver and Gordon Hands, "Does Studying Politics Make a Difference? The Political Knowledge, Attitudes, and Perceptions of School Students," *British Journal of Political Science* 20 (1990):263–88; Elizabeth Frazer, ed., " Political Education," special

issue, *Oxford Review of Education* 25, nos. 1–2 (1999); Orit Ichilov, ed., *Citizenship and Citizenship Education in a Changing World* (Portland, OR: Woburn Press, 1998); J. Kerry Kennedy, ed., *New Challenges for Civics and Citizenship Education* (Belconnen, ACT: Australian Curriculum Studies Association, 1996); Judith Torney-Purta, John Schwille, and Jo-Ann Amadeo, ed., *Civic Education across Countries: Twenty-four National Cases Studies from the IEA Civic Education Project* (Amsterdam: International Association for the Evaluation of Educational Achievement, 1999). In Great Britain, a nationwide civic education requirement has been introduced for the first time.
12. Torney-Purta, Schwille and Amadeo, 1999.
13. John J. Patrick, "Global Trends in Civic Education for Democracy," ERIC Identifier: ED410176, Publication Date: January 1997, ERIC Clearinghouse for Social Studies/Social Science Education, Bloomington, IN. http://www.ericdigests.org/1998-1/global.htm [Exact page number not available on ERIC documents]
14. Finkel, Steven (2003), "The Impact Of The Kenya National Civic Education Programme On Democratic Attitudes, Knowledge, Values, And Behavior," Prepared for U.S. Agency for International Development, Nairobi, Kenya, AEP-I-00-00-00018, Task Order No. 806. Washington, D.C., Management Systems International.
15. Steven E. Finkel and Howard R. Ernst, "Civic Education in Post-Apartheid South Africa: Alternative Paths to the Development of Political Knowledge and Democratic Values," *Political Psychology* 26, no.3 (2005): 333–364.:
16. Niemi and Junn, 1998.
17. Torney-Purta, Schwille and Amadeo, 1999.
18. Finkel and Ernst, 2005.
19. Steven E. Finkel, "Can Democracy Be Taught?" *Journal of Democracy* 14, no. 4 (2003): 138–51.
20. Ibid.

6

Educating Democratic Citizens in Latin America

FERNANDO REIMERS
ELEONORA VILLEGAS-REIMERS

Open societies require shared values, skills, knowledge and dispositions that allow individuals to think for themselves, to value their own freedom and that of others, to exercise agency in pursuing their aspirations and in contributing to their societies, to acknowledge and value differences among members of groups and to be tolerant, and to find productive ways to reach agreements when those differences lead to conflict. Democracy also requires accepted norms to balance individual and collective rights, which are helped by widespread acceptance of the rule of law and of the legitimacy of governments in the belief that public institutions can treat individuals impartially and fairly. This is to say open societies require a normative and regulatory framework that guarantees individual rights and freedoms and balances them against collective rights, and also a set of values and skills that enact those freedoms and support the legal framework and the institutions of democracy. Thus democracy exists as much in the civil liberties guaranteed by the laws as in the minds of individuals and in the social norms and practices that express those liberties in action.

These shared values, attitudes, knowledge and skills, always developing, never complete, constitute the citizenship competencies the aggregate of which form a society's democratic culture. Among the institutions that promote the development of such shared values and dispositions none, with the possible exception of families, is more powerful than schools. In Latin America schools are especially important because a large proportion of the population is of school age. Educational cultures, too, are fluid systems of shared values, continuously in the making. People can learn new systems of shared meanings to replace those that define the existing cultures of education and democracy.

In examining how educational institutions can better align the culture of education with the culture of democracy, we propose a comprehensive framework, which we believe is preferable to one that defines education of democratic values and skills too narrowly, what is traditionally termed civic education. While we subscribe to John Dewey's view that how we teach is what we teach, we also think that the social purposes of schools, including the extent to which they foster a democratic culture, are equally defined by who they teach, what they intend to teach, how well they teach it, who teaches it, in what school climate, and in what sociocultural context. The moral purposes of schools are expressed in all these aspects of the educational process, not just in the open and explicit instructional goals of the curriculum or in the sentences printed in the textbooks. The central argument of this chapter goes beyond positing that civic democratic education should be more than an isolated subject in the curriculum and cut across a range of subjects and grades; our argument is that a culture of democracy is best supported in schools when the purposes of schools are completely aligned and when schools are organized to help students develop democratic competencies.

The school experiences that help students develop citizenship competencies consistent with participating in and maintaining open democracies result from a system of interlocking opportunities, where each layer of opportunity provides further opportunities to develop the capabilities to be free, tolerant and democratic. These capabilities include of course knowledge, both deep knowledge of the basic subjects that are essential to participate in society (language, math, science, economics) and also the specific civic knowledge of the constitution, government institutions, forms of participation and deep knowledge of history. In addition to knowledge these capabilities include also skills, the skills to express one's views, to think for oneself, to hear and understand the views of others, to resolve differences, to negotiate and compromise, to work with others. The capabilities of democratic citizenship include also attitudes and values, tolerance of difference, acceptance of diversity of views, appreciation of freedom. In addition to knowledge, skills and attitudes, democratic capabilities include the disposition to act, the desire to engage with others in solving public problems, the willingness to use one's talents and time to support the institutions that make democracy possible.

At the core of the interlocking system that supports the development of these capabilities in school, at the microlevel, are consistent social interactions and experiences among students, and between students and teachers, that present children and youth with choices, and give them the skills to choose in ways consistent with their short- and long-term aspirations and preferences. Alongside are opportunities to develop skills that are essential to function in a complex modern society. Children need experiences that enable them to read at high levels, for example, because this is essential in most societies around the world in the twenty-first century and because this skill opens up other opportunities.

Learning to read and write, however, offers many opportunities to foster the exercise of freedom: children can read fiction or science books, they can read history or geography, they can develop their writing skills with projects that allow them to express their individual interests and experiences. Their reading choices can include stories and projects that help them learn about human rights; they can learn about the Holocaust in *The Diary of Anne Frank,* or about other parts of the world, or about different cultures. Each student can learn to appreciate and value the many different ways in which the human mind approaches opportunities to create; in so doing they can learn to value freedom. The curriculum can also further develop the skills and dispositions of democratic citizenship by building in explicit times when students can learn what it takes to make democracy work. Students can learn about the individual and collective efforts of historical figures such as Benjamin Franklin, John Adams or Thomas Jefferson in the creation of the American democratic experiment, or they can learn about the role of leaders of social movements like Martin Luther King in the struggle against racial discrimination. They can learn also about comparative efforts around the world to construct open societies, and about the historical experiences of the breakdown of democracy and their consequences for human rights and freedoms. Through systematically providing opportunities in the curriculum to study and engage with relevant curriculum, students can learn to take themselves seriously.

Teachers, of course, need to be both well-educated and capable of fostering freedom of inquiry and independence of thought to support students in developing these capabilities. These classroom interactions should be embedded in an institutional context that respects children and their families. Those entrusted with the task of schooling the young must understand that they are public servants, carrying out an important duty for which they are accountable. Such relationships among teachers, schools, and communities are embedded in a system of institutional norms governing how teachers are selected and promoted, how principals are appointed, and the social climate in the school. Schools that respect students and communities and are models of respect and openness are in turn strong communities, task-focused, and managed in transparent ways.

The system we have described thus includes high-quality and consistent experiences at the microlevel. It includes opportunities to learn about democracy and civil liberties; teachers who value free inquiry and independence of mind; schools that relate to students and their communities in respectful partnerships; school staff who relate to each other respectfully, honestly, and openly; and a larger societal commitment to educating all children at high levels and for democratic life. These interdependent conditions form a system of concentric circles of influence, with children's day-to-day classroom experiences at the core and a broad societal commitment to educating all children as the outermost circle

Applying Our Framework to Schools in Latin America

Using this conceptual model, we now examine the operation of schools in Latin America. We rely partly on the results of a survey administered to students, their parents, their teachers, and their principals in representative samples of schools and third and fourth grade classrooms. These data were collected around 1998 by national ministries of education in collaboration with UNESCO's regional office for education in Latin America. The analyses we present of these data are our own. We rely also on other sources and research, as well as on our own experience studying schools and working closely with ministries of education in several Latin American countries since the mid-1980s.

Broad Commitment to Educating All Children at High Levels

One goal of democracy is to provide all citizens the same opportunities to participate in society and to shape their own destinies. Equal access to an education that provides the opportunity to develop one's mind, skills, values, and knowledge is an essential condition to achieve this goal. Schools in Latin America do not provide equal learning opportunities to all. The reason is not just that individual children learn differently as a result of effort or ability; rather it is that most educational institutions in the region have been better at reproducing or increasing intergenerational social differences than at narrowing those gaps.

Two processes foster this intergenerational transmission of inequality. First, access to schools, particularly to secondary and tertiary education, is significantly more constrained for the children of poor families. The region does not have enough public schools and universities to satisfy the demand for education, or adequate financing mechanisms to enable low-income students to invest time in their education. And many low-income students do not receive an adequate basic preparation that will allow them to succeed in high school, pass college entrance examinations or succeed in college. Second, the quality of basic education is stratified: low-income students often receive education of lower quality.

This state of affairs reflects a society organized in two different groups, with little mobility between them, where social origin is also social destiny. Alas, for most of the last several centuries, the purpose of educational institutions in Latin America has been to perpetuate this difference. This conservative purpose was challenged during the last century by an alternative view that saw schools as capable of reinforcing a different social order, one more urban, industrial, and democratic. The conflict between these two competing educational ideologies has played out variously but has resulted in significant achievements in most countries, including unprecedented educational expansion, the creation of public education systems, and significant intergenerational mobility. Although these gains do not represent an uncontested victory for the liberal project, they have shifted education toward more democratic ideals.[1]

Partly because the idea that all people have the same basic human rights, including the right to be well educated, does not have widespread support in Latin America, blatant educational disparities persist, undermining the formation of social capital and perpetuating divided societies, poverty, and inequality. True, there is universal access to elementary education; but, especially in the poorest regions, the conditions in many schools are dismal and teaching quality is low. Therefore many students learn little, repeat grades several times, fail to develop basic competencies—including literacy and numeracy—and as a result eventually drop out of school or graduate with very weak preparation. Among people fifteen to nineteen years old, 4.4 percent have never attended school, 16 percent dropped out in elementary school, 11 percent dropped out after six years of elementary education, and 6 percent dropped out during secondary education.[2] One in three Latin Americans does not finish high school.

School dropouts come disproportionately from poorer households. Among children living in cities, 43 percent of the school dropouts are in the poorest income quartile.[3] But most children who drop out of school in the region live in villages, where people are even poorer. In rural areas the odds of never entering school are 3.5 times greater than in urban areas; the odds of dropping out in elementary education are 2.3 times greater; the odds of dropping out after elementary education are 1.9 times greater.

Consequently, the levels of educational attainment as a whole are low, and gaps separate the educational achievement levels of different social groups. Since most income inequality relates to educational inequality, these gaps reproduce economic, social, and cultural divides from one generation to the next. For example, among people aged twenty-five to fifty-nine, the average years of schooling attained by those living in cities compared to those living in rural areas was, respectively, ten and four in Bolivia, seven and three in Brazil, eleven and seven in Chile, nine and five in Colombia, nine and six in Costa Rica, and seven and two in Guatemala.[4]

Schools in Latin America not only fail to teach all students; they also fail to teach those who do attend school at equally high standards. In international comparisons of educational achievement, students in Latin America consistently obtain the lowest scores. A recent study of the literacy, math, and science skills of fifteen-year-olds in school in forty-one Organization of Economic Co-Operation and Development (OECD) and middle-income countries found that students in Argentina, Brazil, Chile, Mexico, and Peru (the only Latin American countries included in the study) scored at the bottom of the distribution of scores—along with Albania, Indonesia, and Liechtenstein.[5] One in five students in Argentina, for example, could not identify the main idea in a short text, compared to 2.4 percent of the students in Canada, 4 percent in Spain, and 6 percent in the United States. At the other end of the reading ability scale, only 1.7 percent of the fifteen-year-olds in Argentina could read critically, at the level one would expect from a college student. This compares to 17 percent of students in Canada, 4 percent in Spain, and 12 percent in the United States. The percentage of those without basic literacy skills was just as high or higher in Brazil (23%), Chile (20%), Mexico (16%), and Peru (54%), and the percentage of sophisticated readers was just as low or lower.[6]

Contributing to unequal access to high quality education is the lack of equal access to teaching and learning resources. For example, in a 1998 survey in twelve countries in Latin America, one in four fourth-grade students indicated they did not have a language textbook;[7] slightly more (30%) did not have a math textbook, and one in ten did not have a notebook. Similarly, in many countries in the region, poor children are segregated in schools where they are taught by the teachers with the least preparation and experience and with the least support. Often this segregation occurs in the same school building. In Mexico, for example, where most urban schools run two shifts, it is customary to use the second shift as a placement of choice to give teachers about to retire a second job which will enhance their retirement pay. As a result, teaching staff in the afternoon shifts consists of a highly unstable staff of teachers who are tired, because they are nearly of retirement age and because they also teach in the morning. Knowing this, most parents prefer that their children attend the morning shifts; parent teacher associations set fees for the morning shift that typically are beyond the means of the poorest parents. As a result, there are noticeable differences in the social background of the children attending morning and afternoon shifts in the same schools, with most poorer children attending in the afternoon.

This unequal access to high-quality education hinders the development of a democratic culture because it leads to significant gaps in knowledge and skills for the population at large and for the poor in particular. When the children of the poor attend schools of inferior quality, they learn less and are consequently less likely to proceed to higher levels of instruction. Many thus drop out with low levels of skills. Poorly prepared citizens do not have access to the same jobs, opportunities, and channels of participation and are also less likely to support democracy. A study of the relationship between education and democratic attitudes based on a cross-national survey of forty-eight societies, including Chile, Costa Rica, and Mexico, found that individuals with more years of schooling were more likely to support democracy.[8] A separate study of the same data for the three Latin American countries concludes that while the majority of the adults polled do not trust other people (suggesting low levels of civic culture), the 30 percent who do trust others are significantly more educated and more likely to have reached secondary education and college.[9]

In the United States, Robert Putnam found a similar increasing marginal effect of secondary education on interpersonal trust.[10] Within all levels of education, interpersonal trust in Latin America is low, but it is lower for those with less schooling and in the countries with less educated populations. In a survey administered in seventeen countries in 2002, on average only 19 percent said that most people could be trusted; these figures range from 3 percent in Brazil—with some of the worst educational indicators in the region—to 36 percent in Uruguay, which has some of the highest levels of educational achievement in the region.[11]

Additional evidence of how a weak commitment to equal access and quality of education weakens the development of a democratic culture and the rule of law is the success of political or criminal groups in recruiting young people who are poorly prepared for productive occupations. A recent report that the Shining Path is reemerging in Peru states that the rural guerrilla group was "recruiting a new generation of unemployed youths....With no memory of past violence and few prospects, these youngsters are happy to take the $20 a month wage Shining Path is said to offer."[12] Thus low-quality educational institutions reproduce poverty and social instability.

And of course political conflict in turn reduces educational opportunity, producing still more conflict. In Colombia, school attendance rates are diminishing among poor young people. Among those aged seven to eleven, the percentage attending school among the poorest 10 percent of the population declined from 92 percent in 1997 to 88 percent in 2000; for the next 10 percent of income from 94 to 90 percent; for the next decile from 97 to 89 percent. In all other groups attendance rates increased during this period. Thus, at a time of intense conflict and economic recession, educational inequality is increasing. The increase in these gaps is even more dramatic among those aged twelve to seventeen. Quite possibly the processes underlying these increases in educational inequality are multifaceted.

To sum up, the failure of Latin American countries to provide decent educational opportunities to large groups of the population has undermined democratic culture. It should not be surprising that support for democracy in the region was, at the end of the twentieth century, low and declining, and that satisfaction with democracy is very low: only in Costa Rica, Honduras, Nicaragua, and Uruguay were more than 50 percent "satisfied with democracy." On average, support of and satisfaction with democracy in Latin America are lower than in the European Union, Africa, Asia, and India, and comparable to the levels in Eastern Europe.[13]

Another public opinion study of support for democracy in Latin America conducted by the United Nations Development Program in 2002 reveals that less than half of the population (43%) have democratic attitudes and views, 26.5 percent are definite non-democrats and 30.5% are ambivalent.[14] Particularly disturbing is the finding that support for democracy is weaker among the young: only 40.1 percent of those aged 16 to 29 held democratic views and attitudes, 28.7 percent are non-democrats and 31.2 percent are ambivalent. It is clear that Latin American societies are failing to prepare their young to be free: not all citizens have access to school, and among those who have, not all are equally well prepared. While the twentieth century witnessed government efforts aimed at improving education, those efforts were insufficient. The reforms were timid and misguided, consisting largely of spending more money on the same educational approaches from the past, approaches which we will show in the rest of this chapter are inadequate to foster democratic skills.

Schools That Are Themselves Open Communities

Fostering democratic citizenship requires an educational system that is structured democratically, where participation is not only expected but also encouraged, and where decision making is participatory, transparent, and accountable to the citizens and taxpayers. Educational management and decision making in Latin America, however, reflect an authoritarian culture in which government officials often confuse the public interest with their private interests. Some observers have attributed the underperformance of educational systems in Latin America to the fact that they have been captured by politicians and bureaucrats for their own purposes. Many political organizations have been built using teaching and administrative positions and education budgets to reward supporters. Several of the teacher unions are not democratic professional organizations but political machines that have handsomely rewarded their leaders with power and wealth.

Thus, in the Latin American culture of education, public servants often do not feel accountable to the public that pays their salaries. An analysis of how educational evaluation influences educational decision making in Latin America describes arrogant policy elites that see "little need to bother reading evaluation research or asking those who do for advice." Instead, they believe "they know the answers because their position confers authority on them." They also believe they know the problems and the questions that call for answers."[15] Because they are not held accountable, they can continue their ineffective practices, and the region's education systems continue to underperform.

Ignoring the input of local administrators and communities in the decisions that influence school life is common practice in the region. Schools socialize children into a state of mind where the solution to people's needs is not in the community nor in any individual agency or organization. Instead, they are encouraged to extend their hands in the expectation that the central government—the modern *patrón* in a society of powerful and powerless—will turn its attention to those needs, deciding for the communities and citizens what those needs are and how they should be met.

In Mexico, appointments of teachers, principals, and school supervisors are made by committees that are largely controlled by the teachers' union, the largest trade union in the hemisphere and a very important political stakeholder. Reforms intended to strengthen the profession and reduce the influence of local politicians in educational management have become institutionalized practices that do not embody transparency, accountability, and the rule of merit in advancing the careers of educators. Furthermore, a low proportion of women teachers are promoted to principals and school supervisors; and this even though schools managed by female principals were found to have better relations among staff and between staff and members of the community and higher levels of student academic achievement.[16] While Mexico is among the most inequitable countries in Latin America with respect to gender, similar inequalities are observed in most other countries in the region. Even though approximately 80 percent of third and fourth grade teachers in Latin America are women, only 60 percent of principals are women. It should thus not be surprising that 59 percent of the students completing secondary school believe that women should not participate in politics, in contrast to 15 percent of the fourteen- year-olds who hold the same belief in other OECD countries.[17]

The failure of schools to develop trust, reciprocity, and social capital is reflected in low levels of trust among school staff and students. Fewer than a third of the students trust their teachers "sometimes" and about a third said they did not trust their teacher at all. About a fourth of the students said they constantly had fights with their classmates, and four in five said their classmates harassed them. Teachers often disrespect students, and administrators often disrespect teachers. All too often students learn to mistrust and fear their teachers and classmates rather than trust and respect them.

Relations of Schools to Communities

Reinforcing the deficiencies of schools as models for and promoters of democratic participation are the limited opportunities for parents to be engaged with school. Schools in the region vary widely in the extent to which parents participate in school management committees. Many schools do not even have such committees, and those that do typically involve only school staff. Opportunities for students to participate in school management or student government councils are even more limited.

The limits of parental participation run even deeper. Many parents rarely visit their children's schools. In many countries, fewer than 80 percent of parents visit even once a month. Not only do schools not encourage parents and teachers to participate in their activities and decisions; the larger society also denies this level of active participation more generally.

One way to break this cycle is to provide school experiences that help students, parents, and teachers develop participatory skills. In the United States, psychologist Lawrence Kohlberg and his associates studied how students develop moral reasoning and then developed an approach, called "The Just Community," that involves students in defining school norms.[18] Schools committed to becoming "just communities" adopt a democratic decision-making process in which most major decisions in the school are discussed and approved by every member of the community. Small groups of students, teachers, and administrators organize themselves into committees to examine needs and propose changes, and every member participates in making decisions and implementing projects. Just communities have had very encouraging results: students, teachers, and administrators have been found to have a stronger commitment to taking responsibility for their actions and perceiving their participation as crucial for the functioning of their communities. They learn how to propose changes for their own benefit and for that of other members of the community. In sum, they all learn how to be truly democratic citizens of their schools and in turn make the school organization more democratic. In Colombia, the *Escuela Nueva*, an innovative school model incorporates a strong element of student government, with significant positive consequences in developing democratic capabilities.

Too often the relations of schools with communities reflect an authoritarian tradition of lack of accountability. In a recent survey administered in El Salvador about the most common experiences of citizens with corruption the most common form of corruption experienced was in the form of requests by principals and teachers for illegal fees to enroll children in public schools. The prevalence of this practice was twice as high as requests for bribes in health centers and three times higher than requests of bribes in government offices or by the police.[19]

Well-Prepared Teachers Who Can Serve as Democratic Models, and Who Value Freedom and Diversity

The fact that students in Latin America are not learning at high levels is due only in part to the structural and organizational characteristics of educational systems that reflect an authoritarian and closed culture of decision making. Another factor is poor pedagogy. Teachers are not teaching students well, and in particular are not teaching students to think for themselves and to value the freedom to do so.

In our survey of students in third and fourth grades, only some of the students—on average 65 percent—indicated that they understood their teachers' lessons consistently.

It would be unreasonable to place all the blame for this failure on the teachers. But teachers are one of the most important factors in any educational system, so in this section, we focus on teachers: their own preparation and their role in the preparation of democratic citizens.

Teachers in Latin America could benefit from more and better professional preparation. Most come into teaching with very poor academic preparation; many do not choose the profession, but land in it by default, after having been denied entry into other academic fields. Most of them come from low socioeconomic backgrounds and have a hard time making ends meet. Many teachers work two or more jobs. Many have received no formal education in teaching. Some have only a secondary education. Given the shortage of educators in the region, many schools find themselves hiring anyone willing to teach.

The good news is that an increasing number of teachers have completed at least secondary education, and new accreditation requirements are leading them to the preparation necessary for a teaching certification (which in most countries in the region is now a higher education degree). However, teacher candidates are exposed to very traditional methodologies that reproduce in the classroom the same authoritarian relations that exist in society. Teachers of teachers are not always better prepared than their students and often rely on traditional teaching methods, memorization of facts, and repetition of texts rather than initiative, creativity, or practical applications.

The content of teacher preparation courses and programs varies by country, but virtually none of it includes anything related to education for democracy. Thus, even when the school curriculum begins to target the development of democratic skills, teachers often have not been prepared for this and simply require their students to memorize facts about the constitutions of their countries, without any emphasis on developing the critical thinking, logical reasoning, communication skills, or democratic values that they need to participate in a democratic society.

In addition, the teachers' experiences with democracy are limited, since they are after all citizens of their societies and products of their cultures. It is common practice in the region for teachers simply to do what the school principal says, and for the principal simply to follow orders from his supervisor in the ministry of education, who of course is only following orders from the ministry itself. None of these players has a voice in formulating the policy they carry out; their performance is evaluated according to how efficiently and docilely they follow orders.

Compounding the authoritarian tradition, teachers are often asked to comply with requests that bear no relationship to their students' best interests, or forced to pay fees to teacher unions, participate in partisan political activity, or entertain requests for sexual favors or bribes from their superiors. Teachers have themselves never been taught to question this status quo, and thus by example teach their students that "that's the way the world works." Hence the cycle of nondemocratic practices remains intact, whatever the schoolbooks say, a result reflected in a recent study of civic education in Colombia. Judith Torney-Purta and others found that high-school students had basic knowledge of democratic practices but evaluated them as "not real" based on their experience. These students have learned to identify what the books say as unrealistic and idealistic and in sharp contrast with what they experience in their daily lives, including their experiences in school.[20]

The emphasis in teacher preparation on rote learning, and the limited opportunities for students to learn to think for themselves, both hinder the creation of democratic citizens. When students are taught to parrot poorly understood ideas and to accept that truth rests on authority rather than on evidence and reasoning, how can they value or teach the freedom to think independently? They can learn to value the ability to make choices only if they have opportunities to make them in schools. Students rarely have the opportunity to decide which activity to work on in the classroom, how to approach a problem, which books to read in order to practice reading, or which topic of current events to discuss openly.

Emerging evidence suggests that teachers hold quite intolerant views and have limited understanding of democracy. A survey of teachers in Mexico revealed that only 29 percent consider that citizens must obey the law and only 18 percent believe they should respect the rights of others. One in five teachers would not accept that an indigenous person or a person of another race lived in their home, one third would not accept a person of another religion living in their home and two in five would not accept a homosexual living in their home.[21] These views of teachers both reflect and contribute to perpetuate intolerance among the population at large. A recent study of discrimination in Mexican society found that nine in ten women, disabled, indigenous, homosexuals, elderly, religious minorities and foreigners perceive that they are discriminated against because of their condition. One in three indicates that they have been discriminated against during the last year and one in three indicates that they have been discriminated against at work.[22]

Recent surveys of teachers in Argentina, Peru, and Uruguay confirm high levels of intolerance toward diversity. Twenty percent of teachers in Uruguay, 34 percent in Argentina and 55 percent in Peru would not accept to have homosexual neighbors. There is also high intolerance based on national or ethnic origin. Eleven percent of the teachers in Uruguay, 15 percent in Argentina and 38 percent of those in Peru discriminate against people of other nationalities or ethnicities. There is also high discrimination against those living in slums among 16 percent of the teachers in Peru, 33 percent of those in Uruguay and 52 percent of those in Argentina. There is also discrimination based in religion and immigrant status. One in five teachers in Peru discriminates against Jewish and Arabic people, against Japanese, Chinese, and other Asian people, against Ecuadorians, Paraguayans, and Chileans.[23]

Civic Education Curriculum

In recent years, several countries in the region have begun to develop curricula to promote democratic competencies. While the subject of civic education has been a part of the curriculum in many nations in Latin America for many decades, the dominant conception of civic education focused principally on the institutions of government, emphasized electoral participation and was generally not very engaging. Where the results of such courses of civic education have been assessed they are alarming. A study of the civic skills of fourteen- and seventeen-year-olds in Chile and Colombia shows that while these students know the ideal characteristics of a democracy, they tend to see such knowledge as unrelated to their experience.[24] The study shows that students cannot identify corruption, nepotism, or monopoly of the press as impediments to democracy. The teachers indicate that they are not well prepared to teach this subject. Only half of the Chilean students and 77 percent of the students in Colombia can identify correctly the response to a multiple choice question defining democracy as government by representatives elected by the people. One third of Chilean students believe that democracy is government by experts. In Mexico, where some of the same questions were administered to a large sample of fourteen-year-olds, half of the graduates of secondary school believe that a democracy is the government of experts; only 41 percent identify the correct response to the question.[25] The same study in Mexico reveals that civil education is the subject students like the least. While 24 percent of the students indicate that they enjoy language studies a lot, only 13 percent of them indicate the same about civil education. Many students indicate that their preparation in civil education is weak.

Although this is only an aspect of the larger system of influences through which schools develop democratic skills and dispositions, civic education should be strengthened. Direct and explicit teaching of democratic skills, attitudes, and values is necessary for democratic societies to exist and function, especially when the social climate is not conducive to learning them. It would be especially important to move from a narrow view of civic education as an isolated subject in the curriculum to one that sees the development of democratic citizenship in many different activities in different subjects in the curriculum, including service learning, student governance and opportunities for students to develop the skills to deliberate in all subjects.

In a survey of fifteen Latin American countries in the early 1990s, Villegas-Reimers[26] found that no country in the region had a curriculum that focused explicitly on education for democracy. Most countries had a curriculum on civic education or citizenship education, but these curricula included such a mix of topics—from studies of family structures, to sex education, to the rights and responsibilities of social institutions—that very little, if any, emphasis was given to the effective functioning of democracy.

Two developments, however, are encouraging. One is a recent renewal of interest in developing a curriculum that does emphasize democratic skills. In particular Colombia, Chile, and Mexico are advancing important initiatives in this area. The other is the growing number of NGOs in the region that are working to educate citizens about democracy, including the organizations *Conciencia* and *Participa*, with chapters in several countries. Both have developed curricula to introduce basic knowledge and skills to the young and have also developed programs to encourage adults to become more actively involved in the day-to-day functioning of their societies. Unfortunately, however, the NGOs have had to develop and implement many of these activities outside of schools because they have not received ministry of education approval.

Microlevel Experiences

Providing individualized experiences that can help students develop as independent thinkers in graded schools has always been challenging, as pointed out many years ago by John Dewey and Maria Montessori. In an attempt to provide mass education at low cost, education was standardized and schools adopted a factory model in which the child is not treated as an individual. The very notion of a standard curriculum of instruction is antithetical to the notion that educating means creating conditions for each child to pursue its own path, developing meanings and understandings about the world that reflect its individual interests. And yet the instructional climate students experience is one of the most significant influences in developing democratic competencies.

It is possible, however, to organize education more individually. In learning to read, for example, teachers can depend on a single textbook that every child must use at approximately the same pace or they can rely on a richer set of reading materials, allowing students opportunities to develop their reading skills as they pursue individual interests. Teachers can teach writing skills by asking students to copy from the board or from their lectures, or they can provide students with opportunities to carry out independent research projects and write their own compositions. Teachers can arrange student desks in rows oriented towards the teacher, or they can arrange them in small clusters or circles that promote conversations among students.

To the extent that classroom instruction provides students with more opportunities for individual expression and for individual or cooperative problem solving, they will learn the most valuable lessons: that knowledge is a personal construction, that one can apply one's efforts to learn just about anything, and that anyone can learn. In many classrooms in Latin America, however, instruction is sadly different. Teachers talk most of the time, provide students with low-order explanations, and engage them in low-order cognitive tasks: copying from the board or taking notes from lectures. Students have very limited opportunities to work on research projects that reflect their interests.

For instance, when asked what they did when students made mistakes, only one in four teachers in third and fourth grade said that when feasible they discussed different possible answers to a question, which is potentially one of the richest strategies that might be used to develop students' ability to think at high levels. When they group students in the classroom, only one in five teachers does so based on student interests, suggesting that they see little room for student-directed learning. Teachers have very low expectations about their students' potential educational attainment; one in five expects that most of their students will only finish elementary school, and only two in five expect them to finish high school. Presumably teachers who do not expect their students to go on with their education will see no need to teach them a rigorous and challenging curriculum.

Conclusions

Social change is complex and so is constructing open societies and democratic cultures. Changing societal structures and practices is only possible through the concerted effort of all a society's members. As one of the most important institutions of social change, schools are in a unique position to help transform societies to make them more open, democratic, and just. Only when societies are committed to those goals does this process become possible.

If schools in Latin America are to succeed in preparing democratic citizens who can participate actively in designing and implementing their nations' destinies, the culture of education must change in important ways. These changes include developing curricula that emphasize the development of democratic competencies, designed and taught by teachers who are professionals of the highest quality, who work in an educational system open to all, where participation and accountability is encouraged and expected. These changes are possible and should be the goal of all educational policy in the region. But this will only occur when policy-makers and other leaders in these societies commit themselves to democracy and social justice.

Notes

1. Fernando Reimers "Education and Social Progress," in *The Cambridge Economic History of Latin America*, eds.John H. Coatsworth and Victor Bulmer-Thomas (Cambridge: Cambridge University Press, 2005), vol. 2, 427–480.

2. Economic Commission for Latin America, *Social Panorama of Latin America 2001–2002*. (Santiago, Chile: Author, 2002), 256.

3. Ibid, 114.

4. Ibid., 251–52.

5. Organization for Economic Co-Operation and Development (OECD), *Literacy Skills for the World of Tomorrow. First Results from PISA 2000* (Paris: Author, 2002);OECD, *Literacy Skills for the World of Tomorrow. Further Results from PISA 2000* (Paris: Author, 2003).

6. OECD, *Literacy Skills*, 2003, 274.

7. These figures are our calculations using data obtained by UNESCO in 1998 in a sample of schools.

8. A. Moreno, "Democracy and Mass Belief Systems in Latin America," in *Citizen Views of Democracy in Latin America*, ed. Roderick Ai Camp. Pittsburgh, PA: University of Pittsburgh Press,2001), 27–50, at 35.

9. T. Power and M. Clark, "Does Trust Matter?" in *Citizen Views of Democracy in Latin America*, ed. Roderic Ai Camp (Pittsburgh, PA: University of Pittsburgh Press, 2001), 51–70, at 59.

10. Robert Putnam, "Tuning In, Tuning Out: The Strange Disappearance of Social Capital in America," *Political Science and Politics* 27, no. 4 (1995): 665. Cited in Power and Clark 2001; see note 15.

11. Latinobarometro, 2002, Press Report, http://www.latinobarometro.org

12. *The Economist*, "How Big a Threat Is the Shining Path?" July 17, 2003.

13. Informe de Prensa Latinobarometro, 2002, http://www.latinobarometro.org

14. United Nations Development Program. 2004. *Democracy in Latin America*. New York. http://www.democracia.undp.org/Default.Asp.

15. F. Reimers, "The Social Context of Educational Evaluation in Latin America," in T. Kellaghan and D. Stufflebeam, ed., *International Handbook of Educational Evaluation* (Dordrecht/Boston/London: Kluwer, 2003), 450–51.

16. Fernando Reimers, "Principally Women. Gender in the politics of Mexican Education," in L. Randall ed. *The changing structure of Mexico*. (Armonk, NY: M.E. Sharpe, in press).

17. F. Tirado and Gilberto Guevara. "Educación Cívica. Un Estudio Complementario." México. Mimeograph. 2005.

18. C. Power, "Evaluating Just Communities: Towards a Method For Assessing the Moral Atmosphere of the School," in *Evaluating Moral Development*, ed. L. Kuhmerker et al. (Schenectady, NY: Character Research Press, 1980).

19. Jose Miguel Cruz and Alvaro Martin de Vega. *La percepcion sobre la corrupcion en las instituciones de El Salvador. Los ciudadanos hablan sobre la corrupcion*. San Salvador. Universidad Centro Americana. Instituto Universitario de Opinion Publica, 58. Sixteen percent of those surveyed indicated that they had been asked to pay bribes in public schools.

20. J. Torney-Purta, Personal communication, July 2003.

21. Fundacion En Este País. 2003. Congruencia y Comportamiento Institucional. Encuesta a Maestros de Educación Publica. Mexico. Mimeograph.
22. Secretaria de Desarrollo Social. Mexico. 2005. Encuesta Nacional sobre Discriminacion.
23. Emilio Tenti Fanfani. 2003. Les Immigres a l'ecole. La xenophobie des enseignants en Argentine, Perou et Uruguay. Buenos Aires. Instituto Internacional de Planificación de la educación.
24. Judith Torney-Purta and Jo-Ann Amadeo. 2004. *Strengthening Democracy in the Americas through Civic Education.* Washington, D.C. Organizacion of American Status, 48.
25. Felipe Tirado and Gilberto Guevara. Educación Cívica. Un Estudio Complementario. México. Mimeog. 2005.
26. Eleonora Villegas-Reimers, *Can Schools Teach Democratic Values?* (Washington, D.C.: U.S. Agency for International Development, 1993); E. Villegas-Reimers, *Civic Education and the School Systems of Latin America and the Caribbean* (Washington, D.C.: U.S. Agency for International Development, 1993); and E. Villegas-Reimers, "Preparing the Next Generation of Democratic Citizens," *Revista* (Cambridge, MA: Harvard University, David Rockefeller Center for Latin American Studies, 2002).

Part III
Religion

7

Evangelical Expansion and "Progressive Values" in the Developing World

DAVID MARTIN

Any examination of the relationship between Evangelical (and Pentecostal) expansion in the developing world and the incidence of "progressive values" must begin by estimating the numbers involved and their main geographical locations. Inevitably, the demographics of expansion will be broadly indicative rather than precise, and, since we are interested in a culture, it makes more sense to offer gross estimates in terms of religious constituency rather than the criteria of membership that Evangelicals themselves might prefer.[1]

We must also recognize that the large numbers, perhaps one in three, who pass through the swinging door, and so count as dropouts from the viewpoint of membership, have still undergone a serious change and had a particular kind of experience. So those who are affected in some way also help to create a cultural penumbra. Moreover, the overall Evangelical movement spreads Protestant assumptions across the broader society. That is why the United States is in an important sense a Protestant society, and indeed the only one.

Evangelicalism and Pentecostalism stress a change of heart expressed in commitment to a voluntary organization, and so have an inherent relationship to regimes of competitive pluralism in a religious market. They therefore find, and have helped create, a favorable habitat in the pluralistic societies of North America and sub-Saharan Africa. By contrast, they encounter a resistant environment in the societies of Europe and Asia, where a traditional organic union has long existed between Catholic, Hindu, Muslim, or Buddhist religious practice and the very idea of social belonging. Latin America also had such traditions, inherited from Catholic Spain and Portugal, but now, for complex reasons, it is host to an accelerating pluralism. Catholicism remains hegemonic in the state and elite strata but in society at large has to compete on an open market.

That Evangelicals flourish most in the pluralistic continents of North America and Africa is something of a paradox. North America is the most advanced example of socioeconomic development and Africa the least, so Evangelicals are concentrated at the two ends of the spectrum. Of course, historical contingencies are at work here: Evangelicalism was deeply implicated in Anglo-American culture in its formative period in the 1700s and 1800s, including the moving frontier of the American experience. But it also includes the expanding frontier of the British experience, specifically colonization in Africa. In this very different context, the most advanced type of industrial society encountered in sub-Saharan Africa a kind of pluralism that predated organic unions of church and society. In the course of this encounter, Evangelicalism advanced in partial alliance and intermittent conflict with the traders, soldiers, and administrators of the colonial power. That also meant, inevitably, that Evangelical faith was disseminated as English spread across the globe. It still does, except that Evangelicalism has also achieved a vital relation to a myriad of vernaculars, in particular through Biblical translation and the creation of dictionaries and grammars. Localization complements globalization in a potent combination.

Whatever the differences between Evangelicalism and Pentecostalism, we must still see them as two phases of a faith based on change of heart and thoroughgoing revision of life. A mature and increasingly voluntary Evangelicalism emerged from the revivals and awakenings of eighteenth-century Britain and North America. There it still remains the dominant form of enthusiastic Protestantism, though over time the focus of religious power has shifted from Britain to North America, along with the focus of political power.

In the second half of the twentieth century, Pentecostalism overtook Evangelicalism in Latin America, partly because the latter had been seen as wrapped up in an imported package welcomed by liberal elites but remote from the masses. These elites did not much want the religion but they did associate it with progress. In Africa, Evangelicalism did not confront a resistant union of church and society, and the colonial package, though imported, was widely identified with education, progress, medicine, and new horizons. Moreover, it was carried at least as much by black catechists as by white missionaries. Thus Evangelicalism became indigenous in Africa much more successfully than in Latin America and changed its character in doing so, as well as helping create African Independent Churches. About 1960, Pentecostalism took off in Latin America, and Evangelicalism in postcolonial Africa. A decade or so later Pentecostalism began to challenge Evangelicalism in Africa.

We therefore have two kinds of relationships between the first and second phases of enthusiastic Protestantism. In Latin America and the Caribbean, Pentecostalism becomes the dominant form; in Africa, as well as in India, Korea, and elsewhere, it proceeds in rivalrous tandem with Evangelicalism. Moreover, the vitality of Evangelicalism is now often manifest in charismatic forms, analogous to Pentecostal spirituality. All over Latin America, for example, one encounters Evangelical churches "in renewal."

One way to think about these complicated realities is to remember that the revolutions in communication and geographical and social mobility accelerated enormously in the mid-twentieth century, and on a global scale. The primordial givens of local time and place based on the union of religion and society, and religious hierarchy and social hierarchy, collapsed, to create vast new potential for religious mobilizations based on movement and choice, and operating at the level of culture rather than the state. Here one sees just how markedly Evangelicalism and Pentecostalism differ from Islamic mobilizations seeking to revive an organic union of religion and society based on subjecting the state to religious law and prohibiting competitive pluralism, except by Muslims. Thus where Christian revivalism and Islamic revivalism overlap, as in Northern Nigeria, tension is bound to occur.

The particular potency of Pentecostalism lies in its combination of white and black revivalism in the United States with spiritism and shamanism. It is simultaneously ancient and modern, making it a fit conveyer belt for transitions as it mobilizes depressed strata and marginal ethnicities all over the developing world. It flourishes most among the aspiring poor who are moving out of local hierarchies, with their obligatory deference, into the anonymity and fluidity of the city. Pentecostals are those among the poor who most desire to better themselves in every sense, morally and materially, and their betterment may lead them to repudiate, even demonize, their immediate local culture. From their viewpoint, local traditional culture holds them back and fastens them in place. By contrast, the mainstream churches include many who are sufficiently secure in their status to be more relaxed and to view indigenous cultures with nostalgia. Thus revivals of indigenous cultures are usually set in motion by intellectuals—or by those still largely held in the cultures' embrace.

Another version of Pentecostalism is found in the global charismatic movement that arises either within mainstream churches, including the Roman Catholic Church and Evangelical churches "in renewal," or else appears as Pentecostalism becomes socially mobile. Put crudely, the charismatic movement is a Pentecostalism for the new global middle classes.

Thus we see a very varied market, in which different brands appeal to different sectors, all the way from the Pentecostalism surging forward among marginal status groups and marginal ethnicities in China or Malawi or Ecuador to the charismatic movements of middle classes in Dar es Salaam or Lagos or Singapore—or even within the Lutheran Church of East Africa, and the Egyptian Copts. What they all have in common is a union of release and personal discipline, emotion and control, participation and authority. Therein lies their relevance for both economic and political potential. This is the furthest social reach of the Protestant ethic, with maximum challenge and unique opportunities.

Numbers

Turning to gross estimates of numbers, I might begin with the two continents least pluralistic and most resistant to the evangelical option: Europe and Asia. Again, pluralism in this context refers not to the proximity of different religious communities but to an open market in "religious preferences." In this respect Europe is not pluralistic. Even in Protestant northern Europe one finds state churches which though largely dormant can still inhibit the opening of a free market. The Evangelical sector, inside the state churches and outside them, probably accounts for no more than 5 to 10 percent of a Protestant and post-Protestant constituency of about 100 million people. At the same time, this Evangelical sector is the most vital expression of Christianity in Protestant Europe and, with Pentecostalism, has had some success in Eastern Europe. In Romania, for example, the Protestant community numbers perhaps 3 percent: 2 percent Pentecostal, 1 percent Evangelical, for a total population of 1 million.

Of course, in Asia, Evangelicals and Pentecostals are small minorities set on the margin of huge non-Christian majorities often animated by nationalism and sometimes directly linked to the state. This means that Christianity of whatever kind is largely confined to peripheral status groups and marginal ethnicities. South Korea is exceptional because it is a nation set between China and Japan in which progress and nationalism have been positively related to Christianity, especially the American evangelical type. The Philippines is also exceptional because sociologically and historically it belongs more to Latin America than to Asia. Nearly nine in ten Filipinos are Roman Catholics, with a very heterogeneous and lively evangelical sector.

Where Evangelicalism and Pentecostalism have had the most impact on Asia is in China, as the great trek to the megacity proceeds. They also flourish in the Chinese diaspora from Malaysia to Indonesia where the Protestant ethic seems to find a natural affinity with some of the business and family values of Chinese culture. That affinity can also be traced in both Singapore and Hong Kong. Including the Pacific islands in the overall estimate, Evangelicals and Pentecostals in Asia and the Pacific rim make up a community of perhaps 100 million or more.

In North America, Evangelicalism and its Puritan precursor were equally implicated in the genesis of the "first new nation." Evangelicalism took off in the early years of the republic, while Puritanism became partly transmuted into rationalistic Christianity, especially in New England. The south and southwest of the United States are today fairly solidly Evangelical, as are most African Americans. Up to 20 percent of Latino migrants are also influenced by Evangelical and Pentecostal religion. The United States is of course a Protestant powerhouse, where a born-again population of over 100 million has networks of influence and mission all over the globe. Yet the rapid indigenization of Evangelical and Pentecostal faiths contradicts the notion, so vigorously promoted by nationalist intelligentsias and Anglo-American newspapers of the left, that they are the religious arm of American cultural imperialism.

Notwithstanding the power of North American cultural radiation, Christianity in Africa has become exuberantly indigenous. And since the map of ethnicity runs both inside and across political frontiers, the map of religious affiliation follows suit. At times it leaps across ethnic belonging altogether, particularly in the middle class groups.

The vast proliferation of African Independent churches with some Evangelical or Pentecostal genes lodged in them makes numerical estimates particularly difficult. Perhaps we are dealing with about half the total Christian population of Africa, which means up to 200 million people. Though originally concentrated in English-speaking Africa, the Pentecostal advance is now speeding up in Portuguese- and French-speaking countries, such as Benin, Mozambique, and Burkina Faso.

Latin America originally embodied the pattern of Catholic monopoly, except that the resulting militant liberalism and secularism has never succeeded in reaching the masses as it did in Europe. Latin America, with one or two exceptions like Uruguay, is not disenchanted in the classic Weberian sense, and a syncretistic Catholicism, with an active practice of perhaps not more than 15 percent, has been vulnerable to Pentecostalism. Only three generations ago, Protestants were little more than 1 percent whereas they are now 10 percent, which means some fifty million people. Brazil, Chile, Guatemala, and Nicaragua have large Evangelical or Pentecostal minorities, and since the 1980s even resistant Argentina has witnessed a major charismatic expansion.

The Caribbean once had an Evangelical majority in most English-speaking islands, but this is now superseded by Pentecostalism. As in Africa, Pentecostalism is also making headway in the French-speaking islands, particularly Haiti. Forty percent of Port-au-Prince is Pentecostal.

We are, therefore, considering a massive and expanding sector of global Christianity, moving very fast in Africa to the point of constituting the largest single group in many countries, and in some a national majority, and having had a massive impact in Latin America, as well as discernible consequences in parts of Asia. However, Christianity of an Evangelical kind may have inbuilt limits. It cannot become a universal norm without undermining its own character.

If we add all the gross estimates together in a single gross estimate, we have perhaps half a billion people worldwide, which is a quarter of the Christian constituency, and much more than that as a proportion of active Christians. It makes good sense to regard this as the Christian equivalent of Islamic revivalism, which is also to some extent outside the mainstream and provides an analogous religious discipline for the newly arrived. However, as already suggested, it differs dramatically from Islamic revivalism: it is largely confined to culture, and rarely has ambitions to bring all social life under a single religious umbrella.

To be first and foremost cultural rather than political is an asset, at least initially, since it enables the enclave of personal reformation to concentrate on securing its social base and protecting its boundaries. Once the redeemed salient is secure it can and often does emerge as a political interest group. As such it promotes a moral agenda, so adding to the ensemble of voices seeking an audience. So it accelerates pluralism both religiously and politically, meanwhile affecting economic development and "progressive values."

What Influence?

If there are indeed some half a billion people under the generic head of Evangelicalism, what influence are they likely to have with respect to "progressive values"? Here we should remember that the democratic and economic potential of Evangelically influenced countries in the West took some time to realize, so we should think in terms of generations. Then we must question the direction of causality in the interaction between Protestant Christianity and economic advance, a question that exposes the possibility that a semisecularized Protestantism is most advantageous in economic terms. But that possibility is itself predicated on an earlier buildup of religious and economic resources. Perhaps we can say that, all things being equal, it has certainly helped, historically, to have a critical mass of Protestants, and indeed of Jews, semisecularized or not. To go back three and more centuries, Amsterdam had both, with spectacular results.

Obviously, we are not today dealing with the direct heirs of Benjamin Franklin or with enlightened Scots, or Amsterdam merchants, or the Huguenot dispersion. Joseph Priestley, Unitarian minister, scientist, and utopian seer, is a very long way from Ezekiel Guti, leader of (perhaps) a million-strong Pentecostal church in Zimbabwe, let alone his humblest female follower.

Still, that Zimbabwean woman is imbued with just the same economic virtues and motives for betterment as enlightened Protestants far removed from her in time, place, and status. The contemporary spur may not be Puritan vocation and election, but similar consequences can follow from a rather more democratic doctrine of spiritual gifts available to everyone, irrespective of religious office, or training, or education. These spiritual gifts are realized and acquire purchase under the supervision of a "buried intelligentsia," comprising the most energetic among the poor who run their own show and help create an enclave of fervent participation. Leaders and led speak the same language, which adds to the appeal.

We should also consider the link between Protestantism and Judaism based on the common availability of the Bible. After all, Bible-believing Protestants are not so affected by the evolutionary schemes built into much modern Biblical criticism as to suppose the Hebrew scriptures are less central than the New Testament. This is the source of a persistent philo-Semitism reaching back to the time when Cromwell invited the Jews back into England in 1656 and forward to the Zionism animating Pentecostal movements everywhere, as well as those African movements that explicitly adopt the Zionist label.

Where the earlier Puritanism differs from the later Evangelicalism is in the tendency among some Puritans to adopt an optimistic Unitarianism, whereas Evangelicalism more often mutates toward schemes of psychological self-help and spiritual technology. What begins in a reliance on what Christ has done for sinners has a surprising capacity to end up proclaiming what the righteous have done for themselves. Of course, that too has its economic implications. No one has ever claimed positive thinking is bad for business. I have never forgotten Robert Schuller praying at a conference for "achievers" in Dallas: "O God. You are the greatest achiever of all."

In Brazil, I encountered a small-business proprietor who had graduated out of Pentecostalism to join a kind of religious Rotary where people witnessed to what God had done for them. Over the door of his office was a decalogue of sound business practice incumbent on all employees: be honest, punctual, and frugal, and work hard.

How Do the Protestant Virtues Work?

In discussing how these virtues work out in practice we must remember that these men of God are mostly women. Pentecostalism is a movement of women determined with God's help to defend home and family against machismo, and the seductions of the street and the weekend. They represent female nurture and order over male "nature" and disorder. The male is made subject to the same criteria of discipline and moral responsibility as the female, and his traditional license to move on from one woman to another, leaving each in poverty with a litter of children, is revoked. If the man in the family wants respect, he must earn it, and husbands and wives must work together in partnership to instill right values in their children. One abused woman said she prayed to the Lord to find her "a Protestant even if he is only a rubbish collector."

In all the many interviews Bernice Martin and I have conducted, the theme of virtue rewarded is persistent, alongside the theme of healing. People witness to a healing of the body and a new disciplined energy to achieve goals that hitherto seemed beyond them. Often they describe some crisis of health and circumstance, brought on by dissipation, and the message of Pentecostalism at street corner or on television comes as the light of hope in the darkness of despair. People are assured of a way out, and those groups more inclined to a gospel of health and prosperity assure them of a kind of calculus of consequences or a covenant between them and God. The key is a faithfulness in small things which in God's good providence may one day be greatly rewarded. The buffets of contingency are under divine oversight. Of course, riches also present dangers, of which one must beware, but the dangers can be avoided by those who continue to walk humbly with their God, and in consequence give to other believers and the church.

Merely by recounting this kind of moral economy one hears an echo of how it might also work in the material economy, and one sees why people are attracted in such vast numbers. The chaos of dislocation, especially in the contemporary megacity, is turned into order. The millions who work in the informal economy and in the twilight zones see some light at the end of the tunnel, and share that light with others in similar circumstances. They determine the conditions of their own existence in a common ecstasy of anticipation, singing, shouting and praying "in tongues." They have dreams and see visions of better things to come. Believers believe they count for something in the maddening maze, first of all in the eyes of God but then in the eyes of each other. Eventually when those in the world see "what great things God has done" for them they may even count in society at large.

In the self-selected group of those who seek a better life, and indeed believe that every kind of "good" is connected, all are one in the equality of salvation, and more than equal to the contemptuous "world" outside. That outer world still contains some mutually supporting hierarchies of clergy and class, but in the group all have equal access to the one thing they need: the gift of the Holy Spirit. Through that gift they can exercise their right to speak and "give tongue."

Observers have often commented on the power and authority their leaders enjoy, but in principle it can be visited on anyone. Leaders are people of good standing in the congregation, even though humanly tempted on occasion by the lure of sex or money. Charisma has its dangers, and too much grace and power can lead to disgrace. In general though, this energetic cadre of men are religious entrepreneurs, and their churches, large or small, exemplify the arts of organization, promotion, persuasion, and self-help.

Religious entrepreneurship complements the idea of the self-made man with the idea of the God-made man—or woman. The poor work out how to run things, handle funds, negotiate, deal with officials, erect buildings, conduct choirs, address crowds, and deploy modern technology. These are the areas where they most clearly find a voice. The larger churches often provide classes in the arts of survival and administration. Those who are saved are keen to know how to generate savings and then pass the knowledge on; those who are cleansed from iniquity want to rise "from the dust to the sky." For those who have suffered disrespect, "respectability" is not pejorative.

Naturally, employers prefer workers who can be trusted, turn up on time, seek to improve themselves, and believe in an honest day's work. The middle-class woman prefers a domestic who is clean, will clean, and is more likely to pray than invite in a predatory or violent boyfriend. Whether in factory or domestic employment, evangelical credentials act as a preliminary reference.

The Anatomy of Betterment

Does this mean that Evangelicals and Pentecostals are more likely to succeed in business than others, advancing socially and economically beyond those similarly placed? Are they more open to modernity as they loose themselves from the bonds and ties of locality and from the pressures of more organic forms of society? Are they those who have faith and will travel, finding in their religious groups way-stations as they seek their fortune, or rather their providential reward, far from home?

Not surprisingly, the evidence is equivocal and must be balanced against the amount of time and money taken up by the church and its all-absorbing demands and activities. But for the believer these sacrifices are all part of sinking her own personal investment into creating social capital under her own control. Since so many start from nothing, their first steps must be moral stability and the acquisition of a religious currency of hope and aspiration. Creating order out of chaos may take most of a lifetime, and the investment really works out over generations, especially as children go to school. Generally the advances are modest: tiny increments of security, a refusal to despair or relapse on encountering difficulty. No longer seeing herself as a victim, the believer has God on her side and can recover. But she will certainly be tested; that is part of the deal.

David Maxwell recently studied the members of the Zimbabwe Assemblies of God Africa (ZAOGA), a church that includes up to 10 percent of Zimbabwe's population and has members in several neighboring countries, including Malawi and Mozambique. Maxwell describes the stress on prosperity that animates members of ZAOGA and claims that in some cases this leads to social mobility; it helps others avoid destitution, and overall provides a pattern for benefiting from modernity. Ezekiel Guti, the leader of ZAOGA, had some important contact with the Christ for the Nations Institute in Dallas, Texas, but saw the church mushroom after independence. He uses a vigorous nationalist rhetoric.[2]

Young men and women leave behind a local gerontocracy and reject possession rituals, witchcraft, and peer group violence to pursue literacy and education. Debt and waste are set aside as sinful, and the money that might otherwise go on dissipation is channeled into useful goods and savings. Young people break with the past and local authority.

The economic ethic of ZAOGA turns on a doctrine of the talents that has special messages for women, especially encouraging self-reliance. This is always important because women are so often abandoned or lose their husbands to AIDS. The church makes start-up grants and helps record earnings by computer. Money is not simply accumulated but acquires moral meaning through the ritual cleansing of notes and coins.

Something of the old local authority has returned in the form of the authoritarian charisma of Ezekiel Guti and the church bureaucracy he leads. Still, an atmosphere of fraternal participation remains from the early days of egalitarian fellowship. Dreams and visions of betterment, as well as black pride, continue to motivate hard work for a better future.

The Evangelical and Pentecostal movements appeal to energetic young people keen to deploy modern technology. Historic tensions between science and theology, or between critical scholarship and the sacred texts, are so much background noise compared with the affinity between a technology of the soul and all the means of modern communication. Through radio, television, film, and cassette, Evangelicals and Pentecostals bring to birth "imagined communities" ranging across national borders far wider in scope than actual membership, and in West Africa even secular television feels pushed to emulate the religious style. Evangelicals and Pentecostals are helping reconfigure the transnational networks where people recognize each other by distinctive speech and style.

Thus the new religious movements run along various networks: personal networks among those moving from country to megacity and social ones linking the business and professional classes of the newly arrived in Lagos or Santiago, Singapore or Seoul. Such people may come together in small devotional groups they arrange themselves or they may form a cell in a megachurch in the heart of the city, or belong to a wide-ranging religious association of university or business friends. All over Latin America, sub-Saharan Africa, and other international centers in Asia, including unlikely places like Katmandu, networks of global citizens meet with common needs and shared experiences. Major diasporas also exist in Europe and North America. Characteristically these groups are warm and supportive— and part of an entirely modern ambience promoting family integrity and sound business or professional practice. Some megachurches provide a range of facilities and constitute an all-embracing environment for self-improvement.

Another very different niche exists among marginal and peripheral ethnic groups. Such groups have often suffered a history of conquest or a very partial assimilation into a major civilization, or else find themselves on the border between civilizations, cast in the role of outsider in several directions as national boundaries are drawn. In Latin America various forms of Evangelical Protestantism have appealed to the Mapuche in Chile, to the Maya in Central America, and the Quechua in the Andes, as well as to many smaller ethnicities in Mexico. In Chiapas, for example, with its large indigenous population, 14 percent are Protestants, about double the national rate.

Many of the borderlands of Asian nations are inhabited by marginal ethnic groups that adopt a more distant faith in preference to that associated with the heartlands of Hindu, Muslim, Buddhist, or Confucian civilization. There are conspicuous examples in northeastern India, notably in Nagaland, and along the Chinese, Burmese, and Thai borders. Sometimes religion reconstitutes ethnic identity, but in some valleys of Nepal or parts of inland China, it expresses difference.

Quite often missions provided a script with the scriptures in the vernacular or even a history. For those members of ethnic groups who leave their ancestral regions and join the trek to the city, religion offers home away from home and an outpost of familiarity in the midst of so much that is alien. But religion offers more; it becomes a channel taking a whole people toward modernity, both in terms of educational and medical facilities, and through contact with a global reality wider than the immediate national culture and the pressure it exercises against them.

The dominant groups reluctantly recognize that marginal peoples have found a way to be modern and disciplined. Of course, the alternative is to engage in a full-scale recovery of minority cultural contents, rather as some people in the Russian Federation have turned to paganism as a way to express difference and distance, or as some African Americans have embraced Islam.

Interestingly, it is these leaps over the head of the immediate dominating environment to one of the world religions, rather than a return to paganism or what is constructed as African identity, that lead to modernity and advancement. Those who reject globalization to reconstruct or reassert an older identity either have the intellectual resources and social security that allow such recoveries, or are most distant from the pull of the global. Pentecostals are neither of these, and can hardly afford to reject the opportunities of collective advancement to modernity through a leap of faith. Cultural authenticity and designer tribalism are not their major concern.

Comparisons with the Mainstream

In this context, a question arises about the mainstream churches. Have they abandoned personal conversion, and the power it brings individuals to change their own lives, to focus instead on analyzing victims' experiences? The Methodist Church is a prime example of the shift from conversion to analysis; like other mainstream churches it has suffered from competition from newer bodies that have picked up precisely the emphases it has now abandoned. Indeed, Methodists are not always happy to recognize their theological descendants.

To draw an exaggerated contrast, the newer churches organize their own social assistance, while the mainstream churches foster the ethos of the caring professions and belong to the ensemble of organized welfare and NGOs. One pastor in a poor favela of Santiago de Chile actually said his church existed to make social work redundant. The mainstream churches take up those positions on the center-left characteristic of those who have arrived and exercise influence, whereas the expanding churches quite often take up center-right positions as they search for autonomous spaces where they can engage in self-creation. They have the "Victorian" values of those who aspire, and must rely on their own efforts to achieve their aspirations. They begin with what they themselves absolutely must do rather than prescribe what other agencies ought to do. This makes them ungrateful objects of liberal compassion since they are obstinately proud of their own achievements, however small these may sometimes seem from outside.

Tension is bound to arise between the mainstream churches and their vigorous and assertive rivals, especially as the latter draw away the younger generation. Certainly that tension is present between the mainstream and the new churches in Africa, but one also finds hostility between the churches of the first wave of Protestantism in Latin America and the more successful second wave.

Mainstream Protestant churches found Latin America resistant and unrewarding terrain for so long that the rapidity of Pentecostal penetration has come as a shock, and it has taken them some time to adjust and face the situation with equanimity. At times they have felt more allied to Catholic liberationists than to the Pentecostals. So they are prone to dismiss the Pentecostals, either as versions of American fundamentalism or as an irrational upsurge from deep in the heart of traditional religiosity. Of course, they can hardly be both. The mainstream Protestants are deeply reluctant to admit that the profound emotionality of the revivalist tradition can also bear the fruits of the Protestant ethic.

In fact, the mainstream churches may be at a stage that their rivals will experience later on. John Wesley himself famously predicted that the warmed heart would grow cold again as Methodists enjoyed the fruits of methodical living. The austere chapels that once served as way-stations for people who were deeply moved—and on the move—later acquired Gothic sanctuaries. Increasingly Methodists created educational institutions like Boston University in 1839, to express and promote their arrival socially. From the perspective of this sequence of development, the new churches in the developing world are just late arrivals whose social discipline will soften with time and prosperity.

One waits to see whether the boundaries between church and "world" will weaken and new generations gain educational qualifications or give way to peer-group culture. A Pentecostal intelligentsia is now developing, and it is an open question whether it will become assimilated to the ethos of the secular academy. Is Boston University also a portent of their future?

Para-Protestant Groups

If one accepts the positive relationship among Pentecostalism, social capital, and economic development in the developing world, then something similar would seem to follow for a number of other movements, such as Seventh-Day Adventism, the Jehovah's Witnesses, Mormonism, La Luz del Mundo, and any number of African movements with Zionist and Judaizing tendencies. Such movements spring from two main sources: the Anglo-American world, with its philo-Semitic traditions; and the reading of the whole Bible, which after all consists primarily of the Hebrew scriptures. The two sources are closely connected but not coextensive, and the availability of the whole Bible for the common reader making his or her own interpretation is quite adequate in itself. La Luz del Mundo grows out of a Mexican rather than a U.S. cultural background and so stands apart from the others.[3]

Like Pentecostalism, movements like the Mormons and the Witnesses had their genesis in the United States, and in the eyes of cultural nationalists elsewhere they carry American culture in their wake. There is some truth in this, even though they rapidly indigenize, and especially in the case of Pentecostalism, fresh versions emerge in contexts quite remote from North America. The North American link is significant in terms of contacts, international networks, and the use of English and of U.S. media. Each of these movements is a creation of the American religious imagination. It really is not possible to isolate the religious influence from this more general American influence. Moreover, although cultural nationalists attack Mormons, Witnesses, and Adventists on account of North American links, ordinary people often find such links highly attractive. Authentic natural culture need not be all that important for those whom national intelligentsias nominate as its national carriers.

The Mormons (Church of the Latter-Day Saints) are certainly growing very fast and in 2003 numbered somewhere between twelve and fifteen million. Rodney Stark predicts they are en route to becoming a world religion. Like the Pentecostals, they have found Latin America a responsive mission field over the last half century, and the countries most affected include Brazil and Chile, the Andean republics, and Guatemala. The impact in the Andes and Guatemala suggests some distinctive appeal to indigenous peoples.

The Mormons also have some impact in the Pacific islands. They have a major presence in Tahiti, Fiji, the Cook Islands, Tonga and Samoa, as well as New Zealand and the Philippines. Rodney Stark suggests that Mormons, like Witnesses, flourish in secularized national contexts, such as Uruguay, indicating that they encounter modernity with a relevant message.

The evidence we have about social capital and economic development derives from the general character of such movements as cited in numerous studies: they reject stimulants, alcohol, tobacco, and drugs, and pursue a healthy diet. They also aspire to and provide education, and value work discipline, mutual support, and family stability. What such characteristics imply for better living standards is indicated by the fact that average life expectancy among Mormons is six years longer than for the rest of the U.S. population.

Witnesses number roughly the same as Mormons and are growing even more quickly. They are also spread more widely around the globe rather than having a large proportion of their membership in the United States. Like Mormons, they demand a great deal of effort and commitment from members, including young people who become the more committed through undertaking arduous assignments. Yet such is the dedication of Witnesses that their church continues to grow and easily offsets a high drop-out rate.

Interestingly, the Witnesses' region of greatest success is Latin America, where they number about a million and a half; they also appeal more to Latinos, African Americans, and Asian Americans than to other groups in the United States. Until recently, they suffered considerable persecution because they refuse to serve in the army, acknowledge national symbols, or receive blood transfusions. In spite of the general assumption that Witnesses and similar movements recruit from the uneducated, they are in fact characteristically lower middle class.

Patricia Fortuny's study shows how Witnesses in Mexico provide a framework of support as peasants encounter a complex urban environment. As with Mormons and Pentecostals, women are those initially most interested, but as men are also attracted, they join with their wives in creating a sober family atmosphere, inculcating order, cleanliness, punctuality, and mutual affection.[4]

In the Kingdom Hall, Witnesses feel valued and are able to run their own religious affairs. So with respect to the key cultural traits that create social capital and are consonant with development, Witnesses and Mormons and other Judaizing millenarians make positive contributions. Beyond that, they acquire a sense of participation in a mythic narrative explaining crises as they occur and prefiguring the future. They have been vouchsafed the inside drama, and know how to play their part.

So we return from movements along the margin of Protestantism to the central theme of Evangelicalism proper, noting that we need to add perhaps another 10 percent or more to our overall figure of half a billion to account for Mormons, Witnesses, Adventists, and others.

The Moral Compass in a Plural Society

Bringing together all these various considerations, the heart of the matter lies in the relevance of Evangelical and Pentecostal religion to strata and peoples who are coming to self-consciousness as they are uprooted and encounter global modernity. Religion provides the stabilizers for a difficult journey, above all to the twilight zones and informal economies of new urban agglomerations, but also, for example, for South Koreans and Filipinos crossing the Pacific to the United States and Canada. South Koreans are an advanced example of a process whereby evangelical religion provides the thrust of advancement, though other reinforcements come from Korea's Confucian culture. Korean achievements should give pause to those among their fellow Americans who have sold their birthright of aspiration for the siren-songs of the sixties.

The most dramatic changes are happening at the other end of the scale, among marginal status groups and marginal ethnicities. These are not likely to yield a crop of major entrepreneurs in the near future, but at least they are better equipped to face crises and to seize opportunities. As religious entrepreneurs competing on an open market, where future success rests solely on the individual's shoulders, they find economic values built into their whole operation.

The key motivations are not utilitarian, but depend on providence displacing fate and fortune. Converts have seen the great gulf separating the downward spiral of fatalistic despair from the upward spiral of providential hope. Yet, of course, the utilitarian consequences have their own attraction as part of the advertisement of faith, and people are impressed by the new dignity that comes with the opportunity to participate and lead in the company of those of like mind.

In my analysis here I have put less stress on the possible implications of a participatory style for democracy, important though that is, and more on the ability of those "born again" to meet new challenges. New conditions require second births. The assumption is that "culture matters," and the key lies in the new subjective depth acquired to launch the self successfully in the face of wave after wave of fresh experience.

As people lose their anchorage in stable local hierarchies, the new churches become the rafts taking them, and the whole fraternity of faith, to new destinations. The moral compass of conscience helps them negotiate the whirlpool of expanding choice. To many in the mainstream churches, this is a fundamentalist reaction to modernity; I believe it is more persuasively seen as a creative response to modernity rooted in appropriation of the Biblical narrative. Insofar as it embodies the classical Protestant virtues in company with personal choice and voluntary organization in the sphere of culture, it continues a centuries-old tradition.

A Note to Mainstream Protestants

In principle, mainstream Protestants respect religious variety and seek to appreciate other ways of understanding the Christian message. Yet Pentecostals have been excluded from this charity, for at least two reasons. One is alleged cultural affiliations with the United States at a time of generalized anti-Americanism. Also, they are seen as successful competitors who share neither the mainstream's ecumenism nor its propensity for victim-oriented explanations of poverty and deprivation. As the standard-bearers for the old Protestant ethic, the Pentecostals are stereotyped for espousing the wrong virtues and opting for the wrong social models.

Yet the Pentecostals and similar Evangelical movements are peaceful people engaging positively with modernity, not rejecting it or blowing people up. They are primarily a movement of black women for dignity and self-help—and a challenge to macho culture.

These movements now undermining the mainstream, at least in the third world, are like the movements that undermined what was then the mainstream in Britain's industrial revolution and on the American frontier. And those movements were the forebears of today's mainstream!

Elites around the world tend to feel a protective nostalgia for "traditional" communities, a nostalgia led by anthropologists committed to cultural relativism. But change is inevitable as the poor and dispossessed increasingly become aware that life can be longer, less burdensome, and happier, and discover that Pentecostalism is a viable vehicle to that better life. It deserves better than metropolitan contempt.

A Note to the Pentecostals

Pentecostals are noted for their practicality. Yet as you improve your standards of living, you will spend more time in school and encounter wider horizons. This will test the spirit that raised you up as you confront the enjoyment of affluence and culture. You will also have to deal critically but fairly with the ideologies of intellectuals, which diverge from your own. And you will have to face the challenge of social responsibility: ways in which the mutuality and participation of your church can be realized in the wider society.

The elites believe that the economic virtues no longer matter. But you know better from hard experience in the struggle for survival and a better life. The elites see no need for radical spiritual change and hence cultural change, because they believe that the better life can be achieved by structural changes initiated by the state. But again you know from experience that spiritual and cultural change go together—and how crucial they are.

Notes

1. This chapter relies almost entirely on David Martin, *Tongues of Fire* (Oxford: Blackwell 1990) and *Pentecostalism—The World Their Parish* (Oxford: Blackwell 2001).
2. I describe Maxwell's work in *Pentecostalism,* 145–48.
3. This section on Mormons and Jehovah's Witnesses is mainly derived from publications by Rodney Stark, in particular his contribution, with Laurence R. Iannacone, "The Growth of Jehovah"s Witnesses," *The Journal of Contemporary Religion* 12, no. 2 (1997), 133–58; and his chapters 1 and 2 in James T. Duke ed., *Latter-Day Saint Social Life* (Provo, Utah: Brigham Young University, 1998), 9–28, 29–70.
4. I describe Fortuny's study in *Pentecostalism,* 106–110.

8

Anglo-Protestant Culture[1]

SAMUEL HUNTINGTON

Most countries have a core or mainstream culture shared to varying degrees by most people in their society. In addition to this national culture, subordinate cultures usually exist, involving subnational or transnational groups defined by religion, race, ethnicity, region, class, or other categories that people feel give them something in common. America has always had its full share of subcultures. It also has had a mainstream Anglo-Protestant culture in which most of its people, whatever their subcultures, have shared. For almost four centuries this culture of the founding settlers has been the central and lasting component of American identity. One has only to ask: Would America be the nation it is today if in the 1600s and 1700s it had been settled not by British Protestants but by French, Spanish, or Portuguese Catholics? No. It would not be America; it would be Quebec, Mexico, or Brazil.[2]

America's Anglo-Protestant culture has combined political and social institutions and practices inherited from England, most notably the English language. At the beginning, as Alden T. Vaughan has said, "almost everything was fundamentally English: the forms of land ownership and cultivation, the system of government and the basic format of laws and legal procedures, the choices of entertainment and leisure-time pursuits, and innumerable other aspects of colonial life."[3]

With adaptations and modifications, this original culture persisted for three hundred years. In 1789, John Jay identified six central
elements Americans had in common: common ancestry, language,
religion, principles of government, manners and customs, and war
experience. Americans no longer share a common ancestry, and several of the others have been modified or diluted. For example, to
Jay, the "same religion" undoubtedly meant Protestantism; now we
would have to say Christianity. Though challenged, Jay's components
of American identity still defined American culture in the twentieth
century. Protestantism has been of primary and continuing importance. As for language: although German settlers in Pennsylvania in
the 1700s tried to make German the equal of English, and German
immigrants in Wisconsin in the 1800s tried to use German in schools,
both efforts and others like them, came to naught.[4] At least until
the appearance of bilingualism and large concentrations of Spanish-
speaking immigrants in Miami and the Southwest, the United States
was unique as a huge nation of over 200 million people virtually all
speaking the same language.

The political and legal institutions the settlers created in the 1600s
and 1700s largely embodied the institutions and practices of England's "Tudor constitution" of the late 1500s. Among these institutions were the concept of a fundamental law superior to and limiting
government; the fusion of executive, legislative, and judicial functions, and the division of power among separate institutions and governments; the relative power of the legislature and chief executive;
the merger of "dignified" and "efficient" functions in the chief executive; a two-house legislature; the responsibility of legislators to their
local constituencies; a legislative committee system; and primary reliance for defense on militia rather than a standing army. These Tudor
patterns of governance were fundamentally changed in the United
Kingdom, but their central elements persisted in the United States
well into the twentieth century.[5]

During most of the past two centuries, the United States has in
various ways compelled, induced, and persuaded its immigrants
to adhere to the central elements of the Anglo-Protestant culture.
Twentieth-century cultural pluralists, multiculturalists, and spokes-
men for ethnic and racial minorities testify to the success of these
efforts. Southern and Eastern European immigrants, Michael Novak
poignantly commented, were pressured to become "American" by
adapting to Anglo-American culture: Americanization "was a pro-

cess of vast psychic repression." In similar language, Will Kymlicka argued that before the 1960s, immigrants "were expected to shed their distinctive heritage and assimilate entirely to existing cultural norms," which he labeled the "Anglo-conformity model." If they were thought incapable of assimilation, like the Chinese, they were excluded. In 1967 Harold Cruse declared that "America is a nation that lies to itself about who and what it is. It is a nation of minorities ruled by a minority of one—it thinks and acts as if it were a nation of white Anglo-Saxon Protestants."[6]

These critics are right. Throughout American history, people who were not white Anglo-Saxon Protestants have become Americans by adopting its Anglo-Protestant culture and political values. This benefited them and the country. American national identity and unity, as Benjamin C. Schwarz has said, derived "from the ability and willingness of an Anglo elite to stamp its image on other peoples coming to this country." If the United States has enjoyed "freedom from ethnic and nationalist conflict," it is because of "a cultural and ethnic predominance that would not tolerate conflict or confusion regarding the national identity."[7] Millions of immigrants and their children achieved wealth, power, and status in American society precisely because they assimilated themselves into the prevailing American culture. Hence there is no validity to the claim that Americans must choose between a white, racist, WASPish ethnic identity and an abstract, shallow civic identity that depends on commitment to certain political principles. The core of their identity is the culture that the settlers created, which generations of immigrants have absorbed, and which gave birth to the American Creed. At the heart of that culture has been Protestantism.

"The Dissidence of Dissent"

For over two hundred years, almost all Americans were Protestant. With the substantial Catholic immigration, first from Germany and Ireland and then Italy and Poland, the proportion of Protestants declined fairly steadily. By 2000, only about 60 percent of Americans were Protestants. But even as the proportion of Protestants declined, Protestant culture continued to pervade and shape American life, society, and thought, because moreover, Protestant values deeply influenced Catholicism and other religions in America. They have shaped

American attitudes toward private and public morality, economic activity, government, and public policy. Most importantly, they are the primary source of the American Creed, the ostensibly secular political principles that supplement Anglo-Protestant culture as the critical defining element of what it means to be American.

In the early 1600s, Christianity was the "shaper of nations, even of nationalisms," and states and countries explicitly defined themselves as Protestant or Catholic. In Europe existing societies accepted or rejected the Protestant Reformation; in America, the reformation created a new society. The origins of America "are to be found in the English Puritan Revolution....the single most important formative event of American political history." In America, as the nineteenth-century European visitor Philip Schaff observed, "every thing had a Protestant beginning."[8] America was created as a Protestant society just as and for some of the same reasons Pakistan and Israel were created as Muslim and Jewish societies in the twentieth century.

America, said de Tocqueville in an oft-quoted phrase, "was born equal and hence did not have to become so." More significantly, it was born Protestant and did not have to become so. America was not founded, as Louis Hartz argued, as a "liberal," "Lockeian," or "Enlightenment" fragment of Europe,[9] but as a succession of Protestant fragments, a process underway in 1632 when Locke was born. The bourgeois, liberal ethos that later emerged was not so much imported from Europe as it was the outgrowth of the Protestant societies established in North America. Scholars who attempt to identify the American "liberal consensus" or Creed solely with Lockeian ideas and the Enlightenment are giving a secular interpretation to what are often the religious sources of American values.

America was settled, of course, for economic and other reasons, as well as religious ones. Yet religion was central. Although less important in New York and the Carolinas, religion was a predominant motive in the creation of the other colonies. Virginia had "religious origins."[10] Quakers and Methodists settled in Pennsylvania. Catholics established a beachhead in Maryland. Religious intensity was undoubtedly greatest among the Puritans, especially in Massachusetts. They took the lead in defining their settlement based on "a Covenant with God" to create "a city on a hill" as a model for all the world, and people of other Protestant faiths soon also came to see themselves and America in a similar way. In the seventeenth and eighteenth centuries, Americans defined their mission in the New World in biblical terms.

They were a "chosen people," on an "errand in the wilderness," creating "the new Israel" or the "new Jerusalem" in what was clearly "the promised land." America was the site of a "new Heaven and a new earth, the home of justice," God's country. The settlement of America was vested, as Sacvan Bercovitch put it, "with all the emotional, spiritual, and intellectual appeal of a religious quest." This sense of holy mission was easily expanded into millenarian themes of America as "the redeemer nation" and "the visionary republic."[11]

Protestantism in the United States differs from that in Europe, particularly from those denominations, Anglican or Lutheran, that have involved established churches. Burke noted this difference, contrasting the fear, awe, duty, and reverence Englishmen felt toward political and religious authorities with the "fierce spirit of liberty" among Americans. The American kind of Protestantism, he argued, "is the most averse to all implicit submission of mind and opinion." Though "all Protestantism,...is a sort of dissent,...the religion most prevalent in our northern colonies is a refinement on the principle of resistance: it is the dissidence of dissent, and the protestantism of the Protestant religion."[12]

This dissidence was manifest in the first settlements of Pilgrims and Puritans in New England. The Puritan message, style, and assumptions, if not doctrines, spread throughout the colonies and became absorbed into the beliefs and outlooks of other Protestant groups. In some measure, as Tocqueville said, it shaped "the entire destiny of America." The "religious zeal and the religious conscience" of New England, James Bryce agreed, in "large measure passed into the whole nation." Qualified, modified, diffused, the Puritan legacy became the American essence. While "England had a Puritan Revolution without creating a Puritan society, America created a Puritan society without enduring a Puritan revolution."[13] Unlike the settlers in the three other waves of English settlement identified by David Hackett Fischer, the East Anglian Puritans were predominantly urban artisans rather than farmers and came overwhelmingly in family groups. Virtually all were literate. Many had attended Cambridge. They were also devoutly religious and committed to spreading the word of God. Their ideas, values, and culture diffused throughout the new land, especially in the "Greater New England" of the Middle West, and decisively shaped the way of life and political development of the new nation.[14]

The dissidence of American Protestantism, manifested first in Puritanism and Congregationalism, reappeared in subsequent centuries in Baptist, Methodist, pietist, fundamentalist, evangelical, Pentecostal, and other types of Protestantism. Though these movements differed greatly, they all emphasized the individual's direct relation to God, the Bible as the sole source of God's word, salvation through faith, and for many the transforming experience of being "born again," personal responsibility to proselytize and bear witness, and democratic and participatory church organization.[15] Beginning in the 1700s, American Protestantism became increasingly populist and emotional and less hierarchical and intellectual. Doctrine gave way to passion. Sects and movements multiplied constantly, as the dissenting sects of one generation were challenged by the new dissidents of the next. "Dissidence of dissent" describes the history as well as the character of American Protestantism.

Religious enthusiasm was a distinctive trait of many American sects in the 1600s and 1700s, and evangelicalism, in various manifestations, has been central to American Protestantism. From the beginning, America was, as Martin put it, an "evangelical empire." George Marsden called Evangelical Protestantism "the dominant force in American life" in the 1800s, and Garry Wills says it has always constituted "the mainstream of American religion."[16] In the early 1800s, the numbers of sects, preachers, and adherents exploded. "Young men of relentless energy," says the historian Nathan Hatch, "went about movement-building as self-conscious outsiders." Sharing "an ethic of unrelenting toil, a passion for expansion, a hostility to orthodox belief and style, a zeal for religious reconstruction, and a systematic plan to realize their ideals," they offered "compelling visions of individual self-respect and collective self-confidence" to "common people, especially the poor."[17] Thus "the history of American Evangelicalism is...more than a history of a religious movement," agrees William McLoughlin, the leading scholar of Great Awakenings. "To understand it is to understand the whole temper of American life in the nineteenth century."[18]

Much the same could be said of the twentieth century. In the 1980s slightly under one third of Americans said they were "born-again" Christians, including a majority of Baptists, about one third of Methodists, and more than a quarter of Lutherans and Presbyterians. In 1999 roughly 39 percent of Americans said they were born again. "Contemporary evangelicalism," it was reported, "has been gaining momentum among Americans since the early 1970s." Evangelicalism is now winning many converts among America's largest immigrant group, Latin American Catholics. Numbers of evangelical students are also growing at elite universities; for example, the membership of the evangelical association at Harvard doubled from five hundred to one thousand between 1996 and 2000.[19] As the new millennium began, dissenting Protestantism and evangelicalism were continuing to play central roles in meeting the spiritual needs of Americans.

The American Creed

In 1944, in *The American Dilemma,* Gunnar Myrdal pointed to the racial, religious, ethnic, regional, and economic heterogeneity of the United States, and argued that Americans had "something in common: a social *ethos*, a political creed," which he labeled the American Creed. His term has become the common label for a phenomenon noted by many earlier commentators, and identified by both foreign and American observers as a key element of American identity and often as the only significant determinant of that identity.

Though scholars have defined the concepts of the Creed in various ways, they almost universally agree on its central ideas. Myrdal spoke of "the essential dignity of the individual human being, of the fundamental equality of all men, and of certain inalienable rights to freedom, justice, and a fair opportunity." Jefferson wrote the equality of man, inalienable rights, and "life, liberty, and the pursuit of happiness" into the Declaration of Independence. Tocqueville found people throughout America agreeing on "the liberty of the press, the right of association, the jury, and the responsibility of the agents of government." In the 1890s Bryce summed up the political beliefs of Americans as including the sacred rights of the individual, the people as the source of political power, government limited by law and the people, a preference for local over national government, majority rule, and "the less government the better." In the twentieth century, Daniel Bell pointed to "individualism, achievement and equality of opportunity" as central values of the Creed and highlighted the extent to which in America, "the tension between liberty and equality, which framed the great philosophical debates in Europe, was dissolved by an individualism which encompassed both." Seymour Martin Lipset identified five key principles as its core: liberty, equality (of opportunity and respect, not result or condition), individualism, populism, and laissez-faire.[20]

The principles of the Creed have three outstanding characteristics. First, they have remained remarkably stable over time. Since the late 1700s, descriptions of the Creed have not varied significantly Lipset appropriately concludes that there has been "more continuity than change with respect to the main elements in the national value system."[21] Since the late 1700s, descriptions of the Creed have not varied significantly. Second, the Creed has also commanded the widespread agreement and support of the American people, however practice might deviate from it. The only major exception was the effort in the South to formulate a justification for slavery. Otherwise, the Creed's general principles have been overwhelmingly endorsed by the American people, according to both nineteenth-century observers and twentieth-century public opinion surveys.

Third, the central ideas of the Creed almost universally have their origins in Protestant values. The Protestant emphasis on the individual conscience and the responsibility of individuals to learn God's truths directly from the Bible promoted American commitment to individualism and the rights of the individual to freedom of religion and opinion. Protestantism stressed the work ethic and the responsibility of the individual for his own success or failure in life. With its congregational forms of church organization, Protestantism fostered opposition to hierarchy and the assumption that similar democratic forms should be employed in government. It also promoted moralistic efforts to reform society and secure peace and justice.

Nothing like the Creed was created in continental European societies apart from revolutionary France, or in French, Spanish, or Portuguese colonies, or even in later British colonies in Canada, South Africa, Australia, and New Zealand. Muslim, Buddhist, Orthodox, Confucian, Hindu, Jewish, Catholic, and even Lutheran and Anglican cultures have produced nothing comparable. The extent, the fervor, and the continuity with which Americans have embraced the Creed testify to its place as an indispensable part of their national character and national identity.

The sources of the Creed include the Enlightenment ideas that became popular among some American elites around 1750 and found receptive ground in its century-old Anglo-Protestant culture. Of central importance in that culture were long-standing English ideas of natural and common law, the limits of government authority, and the rights of English people going back to the Magna Carta. To these the more radical Puritan sects of the English Revolution added equality and government responsiveness to the people. "Religion in America," as William Lee Miller has observed, "helped to make the creed and was compatible with it. Here liberal Protestantism and political liberalism, democratic religion and democratic politics, American faith and Christian faith, penetrated each other and exerted a profound influence upon each other." As the Protestant beliefs and the American political creed encompassed similar and parallel ideas, together they forged "the strongest bonds that united the American people during the nineteenth century." As a result, as Jeff Spinner comments, "It's difficult to disentangle what is Protestant from what is liberal in the United States."[22] The American Creed, in short, is Protestantism without God, the secular credo of the "nation with the soul of a church."

Individualism and the Work Ethic

Protestantism in America generally involves a belief in the fundamental opposition of good and evil, right and wrong. Americans are far more likely than Canadians, Europeans, and Japanese to believe that "there are absolutely clear guidelines about what is good and evil" applicable "whatever the circumstances" rather than to believe that no such guidelines exist and what is good or evil depends on circumstances.[23] Thus Americans continually confront the gap between the absolute standards that should govern their individual behavior and the nature of their society—and their own and their society's failure to live up to those standards.

Most Protestant sects emphasize the role of the individual in achieving knowledge of God directly from the Bible without the intermediation of a clerical hierarchy. Many denominations also emphasize that the individual achieves salvation or is "born again" as a result of the grace of God, also without clerical intermediation. Success in this world places on the individual the responsibility to do good in this world. "Protestantism, republicanism, and individualism are all one," as F. J. Grund observed of America in 1837.[24]

Their Protestant culture has made Americans the most individualistic people in the world. For instance, in Geert Hofstede's comparative analysis of 116,000 IBM employees in thirty-nine countries, the mean individualism index was 51. But Americans ranked first with an index of 91, followed by Australia, Great Britain, Canada, the Netherlands, and New Zealand. Eight of the ten countries with the highest individualism indices were Protestant. A survey of cadets in military academies in fourteen countries produced comparable results, with those from the United States, Canada, and Denmark ranking highest in individualism. The 1995 to 1997 World Values Survey asked people in forty-eight countries whether individuals or the state should be primarily responsible for their welfare. Americans, along with Swiss and Swedes, ranked highest in individualism. In a survey of 15,000 managers in seven countries, Americans scored the highest on individualism, Japanese the lowest, with Canadians, British, Germans, and French between them in that order. Thus American managers were "by far the strongest individualists" in the national samples, and "more inner-directed." Americans, believe, the study said, that "you should 'make up your mind' and 'do your own thing' rather than allow yourself to be influenced too much by other people and the external flow of events."[25]

In the American Protestant outlook, the individual is responsible for his or her success; this belief gave rise to the gospel of success and the concept of the self-made man, a phrase first used by Henry Clay in a Senate debate in 1832. "It was Anglo-Saxon Protestants," Robert Bellah says, "who created the gospel of wealth and the ideal of success." As countless opinion surveys have shown, Americans believe that success in life depends overwhelmingly on one's own talents and character. This central element of the American dream was perfectly expressed by President Clinton: "The American dream that we were all raised on is a simple but powerful one—if you work hard and play by the rules you should be given a chance to go as far as your God-given ability will take you."[26] In the absence of rigid social hierarchies, one is what one achieves. The horizons are open, the opportunities boundless, and their realization depends on an individual's energy, system, and perseverance.

The work ethic is a central feature of Protestant culture, and from the beginning America's religion has been the religion of work. In other societies, heredity, class, social status, ethnicity, and family are the principal sources of status and legitimacy. In America, work is. Both aristocratic and socialist societies demean and discourage work. Bourgeois societies promote work. America, the quintessential bourgeois society, glorifies work. When asked "What do you do?" almost no American dares answer "nothing." As Judith Shklar has pointed out, throughout American history social standing has depended on working and earning money by working. Employment is the source of self-assurance and independence: "Be industrious and FREE," Benjamin Franklin said. This glorification of work came particularly to the fore during the Jacksonian era, when people were classified as "do-somethings" or "do-nothings." Shklar comments that "every visitor to the United States in the first half of the nineteenth century" noted "the addiction to work" that this attitude induced."[27]

The right to labor and to enjoy its rewards was among the nineteenth-century arguments against slavery, and the central right espoused by the new Republican party was the "right to labor productively, to pursue one's vocation and reap its rewards." The concept of "the self-made man" is a distinctive product of this American environment and culture.[28]

In the 1990s Americans remained people of work. They worked longer hours and took shorter vacations than people in other industrialized democracies. The hours of work in other industrialized societies were decreasing. In America, if anything, they were increasing. In 1997, on average, an American worked 1,966 hours, a Japanese 1,889, and an Australian 1,867. In Britain the figure was 1,731, in France 1,656, in Sweden 1,582, in Germany 1,560, and in Norway 1,399. On average, Americans worked 350 more hours per year than Europeans. In 1999, 60 percent of American teenagers worked, three times the average of other industrialized countries. Historically Americans have had an ambivalent attitude toward leisure, often feeling guilty about it and attempting to reconcile it with their work ethic. As Cindy Aron argued in *Working at Play*, Americans in the 1990s remained prisoners of the "persistent and continuing American suspicion of time spent away from work."[29] Americans tend to feel they should devote their vacations not only to unproductive leisure but also to good works and self-improvement.

Not only have Americans worked more than other peoples; they have also found satisfaction in and identified themselves with their work more than others. In a 1990 International Values Survey of ten countries, 87 percent of Americans reported taking great pride in their work; only the British reported a comparable number. In most countries, under 30 percent of workers expressed that view. In the early 1990s, some 80 percent of Americans said that to be an American one must subscribe to the work ethic; 90 percent said they would work harder if necessary for the success of their organization, and 67 percent would not welcome social change that would lead to less emphasis on hard work. In their attitudes Americans see society as divided between people who are productive and people who are not.[30]

This work ethic has, of course, shaped American policies on employment and welfare. Dependence on what are often referred to as "government handouts" carries a stigma unmatched in other industrialized democracies. In the late 1990s, unemployment benefits were paid for five years in Britain and Germany, two years in France, one year in Japan, but only six months in the United States. The move in America in the 1990s to reduce and, if possible, eliminate welfare programs was rooted in the belief in the moral value of work. "Getting something for nothing" is an immense source of shame. "Workfare," as Shklar points out, "is about citizenship and whether able-bodied adults who do not earn anything actively can be regarded as full citizens."[31]

In the 1890s Polish immigrants to America were overwhelmed by the amount of work expected of them. "In America," as one wrote in a letter back home, "one has to sweat more during a day than during a whole week in Poland." In 1999 a Cuban-American, Alex Alvarez, warned new Cuban immigrants of what they confronted in America:

> Welcome to the capitalist system. Each one of you is responsible for the amount of money you have in your pocket. The Government is not responsible for whether you eat, or whether you're poor or rich. The Government doesn't guarantee you a job or a house. You've come to a rich and powerful country, but it is up to you whether or not you continue living like you did in Cuba.[32]

Moralism and the Reform Ethic

Politics in America, as in other societies, has been and remains a politics of personality and faction, class and region, interest group and ethnic group. To an extraordinary degree, however, it also continues to be a politics of moralism and moral passion. American political values are embodied in the Creed, and efforts to realize those values in political behavior and institutions are a recurring theme in American history. Individually Americans have the responsibility to pursue the American dream and achieve what they can through their talents, character, and hard work. Collectively they have the responsibility to insure that their society is indeed the promised land. In theory, success in the reform of the individual could remove any need for the collective reform of society, and several great evangelists opposed social and political reforms precisely because they were not directed to regenerating the individual soul. In practice, however, the four Great Awakenings in the history of American Protestantism have been closely related to great periods of political reform. These manifestations of "creedal passion" have been fundamentally shaped by the dissenting, evangelical nature of American Protestantism.

The Great Awakening of the 1730s and 1740s was one of many political, economic, and ideational factors that came together to create the American Revolution, along with Lockeian liberalism, Enlightenment rationalism, and Whig republicanism. Led by George Whitefield and other revivalist preachers and provided with doctrine and justification by Jonathan Edwards, the Awakening swept across the colonies, mobilizing thousands of Americans to commit themselves to a new birth in Christ. This religious upheaval laid the basis for the political upheaval that followed. Although a revolution might well have occurred without the Awakening, the Revolution that did occur was grounded in the Awakening and significantly shaped by it. "The evangelical impulse," as the Harvard scholar Alan Heimert said, "was the avatar and instrument of a fervent American nationalism. In the evangelical churches of pre-Revolutionary America was forged that union of tribunes and people that was to characterize the early American Democracy." Substantial proportions of Congregationalists, Presbyterians, and Baptists, involving close to half of the American people, "entertained millennial ideas," and these "millennialist denominations were also those that most solidly backed the American Revolution."[33]

Although Americans did not all support it to the same degree, the Awakening was still the first popular movement to engage people from virtually all sects and denominations throughout the colonies. Preaching from Georgia to New Hampshire, the charismatic George Whitefield became the first truly *American* public figure. The experience and environment he created formed part of the background of the transcolony political movements that led to independence. It was the first unifying experience for Americans, generating a sense of national, distinct from provincial, consciousness. "The Revolution," John Adams observed in 1818, "was effected before the war commenced. The Revolution was in the minds and hearts of the people; *a change in their religious sentiments of their duties and obligations.*" (Italics added.) Echoing Adams, William McLaughlin concluded in 1973 that the Great Awakening was "the beginning of America's identity as a nation and the starting point of the Revolution."[34]

The Second Great Awakening of the 1820s and 1830s was "evangelical and revivalist," in effect the "second American revolution."[35] The Methodist and Baptist churches expanded tremendously, and many new sects and denominations formed, including the Church of the Latter Day Saints. Preaching the need to "work as well as believe," Charles G. Finney recruited tens of thousands of people into American churches and generated a "mighty influence toward reform." Societies were formed "to advance" a multitude of causes, among them temperance, Sunday schools, peace, prison reform, and education. Others aimed "to save sailors at the ports and along the canals; to fight the use of tobacco; to improve the diet" and "to stop prostitution."[36] The most important child of the Awakening, however, was the abolitionist movement, which in the early 1830s placed the slavery issue squarely on the national agenda, and for the next quarter century aroused and mobilized people in the cause of emancipation. When war came over that issue, soldiers from both North and South marched off to fight sure that their cause was God's cause. The depth of the religious dimension in that conflict is reflected in the immense popularity in the North of the "Battle Hymn" crafted by Julia Ward Howe, which begins with a vision of "the glory of the coming of the Lord" and ends invoking Christ: "As He died to make men holy, let us die to make men free."

The third Great Awakening got underway in the 1890s and was intimately linked with the populist and Progressive drives for social and political reform. The latter were suffused with Protestant morality; as in previous reform periods, the reformers stressed the moral necessity of eliminating the gap between institutions and ideals and creating a just and equitable society. They attacked the concentrated power of corporate monopolies and big city machines and advocated antitrust measures, women's suffrage, prohibition, regulation of railroads, the direct primary, and the initiative, referendum, and recall. Support for these reforms was strongest in the Midwest and far West, the areas of "Greater New England" to which the descendants of the

Puritans had migrated and where the intellectual, social, and religious legacy of the Puritans predominated. In general, participants in the Progressive movement believed in the superiority of "native-born, white Americans;…of Protestant, indeed Puritan, morality; and…of a kind of populism, of some degree of direct control over the state and city machines, which, it was alleged, were dominated by the 'interests.'"[37]

The fourth Great Awakening originated in the late 1950s and 1960s with the growth of evangelical Protestantism, and Sidney Ahlstrom argues, "left the human landscape…profoundly changed."[38] It is associated with two reform movements in American politics. The first, beginning in the late 1950s, focused on the most obvious gap between American values and American reality: the legal and institutional discrimination against and segregation of America's black minority. Then, in the 1960s and 1970s, it led to the general challenging of the institutions of established authority, focused on the conduct of the Vietnam War and the abuse of power in the Nixon administration. In some cases, Protestant leaders and organizations, such as the Southern Christian Leadership Conference, played central roles. Other organizations of the time were entirely secular in definition but equally intense in their moralism. For example, the New Left of the early 1960s "begins from moral values which are held as absolute," as one leader put it.[39] The second and later manifestation was the conservative drive for reform in the 1980s and 1990s focusing also on the need to reduce governmental authority, social welfare programs, and taxes—and simultaneously attempting to expand government restrictions on abortion.

Dissenting Protestantism has marked American foreign policy as well as its domestic politics. In conducting their foreign policy, most states give overwhelming priority to what are generally termed the "realist" concerns of power, security, and wealth. When push comes to shove, the United States does this too. But Americans also feel the need to promote in their relations with other societies and within those societies the moralistic goals they pursue at home. In the new republic before 1815, America's Founding Fathers debated and conducted its foreign relations overwhelmingly in realist terms. They led an extremely small republic bordered by possessions of the then great powers, Britain, France, and Spain, which were for most of these years fighting each other. As they fought indecisive wars with Britain and France, intervened militarily in Spain's possessions, and doubled the size of their country by purchasing Louisiana from Napoleon, America's leaders proved themselves adept practitioners of European-style power politics. With the end of the Napoleonic era, America was able to downgrade its realist concerns with power and security and pursue largely economic objectives in its foreign relations while concentrating its energies on expanding and developing its own territory. In this phase, as Walter McDougall has argued, the purpose of Americans was indeed to make their country the promised land.

Around 1900, however, America emerged as a global power. Now it had to face the realities of power politics, and learn to compete in a hard-nosed way with the other world powers. But that new status as a great power also enabled America to begin to promote abroad the moral values and principles on which it had aspired to build its society at home. The relation between realism and moralism thus became the central issue of American foreign policy in the twentieth century, as Americans, in McDougall's words, redefined their country from "promised land" to "crusader state." In the twenty-first century, the central issue for America is how to reconcile its role as a crusader state, fueled by its latest religious revival, with a world that is culturally pluralistic, non-Western, non-Protestant, and non-liberal.

Notes

1. This chapter derives from chapter 4 of Samuel Huntington, *Who Are We? The Challenges to America's National Identity* (New York: Simon & Schuster, 2004).
2. In this chapter, I will often say "America" for "United States of America." I trust the context will make my meaning clear.
3. Alden T. Vaughan, "Seventeenth Century Origins of American Culture," in *The Development of an American Culture*, ed. Stanley Coben and Lorman Ratner, 2nd ed. (New York: St. Martin's Press, 1983), 30–32.
4. James A. Morone, "The Struggle for American Culture," *PS: Political Science & Politics*, 29 (1996): 428–29; John Higham, *Send These to Me: Jews and Other Immigrants in Urban America* (New York: Atheneum, 1975), 180.
5. Samuel P. Huntington, *Political Order in Changing Societies* (New Haven, CT: Yale University Press, 1968), 93ff.
6. Anthony D. Smith, *National Identity* (Reno: University of Nevada Press, 1991), 150; Michael Novak, *Further Reflections on Ethnicity* (Middletown, PA: Jednota Press, 1977), 26. Will Kymlicka, *Multicultural Citizenship: A Liberal Theory of Minority Rights* (New York: Oxford University Press, 1995), 14, levels the same charge against Canada and Australia; Harold Cruse, *The Crisis of the Negro Intellectual* (New York: Morrow, 1967), 256.
7. Benjamin C. Schwarz, "The Diversity Myth," *Atlantic Monthly* 275 (May 1995), 57–67.

8. Adrian Hastings, *The Construction of Nationhood: Ethnicity, Religion and Nationalism* (New York: Cambridge University Press, 1997), 187, and chapter 8 generally; Samuel P. Huntington, *American Politics: The Promise of Disharmony* (Cambridge, MA: Harvard University Press, 1981),154; Philip Schaff, *America: A Sketch of Its Political, Social, and Religious Character* (Cambridge, MA: Harvard University Press, 1961), 72.

9. Louis Hartz, *The Liberal Tradition in America* (New York: Harcourt, Brace, 1955); William Lee Miller, "Religion and Political Attitudes," in *Religious Perspectives in American Culture,* ed. James Ward Smith and A. Leland Jamison (Princeton, NJ: Princeton University Press, 1961), 85; Huntington, *American Politics* 154.

10. Jon Butler, *Awash in a Sea of Faith: Christianizing the American People* (Cambridge, MA: Harvard University Press, 1990), 38–66.

11. Sacvan Bercovitch, *The Puritan Origins of the American Self* (New Haven, CT: Yale University Press, 1975), 44ff; Hastings, *The Construction of Nationhood,* 74–75; Morone, "The Struggle for American Culture," 426.

12. Edmund Burke, *Reflections on the Revolution in France* (Chicago: Regnery, 1955), 125–26; Burke, "Speech on Moving Resolutions for Conciliation with the Colonies." in *Burke's Politics,* ed. Ross J. S. Hoffman and Paul Levack (New York: Knopf, 1949), 69–71.

13. Morone, "The Struggle for American Culture," 429; Alexis de Tocqueville, *Democracy in America* (New York: Vintage, 1945), 2:32; Huntington, *American Politics* 153; James Bryce, *The American Commonwealth* (London: Macmillan, 1891), 2:599.

14. David Hackett Fischer, *Albion's Seed: Four British Folkways in America* (New York: Oxford University Press, 1989), 787; Kevin P. Phillips, *The Cousins' Wars: Religion, Politics, and the Triumph of Anglo-America* (New York: Basic Books, 1999), .xv and passim.

15. John C. Green et al., *Religion and the Culture Wars: Dispatches from the Front* (Lanham, MD: Rowman & Littlefield, 1996), 243–44.

16. George M. Marsden, *Fundamentalism and American Culture: The Shaping of Twentieth Century Evangelicalism, 1870–1925* (New York: Oxford University Press, 1982), 6; Garry Wills, *Under God: Religion and American Politics* (New York: Simon & Schuster, 1990), 19.

17. Nathan O. Hatch, *The Democratization of American Christianity* (New Haven: Yale University Press, 1989), 4.

18. William McLoughlin, ed. *The American Evangelicals, 1800–1900; An Anthology* (New York: Harper & Row 1968), 26, quoted in Bellah, *Broken Covenant,* 46.

19. George Gallup, Jr. and Jim Castelli, *The People's Religion: American Faith in the 90's* (New York: Macmillan, 1989), 93. For other estimates, see Cullen Murphy, "Protestantism and the Evangelicals," *The Wilson Quarterly* (Autumn 1981), 107ff; Marsden, *Fundamentalism and American Culture,* 228; *Boston Sunday Globe,* February 20, 2000, A1.

20. Alexis de Tocqueville, *Democracy in America,*1:409; Bryce, *American Commonwealth,* 2: 417–18; Gunnar Myrdal, *An American Dilemma* (New York: Harper, 1944); 1:495, Daniel Bell, "The End of American Exceptionalism," in *The Amer-*

ican Commonwealth 1976, ed. Nathan Glazer and Irving Kristol (New York: Basic Books, 1976), 209; Seymour Martin Lipset, *American Exceptionalism: A Double-edged Sword* (New York: Norton, 1996), 63–64.

21. Seymour Martin Lipset, *The First New Nation: The United States in Historical and Comparative Perspective* (New York: Norton, 1973), 103.

22. William Lee Miller and John Higham, "Hanging Together: Divergent Unities in American History," *Journal of American History* 61 (1974), 15; Jeff Spinner, *The Boundaries of Citizenship* (Baltimore: Johns Hopkins University Press, 1994), 79–80.

23. Lipset, *American Exceptionalism,* 63–64.

24. Francis J. Grund, *The Americans in Their Moral, Social and Political Relations* (New York: Johnson Reprint, 1968), 355–56.

25. Geert Hofstede, *Culture's Consequences: International Differences in Work-Related Values* (Beverly Hills, CA: Sage, 1980), 222; Henry van Loon, "How Cadets Stack Up," *Armed Forces Journal International* (March 1997):18–20; Lipset, *American Exceptionalism,* 218; Charles Hampden-Turner and Alfons Trompenaars, *The Seven Cultures of Capitalism* (New York: Doubleday, 1993), 48, 57. See also Harry C. Triandis, "Cross-Cultural Studies of Individualism and Collectivism," *Nebraska Symposium on Motivation 1989* (Lincoln: University of Nebraska Press, 1990), 37: 41–133.

26. Robert N. Bellah, *The Broken Covenant: American Civil Religion in Time of Trial* (Chicago: University of Chicago Press, 1992), 76; John G. Cawelti, *Apostles of the Self-Made Man* (Chicago: University of Chicago Press, 1965), 39ff; Bill Clinton, remarks to Democratic Leadership Council, 1993 quoted in Jennifer L. Hochschild, *Facing Up to the American Dream,* 18.

27. Judith N. Shklar, *American Citizenship: The Quest for Inclusion* (Cambridge, MA: Harvard University Press, 1991), 1–3, 67, 72–75.

28. Roger M. Smith, "The 'American Creed' and American Identity: The Limits of Liberal Citizenship in the United States," *Western Political Quarterly* 41 (June 1988):239, citing Eric Foner, *Free Soil, Free Labor, Free Men: The Ideology of the Republican Party before the Civil War* (New York: Oxford University Press, 1970); Cawelti, *Apostles of the Self-Made Man,* esp. 39ff.

29. Cindy S. Aron, *Working at Play: A History of Vacations in the United States* (New York: Oxford University Press, 1999), 236; International Labor Organization Study September 1999, cited in *The Daily Yomiuri,* September 7, 1999, 12; *Prospect,* no. 49 (February 2000), 7, citing *Boston Review,* December 1999–January 2000.

30. Daniel Yankelovich, "What's Wrong—And What's Right—With U.S. Workforce Performance," *The Public Perspective* 3 (1992): 12–14; "American Enterprise Public Opinion and Demographic Report"; Jack Citrin et al., "Is American Nationalism Changing? Implications for Foreign Policy," *International Studies Quarterly* 38 (March 1994):13.

31. *New York Times,* May 9, 1999, WK5; Shklar, *American Citizenship,* 98.

32. Hochschild, *Facing Up to the American Dream,* 228–29; *New York Times,* February 11, 1999, p. A1.

33. Alan Heimert, *Religion and the American Mind, From the Great Awakening to the Revolution* (Cambridge, MA: Harvard University Press, 1966), 14, 19; Ruth

H. Bloch, *Visionary Republic: Millenial Themes in American Thought, 1756–1800* (New York: Cambridge University Press, 1985), xiv.

34. John Adams, letter to Hezekiah Niles, February 13, 1818, in Adrienne Koch and William Peden, eds., *The Selected Writings of John and John Quincy Adams* (New York: Alfred A. Knopf, 1946),.203.

35. Bellah, *Broken Covenant*, 44–45.

36. William W. Sweet, *Revivalism in America: Its Origin, Growth, and Decline* (New York: Scribners, 1944), 159–61.

37. Alan P. Grimes, *The Puritan Ethic and Woman Suffrage* (New York: Oxford University Press, 1967), 102.

38. Sidney Ahlstrom, "National Trauma and the Changing Religious Values," *Daedalus* 107 (Winter 1978):19–20.

39. Al Haber, quoted in Edward J. Bacciocco, Jr., *The New Left in America* (Stanford, CA: Hoover Institution Press, 1974), 228–29.

9

The Development of the Jews

JIM LEDERMAN

Modern Jewish history began in 586 BCE when Nebuchadnezzar and the Babylonians conquered the kingdom of Judea. It is a story of experimentation, regression, self-interest, and opportunism; religious, feudal, and colonialist oppression; repeated failures in governance, and occasional, lasting, universally relevant insights. The traits, values, beliefs, and actions that led to the Jews' social and economic development were only rarely the result of a revolution in thinking and practice. For the most part, their culture was the product of willful, incremental, and cumulative change.

The Judeans carried with them into Babylonian exile a number of concepts—many fundamentally different from those prevalent in the nations surrounding them—that would prove essential to their future survival. These included a realization that leadership is fallible, an evolving codex of law, a tradition of social and political criticism, a growing belief in the idea of personal responsibility before God, and the beginnings of messianism.

The exile was relatively short and was canceled by Cyrus of Persia when he conquered Babylon in 538 BCE. However, only a minority of these former Judeans took advantage of their newfound liberty and returned to the Land of Israel. From then on, the fate of the Hebrews would not be completely bound up with one geographic locale. In Egypt, a sizeable community of Judeans that had sided with the Egyptians against Nebuchadnezzar had taken up residence, especially in the Nile Delta and Aswan. The Diaspora had begun, and with it the need for a common language of discourse, secure lines of communication, and a system of jurisprudence to settle commercial disputes that might otherwise disrupt the flow of information, services, and goods. Commerce with the great civilizations of Mesopotamia, the Nile Valley, the Hellenic world, and imperial Rome meant that the merchant class had to become multilingual. Mass multilingualism would become a defining national characteristic for other reasons as well. Unlike some other cultures before and since, the Jews rarely resisted learning other languages.

A reformed, posttribal group identity was also required. It was decided that henceforth higher social value would be placed on national unity and strength than on individual or tribal gain. To promote this value, the Jews needed a new form of governance, one that would be accepted nationally and whose decisions would be binding nationally. Thus was reinvigorated a concept that had evolved during the Babylonian exile: self-rule through scholars' continuous interpretation of Mosaic Law. Once established, it was inevitable that the new governing body, called the Sanhedrin, would also become involved in initiating new laws, to deal with the uncertainties caused by rapid social and economic change. The Sanhedrin was abolished by Emperor Theodosius II in 425 CE, but the principles of law and self-governance it established remained part of the Jews' collective consciousness and continue to be used, in a modified form, today.

The introduction of scholarship as a profession open to anyone was to also have a profound effect. It inaugurated the idea of a state- or community-supported meritocracy: a new vehicle for social mobility for those who lacked hereditary credentials for public office, or business acumen, or financial capital. There was to be no formal separation between religion and state, but there was a definite division of labor. The rabbis and scholars were charged with creating laws through biblical interpretation and reinterpretation and with teaching and adjudicating disputes. This was as close to the Platonic ideal of the philosopher king as any nation has ever attained. What might be termed the "lay leadership" was mandated to manage the community's everyday affairs.

The format for self-governance that the rabbis adopted is worthy of particular note. They sat as a kind of combined commission of inquiry, legislature, and judicial court. Their deliberations were open to all who would come and listen. Anyone with relevant information and/or arguments—including apostates and non-Jews—could present evidence. Documents signed in other jurisdictions were also admissible. From their actions, it is clear that the rabbis believed that open debate, not closed-door deliberation, was the best vehicle for allowing all issues to be raised and discussed. By encouraging all voices to be heard, they could reach mass consensus, which would in turn reduce the number of excuses for future law-breaking. True validation of the law and obedience to it would come with widespread individual internalization of the court decisions.

In retrospect we can say that the process was guided by three principles. All laws and all precedent-setting interpretations of the law were to be clear and transparent, and not subject to temporal whim or short-term considerations. The process of law making and interpretation was to be transparent as well. And in order to be validated, laws had to be seen as equally applicable, fair, reasoned, balanced, and proportionate. The deliberations in Judea produced the Mishnah, the basic compendium of civil and religious law. Additions and commentaries, especially in Babylonia, produced the Talmud.

Today, when we look at all the principles, discussions, and decisions as a single, comprehensive whole, we see that the rabbis believed that a lack of transparency leads not only to corruption but also to the kinds of socially destabilizing conspiracy theories that were endemic to the nations around them. Conspiracy theories allow people to disengage from public policy-making, believing they cannot influence events. This may have suited the needs of the neighboring autocrats, but it would have undermined the rabbis' aim of encouraging individual activism in support of group-validated norms. Thus, conspiracy theorizing would not only have reduced decision-making input, it would also have created among Jews the same epidemic of pathological fatalism that infected the masses in many of the nations surrounding them.

The Babylonian Talmud

The completion of the Babylonian Talmud in about 500 CE enshrined forever the principles that would make Jews everywhere a progress-prone people when and if they chose to set progress and adaptation as a group objective—and when and if their neighbors permitted them to advance socially, economically, and culturally. Foremost among these principles was mandatory, universal literacy—for women too. Everyone, without exception, was expected to know and obey the law.

By its very existence the Talmud also introduced the concept of knowledge as a portable commodity that should be accessible to anyone. Unlike the Greeks and later the Christians, the Jews ensured that human discoveries and intellectual endeavors would no longer be the private preserve of an elite. In fact, as Christian, Zoroastrian, and later Muslim persecutions of the Jews increased and Jews dispersed throughout Europe, western and central Asia, and North Africa, portable knowledge in any form—what we today call intellectual property—would become to Jews the ultimate measure of personal wealth. While real property could be burned or stolen, knowledge or skill could be kept safe in the mind of anyone who survived.

The most obvious and characteristic trait among Jews for centuries was multilingualism. All Jewish children who were capable of attending classes were taught two languages in primary school: the Hebrew of the Bible and the Mishnah, and the Aramaic in which the Talmud was written. To this would be added the local vernacular as well as, wherever they developed, "Jewish" vernaculars such as Yiddish in Eastern Europe, Mougrabi in North Africa, and Ladino in places to which the Jews were expelled from Spain in 1492. In cosmopolitan cities such as Alexandria and nineteenth-century Warsaw, they would add the languages used in international trade. And in war-torn places like the plains of Poland, they added fluency in the language of the most recent occupying power.

This multilingualism enabled Jews to have access to and to build their individual and collective treasury of all the knowledge available at the time—as long as it was in a language they understood. Access to knowledge, especially proprietary information gained from afar, enabled them to enter such diverse fields as trade, medicine, and specialized manufacturing, where intellectual property is the most important form of capital.

While literacy and access to the knowledge previously accumulated by other cultures were necessary preconditions for progress, they were insufficient predictors of economic and social advancement. To these two traits must be added what most modern economists see as the essential prerequisite for economic and social development: adherence to the rule of law. Moreover, the principle that underlay Jewish law was that almost anything that was ethical and not specifically forbidden by law or precedent was permissible. Thus, for example, the Catholic prohibitions on teaching the discoveries of Galileo and Copernicus entirely bypassed the Jews. The didactic and dialectic nature of Talmudic-style debate, in which all Jewish children were raised, fitted in easily with the development of the modern scientific method. The Talmudic quotation emblazoned above the ark of the Torah in many synagogues, "Know before whom thou standest,"[1] was an invitation and even a commandment to explore and investigate the God-created natural world. This stood in stark contrast to the later Muslim concepts of fatalism and resignation and the Catholic concept of submission to authority.

Thus Jews gave themselves almost complete local autonomy in matters such as customs and modes of self-governance. While not democratic in the modern sense of the word, their political system was generally consultative, consensual, and cooperative. Still, during times of great duress they tended to regress and to rely on oligarchs for communal leadership, or to seek solace in hereditary hierarchies, of which Hassidic rabbinical "courts" are the best current example.

Judaic Culture

Social status and social mobility were predicated on an individual's personal accomplishments and his pursuit of excellence. Scholarship remained the highest social value, but skilled, knowledge-based employment came a close second. Economically, individuals were allowed to retain and build on their capital, and interest was allowed. Far greater deference was given to earned income than to inherited wealth, unless the individual used some of the windfall for important social purposes. Formal punishments for breaches of group behavior—such as shunning, banishment, and excommunication—existed but were rarely applied. The strongest penalties were often popular ones: having one's ideas dismissed out of hand and, worst of all, being ignored as a person of no account.

Learning, even for its own sake, was defined publicly as legitimate work—even though the families involved might look askance at the idea. Importantly, though, most of the underlying skills and disciplines needed for productive study were easily transferable to professions and trades. In this, the Jews still differ significantly from other cultures. The British speak of "reading" a subject at university as though it were an avocation for the leisure class. Americans "study" a subject to pass an examination. Traditional Jews, however, always "learn" a subject, believing in the need to internalize what is taught or read. Moreover, while education in many other cultures is performance-directed through the imposition of centralized testing, traditional Jewish education emphasizes learning how to learn so the learner can continue laboring outside the confines of formal schooling.[2]

Community investments concentrated on education, maintenance of cemeteries and ritual baths, and aid to the financially distressed. During those times when nobles held whole towns to ransom, and slavery and kidnapping were common, the Jews felt an overwhelming imperative to redeem the captive or slave by paying communally raised funds. Since prayer could take place anywhere, synagogue construction was a relatively low priority, undertaken only when funds were sufficient. Most synagogues were initially built as schools or as adjuncts to existing schools.

By this time, several identifiable group and individual personality traits had been established, defining personal behaviors, the product of group priorities, that many non-Jews took and still take to be arrogant, abrasive, insulting, or just impolite. However, in hindsight, they were critical to national survival and, when external circumstances permitted, allowed the Jews to flourish. These included a preference for deference that was earned over courtesy that was expected; cleanliness, hygiene, and ritual purity over tidiness; intellectual precision over punctuality; immediate interruptions to correct mistakes over staid politeness; direct, even blunt speech over euphemisms and generalities; self-selection of leaders over managerial authority. During periods of severe distress and persecution, however, Jews sometimes abandoned such behaviors, and intense orthodoxy took hold as a palliative for pain and anguish. During periods when group survival was at stake, intragroup competition was frowned upon. In times of relative freedom, these suppressed behaviors would return to blossom like hibernating flower seeds in the desert after the first rains.

Without an autonomous, physically defensible territorial base, the Jews' development was highly influenced by their environment. Persecution was rife. During the second millennium of the Common Era, hundreds of thousands of Jews were killed simply for being Jewish. In both Muslim and Christian countries, they were subject to restrictions and punitive taxation. Often they were given the choice of conversion or death. They were expelled from fundamentalist

Almohades-controlled Spain in the twelfth century, from England in 1290, from France in 1394, and from Catholic Spain in 1492. In Germany and central Europe, they were subject to almost continuous decimation by mobs. But each time tragedy struck, they were able to rise and rebuild once circumstances altered.

Survival—and Change—in Jewish Tradition

It is worth examining some of the elements and processes that were essential for survival under the extreme conditions in which the Jews lived, and especially those critical for renewal. The decimations inflicted on the Jews left a body of true believers who would remain faithful to their precepts. But belief alone was not enough when faced with the most ruthless and hateful instruments of state. The Jewish form of messianism rejects passivity and fatalism, concentrating instead on forward-looking activism. The Jews believe that only through mass social enterprise that helps fulfill the prophetic injunction to "do justice, love mercy and walk humbly with your God" can they make the world fit for the Messiah, hasten his arrival, and find group redemption.

Jews always had Hebrew as a common written and oral language. Any available knowledge could be transferred from one Jewish community to another, allowing them to trade, even under the harshest circumstances. Rigid adherence to grammatical rules prevented the growth of dialects. Hebrew was mutable enough to absorb new words but fixed in its overall structure. Thus when one community, recovering from a period of isolation or oppression, needed knowledge to catch up rapidly on world developments in science, the humanities and other fields, it was readily available from elsewhere in the Diaspora. Today English plays the same role.

Community life revolved around the synagogue, often a school or room in a teacher's home. Instead of building centralized cathedral or mosque-type buildings, a community of any size would have a multitude of synagogues or prayer quorums that also provided amiable and amicable social environments. The synagogue functioned not just as a place of worship but also as a community center, labor exchange, health referral center, and school.

The nature of Jewish family life also fostered communal stability. The commandment to "be fruitful and multiply" helped sustain communities after they were decimated by mob violence. Families knew the community would care for widows and orphans if no relatives could assume responsibility. The institution of the matchmaker became almost sacrosanct. Relatively early marriage also reduced communal turmoil. Polygamy was forbidden to European Jews and was frowned on among Jews in Muslim-controlled countries unless the husband was wealthy enough to treat all his wives equally. Therefore there were few desperate young men without a woman—and few women without male or communal support. Husbands with families are usually less prone to violence, less footloose, and less willing to take unnecessary risks. The ready availability of divorce—by mutual consent and based on a prenuptial contract that stipulated payments to the wife—provided an outlet for intolerable family tensions.

Jewish development over two millennia appears on the surface to have consisted of short eruptions of indigenous innovation. A closer look demonstrates that the level and extent of change was closely linked to the Jews' environment. The more open the surrounding society was to intercourse, the greater was the level of Jewish originality and invention. When societies contracted into themselves, Jews suffered as outsiders. Personal contact, continuous local intellectual input, and relative freedom from want or persecution were necessary for development but insufficient; without additional input, intellectual incest could result. So a crucial source of innovation was translation into the vernacular (not the language of the elite, if one existed) of foreign language texts by the surrounding society. Translation was not only a signpost for the level of openness to different and avant-garde ideas in that society; it also provided access to new knowledge for Jews to contemplate and digest with the aid of their own intellectual frameworks.

The relative openness of the surrounding society also helped to determine Jewish communal thought processes that, in turn, influenced the pace of change. The greater the degree of rationalism in the environment, the more rapid was Jewish intellectual development. Throughout Jewish history, there were periods when either rationality or orthodox word-literalism was in the ascendant. Certainly, there were no formal restrictions on rationalism. As early as the tenth century, the "genius of the age," Saadia Gaon, declared that rationality and faith were not mutually exclusive. Five centuries later, Maimonides, the greatest philosopher of his time, directly confronted the teachings of Aristotle.

In general, progress-resistant orthodoxy was particularly strong during periods of duress and isolation, when people needed to cling to fixed ideas and patterns of behavior in order to ride out the surrounding storm. On the other hand, in freer societies Jews needed to confront the ideas swirling around in the open and so placed more importance on reason. At such times Jewish scholarship focused on what came to be euphemistically termed "supplementing" the Talmud. Often this was not just explanation or clarification but wholesale innovation designed to bring Jewish thinking up to date without abandoning the bedrock of tradition. When neither reason nor orthodoxy could provide an adequate response to distress, Jews tended to latch on to the words of charismatic false messiahs—until their real identities were uncovered, leading to psychological trauma and collapse among their followers that sometimes lasted for generations.

The level of personal reliance on mysticism—a direct offshoot of religious orthodoxy that began in tenth-century Babylonia—does not seem to have been necessarily influenced heavily by external economic conditions. It crossed time periods and socioeconomic lines. Still, its impact has been substantial. Surveys conducted by the Bank of Israel and the Israeli Central Bureau of Statistics indicate that those ultra-Orthodox who have mystical beliefs are less open to innovation and are less economically productive, by a very substantial margin, than neighbors on the same street or even in the same apartment building. Not only do mystics not add to the common weal; they can seriously drain communal resources by demanding payments for their basic sustenance. And, especially during times of distress, mystics can have an influence disproportionate to their numbers.

Such was the case in 1567 when Joseph Karo, a mystic scholar in the Galilean town of Safed, published his book on Jewish law, *Shulchan Aruch*, or The Table is Set. A monumental piece of scholarship, the book had disastrous consequences for Jewish cultural and economic development for centuries to come. In it Karo assembled all the laws, customs, and regulated behaviors produced by scholars before him and declared that their project was now complete and their decisions inviolable. This "how-to" manual of Jewish practice was accepted by most Jews of the time, and to many orthodox Jews today it is still the final word. For centuries it effectively closed the door on Talmudic "supplementalist" intellectual challenge and adaptation. Scholarship degenerated into narrow scholasticism, and rabbis who practiced these excursions into minutiae became more isolated from the common people and their problems and more conservative, absolutist, and autocratic in their legal judgments. The common people were left without activist religious and social leadership.

But the Jews were saved from intellectual calcification and the inevitable economic ruin it creates by the traditionally malleable nature of their approach to human authority in matters of personal belief and conscience, and by their belief in the fallibility of every man and woman. Among Jews, human authority was and remains individually selected, and excommunication is difficult.

The first mass revolt against rabbinical isolation, asceticism, and narrow-mindedness was not an attack on orthodoxy as such. The time was 1636. Jews throughout Eastern Europe were facing pogroms, famine, and destitution. The great scholars had no response. They shut themselves up in their studies. The leader of the rebels, who came to be known as the Baal Shem Tov ("The Owner of a Good Name"), was a pious, unassuming, mystical lime-quarrier from the Carpathian mountains who preached a simple message: Every human occupation was a form of worship, God should be worshipped with joy, and even an ignorant person who worshipped God with joy would find more acceptance in the eyes of the Almighty than a dry scholar. The idea that legitimate, God-sanctioned happiness could arise from any day-to-day action, even menial labor, caught on like wildfire and spread rapidly to become a mass movement that the Baal Shem Tov's followers called Hassidism or Pietism.

The anti-Orthodox *Haskala*, or Enlightenment, movement began a century later. Its originator was Berlin-based Moses Mendelssohn (1729–86), a fervently rationalist scholar, philosopher, and practicing Jew. He believed that nationality and state citizenship were divisible. The Jews, he asserted, should acquire full civil and political emancipation (with all the duties and responsibilities that true citizenship entailed) while remaining committed to their Jewish national identity. To that end, they should become fully at home with the German language and its secular, post-Reformation culture. This would entail restructuring the Jewish education system to include modern science and humanities.

The reaction came quickly. Orthodox rabbis feared assimilation and loss of autonomy if the separate Jewish courts that had tried civil matters between Jews were to be abolished. They launched a virulent campaign against change. Neighboring Christians were of mixed views: reactionaries opposed giving Jews any new rights, while others acquiesced to civil but not political emancipation. Still others believed that what the Catholic Church had failed to accomplish over centuries by forced conversion could now be accomplished through legislation that would encourage Jews to assimilate.

These conflicting approaches, combined with the influence of the American Constitution and the introduction of the Napoleonic Code in some parts of Europe, created a raft of incoherent and often contradictory civil and political reforms in western and central Europe. In many regions, even after legal reforms, medieval restrictions remained on residence, entry into professions, and admission to guilds. Many Jews took the path of least resistance and assimilated or converted; composer Felix Mendelssohn was one of them. The models for these ex-Jews were the German Protestants and the secular French deists.

In Eastern Europe, where the conservative Catholic and Greek Orthodox churches prevailed, change was slower for Jews and non-Jews alike. There the Jews saw no attractive local economic or social models to emulate. By the mid-nineteenth century, four schools of Jewish thought had emerged: traditional Orthodoxy (which the Hassidim called *Misnagdim*), Hassidism, Hebraism, and Yiddishism (or Bundism). The reform movement in Germany had been a top-down elitist enterprise by scholars. In eastern Europe, where the majority of European Jewry lived, the Orthodox remained hierarchical, while the progressivists were bottom-up revisionists. The Hebraists modernized and revived the Hebrew language and became the precursors of the Zionists. The Yiddishists believed in local political and civic reform and preached adaptation to the surrounding environment. Within just a few decades, these two latter groups produced an astonishing flowering of translation, original literature, and philosophical and political debate.

The Jews in America

But Christian reaction and anti-Semitism left residues. After pogroms in eastern Europe, a mass immigration to America began in the 1880s. The notorious Dreyfus trial, in which a French Jewish army captain was tried and sentenced unjustly for treason based on false evidence by anti-Semites, led directly to the advent of political Zionism. In North African Muslim countries, untouched by the Reformation and the subsequent chaos, there were no mass movements. In the areas of French metropolitan rule and French influence, the Alliance Israelite made modern, French-speaking schools available to the Jewish bourgeois elite, and with them, French culture, translations, and progress. The ancient Jewish civilization in Iraq only began to modernize with the British occupation following World War I.

In America, with its legal freedoms, the Jews achieved levels of success and innovation they had not seen since the pre-Mishnaic period. A core of successful Spanish-Portuguese and German Jews had been in America before the mass migration. Most engaged in banking, trading, and merchandising. Almost all had adopted the manners and many of the outward appearances of the surrounding WASP elite. The sudden arrival of waves of poverty-stricken Jews, unlettered in English or German, created consternation, even revulsion. Almost immediately, though, the Diaspora system of self-governance and community assistance swung into action, providing education, material and spiritual assistance, and community services.

The goal of almost all the new arrivals was to enter the middle class within one generation. To that end, dual-income families with a reduced number of children became the norm. Savings were invested in businesses and education, not spent on conspicuous consumer goods. Unencumbered by any strong tradition of primogeniture, families with limited funds for higher education could choose to send the most talented—not necessarily the oldest—on to higher education.

Nonetheless, already familiar, if now informal, restrictions on housing, jobs, and education remained. Jews were excluded from certain residential areas, and from professions and trades such as the police or locomotive engineering. They were limited in professional studies (Yale, for example, only dropped its quota system in 1962) and were refused membership in private clubs whose priority was business networking. Partly out of necessity and partly out of communal attachment, Jews tended to congregate in urban areas, creating a critical mass of self-reinforcing, group-assisted, progressive inventiveness. The result was a burst of competitive entrepreneurship based on intellectual capital, hard work, and innovation—first among Jews themselves and only then face-to-face with the wider population.

The results were astonishing. By the end of the second millennium, little more than a century after the mass migration began, Jews, who made up only 0.021 percent of the world's population and about 2 percent of the North American population (depending on the definition of a Jew),[3] had won about 15 percent of all Nobel prizes. To give but a few other examples of adaptation and success: In the United States, the median income of Jewish households is $54,000 compared to a national average of $42,000, and 36 percent of Jewish households earn more than $75,000 per year versus 18 percent of American households as a whole. Overall, 60 percent of Jewish adults occupy high-status and education-intensive jobs such as those in the free professions and technical professions, and in management, business, and finance, compared to 46 percent of the American population as a whole. And education: 55 percent of American Jews hold a bachelor's degree, compared to the national average of 29 percent, and 25 percent hold graduate degrees, compared to 6 percent of the rest.[4] As of 1999, 30 percent of Supreme Court law clerks and 26 percent of law professors were Jewish.[5]

In the arts, during the twentieth century, Jews dominated classical music performance, wrote some of the best and most successful novels, and can even be said to have created the "American Dream"[6] and American pop culture by inventing those most quintessential of American communications media: Hollywood, mass television, and the modern Broadway musical.

It is foolish to generalize about members of any culture—most of all, the fractious Jews. There are no defining dogmas and too many gradations of belief and practice to allow blanket judgments. In terms of religious practice, Jews today can be roughly subdivided into several categories. The ultra-Orthodox, both Misnagdic and Hassidic, live for their religion. It dominates every aspect of their lives. Its adherents see their form of religion, with its voluntary enclaving and its relative uniformity of belief and action, as a familylike, God-protected safe haven from vicissitudes and external dangers. With certain notable exceptions, they are the Jews most isolated from their surrounding societies and the least willing to adapt and change, and are thus the most progress-resistant.

For the Modern Orthodox, religion does not prevent them from partaking of aspects of modern life that do not conflict with traditional law. They tend to gravitate to teaching, the professions, and basic science, where they can control their own time and set their work schedules to avoid conflict with their beliefs and practices, such as keeping the Sabbath and the holidays. To liberals, who usually affiliate with the Reform, Conservative, and Reconstructionist movements, religion is a guide to life, but one that is adaptable to new circumstances. People who label themselves as "cultural" or "secular" Jews reject formal religion or theism but find meaning in some values that arose from the religion. Those who have assimilated or converted to other religions still retain commonalities with Jews. Many have internalized values and patterns of behavior they learned from family members earlier in their lives. This group, in particular, demonstrates that some Jewish values, especially those most useful in daily life, transfer to other cultures.

That the Jews have outperformed the Protestants—the inventors of the modern capitalist system—in aggregate, measurable terms has perplexed and even exasperated many economists and historians. The Nobel Prize winner Milton Friedman[7] has struggled to grasp why Jews, who have done so well under capitalism, consistently vote for centrist or left-of-center political parties, especially on domestic issues. Friedman and others ascribe this phenomenon to Mishnaic Law, and to the fact that many Jews are intellectuals, a group that tends to be leftist. They also say Jews are reacting to stereotypes of them common in nineteenth-century Europe, ranging from their alleged control over world finances and banking, to their allegedly being dirty, slovenly, and poor.[8] Each of Friedman's arguments can be refuted. Most Jews today know little of traditional Mishnaic and Talmudic law; not all Jews are intellectuals, and not all intellectuals are leftists; these stereotypes did not apply to North African or Iraqi Jews, who have been equally successful in the world of commerce or philanthropy once they arrived in a receptive environment in France, Canada, or Israel.

The answer would appear to be much simpler, and it has important implications for other cultures seeking economic and social development. The capitalist system cares little about personal beliefs, presumptions, and assumptions. It is sensitive primarily to personal behaviors that can be altered without undermining cherished beliefs and other cultural values. Modern Orthodox Jews are a particular case in point. The financial success of Asians who have recently reached the United States is another example.

Although their stories are peopled by vastly different characters, the folklore of Protestants and Jews is remarkably similar. They revolve around ordinary people, caught in extraordinary situations, who emerge victorious. They honor plucky individuals who can stand up to seemingly insurmountable odds and emerge successfully through actions, imagination, adherence to ethical norms, or hard work. In terms of theological and social beliefs—and beyond the obviously divisive question of whether Jesus Christ is the Savior—Jews and Protestants could not, it is true, be more different. Protestantism believes in individual salvation; Judaism is based on the possibility of group redemption.

As a result, Protestantism was highly influenced by Hobbesian concepts of egocentric and utilitarian markets, while Jews believe in strength and survival arising from individual efforts that strengthen the group. Protestantism believes that the yields of the earth are gifts of God; Jews believe that humans were given dominion on earth as a trust, to be protected and improved. Protestant culture is founded on certainty of belief; Jewish Pharisaic culture is based on perpetual uncertainty about everything except belief in one God. Despite these fundamental differences, however, there is a neo-Darwinian convergence in certain of their public behaviors.

Jews combine perpetual uncertainty with a feeling of responsibility to the immediately surrounding group, which, in turn, becomes a broader feeling of personal responsibility for all the citizens of the country where they live. This combination of uncertainty and individual responsibility has led Jews to vote in disproportionately higher numbers than the surrounding population in almost every democratic country where they are citizens.

Jewish newspapers and magazines are preoccupied by three subjects that focus on national uncertainty: the rise in global anti-Semitism, the fate of Israel, and high levels of assimilation that threaten to undermine group strength. Polls indicate that 72 percent of American Jews believe that they share a common destiny with Jews in Israel[9] and elsewhere. The idea of group identity and common sense of destiny has been reinforced by such recent events as the Holocaust, Israel's interminable wars, terror attacks on Jewish targets worldwide, and September 11. But if pollsters had asked American Jews about having a common destiny with the rest of American society, one can conjecture that the percentages would have been similar, if not higher.[10] This is a far cry from the polar-opposite, idealized American belief in the supremacy of the "rugged individualist."

The Centrality of Tikkun Olam

Central to Jewish beliefs is the concept of *Tikkun Olam*, "repairing the world." Almost by definition, this demands individual civic participation and social, economic, and political innovation—and even contrarianism. Jews have been at the forefront of the battle for racial equality and religious tolerance. Beyond avoiding judgmentalism about other groups' morals, this attitude has other economic benefits. For nothing more distorts free markets and creates greater market inefficiencies than ignorance of others' needs, intellectual blindness, and practices that unilaterally exclude certain types of human capital because of irrational prejudice.

As emphasized above, Judaic culture is centered on law, which can be amended or reinterpreted as needs arise. Jews have a long tradition of self-criticism and a belief in human fallibility in interpreting the will of God. A close reading of data on the jobs that Jews tend to fill indicates that almost all such professions—from doctors, merchants, and teachers to lawyers and scholars who must constantly undergo peer review—are based on human contact, communication, and feedback. Israeli experts on cross-cultural problems that emerge following business mergers with foreign firms have found that Israelis demand much more, and more constant, feedback than do individuals in other cultures.[11] In addition to helping lessen uncertainty, feedback also leads to constant midcourse corrections in rapidly changing social and economic environments—yet another decided market advantage.

One feature of Jewish communal life that is crucially important to development is the pride the group takes in individual members' achievements in business, science, and the humanities. In some societies, this sort of group behavior and interest in the individual is viewed as a source of destabilizing envy. Jews, however, reward successful individuals with lavish and supportive feedback and use them as models for themselves and their children.

It is no wonder, therefore, that in that most competitive, intellectually risky, individualistic, ruthless, imaginative, innovative, bottom-up, cross-cultural, status-driven, consumer-oriented, feedback-craving, market-driven of all businesses, the mass media, Jews have achieved their greatest successes. Today, most of the largest mass media outlets, including CBS, NBC, ABC, and most of the major Hollywood studios, all founded by Jews, have been sold to international conglomerates. Still, as of last count, fully 56 percent of Hollywood executives and producers involved in the largest grossing movies were Jews.[12]

History shows that Jews tend to be most successful in intellectually open, free-market societies governed by the rule of law. But what makes the Jewish case particularly interesting is that, except for the unusually privileged, Jews have succeeded more than the surrounding population under almost all types of political and economic regimes—communist, socialist, capitalist, democratic, or authoritarian—as long as local laws and regulations were not directed specifically against them.

Jewish tradition holds that life, and living in the world, is essentially an incomplete, individual and group "work in progress." Death is not sought. There are no wakes or forms of ancestor worship in Judaism, only mourning for loss. Final judgment is based on the sum of a life as it was lived. With the exception of mystics, to the vast majority of Jews the dead are not intermediaries, merely historical examples. The typical honorific given to someone who has passed away is *Zachur La Tov*, "May he/she be remembered for good."

All human activities and policies must, therefore, be directed toward the living and the living-to-be—and thus must also be future- and long-term oriented. This, in turn, demands continuous social entrepreneurship and social engineering that will only end with the coming of the Messiah. Belief, according to Jews, is insufficient to discharge the human obligations delineated in the covenants God has made with humankind. Therefore, everyone is obligated to participate in activism to improve the world. The guide to what should be done, and the ways it should be done, are embodied in a code of laws to which everyone must adhere—especially the Jews themselves.

The basic rules of ethical behavior are believed to be immutable. However, implementation is subject to conflicting views and interpretations, debate, and change. Jews do not automatically disdain uniqueness or novelty, and their appreciation for the potential value of invention carries over into almost all aspects of human activity. New ideas, though, are subjected to a rigorous process of selection. Although the traditional literature does not describe the procedure in these terms, Jews approach new problems or situations by using a multistage technique: proposition, referral to previous sources, argumentation, systemization, debate, legalization, institutionalization, examination over time, and finally validation through mass internalization of beliefs and practices.

Jews experience existential tensions between innovation based on rationalism and protective orthodoxy; between desires for group survival and for individual expression; and between regulation and creative freedom. But they do not see these ideas as mutually exclusive.

It is the Jews' learned ability to function within this matrix of tensions that has enabled them to fully integrate their concepts of social justice within a framework that also includes fierce intellectual and economic marketplace competition.

Leadership is self-selected and devolves to those who exhibit continuing merit in belief and practice. Merit is assigned based on proof over time. It is an award that can be withdrawn. While Jewish law requires obedience to the sovereign (in democracies this includes the will of the majority), this does not preclude the idea that one can be a member of a loyal opposition without being treasonous.

At any one time, a half-dozen or more rebellions or debates of greater or lesser import among Jews may be underway. In the last decade, for example, traditional Jews have engaged in a bitter debate about the role women can play in leading worship. In the secular arena, a major "silent" Jewish rebellion against majority rule in the United States is currently underway. The sovereign majority, through its representatives, has declared a cut in taxes, which has meant a decline in educational services. As a result, although they adhere to their legal obligation to pay property taxes for services they do not use, rapidly increasing numbers of Jews are deserting the public school system (which they ardently supported in the past) and are sending their children to Jewish day schools. Principals at these schools report that, unlike in other religious or private school systems, many of these newcomers are not seeking increased spirituality or social prestige for their children, but rather a higher (and usually more financially costly) level of education. Since quality education is a group priority by consensus, the community as a whole—even those with no personal stake—voluntarily bears some of the additional costs.

Critical to the success of any initiative is the ability to reach group consensus. If that fails, the fall-back position is invariably desertion from the current leadership, and either isolation or the formation of a new subgroup within the framework of the tradition. In most cases, Jews frown upon violence and law-breaking in the service of ideals. But they also reject passivity and fatalism. Instead, they engage in vigorous ongoing dispute over the terms for permitting the use of violence in self-defense, and the timing of, rationale for, and tactics to be used in nonviolent protest.

Central to *Tikkun Olam* is the belief in the need to establish a level playing field for everyone. Jews generally reject utopian egalitarianism as denying the God-given uniqueness and creativity present in each individual. Instead, the purpose of almost all Jewish law that does not deal directly with behavior toward the Divine is to encourage fairness in human relations. Quality education even for those with natural and economic handicaps; immediate feedback to encourage corrections in thought and behavior; universal adherence to criminal, commercial, and tort law; and independent adjudication of disputes are considered essential resources to achieve this ideal.

Activism to "repair" human-created law where it is faulty or inadequate is deemed to be an obligation. For the most part, behaviors are viewed as means that can be altered, not objectives in themselves. Individual and group self-criticism, self-assistance, and a willingness to battle corruption are perceived to be required traits and assets. Notably, among Jews, in almost all matters, immediate responsibility for creativity and action lies with the individual, but long-term success belongs to the group that sets the norms that foster accomplishment.

Notes

1. *Berachot*, 26b.
2. A recent, internally published survey by the Israeli Ministry of Education found that in schools where a combination of traditional Jewish and modern methods of teaching were used, students performed significantly better on standardized tests for mathematics, science, and reading comprehension than did students in purely secular schools that used only methods common elsewhere in the world.
3. Sergio Della Pergola, "World Jewish Population 2001," http://www.icj.huji.ac.il/demog/dmg_worldjpop_01.htm
4. "National Jewish Population Survey," 2004, http://www.jewishdatabank.org
5. Eugene Volokh, "Rule of Law: Racial Politics at the Supreme Court," *Wall Street Journal Interactive Edition*, October 12, 1998.
6. Neal Gabler, *An Empire of Their Own* (New York: Crown Publishers, 1988).
7. Milton Friedman, "Capitalism and the Jews," in *Morality of the Market: Religious and Economic Perspectives,* ed. W. Block, C. Brennan, and K. Elzinga. (Vancouver, BC: The Fraser Institute, 1985), 401–408.
8. See also: Derek J. Pendlar, *Shylock's Children* (Berkeley, University of California Press, 2001).
9. National Jewish Population Survey (NJPS).
10. Indirect evidence for this supposition comes from the NJPS finding that American Jews give substantially more money to non-Jewish charities than they do to Jewish charities.
11. Judy Maltz, "Bridging the Cultural Divide," November 19, 2003, http://www.Globes.co.il.
12. Seymour Martin Lipset and Earl Raab, *Jews and the New American Scene* (Cambridge, MA: Harvard University Press, 1996), 26–27.

10

Culture Begins with Cult

The Surprising Growth of the Catholic People

MICHAEL NOVAK

At the beginning of the twenty-first century, to almost universal surprise, the Roman Catholic Church is among the fastest growing of the major world religions. With just over a billion members today, by 2025 it is projected to approach 1.5 billion, just about two-thirds of all Christians and one-fifth of all humans. For example, from 120 million in 2000, Africa is predicted to have 228 million Catholics in 2025; similarly Latin America's Catholic population will rise from 461 million to 606 million and Asia's from 110 million to 160 million. Only Europe will see its Catholic population fall, from 286 million to 276 million. At that point the Church may in fact surpass the nation of China as the single most populous entity on earth, worldwide in scope and embracing within itself, in all their variety, nearly all cultures.

Most of this growth is taking place in Africa, Latin America, and Asia. Among the top five Catholic populations, only Italy, with nearly 56 million Catholics, is in Europe. The others lie along different missionary trails of the modern age, led by Brazil (144 million), Mexico (124 million), the United States (65 million), and the Philippines (63 million). Among the top fifteen Catholic countries today, five are in Europe, two in Asia, and one each in Africa and North America. But these groupings will change radically.

Also overlooked is the awesome persecution of Christians in Africa by a newly aggressive Islam pressing downwards from the north. Incited by politicized activists, Muslim mobs are burning churches, murdering, and carrying off into slavery Christian victims who now number in the millions. Worldwide persecutions during the past century have exceeded in ferocity and variety those of any time in the past. Robert Royal writes that "the twentieth century, by any measure, presents a brutal spectacle that may be remembered historically as one of the darkest periods of martyrdom."[1] Historically, a season of martyrs has been a harbinger of great growth for the church. From present trends in both conversions and population growth, demographers are already projecting an entirely unexpected rate of growth.

As I will argue in the rest of this chapter, the basic doctrines of Catholicism fit well with both democracy and capitalism, though Catholic cultures have sometimes resisted one or both of them in the past. By looking again at these basic doctrines and finding ways to share them with the poor in Catholic societies, we may begin to help them use capitalism, as so many millions of others have, to break the chains of their poverty.

The Catholic Cult: The Eucharist

The Catholic Church has often demonstrated its capacity to shape culture. At the heart of any culture is its central cult, a dramatization of one possible answer to the riddle of human existence. The cult around which Catholic cultures are formed celebrates the breathtaking offer by the creator of the universe to share with human beings his friendship, if they choose to accept it. This lord desires the friendship of free women and men, a friendship they are supposed to enter into not under coercion or duress, but in uncoerced personal and political liberty ("Give to Caesar the things that are Caesar's, and to God the things that are God's"). God freely made us and freely sent his son to unite us to himself (we did not merit it), and his son freely accepted the sacrificial destiny assigned him (he did not have to). Correspondingly, the offer God makes to human beings is also addressed to our freedom of choice. This appeal to our liberty is the meaning of the sacrifice of the cross, freely undertaken by Jesus and daily renewed on every Catholic altar in the world.

At the heart of the Catholic cult, then, lies liberty. Its crown is friendship or, as St. Augustine portrayed it in his *City of God*, the invisible bond among those united in the gift of God's love. Catholics call their cult the Eucharist (the giving of thanks), the sacrifice of the Mass, the reenactment of Calvary, and even, for one of its climactic parts, communion. In it, all creation is summed up and offered to the creator in common prayer: "The Eucharist is all creation, redeemed and at prayer." The sun never sets on the continuous reenactment of this action around the globe.

Of course, humans being what we are, in this action the sinner is at the heart of the church. It is as a body of sinners that the church prays. In this respect, the Catholic Church is not a good home for utopians; nor, in another respect, is it a comfortable home for puritans.

Another distinctive feature of the Catholic people is its internal cultural variety. The daily recurrence of Christ's sacrifice at the Mass is so powerful a central cult, and the careful nurturing of the clarity of the creed so highlights the necessary things, that large and significant adaptations to time and place and to individual cultures are part of the church's normal practice worldwide. In other words, the term *Catholic* actually signifies both worldwide commonality and local concreteness. The Church in Poland is different in feeling from that in Italy, as the Church in Nigeria is different from that in Australia. Yet it is easy for pilgrims from all such places to come together as one in St. Peter's Square, united under the Bishop of Rome. They also renew their unity at Mass, wherever they may be on the globe.

The strength of this internal structure is obvious in the recent promotion and defense of democracy and universal human rights, especially under Pope John Paul II, in places as diverse as Chile, the Philippines, Eastern Europe, Africa, and (regarding the unborn) Western Europe and America. Its weakness becomes apparent in the relatively uneven record of Catholic cultures in adapting to a capitalist economy. During the nineteenth century, harsh experiences with the anti-Catholic democracies of Europe loomed large in the Vatican's mind, while the fairly benign democratic experiment in the United States, praised by Leo XIII, seemed remote. Beginning with Napoleon's invasion of Italy, two popes were dragged away in wagons into captivity in France, and their successors were put at risk of life and limb for more than a century. After bitter experiences under the boot of Continental democracy taught it to oppose democracy during the long nightmare from the French Revolution through the 1920s, the Church changed course during the twentieth century. Recently, a third wave of democratization has begun in Catholic cultures on several continents, as Samuel Huntington describes:

Two (Portugal and Spain) of the first three third wave countries to democratize were Catholic. Democratization then swept through six South American and three Central American countries. It moved on to the Philippines, the first East Asian country to democratize, doubled back to Chile and affected Mexico, and then burst through in Catholic Poland and Hungary, the first East European countries to democratize. Catholic countries were in the lead in every region of the world, and the most Catholic region, Latin America, was the region that democratized most fully. Overall, roughly three quarters of the countries that transited to democracy between 1974 and 1989 were Catholic countries.[2]

Moreover, at the highest level, in the sustained body of reflection embodied in his social encyclicals and brought to a magisterial summary in "On the Hundredth Year," John Paul II highlighted as the engines of human development not only democracy and capitalism, but all three fundamental human liberties: first religious and cultural liberty, then political liberty through democracy and the rule of law, and under these economic liberty through a free and creative economy. As the beacons of a proper "moral ecology," he lists the guiding themes of human solidarity, the common good, social justice, the dignity of the human person, and the principle of subsidiarity.[3]

He explores the social destination of all the goods of the earth and the origin of the right to individual property. He sees society as a community of free persons, and describes the subjectivity of the person: individuals can understand and choose, and express those abilities throughout their social life. The value is not merely in the steel produced by the worker, but the intelligence and will the worker pours into his work—an aspect of work the Marxists overlooked. All these themes are part of the "moral ecology" or "human ecology" of a culture, that whole ethos within which humans work out their free destiny.

Given the intellectual leadership of John Paul II, the Church is well positioned to face the huge tasks of economic and political development that lie ahead. Flat on its back after the French Revolution, then threatened for decades with shrinkage in its body of believers, as the new millennium begins the Church has rebounded spectacularly both in numbers and in intellectual self-confidence. Just a few decades ago, as the French political philosopher Pierre Manent wisely observes, the future of democracy seemed assured and that of the Church doubtful. But today it appears that the Church has adapted far more easily to democracy than democracy has to the urgent demands of its own moral and cultural disorder:

> Thus, the political submission of the Church to democracy is, perhaps, finally, a fortunate one. The Church willy-nilly conformed herself to all of democracy's demands. Democracy no longer, in good faith, has any essential reproach to make against the Church. From now on it can hear the question the Church...alone poses, the question *Quid sit homo*—What is man? But democracy neither wants to nor can respond to this question in any manner or form. On democracy's side of the scale, we are left with political sovereignty and dialectical impotence. On the Church's side, we are left with political submission and dialectical advantage. The relation unleashed by the Enlightenment is today reversed. No one knows what will happen when democracy and the Church become aware of this reversal.[4]

Still, in actual practice, the Church's dispersion into many different cultures and historical streams around this planet inevitably results in uneven progress among the more or less Catholic nations. Many largely Catholic cultures aspire to democratic political life, but are not yet prepared to understand or to welcome capitalist development.

Catholics and Anticapitalist Traditions

Given their many different historical experiences, then, Catholic people in the less developed world face at least four major streams of resistance to capitalism. First, and perhaps easiest to understand, are the anticapitalist reflexes of those cultures that lived under communism for up to seventy years. The second resistance comes from those who experienced five hundred years of agrarian feudalism in the Holy Roman Empire, in Latin Europe, and in the American colonies of Spain and Portugal.

Third, all through Africa, many necessary cultural and political preconditions of a capitalist economy have barely been met, if at all. Almost entirely lacking, for instance, are a stable rule of law, widespread personal ownership of property, and a male culture of work and self-improvement. In many countries, men were expected to be warriors and hunters, while women performed most of the agricultural labor. Along with Africa, in this same category, many Asian cultures have only recently come to expect progress and, family by family, the urgent desire "to improve one's condition."

Fourth, one of the least helpful inheritances from British, French, and American progressives during the past century has been their exportation to the less developed world of a soft sort of Fabian socialism. This unfortunate foreign export infused Third World elites with a powerful anticapitalist prejudice and an excessive expectation of benefits from the state. Many Catholic bishops and professors in such places stubbornly resist liberal ideas as antithetical to their own desires for community and collective responsibility. They feel their own model is morally superior to Anglo-American liberalism.

A word on this latter point may be helpful. Early in the last century the Spaniard Felix Sarda y Salvany produced a little book entitled *Liberalismo es Pecado,* translated as *Liberalism is a Sin.*[5] In it he distilled the long-smoldering animosity of the Iberian nobility toward the merchant culture of the Anglo-Americans, because of what the Iberians saw as extreme individualism and preoccupation with material progress. Claiming moral substance, civility, and honor for the old order, and lacking de Tocqueville's balance and even-tempered judgment, Sardy y Salvany saw only selfishness and self-interest in the new democratic order. Down through the years and even recently in the work of Ortega y Gasset, the Iberian world abounded with polemics against the mass society, consumerism, materialism, and vulgar culture represented nowadays by McDonald's and MTV. Today, the rise of democracy and an entrepreneurial culture is rather markedly transforming the world.

In Western Europe, Canada, Australia, and the United States, meanwhile, many Catholic clergy are the sons or nephews of labor unionists and influenced by other family members whose political leanings are not a little suspicious of, or hostile toward, business. Among Latin American clergy these suspicions and hostilities are fairly routine. Only the rare prelate or highly placed clergyman seems to have grown up (as Pius XI did) as the son of an entrepreneur-owner of a small business. The result is a fairly widespread lack of sympathy for capitalist activity.

So it can hardly be a surprise, only a severe disappointment, that during the late 1990s Jesuit colleges all over Latin America sponsored essay contests on the evils of "neoliberalism." That term, not carefully defined, is loosely associated with such shibboleths as the IMF, Reaganism, Thatcherism, and "the Chicago School." No criticisms were solicited about the corruption and economic irresponsibility of precapitalist Latin American regimes, sometimes militaristic, sometimes democratic, and sometimes both by turns. The Jesuits' criticism was directed only outwards, toward attempts to reform Latin American traditions, particularly reforms from the dreaded "liberal" direction.

Thus, even though the democratic idea has been winning favor on the Latin American left, which had long shared Marxist suspicions about democracy, the conviction that a capitalist economy is a necessary (but not sufficient) condition for the success of democracy is still very far from having taken root. Meanwhile, the Latin American right, rooted in land ownership, is often anticapitalist for ancient, traditionalist reasons. The land-owning interest fears and resists a newly emerging entrepreneurial class that might eventually threaten inherited sources of power and wealth.

Partly as a result of this double assault on capitalism, from both left and right, democratic experiments in Latin America are likely to be short-lived. Without plenty of new enterprises to generate economic growth across all social strata, popular discontent continues unabated, generation after generation. Tens of millions of Latin Americans, no longer content with the bare subsistence of farming life, stream toward the cities to seek opportunity. But there they are frustrated because they find few factories to employ them. No longer campesinos, they have yet to become proletarians working in industry. Most are entrepreneurs living hand-to-mouth, usually as *ilegales* or *informales,* as Hernando de Soto has pointed out in *The Other Path.*[6]

The culture around the Latin American poor so far offers little support, moral or legal, to entrepreneurship: neither legal status through cheap and easy incorporation, nor accessible credit via small loans, nor secure property rights, nor education in entrepreneurial skills and economic literacy. It does not even offer them praise and honor, but rather shame and legal rejection. Traditionalist mothers think working for the government bears honor, but business and entrepreneurship are held in bad odor—and known to be highly insecure, when political tides turn.

Latin America is already home to more Catholics than anywhere else on earth, and will continue to have the largest group of Catholics for the foreseeable future. Therefore, their lingering hostility to capitalism, which must be present for democracy to succeed, is a matter for grave concern.

Catholicism, Democracy, and Culture

Beginning in the late 1990s, the Pontifical Academy of Social Science (PASS), a stellar panel of international experts, conducted a seven-year study of democracy, with special attention to the Catholic experience around the world. It came to some quite remarkable generalizations, which it published in three successive volumes.[7] The academy asked me, as an outside expert, to evaluate these studies and propose new directions. In constructing my evaluation, I emphasized that democracy depends on culture. At the heart of democracy lies the practice of self-government, by which citizens through their own associations achieve their own ends, private and public, without always turning to the state to take care of them. Self-government, in turn, depends upon certain cultural understandings and practices, culturally supported and culturally disciplined. Although the idea has frequently been expanded upon since, perhaps no one caught the essence of the matter as vividly and succinctly as Alexis de Tocqueville:

> Europeans exaggerate the influence of geography on the lasting powers of democratic institutions. Too much importance is attributed to laws, too little to mores. Unquestionably those...three great influences [geography, laws, customs]...regulate and direct American democracy; but if they are to be classed in order, I should say that the contribution of physical causes is less than that of the laws, and that of laws less than mores.[8]

Capitalism and Anticapitalism

No similar study has been made by the Pontifical Academy, or any other Catholic body that I know of, concerning the question: If democracy is the political system the church now recommends to the Catholic people as most consistent with the gospels, which economic system ought it to recommend, and under what conditions? Of course, Pope John Paul II asked precisely that question three times in "The Hundredth Year," and based his final answer on the meaning of the capitalist system:

> If by "capitalism" is meant an economic system which recognizes the fundamental and positive role of business, the market, private property and the resulting responsibility for the means of production, as well

as free human creativity in the economic sector, then the answer is certainly in the affirmative, even though it would perhaps be more appropriate to speak of a "business economy," "market economy" or simply "free economy." If by "capitalism" is meant a system in which freedom in the economic sector is not circumscribed within a strong juridical framework which places it at the service of human freedom in its totality, and which sees it as a particular aspect of that freedom, the core of which is ethical and religious, then the reply is certainly negative.[9]

As the church showed caution in observing the fruits and demerits of democracy before committing fully to it, John Paul II also moved, with caution, to state the essential understandings that lie behind a capitalist economy. He was careful to think through these concepts within the horizon both of faith and of the long Catholic intellectual tradition, pushing the latter into new territories.

Still, some energetic resistance to capitalism remains within the church, and even in the Vatican itself. Many of the Latin clergy, especially, interpret capitalism as a malignant form of that much-dreaded nineteenth-century menace, antireligious liberalism, which they see as relying on an ideology of materialism, atomic individualism, and relativism. The Jesuits are notably anticapitalist, especially in Latin America and Asia. The Latin Americans and clergy from such Latin nations as France, Spain, and Italy, tend to dismiss capitalism as a Protestant Anglo-Saxon disease, neither genuinely Christian nor even minimally moral. Indeed, efforts to argue that at least capitalism does succeed in lifting up the poor, are typically answered with statements to the effect that yes, it works, but the means it uses are still immoral.

Although the two currents rush downstream in the same direction, and at some points flow into each other, the Catholic anticapitalist critique cannot be reduced to a simple Marxist critique. For instance, the Catholic left parts company with the Marxists in holding firmly to the fundamental right to private property. Besides, traditionalists on the right have done at least as much as leftists to shape Catholic anticapitalism. The paternalism of the traditional aristocracy and the landholding gentry dovetails quite nicely with socialist authoritarianism. Both oppose uncontrolled free markets and unmanaged individual opportunity for all. The assumption of both right and left seems to be that the poor are not yet ready to compete on their own, that they still need guardians. Their dispute revolves around which guardians the poor should turn to.

Many Catholics, left and right, hold the view that what economists call "self-interest" is only a form of primordial selfishness, directly contrary to the two great commandments to love one's neighbor and to love God. They say that the profit motive is an expression of greed, one of the seven deadly sins. They insist that capitalism benefits only the rich, and grinds down the poor. They say that capitalist individualism turns each person into a solitary atom, *homo homini lupus*. They say that capitalist advertising breeds hedonism, envy, greed, lust, a love for luxury, and moral vacuity. They argue that capitalism makes buying and selling into the organizing principle of virtually every sphere of life, even the churches and the universities and hospitals. They insist that it destroys leisurely meals and delicate cuisine, in favor of fast foods and a hurried, frantic lifestyle, and brings about a severe flattening of good taste. Capitalism, they add disdainfully, breeds vulgarity of every sort, and puts up ugly boxy buildings disfigured by omnipresent billboards and neon lights. When they compare it to the beautiful tastes and high styles of aristocratic cultures, and even to simple peasant life, they find capitalist living hateful. Besides, they believe that capitalist wealth arises from the exploitation of the miserable poor overseas and in capitalist urban centers.

To set forth a positive theology of capitalist purposes, institutions, and methods requires a great deal of patience and a willingness to meet this long series of accusations—and many others—one by one, sorting out what is true in each from what is outrageous or simply contrary to fact. Anticapitalist critics must present their own better alternative for lifting up the poor. The issue is not who can imagine a prettier paradise. The question for anticapitalist Catholics is this: What do you have to offer, considering this world as it is, that will raise up more of the poor from poverty, so that they might by the millions come to share the material goods suited to their human dignity and God-given talents? One can read dozens of volumes of the liberation theology from the 1970s and 1980s without finding a single page of concrete proposals on how to move the poor out of poverty. The traditionalist Catholic regions did not succeed in doing that, and neither did the multitude of socialist experiments in the twentieth century.

Yet in Hong Kong and South Korea, Taiwan and Singapore, formerly among the poorest nations, capitalist methods have helped large majorities to rise out of poverty with impressive speed. The same is true of Ireland since the mid-1980s, and a similar dynamism appears to be slowly but steadily bringing prosperity to most people in Poland, Slovakia, Lithuania. and some other formerly Communist nations of central and eastern Europe, where cultural factors and the rule of law have been in favorable alignment.

By contrast, although much progress has been made in Latin America since 1989, in the shift away from traditional state-centered mercantilism to more liberal economies, reforms have been halfhearted and incomplete, often not given full popular support. Latin American elites of both right and left remain steeped in anticapitalist prejudices and strongly entrenched in their own inherited privileges and self-interests.

Catholicism and Culture

In an earlier study of the cultural factors that defeat democratic and capitalist development, Lawrence Harrison and colleagues developed a table of fourteen basic attitudes which either facilitate or torpedo the liberation of the poor from poverty and political oppression. Among the favorable ones are future orientation, belief in personal empowerment, the work ethic, and respect for competition. Those same cultural differences separate those Catholics who favor democracy and capitalism from those who resist them, and who especially resist capitalism.

Pope John Paul II articulated virtually all fourteen of these attitudes that favor the development of democracy and a dynamic capitalist economy. These attitudes encourage the poor "to acquire expertise, to enter the circle of exchange, and to develop their skills in order to make the best use of their capacities and resources."[10] And now Catholic thinkers, writers, and political leaders in many nations are marshaling arguments behind these attitudes, and undermining the arguments of "the cultural despisers of capitalism."[11]

The long, dark experience of Communism in Poland and the rest of eastern Europe led many to search ardently for an alternative to socialist thinking. The buoyancy of the Anglo-American economies during the 1980s and 1990s, and the positive examples of the Four Asian Tigers, and the Irish Tiger, added powerful empirical arguments to the democratic and capitalist project. I do not think that the long-term issue is in doubt, but clearly the intellectual struggle will be fierce for at least two or three more decades.

Meanwhile, as I proposed to the PASS, it would be highly useful to prepare a handbook or catechism of democracy and economic development for Catholic peoples in the developing countries, and even in the developed ones. We need a usable inventory of the habits (virtues) that a people must develop if it wishes to experience economic and political progress.

Consider four vices that would poison any hope of a culture of liberty. Were any group of leaders or nations to proceed with arrogance, as if they were all-seeing and all-knowing, others would be repulsed and driven into stern resistance. When governments and institutions begin suppressing inquiry and evidence, others are driven to rebel. Were any people or nation to enslave, demean, or exploit others, they would earn the contempt of onlookers and the fierce resentment of those so demeaned. Were any people or nation to treat other peoples highhandedly, doing to them what it would not tolerate being done to itself, other peoples would look on with disgust. No doubt other vices can destroy an amicable society. Let us begin with these four, and turn them into their opposite virtues.

From these vices, which are especially offensive to modern peoples, we may derive four new cardinal virtues—hinge virtues on which at least a rudimentarily sound moral ecology for the whole human race might turn. Though the names are not nearly so significant as the realities, I call them cultural humility; respect for the regulative ideal of truth; the dignity of the individual person; and human solidarity.

1. *Cultural humility,* that is, a proper sense of one's own fallibility, past sins, limits, and characteristic faults, does not require that one embrace cultural relativism. Humility means being aware that in my truth, there is some error, and in the errors of my adversaries, there is bound to be some truth.

2. *Truth as a regulative ideal* does not mean that any one person possesses the truth, but only that all of us live under the constraints of evidence and reasoned argument. Those in the West who play with the idea that relativism is crucial for liberty are playing with fire. Where relativism flourishes, thugs eventually seize leadership; without truth, power rules. Against the thugs, one cannot hold the banner of relativism and shout "Injustice!" To that they will reply, "Says who?" And one cannot say, "Those charges are false!" for there will no longer be any such thing as "true" or "false." It is now power, power alone, that speaks.

Thus truth as a regulative ideal is crucial for a civilized society. It is necessary if people are to have respect for one another, and to submit opposing judgments to the light of evidence. The concept facilitates conversation in the light of evidence. Civilized persons converse; they argue, they reason with one another. Barbarians club one another.

3. In response to the barbarities of the twentieth century, the Catholic Church has come to emphasize the dignity of the individual person. All of Christianity has insisted that every single human is loved by the creator, is made in his image, and is destined for eternal friendship. Following Judaism, Christianity made human dignity a concept of universal application. "Inasmuch as ye have done it unto one of the least of these my brethren, ye have done it unto me" (Matt. 25:40). Christianity made it a matter of self-condemnation to use another human as a means to an end. A person is more than an individual.

4. *Solidarity* is the special virtue that makes each individual aware both of inalienable personal responsibility and of belonging to the whole human race, of being brother or sister to all others, of living in community with all other humans in God. Solidarity points simultaneously to the personal responsibility and initiative of the human subject and to communion with others. It is radically different from what socialists meant by collectivization. Solidarity awakens, and does not lull, individual conscience. It evokes responsibility, enlarges personal vision, and connects the self to all others as self-to-self, not as a unit in lock-step.

The authors of our Declaration of Independence, for example, spoke of human persons as "endowed by their Creator with inalienable rights," and strove to invent institutions worthy of human dignity. This vision implies both that each individual is incommensurable, and that every member of the human community shares in the common endowment. On one side, then, a self-enclosed individualism, heedless of others, demeans the calling of the human person. On the other side, so does any vision of the common good as a mere sum of individual goods (or the greatest good for the greatest number). The common good of a society of persons consists in treating each person as an end, never as a means. To arrange the institutions of human society to insure this for everyone is by no means easy.

From these four "cardinal" virtues of social well-being flow others, necessary for political, economic, and cultural liberty but too numerous to examine here. A free polity, for example, requires dispositions of character that build a high degree of social trust. Economic success depends upon initiative and creativity, habits of enterprise and invention, innovation, risk-taking, creative imagination, and practical skill in turning mere ideas into realities. The habit of enterprise is the inclination to notice what other people do not yet see, so as to bring into reality things not before seen. It is the ability to foresee both the needs of others and the combinations of productive factors most adapted to satisfying those needs. The virtue of building community involves the capacity to maintain in oneself and to inspire in others a certain level of creativity, teamwork, and morale. The virtue of practical realism develops goals, strategies, and tactics to carry out the activities of business (or government and community) in light of circumstance and contingency.

In the political realm, citizens require the inner virtues that enable them to exhibit self-control and self-government. Each citizen needs an internalized inner policeman—conscience—which guides him or her to act lawfully even when no one is looking. People exercise the virtue of social justice when they join with others to improve the institutions of society. The principle of self-interest, when rightly understood, attaches natural instincts of self-interest to worthy and socially beneficial projects, teaching people that their own self-development depends upon their becoming social beings.

In addition, peoples new to democracy and capitalism have much to learn about the practical nature of compromise, being a loyal opposition, the role of associations in the practice of self-government, skills in coalition building, the ability to keep profit/loss accounts, and the voluntary cooperation of free persons in common projects.

In a word, we need a few simple handbooks that explain to peoples in many cultures—and at many levels of development—the ideas, practices, and institutions they need to make democracy and capitalism work. Many of these are not obvious, but are rather the product of long and painful experience and experimentation. Moreover, the powerful interests, prejudices, and arguments thrown up in resistance to them must be unmasked or patiently punctured, one by one. A set of little "catechisms"—frequently asked questions on each of these main subjects—would be invaluable, especially to people who are genuinely confused and genuinely inquiring, and eager to find the best path for the human development of their country or region.

A Plan of Action

What should the Church, both laity and clergy, do to help all the Catholic people move into "the circle of development," especially economic development? The primary vocation of the clergy is not to lead the Catholic people into worldly prosperity and political liberty; these days, that task is mostly assigned to the laity. In fact, Catholic sisters worldwide direct a larger health service than all but a handful of national health services. Many Catholic laypersons lead major public institutions, as presidents, prime ministers, justices, and other high officers of the state. Hundreds of Catholics are university presidents, and thousands of Catholics head companies, labor unions, and newspapers. Thousands more are television executives, movie stars, and scientists, generals, poets, heads of think tanks, brokers, financiers, and leaders of every secular description.

For the first time in history, lay Catholics are in a position to establish an Initiative for the Poor, a major organized effort to stimulate economic development among the world's poor. The current roadblock is that many existing Catholic organizations and lay leaders appear to believe more in redistribution, caretaking, and what might be called remedial "welfare" than in stimulating economic enterprise, activism, and economic growth in the small-business sector, from the bottom up. This appearance may be deceiving. But public appeals from Catholic Relief Services, Caritas, and the Catholic Campaign for Human Development, and from various religious orders, seem to emphasize charity and handouts, rather than capitalist transformation.

Consider this proposition: *The best way to liberate the poor is grassroots capitalist development.* Perhaps only a minority of today's Catholic leaders, clerical or lay, hold that proposition as empirically sound. But that is the minority with which we must begin. The greatest of all acts of charity is to teach the poor how to escape from the prison of poverty. Equally crucial is to teach the badly governed how to build limited governments on democratic bases: the consent of the governed, the rule of law, respect for the rights of individuals, and checks and balances. The societies that successfully raise up the poor begin with a set of sound economic principles, and nurture the required habits and practices. Economic reform begins with knowledge. That is why communicating this knowledge is so great an act of charity.

Of course, it would be very helpful if the Vatican, along with regional councils of bishops, put the weight of their own knowledge and will behind the formation of an Initiative for the Poor. Such action would speed the spread of ideas and practices that lead those at the bottom of society to create wealth rapidly. Failing that, leaders of business must create such an organization, finance it, and direct it. This might be a task for the Knights of Malta, an organization of hospitallers and warriors founded in Jerusalem about 1080, which now claims 10,500 members worldwide. The Knights and Dames of Malta recruit eminent Catholics from every walk of life; their main mission today remains supplying medical aid at times of disaster and sudden need, along with food and other forms of assistance. Yet the talents of this organization and its worldwide scope would suit it for the more dynamic, fundamental role in reducing poverty represented by the Initiative for the Poor.

This initiative need not create a new bureaucracy; I hope it will not. But it will require funds to prepare teaching guides and field advisors to demonstrate how the creation of wealth gets underway. Someone must organize seminars that target local elites and poor people alike, to show how they can change institutions and habits, and offer technical support to assure that local projects do succeed in stimulating new small businesses.

Let me cite two examples from Bangladesh. Rose received a $100 miniloan from an American missionary to purchase seedlings, fertilizer, and a few tools so she could begin to grow flowers. Bangladesh is a nation of much sun and water, so Rose has flowers growing nearly year-round. Every two days her daughter takes them into Dhaka, the nearest city, where they sell quickly. With the money raised, she has paid back her loan and has been expanding her production. Her example has inspired other village women; together, they have nearly doubled the village's annual income.

In another village, Tahmina purchased a cell phone with an even smaller loan. Her ability to telephone various markets in nearby cities to check current prices has greatly helped her husband's business. Neighbors also pay her small sums to use her phone; she has become a telephone exchange for the entire village.

The effort to precipitate economic growth from the bottom up has now succeeded in many regions. One crucial case to study is Germany after 1945. Another is that of the Four Little Tigers of Southeast Asia: South Korea, Taiwan, Singapore, and Hong Kong. A third is Ireland during the 1980s; a fourth is Chile.

If Catholics are serious about liberating the poor from poverty, they must become serious about ground-level capitalist development. Small business is the key to job creation. Encouraging tens of millions of small entrepreneurs in the world's poorest regions is the top priority of social justice in our time. For social justice means concerted, cooperative efforts (the "social" dimension of the virtue) to improve the condition of the earthly city by liberating the poor from immemorial poverty (the "justice" part). Poverty limits the range of human development. That is why lifting the restrictions imposed by poverty on the back of the poor is a crucial step toward helping them to become all that God wants them to become.

Notes

1. Robert Royal, *The Catholic Martyrs of the Twentieth Century: A Comprehensive World History* (New York: Crossroad/Herder & Herder, 2000), 1.
2. Samuel Huntington, *The Third Wave: Democratization in the Late Twentieth Century* (Norman, OK: University of Oklahoma Press, 1991), 76.
3. In *Centesimus Annus* (*CA*), or On the Hundredth Year, 48, John Paul describes the principle of subsidiarity: "a community of a higher order should not interfere in the internal life of a community of a lower order, depriving the latter of its functions, but rather should support it in case of need and help to coordinate its activity with the activities of the rest of society, always with a view to the common good." The text of this encyclical is available at: http://www.vatican.va/holy_father/john_paul_ii/encyclicals/documents/hf_jp-ii_enc_01051991_centesimus-annus_en.html.
4. Pierre Manent, "Christianity and Democracy," in *A Free Society Reader: Principles for the New Millennium*, ed. Michael Novak, William Brailsford, and Cornelis Heesters (Lanham, MD: Lexington Books, 2000), 125. First published in *Crisis*, February 1995.
5. Felix Sarda y Salvany, *El liberalismo es pecado* (Barcelona: Libreria e Typografia Católica, 1887). Originally published in English in 1899 by B. Herder Book Co., St. Louis, Missouri under the title *What Is Liberalism?* and reprinted in 1979 and 1989 by TAN Books and Publishers, Inc. Retypeset by TAN Books and Publishers, Inc. in 1993, under the title *Liberalism Is a Sin*.
6. Hernando de Soto, *The Other Path: The Economic Answer to Terrorism* (New York: Basic Books, 2002).
7. *Proceedings of the Workshop on Democracy* (1998); *Democracy: Some Acute Questions* (1999); and *Democracy: Reality and Responsibility* (2001). Available on the Vatican Web site, http://www.vatican.va/roman_curia/pontifical_academies/acdscien/own/documents/rc_acdsci_doc_20001003_publications_social_en.html.
8. Alexis de Tocqueville, *Democracy in America* (New York: Harper Perennial, 1988), 308.

9. John Paul II, *CA*, 42.
10. John Paul II, *CA*, 34.
11. The writings of many of these leaders have been compiled in Michael Novak, William Brailsford, and Cornelis Heesters, eds., *A Free Society Reader* (Lanham, MD: Lexington Books, 2000). In Italy, see the works of Dario Antiseri and Flavio Felice; in Slovakia, Juraj Kohutiar; in Poland Ryzard Legutko.

11

Reimagining the Orthodox Tradition

Nurturing Democratic Values in Orthodox Christian Civilization

NIKOLAS K. GVOSDEV
With a Response by Georges Prevelakis

Can the values, historical experience, and theological outlook of Orthodox Christianity play a positive role in strengthening democratic governance, promoting social justice, and encouraging prosperity? Answering this question is by no means simply an academic exercise. Several countries in the traditional Orthodox world, among them the Russian Federation, Ukraine, and Georgia, are engaged in political and economic transitions whose final outcomes remain uncertain. Other "Orthodox" states, among them Cyprus, Romania, and Bulgaria, are joining Greece (already a member of NATO and the European Union) to form an "Orthodox bloc" within the political and economic institutions of the Euro-Atlantic community, the very core not only of Western civilization but also of the world's advanced industrial democracies.

A distinction should be drawn between Orthodox Christianity as a religious faith with adherents throughout the globe and an "Eastern Christian civilization, which arose under the influence of Orthodoxy."[1] The latter is my focus here. In the twenty countries of the Orthodox "cultural zone" (eastern Europe, western Asia, and the

Eurasian plain), the majority of the population is nominally Eastern Orthodox, or Orthodoxy is considered a "national" faith. There,
traditional culture took its cultural, artistic, legal, and philosophical
influences from the Eastern Roman or Byzantine empire centered at
Constantinople.[2]

Like other historical Christian traditions that functioned as state
churches (such as Roman Catholicism, Anglicanism, and Lutheran-
ism), Orthodoxy's dominant outlook on the ideal form of human
governance, since the Emperor Constantine "established" Christianity in the early fourth century, was that human monarchy and a hierarchical social structure mirrored the divine order. Bishop Eusebius
of Caesarea, an advisor to Emperor Constantine, wrote of the emperor that "invested…with a semblance of heavenly sovereignty, he
directs his gaze above, and frames his earthly government according
to the strength of the pattern of that Divine original, feeling strength
in its conformity to the monarchy of God."[3] The Byzantine historian
George Ostrogorsky concluded, "As the emperorship was an emana-
tion of divine power, it was bound to gather up the whole power on
earth, and its authority could not be impaired by any other inner or
outer force."[4] These ideas were reinforced in medieval Russian political thought by church figures such as St. Cyril of Beloozero and St.
Joseph of Volokolamsk, who believed that a strong autocratic monarchy was essential to restrain evil, enforce justice and morality, and
safeguard the existence and well-being of the church.

Moreover, although Orthodoxy shares with its Western Christian
counterparts a common origin in the Greco-Roman-Semitic fusion
of antiquity, Eastern Christian civilization did not evolve in the same
fashion as Western Christendom. In the West, repeated struggles for
authority between popes, emperors, and kings in the High Middle
Ages and the diffusion of power within the feudal structure and
among autonomous guilds and corporations led to a great deal of
intellectual speculation about natural rights and the origins of civil
authority. The resulting discourse about rights helped push Western
civilization in the direction of political democracy and free-market
institutions. While a few similar speculations occurred in the Byzan-
tine/Orthodox world, they never achieved the critical mass needed to
influence the evolution of the state. When such ideas began to penetrate the Orthodox world, beginning with Russia in the eighteenth
century, they were often presented as standing in opposition to traditional Orthodox practice.

The task facing the Orthodox in the modern era is to graft new institutions and forms onto an indigenous, existing tradition, to see tradition as not simply a binding code from the past but also an ongoing and dynamic heritage. In the nineteenth century the Slavophiles, a group of Russian Orthodox intellectuals, opposed attempts in Russia to emulate Western models and institutions. They did not, however, preach blind obedience to the past, acknowledging that "it was not [Byzantium's] fate to present history and the world with the model of a Christian society."[5] Similarly, Vasilii Bolotov, a leading Russian theologian discussing reform wrote in 1906 that "there is no greater mistake than the attempt to restore the ecclesiastical order of a distant past." Reforms must "correspond to the needs of the present time," and take advantage of current improvements to be "regarded as truly canonical," whatever the historical precedents. Thus, "church history is only a useful record; it is in no way a code of laws."[6]

The Orthodox world, including the church and other organizations, has several assets that will help it strengthen democratic governance. The Orthodox countries already have significant experience with democratic and free-market institutions. Seventy percent of the countries in the "Orthodox" zone are classed by Freedom House as electoral democracies, and four-fifths were characterized as "free" or "partly free" with regard to their political and economic institutions. And though it is fair to ask whether, on balance, this progress occurred because of Orthodoxy's cultural and historic legacies, or in spite of it, it can hardly be argued that *nothing* within the Orthodox tradition before the modern period has been useful in this regard. Orthodox anthropology conceives of the human being as a creature possessing free will, personal autonomy, accountability, and the capacity for rational choice.

These ideas were repeatedly stressed by the leading fathers of the church, such as Saints Basil the Great, Gregory the Theologian, and John Chrysostom, creating the intellectual basis for modern political and economic systems. Their views were codified in the authoritative *Expositions of the Orthodox Faith*, assembled by St. John of Damascus in the eighth century. Indeed, John Chrysostom, working from the assumption that the human being is free and autonomous, anticipated the theory of the social contract, that governments are created by the will and the consent of the governed for mutual security, observing "that from of old all men came to an agreement that governors should be maintained by us, because to the neglect of their own affairs, they take charge of the public, and on this they spend their whole leisure, whereby our goods are kept safe."[7]

Historical precedents also provide support for modern institutions. The city-states of northern Rus, especially Novgorod and Pskov, developed representative political institutions and advanced commercial structures during their heyday in the eleventh to fifteenth centuries, akin to the Catholic commercial republics of medieval Italy and Flanders. But they defined themselves as Orthodox polities, indeed as democracies established by God. Other examples—the Cossack "republics" of the sixteenth to eighteenth centuries, the autonomous cities of the late Byzantine empire, and self-governing villages in the Balkans—all can be seen as precursors to modern institutions.

Some political leaders in the Orthodox world have sought to ground modern institutions in a reinterpretation of their own cultural inheritance. Just as Roman Catholic thinkers find support for democracy and the free market in the historical experience of the mercantile republics of the medieval West, their Orthodox counterparts are seeking to do the same. In Russia, the governor of the Novgorod oblast, Mikhail Prusak, believes that it is essential to redefine reform as a "return" to past values, and that by constructing new institutions with reference to past experiences and traditions, it has "eased the shock of cultural discontinuity, broadened the social constituency in favor of reforms, and contributed to dramatically higher levels of confidence in local government."[8] In 1999 Governor Prusak made the case that Russia could in fact embrace new political and economic institutions by placing them in the proper historical and cultural context: "Our generation can return to the principles of our ancestors. Self-government, elections, public accountability of authority, private property, individual liberty—the very cornerstones of the Novgorod Republic—are regaining their former significance."[9] These ideas have found a receptive audience among the political, business, and intellectual elites in many regions of Russia.

Indeed, drawing upon these patristic and historical resources, some within the Orthodox Church are beginning to reconcile its traditional outlook with modern institutions. One of the pioneers in this regard was Archbishop Makarios of Cyprus, who ended up serving as both primate of the church and president of the republic. In 1974, he observed that "in Cyprus...the archbishop, like the bishops, is elected directly by the people, with universal suffrage. In other words, in Cyprus, the archbishop isn't only a representative and administrator of the church, he's also a national figure. The ethnarch." In his opinion, he continued, "the church should interest itself in all aspects of life—the Christian religion doesn't confine itself to taking care of the moral progress of men, it's also concerned with their social well-being."[10]

In recent years, the Orthodox Church in the Russian north has also engaged in a process of reimagining its tradition. Originally, Russian sociologist Sergei Filatov observes, it "developed a tradition of the freedom and dignity of the individual." Now, he says," the local people are resurrecting this tradition, recognising the individual's own responsibility towards church, state and society," and "the development of Orthodox church life in this region shows that the bureaucratic Moscow style of church governance has not destroyed these northern religious traditions."[11] This church has many active lay organizations, among them Sunday schools, youth movements, and charitable sisterhoods. It works closely with educational and cultural institutions in developing shared curricula, and has forged strong connections with the region's political, business, and cultural leaders. A synergy has emerged between Orthodox church activists and democratic political reformers; a stress on decentralized structures of authority, free elections, and local self-government, as well as tolerance of diversity, defines both church and state institutions in the region. Churchmen, politicians, and intellectuals all promote the idea that the north is an "heir to the Novgorodian tradition of political and religious freedom."[12]

These efforts to reimagine the tradition have also begun to be codified in official statements by the Orthodox Church. Prior to the 2000 elections in Yugoslavia, the Synod of Bishops of the Serbian Orthodox Church issued this declaration:

> We feel obligated once again to summon the responsible representatives of the government, as well as all other participants in the elections, to do all within their competence so that the elections will proceed in an orderly and peaceful way, and that the results will be a true expression of the will of the people. For the ancient wisdom wisely holds: "The voice of the people is the voice of God."[13]

Similarly, before the 2000 presidential elections in Russia, Patriarch Aleksii II of Moscow declared that "every citizen, especially the Orthodox, is called to assume responsibility for…the country and the people, for their present and their future....The Lord has placed their fate in the hands of the people, who are endowed with the God-resembling freedom."[14]

In its authoritative "Bases of the Social Conception of the Russian Orthodox Church," adopted in 2000, the Bishops' Council endorsed, with qualifications, the democratic system of government and freedom of conscience. The document spells out several democratic tenets that the church agrees with, including the following: governments are formed with the consent of the governed (III.1); the people have the right to determine their own social and political institutions, so the church does not give preference to any specific form of government (III.7); scriptural and patristic references to monarchy are to be understood to refer metaphorically to government in general rather than as endorsement of a specific type of governance (V.3); Orthodox Christians are called to participate in affairs of state (II.3, V.3), including voting (V.2); and governments must secure an "autonomous sphere" of freedom for the individual, based upon fundamental rights to belief and life, complemented "by other, external ones, such as the right to freedom of movement, to obtain information, and to create property both to possess and utilize" (IV.6).[15]

Some bishops have used this "social doctrine" to encourage their flocks to participate actively in the political system. Archbishop Manuil, the head of the northern Russian diocese of Petrozavodsk and Karelia, notes that "government is a reflection of ourselves" and that "the church calls its faithful to participate actively in the life of society—its political, social and cultural life.... The hierarchs do not have any right to agitate for any particular" party or candidate, "but voting, taking part in elections is necessary, and I speak about this in all my sermons."[16]

Adopting statements is a positive first step, but the social and political environment will not change unless there is a corresponding reform of institutions. One can point to long-standing traditions within the Orthodox Church of Cyprus, where hierarchs are elected and where communities and dioceses enjoy a great deal of autonomous self-administration, as one factor assisting the consolidation of democratic institutions. Similar patterns in the Balkans and among the Orthodox of Estonia and Finland have also helped to reinforce democratic governance. In contrast, the less even pace of democratization in post-Soviet Russia, Ukraine, and Belarus may be traced, in part, to the unwillingness of church leadership to fully implement reforms adopted at the 1917–18 Moscow Council that had been designed to increase lay participation in church affairs. In theory, the Russian Orthodox Church is supposed to be governed at both the national and diocesan levels by mixed clergy–laity councils with elected delegates—and bishops were likewise supposed to be elected rather than appointed. The Soviet state blocked or eviscerated many of these provisions, and even today few of these regulations have been implemented.

Thus, a noticeable gap still exists between the "Orthodox world" and the "West" in terms of consolidation of democratic values, respect for human rights, and the smooth functioning of economic institutions—including the elimination of corruption. Some of this can be traced to a stronger "communitarian" strain in Orthodox culture. Orthodox thinkers usually refer to this as "conciliarity" (in Russian, *sobornost'*), a greater emphasis on consensus over competition and the importance of maintaining group cohesion and harmony. Some of it, however, also results from an unwillingness to actively reshape the culture.

Take the question of religious freedom, arguably the foundation for all other social and political rights. The Orthodox Church accepts the idea that faith must be freely chosen. The Ecumenical Patriarch of Constantinople Bartholomew recently reiterated that "the Orthodox Church does not seek to convince others of any one particular understanding of truth or revelation." He continued, "Whenever human beings react to the perspectives and the beliefs of others on the basis of fear and self-righteousness, they violate the God-given right and freedom of others to come to know God and one another in the manner inherent to their identity as peoples."[17]

Still, many in the Orthodox world are unwilling to accept the primacy of individual choice over the cohesion of the collective. While endorsing the principle of individual choice, in practice they place several conditions on how that choice can be exercised. Patriarch Aleskii made this very clear as he responded to a question on his understanding of religious freedom:

Respecting the right of every individual to confess a religion or to confess no religion, the church must decisively protect...against the negative influence on society of totalitarian sects, which divide families, which inculcate hatred in children for their parents, which discredit in the eyes of the youth an understanding of civic responsibility and patriotism. Our Lord warned us, "Every kingdom that is divided within itself falls; and every city or home that is divided within itself cannot stand" (Matthew 12:25).[18]

Indeed, many within the Russian Orthodox Church understand religious freedom in terms of collective rather than individual rights; that is, the right of "traditional" communities to exist side by side rather than for individuals to have the ability to change faiths. This perspective reinforces a premodern, progress-resistant worldview that emphasizes identification with a narrower community and discourages individual choice.

Several other challenges have hampered the Orthodox tradition from fully evolving to endorse modern political and economic institutions. While the Moscow Council of 1917–18 was similar in many ways to the Second Vatican Council of the Roman Catholic Church in its attempts to adapt Orthodox teaching and practice to modern realities, its decisions were largely stillborn once the Soviet state unleashed its persecution of religion. And while the intellectual heritage of the council was carried into exile and has profoundly influenced Orthodox theology, several challenges at the mass cultural level have inhibited the process of modernization.

Indeed, one can observe the tension between an "intellectual" or "theological" Orthodoxy and the "folk" or "popular" Orthodoxy, which may contain a number of pre-Christian elements. At times the intellectual and the folk traditions stand in radical opposition to each other. Take, for example, the question of women's ministries in the institutional church. Within the "intellectual" tradition of the Orthodox Church, great emphasis was placed on spiritual equality between the sexes. Chrysostom himself contrasted "traditional" gender roles in secular society with equal participation in the work of the church: "It is accepted that the woman should remain at home and man occupy himself with the interest of the city.... but in labors concerning the church...woman surpasses man in valor" and endurance. Women should not "think that zeal and labor for the good of the church is foreign to your sex."[19]

Nevertheless, the diaconal, teaching, and service ministries of women in the Byzantine period were largely an urban and upper-class phenomenon. Among the lower classes and in rural areas, other ideas—about female "purity" and "proper" gender roles, often pre-Christian in origin—eviscerated many of the women's ministries from the life of the church, even to the point of removing them from books of canon law. Both progressive and patriarchal positions can find support within the Orthodox tradition. On a host of social issues, Orthodox continue to debate which traditions represent the "authentic" Orthodox voice.

In fact, one can point to a dramatic divide in Orthodoxy, between an intellectual tradition that can serve as the basis for a "progress-prone" culture, and the historic and popular interpretations of Orthodoxy that reinforce elements characteristic of a "progress-resistant" culture.[20] The patristic writings stress the value of work and the need for personal responsibility and emphatically reject fatalism. Popular expressions of Orthodoxy, on the other hand, seem to encourage passive acceptance of one's fate, the value of conformity, and a decidedly "magical" approach to the world.

This debate is complicated in many of the countries of the Orthodox zone because of the enforced secularization of the Communist era. In the Russian Empire before 1917 and in many of the Balkan countries such as Romania (before 1945), the church's relationship to the surrounding state and society was widely and openly debated. Today, however, the church's forced expulsion from society in Communist countries has produced a class of people who are well educated in secular matters but have only a rudimentary knowledge of the Orthodox tradition, and of its rituals and customs far more than its theology and ethics.

Thus many profess a nominal Orthodox identity without being familiar with the church's teachings. This gap is further reinforced by low levels of church attendance. Though up to 70 percent of Russian citizens identify themselves as Orthodox, surveys consistently show that only about 5 to 10 percent are active members of the Orthodox Church. This pattern is mirrored elsewhere in the Orthodox world: 6 percent of Greeks, 7 percent of Serbs, and 10 percent of Georgians and Ukrainians are active churchgoers. In contrast, 45 percent of Romanians and 48 percent of Cypriots attend regularly.

It is not surprising, then, that many Russians—and by extension, other eastern Europeans—do not believe that Orthodoxy has much to contribute to solving current social and political problems, despite the church's issuing of documents like the "Social Doctrine."[21] This skepticism is particularly inopportune at a time when eastern Europeans face "the task of rebuilding [their] cultural identity and [their] social, political and economic institutions from scratch."[22] Moreover, it opens up a dangerous possibility: that the Orthodox tradition will cease to be a living, evolving cultural force and may instead become a museum institution, faithfully transmitting a premodern past. The church's continuing use in its liturgy of archaic forms of Greek, Arabic, and Church Slavonic rather than the modern vernacular is one of the most visible signs of this tendency. It also has strong roots in the recent Orthodox past, when the church was seen as the repository of a "Golden Age," the guardian of a past cultural heritage in danger of being completely lost. This was the role Orthodoxy played during the centuries when the Ottomans occupied the eastern Mediterranean region, and, to a lesser extent, during the Communist period. The negative side of this role, however, is that "unable to keep up with the West," Orthodoxy may choose to fence itself off and focus on preservation rather than evolution.[23]

In fact, a current snapshot of Russian Orthodox life would reveal several of the features that Daniel Etounga-Manguelle has identified as the main impediments to progress and modernization: highly centralized, vertical traditions of authority; a focus on the past as opposed to the future; an intellectual life characterized by irrationality and fatalism; and the suppression of individual initiative and achievement.[24] This is why, in certain dioceses of the Russian Orthodox Church, reforms are being promulgated in the educational system. The Rev. Aleksandr Ranne, head of the Novgorod diocese's department for religious education, observes that "the church should have value in the eyes of the contemporary individual not simply because of its...history and the glorious pages of the past, but because of the power of God's redeeming will."[25]

Reform, however, competes with another option: Westernization. Why should a nation make the effort to reform a traditional culture when it can simply import Western institutions and substitute Western norms and values? Ever since Peter the Great instituted his reforms, politicians and intellectuals in the Orthodox lands—first in Russia, then in the Balkans and the Middle East—have considered Westernization the path to modernization.

The problem here, however, is that transplanted institutions and values must sink roots in their new environment if they are to thrive. This is why, particularly in the early 1990s, one found an emphasis on "replacing the soil." In evaluating that approach, Nicolai Petro described "the prevailing attitude" that "Russian culture was deficient, incapable of generating the values needed to support the transition to democratic systems of governance and free markets." He believes that "the over-idealization of the West, and especially of America," is one reason "for the current backlash against American culture one observes in contemporary Russia."[26] It is also evident in the reaction of voters in Russia; those political parties and movements that have advocated the complete adoption of Western models as a guide for political and economic reform have been largely displaced by centrist reform parties that advocate a distinctive Russian approach to these questions. On the other hand, the Cypriot experience shows how British-derived democratic political institutions can thrive in a traditionally Orthodox nation, in part because these newer forms meshed well with historic practices, such as local self-government in villages and parishes and the election of bishops by clergy–laity councils.

Moreover, the historical experience of the Orthodox world with Westernization is not that the latter succeeded in replacing traditional culture, but that Western and traditional cultures ended up coexisting side by side. This tendency has been most pronounced among Greeks, who conceive of themselves as the heirs of both the "originators" of Western civilization and the Byzantine Empire. A Greek therefore navigates between a modern, "progress-prone" Western world and its values (the world of the "Hellene"), and traditional Orthodox culture, with many "progress-resistant" elements (the world of the "Romios"—a term for those in the Byzantine Empire who continued the ways of the old Roman Empire). As Patrick Leigh Fermor remarked, "inside every Greek dwell two figures in opposition, namely, the Romios and the Hellene, though all Greeks are in fact an amalgam in varying degrees of both, contradicting and completing each other."[27]

This process of adaptation will likely continue for the foreseeable future. Though ignorant of their own tradition, the masses within the Orthodox world remain attuned to what they perceive to be their own culture and to what appears to be foreign. Metropolitan Kirill described the need to understand that "Eastern Europe does not want to blindly follow rules developed some time ago by someone without its participation and without consideration of its inhabitants' philosophy of life simply because these rules are applied at present in the materially prospering countries of the West."[28] This explains why Russian political parties across the spectrum—from the Communist Party on the left to the bloc headed by Zhirinovskii on the right, and every centrist, prodemocratic, and proreform party in the middle—regularly seek the imprimatur of the Russian Orthodox Church, as the titular representative of Russian values and mores, as evidence that they are indeed working for the popular welfare and Russia's national interests.

In the end, much depends on two separate but interrelated processes. The first is whether the guardians of the Orthodox tradition—not simply the clergy but also its intellectuals and activists—are prepared to actively reimagine the Orthodox tradition in ways that are more conducive to supporting democracy and free market institutions. The second is whether the bulk of the populations of the Orthodox world—especially the unchurched—will accept this reimagination as a legitimate expression of their traditional culture. Again, the answer is unclear. The experience of the Russian north demonstrates that it is possible to engineer a broad consensus in favor of reform and modernization while crafting a link to traditional culture and national identity. Yet the experience of the Greeks in the modern era also points to the possibility of simultaneously maintaining a traditional, progress-resistant culture alongside a modern, Western, progress-prone culture.

Lawrence Harrison observes:

> Religious reform can be a potent agent of positive cultural change when it: (1) stresses the future and the concept of progress, (2) encourages an ethical code that helps to extend the radius of trust in society, (3) discourages authoritarianism and (4) encourages the belief that human beings can control their destinies.[29]

Is such reform possible within the Orthodox Church, and more specifically the Russian Orthodox Church? And can it have a correspondingly positive effect on the larger culture? The Novgorod experience suggests that it is possible. A successful reengineering of the culture at the local level has produced tangible results. The gross regional product has grown an average of 4 percent every year since 1995. Novgorod has the second lowest investment risk in Russia, out of eighty-nine regions. While foreign direct investment is only 5 percent of all investment in Russia, in the Novgorod region it is half. Novgorod ranks as one of the more democratic regions of Russia and is in the top quarter of all Russian regions for the number of civic associations and nongovernmental organizations. Meanwhile, the Orthodox Church has experienced a genuine revival, but not at the expense of denying religious freedom to others: outside observers call the Russian north the "most ecumenical region in the whole of Russia."[30]

It remains to be seen, however, whether the revival that has occurred in Novgorod and other northern regions will be transferred to the national church as a whole. A May 2000 conference at St. Andrew's College in Moscow, "The Rebirth of Religion and the Birth of Democracy in Russia,"[31] addressed the question of church reform. Rev. Sergei Hackel called attention to the "persistence of absolutist patterns of government" in Orthodoxy and the need to take up the reformist program of the 1917–18 Moscow Council. Rev. Vladimir Fedorov cited popular ignorance, pessimism, and maximalism as factors that have hindered revival in the Russian Church. Rev. Veniamin Novik noted that the church needed to "renounce the exaggerated collectivism of Russian culture" in favor of embracing "a Christian personalism in which respect for individual freedom is uppermost." The conference's final document observed that "religious revival in Russia can also be a democratic renewal," but it warned that "ignorance, passivity and inadequate education are important barriers to renewal of church and society."

Herein lies the challenge for the Russian Orthodox Church. Many regions of Russia have signed cooperation agreements with the Orthodox Church to develop curricula covering what would be termed "character education" in the United States and describe the role of the Orthodox Church in Russian history and culture. In some cases, such as in Novgorod, an emphasis has been placed on those elements of Russian history and culture that support modern institutions. However, "The Foundations of Orthodox Culture," a draft curriculum prepared by the Ministry of Education for a nationwide program and released in November 2002, has raised some concerns. Apart from the question of whether such a program is constitutional (although the courses will be optional), the curriculum's content is problematic for those hoping that the central leadership of the Russian church will follow the recommendations made at the St. Andrews conference. Religious organizations are predictably concerned about the sections dealing with other faiths, which reflect a nineteenth-century, antiecumenical attitude toward other religions, raising very real concerns about whether this curriculum will promote tolerance and mutual respect.

Of even greater concern is how the curriculum presents the tradition. It emphasizes the Muscovite legacy of the Orthodox experience in Russia, with its emphasis on statism and ritualism, at the expense of the more democratic and tolerant periods of early Rus and the medieval Russian north. In terms of political theology, the students are expected to study the life of the Emperor Constantine and of the medieval Moscow princes; nowhere does the curriculum address Orthodoxy's potential compatibility with modern democracy. They would also study the 2000 "Bases of the Social Conception of the Russian Orthodox Church," but with little consideration of how the Orthodox tradition might be able to evolve from a premodern, collectivist outlook to one in touch with modernity.

The deputy head of the government administration, Aleksei Volin, has openly criticized the curriculum, which he says "reeks of medievalism and obscurantism."[32] The Rev. Kiprian Yashchenko, dean of the pedagogical department at St. Tikhon Orthodox Theological Institute and one author of the course, says they are revising the materials to take some of these concerns into account, noting that if the program "does not create a field for thinking, then we will definitely kill the cause."[33] Still, the danger remains that this program may reinforce the tendency to view Orthodoxy as a component of historic Russian culture but with little relevance to current life, thus helping to reinforce the xenophobic aspects of Russian nationalism.

Canon Michael Bourdeaux, a longtime observer of the Russian Orthodox Church, opined: "Despite the problems confronting the Russian Orthodox Church today, and the issues that cloud its past, many positive things are happening. Perhaps, through them, it will find the confidence to embark on a new era."[34] The foundation for reform exists, but it is not yet clear whether construction will begin.

Greece: Orthodoxy, Culture, and the Economy
A Response to Nikolas Gvosdev

Georges Prevelakis

Greece is perceived as a country with chronic economic difficulties. Considered "underdeveloped" during the 1950s, 1960s, and 1970s, even today it is the "bad pupil" of the European Union. As the only Christian Orthodox country in the West during the Cold War, can Greece be a useful case study for anticipating the fortunes of post-communist Orthodox countries? We will see that only to a small extent can the Greek case be interpreted through the prism of religious culture; in respect to economic goals and modernization, however, religion has more often had a positive than a negative influence.

First we must distinguish between Greece and Greeks. Comparing the wealth of Greek ship owners during the 1950s and 1960s with the state of the Greek economy in the same period shows that the two do not always move in tandem. Outside Greece, Greeks generally succeed economically. In that way they are more comparable to Jews, Armenians, Lebanese, or Chinese than to other Orthodox Christians. Like these groups, they live in a diasporic culture that often prompts individuals and families to benefit from global networking.

Is this attribute "Greek," "post-Ottoman," or simply Mediterranean? Greek economic networks are founded on anthropological elements similar to those of other Mediterranean diasporas. They do, however, have some distinctive characteristics, including the continuity myth, the role of the Greek state, the global influence of the Greek language (on the classics, scientific vocabulary, Christianity) and the structuring function of the Greek church (under the Constantinople patriarchate).

The Greek state was not created, as is usually thought, to satisfy the political needs of a preexisting Greek nation dominated by the "Turks." Rather, it emerged—together with the nation—because of an imperative European need. Modernity's rupture with the past required it to idealize a Golden Era of Antiquity: the Enlightenment as a return to a remote past rather than as an adventure toward an unknown future. The reincarnation of Ancient Greece in the form of a modern nation-state served as a tangible justification for this project.

Modern Greece was therefore created to serve Europe ideologically. Its symbolic role was its main source of political capital and principal economic asset. As the 2004 Olympic Games have shown, Greece is still a myth-selling enterprise. Servicing its European and American clientele and seeking the best prices for those services has been much more important than developing industrial or other activities. It is in this context that we should understand the inefficiencies of the Greek economy.

This interpretation can explain such apparently puzzling episodes as the recent "Macedonian question." For Greece, historical mythology is a more valuable resource than oil is for the Gulf countries. The benefits coming in from outside (American aid in the 1950s,

European funds in the 1980s and 1990s) are distributed among the "shareholders" of the national myth: the inhabitants of Greek territory. This process is regulated through an elaborate political, electoral, and bureaucratic machine that involves the state, patronage, and corruption. Having functioned for more than two centuries, it has created an original political culture. This culture creates major obstacles to productive economic development but also generates income on a massive scale. The know-how it represents is evenly distributed among the elite (power to attract support from the West) and the simple people (capacity to obtain their share from the political leadership).

From this brief analysis of the two categories of state and diaspora, it is obvious that religion has a much more complex influence than usually thought. The Greek case does not confirm the hypothesis of an Orthodox Christian family in respect to economic behavior. There are as many differences from other Orthodox Christians as there are similarities, and the Greeks can be successfully compared to populations of other religions. Again, to the extent that religious culture plays a role in the economy, it is generally positive.

The Greek Orthodox Church has a strong charitable function, inherited from the *vakf* system in the Ottoman Empire. In order to maintain this role, the church in diaspora depends on donations from its wealthy members. Not surprisingly, it encourages economic achievement. Its message is clear: *enrichissez-vous*, get rich. A complex system of distinctions rewards wealthy philanthropists. In the United States, the favorable social and ideological environment has helped transform the Greek-American church into an important economic actor and a key source of financial support for the Patriarchate of Constantinople. Protestant values absorbed from the environment, combined with the tradition of social promotion inherited from the Ottoman past, have led to a Greek-American cultural profile that guarantees economic efficiency: Greek-Americans work hard so that they can obtain status through religious philanthropy.

Inside the Greek state, Orthodoxy has sometimes, but not always, functioned as a brake on modernization. Scholarly authors who defend "orthodox" Orthodoxy criticize the church that is associated with the Greek state as too much influenced by Protestant values. (The relations between this autocephalous Greek Orthodox Church and the Constantinople Patriarchate are too complex to be discussed here.)

Orthodox culture inside Greece is thus far from monolithic. Orthodoxy has, however, played another fundamental role: it has been the major element of the modern Greek national identity and in that sense has made an essential contribution to nation-building. As we saw before, the alternative element, the reference to Ancient Greece, is an exportable good rather than "glue" for the national community. Orthodoxy's role in the Greek economy has thus been indirect but essential. Without a strong national identity, the country would have had no stability, therefore no economic progress. The Orthodox Church, in spite of its traditionalistic appearance, has functioned as the major factor in modernization by filling in the vacuum of an artificial neoclassical national identity.

Notes

1. Remarks of Metropolitan Kirill of Smolensk, Chairman of the Department of External Church Relations of the Moscow Patriarchate. "International Integration and Civilizational Diversity of Humanity," Inaugural Meeting of the European Council of Religious Leaders, Oslo, Norway, November 11, 2002.
2. Based on those norms, the twenty countries comprising "the Orthodox world" are usually considered to be Albania, Armenia, Belarus, Bosnia-Hercegovina, Bulgaria, Cyprus, Eritrea, Estonia, Ethiopia, Finland, Greece, Lebanon, Macedonia, Moldova, Romania, the Russian Federation, Syria, Ukraine, and Yugoslavia (Serbia-Montenegro). Poland, Lithuania, Latvia, and Kazakhstan also have large Orthodox communities and are represented in the European Inter-Parliamentary Assembly of Orthodoxy. For a definition of the zone of Orthodox Christian civilization in terms of the "Byzantine Commonwealth," see Dimitri Obolensky, *The Byzantine Commonwealth* (Crestwood, NY: St. Vladimir's Seminary Press, 1971), 13; John Meyendorff, *Imperial Unity and Christian Divisions* (Crestwood, NY: St. Vladimir's Seminar Press, 1989), 5; Garth Fowden, *Empire to Commonwealth: Consequences of Monotheism* (Princeton, NJ: Princeton University Press, 1993), 128.
3. Taken from Eusbeius' "Oration" before the Emperor Constantine (335), and quoted in Nikolas K. Gvosdev, *An Examination of Church-State Relations in the Byzantine and Russian Empires* (Lewiston, NY: Edwin Mellen Press, 2001), 22.
4. G. Ostrogorsky, "The Byzantine Emperor and the Hierarchical World Order," *Slavonic and East European Review* 35 (1956), 4.
5. Alexei Khomiakov, quoted in Nikolas K. Gvosdev, *Emperors and Elections: Reconciling the Orthodox Tradition with Modern Politics* (Huntington, NY: Nova Press, 2000), 6.
6. Quoted in Gvosdev, *Emperors and Elections*, 3.
7. Quoted in Gvosdev, *Emperors and Elections*, 44. This quote is drawn from Chrysostom's *Homilies on St. Paul's Epistle to the Romans*.
8. Nicolai N. Petro, "A Russian Model of Development: What Novgorod Can Teach the West," in *Civil Society and the Search for Justice in Russia*, eds. Christopher Marsh and Nikolas K. Gvosdev (Lanham, MD: Lexington Books, 2002), 44.

9. Mikhail Prusak, *Reform v Provintsii* (Moscow: Veche, 1999), 96.
10. This interview was conducted by the Italian journalist Oriana Fallaci and was later published as part of a collection in *Interview with History* (London: Liveright, 1976).
11. "Keston Survey of Religion Across Russia Goes on Sale in Moscow," *Keston News Service*, April 26, 2002. The book in question is *Religiya i obshchestvo: ocherki sovremennoi religioznoi zhizni Rossii*, edited by Sergei Filatov.
12. Theodore Karasik, "Russia's Northern Cities," *Johnson's Russia List*, no. 4029 (January 12, 2000).
13. "Appeal of the Holy Synod of Bishops," no. 1966 (September 21, 2000).
14. "Television Appeal of the Most Holy Patriarch of Moscow and all Rus' Aleksii II in Connection With the Elections for President of the Russian Federation," March 25, 2000. Distributed by the Communications Service of the Department of External Church Affairs, Moscow Patriarchate, and archived at http://www.russian-orthodox church.org.ru/nr003241.htm. (Accessed October 31, 2001)
15. The complete text of the document is contained on the website of the Moscow Patriarchate, at http://www.russian-orthodox-church.org.ru/sd00r.htm.
16. Comments of the archbishop can be found on the diocesan website (in Russian) at http://eparhia.onego.ru/rodmanl.htm.
17. "Statement of His All Holiness Ecumenical Patriarch Bartholomew For the Forthcoming United Nations Durban World Conference Against Racism, Racial Discrimination, Xenophobia, and Related Intolerance," March 17, 2001. (A copy is archived at http://www.orthodoxa.org/GB/patriarchate/speech/statement.htm)
18. Interview in *Rossiiskaya Gazeta*, January 6, 2001.
19. Quoted in Matushka Ellen Gvosdev, *The Female Diaconate: An Historical Perspective* (Minneapolis, MN: Light and Life Publishing, 1991), 10.
20. A typology of the two types of culture is provided in "Culture Matters: How Values Shape Human Progress," Presentation and Discussion with Lawrence E. Harrison," at the Canadian Centre for Foreign Policy Development, October 6, 2000, Ottawa, Canada, and archived at http://dsp-psd.communication.gc.ca/Collection/E2-227-2000E.pdf.
21. See my "The New Party Card? Orthodoxy and the Search for Post-Soviet Russian Identity," *Problems of Post-Communism* 47, no. 6 (November/December 2000), esp. 31, 32.
22. Petro, 42.
23. Schmemann, 283, 284.
24. As found in Lawrence E. Harrison, *Underdevelopment Is a State of Mind: The Latin American Case*, rev. ed. (Lanham, MD: Madison Books, 1985, 2000), xxiii–xxiv. See Etounga-Manguelle's chapter in *Culture Matters*.
25. A full report on the church educational system in the Novgorod diocese is available at the diocesan website (in Russian), at http://www.novgorod.ru/rus/cult/eparhia/articles/39.htm
26. Petro, 46.
27. Quoted by John Leatham in his "translator's note" to Helene Ahrweiler, *The Making of Europe: Lectures and Studies* (Athens: Livanis Publishers, 2000); see also Leonard A. Stone, "A Dialogue of Past and Present: The Construction and

(Re)presentation of Greek National Identity," *Perceptions* 4, no. 2 (1999) for a discussion of how Greeks have moved between these two poles.

28. "International Integration and Civilizational Diversity of Humanity."
29. Harrison, 171.
30. Petro, 43–44.
31. This conference was sponsored by St. Andrew's Biblical-Theological College, an independent Orthodox institution in Moscow, and its findings are archived at http://www.standrews.ru/eng/news/conf.html.
32. Andrei Zolotov, Jr., "Schools to Teach Orthodox Culture," *Moscow Times* (November 18, 2002).
33. Zolotov.
34. Bourdeaux, 23.

12

Market Development, Political Change, and Chinese Cultures

ROBERT P. WELLER

As one might expect from a place with such a long history and complex society, Chinese culture contains many strands. Even some stereotypically core features of Chinese culture have varied widely. We see, for example, strong lineages in some areas, with ancestor worship strictly patrilineal. Other areas, however, had no lineages and hardly seemed patrilineal at all; families in the Taiwanese village where I first did research typically worshipped two or three surnames on their altars, coming from both the male and female lines. Chinese society also had cultural resources for quite varying economic attitudes. Imperial China had a strong state that gave very low status to merchants and favored central economic control, yet it also allowed extensive market development where merchants thrived. A cultural emphasis on hierarchy and consensus was met with strongly individualistic streams and chronic structural conflicts, even within the family.

These cultural strands, which I will expand on below, constantly interacted with each other and with broader economic and political processes. Thus, to cite a trivial example, those Taiwanese villagers who worshipped their mothers' or wives' ancestors along with their own paternal ones did not have a fundamentally different idea of kinship from their neighbors who organized into strict patrilineages.

Instead, they were reacting to their broader conditions of life. As relatively recent migrants they did not own much land (which forms the economic core of a lineage), they had very shallow genealogical histories, and they relied heavily on relations through marriage to create social networks. The culture of Chinese kinship allows both patterns, although certain conditions can cause one pattern to dominate. Culture does not directly create this kinship system, the way a mold turns out identical plastic toys. Instead, culture shapes the possible lines of development in interaction with other local conditions.

In the analysis that follows I examine some of the cultural features that appear closely related to successful market economies, to political democratization, or both. These include individualism, a work ethic, highly valued education, civility, and trust with its associated social capital. In each case, I will begin with the multiple possibilities that lie within Chinese economic and political cultures, and the ways they have shaped and been shaped by social change.

In order to be useful in today's world, these cultural features need not necessarily match those that the West has identified in its own history. More than one path may lead to market success and to democracy. Ample evidence of alternate modernities and alternate civilities already exists in East Asia, and in this chapter I will continue to explore those possibilities. I will conclude with some speculation about the possible policy implications of this approach, which takes culture seriously, but only in a carefully grounded local context.

Chinese Cultures and Market Behavior

Max Weber took a long look at imperial Chinese economic culture and concluded that it offered little potential for capitalist development beyond the simple merchant capitalism of trade for profit.[1] He noted that the early Chinese economy had many features in common with medieval Europe, but that it had not had Europe's capitalist revolution. One reason for this, he argued, was the successful creation of an imperial state over two thousand years ago, putting an end to a period of interstate competition that had driven rapid change in both material culture and thought in the centuries before the Qin and Han Dynasties.

One consequence of this, in Weber's view, was that systems of thought never developed that might offer the driving tension that

Protestantism provided in Europe. Daoism left people living in an "enchanted world," while Confucianism consistently downgraded the world of the market. Merchants thus ranked lowest in a Confucian class hierarchy, inferior to scholars, peasants, and artisans. During some periods, they were not even allowed to take the civil service examinations. China viewed itself in many ways as a tributary state, with the larger economy working primarily through centralized redistribution, supported largely by rural tax payments and corvée labor. Merchants, in this view, were social leeches who profited from the productive labor of others.

This Weberian understanding was enormously influential among China scholars in the 1950s and 1960s, but it has not stood the test of time. First, of course, this line of analysis failed to predict or explain the tremendous economic successes of many Chinese societies in the last half of the twentieth century, including Hong Kong, Taiwan, Singapore, and many Chinese overseas communities. Just as importantly, it did not sufficiently recognize either China's enormous commercial development, especially over the past millennium, or the cultural features that were part of that development.

Small-scale production of commodities for markets has been a standard feature of Chinese life for many centuries. Some areas saw mass production of commodities like porcelain or silk for long-distance trade. Even a frontier backwater like Taiwan, which only became a province in 1884, lived primarily by the market. By about 1900, many of its farmers were producing high-grade rice which they exported to the mainland and to southeast Asia, buying cheaper rice on the market for their own meals. They also exported tea, camphor, sugar, and other commodities for the world market. Late imperial mainland China had extraordinarily well-developed land and labor markets in many areas.

While the degree of commercial development varied widely over space and time, the overall commercialization meant that a sophisticated cultural infrastructure developed for dealing with markets. Share-holding corporations, for example, were widespread. They were not just common in business arrangements, but formed the legal basis of many village-based organizations like community temples or lineages. Chinese were also intimately familiar with contracts, and it is still very easy to find peasant households that have retained Qing Dynasty contracts for land sales, property arrangements when families divided, and many other purposes.

China's legacy of economic culture is thus complex and multiple. It contained elements of centralized state control and elements of market freedom. It varied over time and space, with peripheral areas often having less commercial development. Attitudes toward the economy also varied by class, especially because the political elite was trained in Confucian philosophy. To some extent, though, nearly every individual could access this range of market cultures, acting sometimes in accord with the state-centered model and sometimes with the market-based model. Even local worship of deities reflected this complexity. Put simply, most people worshipped deities who drew their authority from a kind of feudal model of enfoeffment by the emperor, and whose power echoed the kinds of power the secular government exercised. These were deities dressed as imperial officials, in temples that resembled a magistrate's official offices, addressed often through preprinted petition documents like those used by the government. Yet the act of worship also always involved the exchange of cash in the form of "spirit money" (*ming qian*) printed on cheap paper and burned for the benefit of the deities. Many interactions with deities took the form of contractual promises to deliver services in exchange for gifts to the temple or other vows of piety.

Individualism

To Weber, Calvinism had facilitated the capitalist revolution in part by freeing the individual from the "sib fetters" of family and kinship, and thus allowing a new range of social interactions based on individual responsibility and trust beyond personal ties. Important sources for individualism had long existed in Western cultures, from both religious and classical republican sources, but individualism grew to its current culturally dominant position only with the triumph of market capitalism. More communal versions of the self largely gave way to the idea of an autonomous individual. One worry about China's economic future from Weber through the development theory of the 1960s was that a Confucian emphasis on harmony and hierarchy, on the fundamentally social nature of the self, would prove incompatible with market economics.

Like an earlier Europe, though, China in fact had many lines of thought about the self, some of which emphasized a high degree of individual autonomy. Confucianism certainly did emphasize harmony and hierarchy, taking an idealized image of the patrilineal family as a metaphor for society as a whole, and emphasizing how actions must accord with people's proper roles. "The nail that sticks up gets hammered down," as the proverb goes.

But there is another side to this. As William de Bary says, "Confucian ethics, instead of being primarily a social or group ethic, as it is often referred to, starts with self-cultivation, and works outward from a proper sense of self to the acceptance of reciprocal responsibilities with others."[2] Those responsibilities could include challenging both harmony and hierarchy. Confucian officials had a duty to remonstrate with an emperor following improper policy, for instance. They were morally obliged to disagree with mistaken authority, and China has honored officials who suffered, sometimes at the cost of their lives, in carrying out this responsibility. An annual festival still commemorates Qu Yuan, whose remonstrance led to his suicide two millennia ago. The tradition has continued through today, in the posthumous rehabilitation of officials, like Liu Shaoqi or Peng Zhen, who dared to disagree with Mao Zedong.

Other ideas also offered resources for individualism. Daoists tended to celebrate eccentrics, like the Eight Immortals—some known for their appearance as beggars, some for their indulgence in women and wine, but none of whom showed much attachment to the communal virtues of family or state. Buddhists had a rather different reputation for individualism, particularly visible in the frequent criticism that they avoided communal responsibilities (filial piety above all) by leaving the family to cultivate themselves.

Popular worship of spirits also picked up on these themes, allowing for both highly communal and highly individualized notions of self. In the realm of gods, temples often promoted images of gods as parallels to secular bureaucrats, given ranks and titles by the earthly emperor in a feudal process that reinforced the cosmic power of the state. On the other hand, many deities were associated with violence and asocial behavior. Ghosts, generally thought of as the spirits of the unworshipped dead, were the extreme form of unincorporated spirits. Often nameless, they affected the living by causing illness or other problems. They could be bought off with offerings, and they would also grant wishes on a kind of contract basis. Asocial, atomized, amoral, they would do anything. It is no coincidence that ghost temples grew particularly large and popular during the period of Taiwan's most rapid market growth in the 1980s.

This issue of ghosts brings up the two sides of individualism. Chinese ghosts do offer an image of individuals unfettered by social ties, whose relationships are above all based on market and contractual exchanges. On the other hand, they also tend to be malevolent and unreliable exactly because they lack the control of broader communal and social ties. In the same way, individualism is an important underpinning of market success, but also sometimes leads to self-serving behavior—greed, corruption, crime—that undermines the market system. Individualism may be one key to a thriving market economy, but only if it is somehow embedded in the broader society. Even in the United States individualism has broader social supports, as Granovetter and others have argued.[3]

The key, then, is less having the cultural resources to develop a Western-style individualism than having the resources to combine an ethic of individual achievement with broader social values. It may well be that thriving market economies are compatible with a wide range of such combinations. Indeed, a kind of networked capital seems to have developed in most Chinese societies, including most recently the People's Republic under the economic reforms. This is a form of social capital built around interpersonal relationships or *guanxi*. These relationships overlap with but are not identical to the ascribed and particularistic ties that Weberians saw as an obstacle to market development. They include ties of kinship and neighborhood, but even these are fundamentally socially constructed in China. Beyond the immediate family, such ties create an easier path for the development of *guanxi*, but there are no guarantees. Trustworthiness (*xinyong*) is as important a consideration as blood; in this sense even kinship networks are selective. Other kinds of ties, like classmates or just friends (both accepted Confucian relationships with a long history), are even more obviously constructed.

Many studies have documented the importance of such ties in Chinese business arrangements in Hong Kong, Taiwan, and overseas Chinese communities in Southeast Asia.[4] More recent studies show the same kind of thing developing in China itself now that the market economy is opening up.[5] While some have suggested that this reliance on interpersonal ties discourages the development of very large companies, the evidence is now overwhelming that this particularly Chinese adaptation to capitalism has worked very well. Even if it is true that large corporations are more difficult to organize under this system, it is no longer clear that large corporations are necessarily superior in the current economy dominated by innovation and market flexibility.

Work Discipline and Savings

For Weber, Protestantism created an inherent tension with the world: Calvinism led not to the fatalism one might expect from its belief in predetermination, but to a constant pressure to prove oneself to be among the elect through success in the secular world. Work became an end in itself, as people lived to work instead of working to live. Capital accumulation for reinvestment was a natural byproduct, because people no longer consumed as conspicuously. Weber recognized that this was an ideal type, and that market capitalism would eventually drive this sort of behavior using the "iron cage" of its own logic, with no need for Calvinism.

Still, in his view the Protestant tension with the secular world had been a crucial driver of early modern capitalism. One reason he was pessimistic about China's economic possibilities was that he saw no moral tension to drive people toward ever more efficient ways of working. Neither Confucianism nor Daoism, he argued, lifted the Chinese out of their "enchanted world" in a way that would drive new forms of secular behavior. This claim, however, always ran up against the empirical problem that Chinese seem to work very hard indeed, and that they show high rates of savings. Thomas Metzger wrote an extended analysis of possible Confucian sources for a tension with the world that would parallel Weber's analysis of Protestantism, based on the neo-Confucian demand to constantly reform the self.[6]

While it is not clear how this philosophy would have influenced the behavior of ordinary people in China, Harrell has argued that quite different factors promoted hard work and high savings rates.[7] Filial piety demands that people provide for their descendants—not just their children, but an entire patriline that extends, in principle, forever. Informants will often offer just this explanation, and they see it realized concretely through practices like the creation of large lineage estates that could generate significant income. They work hard and save so that their descendants will prosper forever.

None of this led to a capitalist revolution comparable to Europe's, in part because of the broader political system that encompassed these values. Still, they would be important causes of China's eventual comfort with market capitalism. They are not really functional equivalents of the Protestant ethic—the logic driving them is quite different—but they have been crucial to the market success of many Chinese societies.

Education

Education was not one of the areas that Weber particularly stressed, but most current development professionals give it a high priority. Some of the reasons are common sense: all but the worst jobs require basic literacy and numeracy, and this trend is only increasing. Small entrepreneurship, which is frequently an engine for growth, benefits particularly from education. Other reasons stem from the regular correlation between educational levels and many indicators of development, including high income, good health, and low birth rates.

Societies can institutionalize education in ways that offer little direct effect on secular change, which is probably why Weber did not emphasize it. All of the societies that Weber compared systematically to Europe (China, India, and the ancient Near East) had traditions of literacy and even of virtuosic textual mastery. There is a great difference, though, between education as the extraordinary skill of the monk or the government clerk, and education as a way of opening up the world to the broader society. That is why the Protestant move to encourage everyone to read and interpret the Bible directly was so radical, especially paired with the development of the printing press.

Even by this measure, though, late imperial China does not look bad. While it is true that the upper reaches of Confucian educational competence were both extraordinarily virtuosic and limited to a very small group, we have increasing evidence that a broad range of the male population (and a much smaller range of the female) were somewhat literate. In addition, numbers of schools had expanded enormously and the publishing industry included new genres aimed at a popular audience, like religious morality books (*baojuan*). This occurred before the major influx of Western influences in the nineteenth century.[8]

Just as importantly, Chinese understandings of social life emphasized the ideas that education was a key to social mobility and that it was in principle available to anyone. Unlike a genuinely feudal system, late imperial China offered everyone the imaginative possibility of going from rags to riches based on hard work and study—Dale Carnegie with Chinese characteristics. Few achieved this, of course, but the existence of the idea was crucial. Education and its possibilities were crucial to the ways people thought about social status, but the entire economic system also allowed for the possibility of significant mobility, both upward and downward. Most land, for example, could be bought and sold on the open market by late imperial times, and peasants were not tied to the land, unlike their contemporaries in Russia or Japan.

As with any cultural value, however, many other factors also contribute to shaping behavior. People recognize the potential value of education, but must balance it against other needs and opportunities. The People's Republic of China, for example, saw an extended period where people put a high value on education because it was one of the few paths up to Communist Party membership, and thus to a possible life of power and privilege—not too unlike the situation in late imperial times. After the economic reforms of the 1980s, however, new paths to upward mobility opened outside the party. In addition, the return to family contracting of agricultural land and the general decollectivization in the countryside meant that families suddenly needed labor power at home. School attendance dropped because the opportunity structure of education had changed, even though its cultural value remained.

Economic Culture in Practice

On the eve of the major Western influx in the nineteenth century, China already had a long familiarity with markets and commodity production. All levels of society were familiar with contracts and shareholding arrangements, and they shared cultural elements that would coexist easily with the demands of the market economy that would come to dominate by the end of the twentieth century. On the other hand, they also had a set of values that downgraded mercantile success, and that channeled the best and brightest into politics and away from economics. These values themselves determine behavior only as people make decisions under the constraints of daily lives. Thus various aspects of this complex and sometimes contradictory tradition could come to the fore, depending on the changing structure of society as a whole.

One of the most dominating influences has been the structure of the state, which underwent radical transitions over the course of the twentieth century. Culture helps shape political systems themselves, but that should not lead us to underestimate the effects of political change on culture. The work ethic I have discussed, for example, has developed in different ways in various Chinese contexts. Many overseas Chinese develop the ethic to a degree that is even stronger than it was at home. Like many voluntary migrants, of course, they were not a random sample of the population. Migration selects for entrepreneurial characteristics like willingness to take risks and to work very hard. In addition, most of the early Chinese migrants intended to return home eventually. They were trying to build up family estates in a dramatic way.

While migrants were working long hours in difficult circumstances in Chinatowns around the world, however, urban workers in China under the planned economy were evolving in the opposite direction. No one could visit China even as late as the mid-1980s without noting the extraordinarily surly and unhelpful workers who staffed state-owned restaurants or bookstores. Economists complained that there were three or four workers for every job, leading to enormous expertise in the arts of malingering. At the heart of this was the policy of giving people an "iron rice-bowl"—a metaphor for an unbreakable source of income, a job from which they could not be fired. As state-owned enterprises began to lay off workers in the 1990s, many of their employees balked at the thought of the very different kind of life that would be required in the world of market competition.

Culture and values are not passed down automatically, like genes. They must be reproduced in each new generation, which opens up the possibility of reworking culture in times of change. To some extent, this has already happened with the work ethic. When I was asked to consult about the massive unemployment that would result when a European firm took over a Chinese steel factory, I found that the employees seemed to have little interest in diving into the sea of market risk, and much more interest in protecting their privileges as socialist workers. The laborer-elite of the planned economy was never a majority of the population, but it did show evidence of real cultural change away from a work ethic value. At least by anecdotal evidence, the most successful entrepreneurs in the market economy that has opened up are either well-connected officials or people who had been in marginal positions; they are much less likely to be the old privileged class of workers in state-owned enterprises.

Chinese patterns of networked capital—the reliance on personal ties in market relationships—also varied in their effects. They have become important primarily when the broader political context allows relatively free economic activity but does not offer it significant support. This has been the case for overseas Chinese communities in much of southeast Asia, although interesting variations occur. It was also true for Taiwan under the Nationalists. Most of these cases saw a few large businesses with very close government ties; in Taiwan a significant number were owned directly by the state or the Nationalist Party. The vast economy of small producers, however, was generally left to its own devices. Small entrepreneurs had little or no access to legally sanctioned credit, for example, because banks would not make loans unless the borrower already had significant collateral. This encouraged a boom in rotating credit associations, postdated checks, and other social mechanisms with no underpinning in the legal system. People relied on personal forms of trust because they lacked institutionalized forms.

Identical relationships are developing in the People's Republic today with the economic reforms. Large entrepreneurs have very close political ties, while the small ones are left on their own. The result has been an economic pattern that looks quite different from development out of a partially shared cultural background in Japan or South Korea, where a few very large corporations dominate the economy. We also have evidence, however, that Chinese will begin to rely on more purely market-based relationships, even in the absence of strong interpersonal connections, when the political and legal systems encourage it, as in Taiwan or Hong Kong in the last few years.[9]

This general reliance on personalistic ties has worked more successfully than modernization theorists expected. The explanation is largely that Chinese consciously create those ties based on ideas of trustworthiness (*xinyong*). They are not simply ascribed relationships predetermined by crusty tradition. In this case, premodern social ties have adapted themselves quite easily to modernity.

On the other hand, personal solidarities also form the core of corruption. The late imperial government recognized this in its fear of cliques and its avoidance rules that prevented officials from serving in their home areas. These mechanisms still did not prevent enormous amounts of rent-seeking by late Qing officials. The cultural ties that have served so well in developing small entrepreneurs in most Chinese societies have also formed natural lines of corruption. While graft is never an easy topic to study, it is clear that the People's Republic in the reform period has experienced enormous increases in corruption, with raw bribery often phrased exactly in the gift-giving language of traditional Chinese reciprocity. This rapid increase in corruption has to do with new economic policies that still have a weak basis in the rule of law or in broader social relationships.

Chinese Cultures and Political Behavior

Chinese tradition seems to offer few possible roots for democracy. China's various political systems—imperial, nationalist, and Communist—were all designed to be thoroughly driven from top to bottom, right up to the waning years of the twentieth century. The imperial system never had the slightest intention of working democratically, and both the Nationalist and the Communist Parties who ruled China for most of the twentieth century shared an essentially Leninist understanding of how the single-party state should work. Both paid lip service to the ideas of democracy, in their very different ways, but both in fact institutionalized powerful authoritarian rule.

Even at the village level, China had no institutional mechanisms of self-government. In late imperial times, the magistrate held all legal authority, and any village-level organization served to further his social control or ability to tax. The main techniques for this during the Qing were the *bao-jia* system, which organized people into units of ten, with mutual responsibility for surveillance and monitoring behavior, and the village contract (*xiangyue*) system, in which the magistrate or local elites would read an imperial statement about moral behavior. In practice, local elites like large landlords tended to control villages and would work closely with magistrates.

This pessimistic conclusion, however, cannot be the whole story. Taiwan lifted its decades-long "state of emergency" in 1987, legalized opposition political parties, and embarked on a rapid and remarkable course of democratization. This has been successful by almost any measure, leading ultimately to the election of a president from outside the Nationalist Party. No one could have imagined this two decades earlier. As with economic behavior, this success has important cultural precursors even without any kind of democratic tradition. Similarly again, those cultural elements are no guarantee of success, but simply offer a potential line of development that can only be realized under certain circumstances.

Civility

Democracy requires a set of values and social understandings as well as an institutional structure. China and Taiwan certainly lacked the institutional traditions, but they did not lack the kinds of community resources that Robert Putnam's work on social capital identifies as crucial to democratic development. These resources are the social bonds that allow the creation of a public sphere and eventually a civil society. I will discuss two such resources in particular: civility and trust.

The concept of civil society had no real equivalent in China until it was imported in the twentieth century. Even now the term has several competing translations. The "civil" half of the term, however, has a long and important Chinese tradition. Quick definitions often take civil society as those social organizations that fall between the family and the state. But not all such social organizations are civil. Gangsters, lynch mobs, and terrorist cells all fall between family and state. We must expand the quick definition by adding at least two other aspects of civility. First, these organizations must allow room for other groups whose agendas may differ. Second, they must accommodate, and be accommodated by, the state structure.

Two core Chinese concepts with long histories capture a great deal of this meaning of civility: *wen* and *li*. *Wen* literally means writing, but was used in many ways that overlap with "civil" and related words in English, including *wenming* (civilization) and *wenhua* (culture). Referring to officials, it indicated civil authorities, as opposed to the military. *Li* is usually translated as ritual or propriety. It included a wide range of behavior from the imperial rituals of the state cult to simple courtesy. Some of the greatest neo-Confucian thinkers, including Zhu Xi and Sima Guang, wrote manuals of *li* for household use, which included everything from how to conduct weddings to the proper format for writing letters or using calling cards. Ritual and courtesy are in many ways the same thing, and they meet a core need of civility: they allow people to interact and cooperate in spite of differences in interests, backgrounds, and even cultures. The imperial Ministry of *Li* was thus responsible for diplomacy, among other things.

These concepts of civility provided a resource for some amount of tolerance in late imperial China. In practice, however, they could become tools of political control as easily as they could develop into sources for civil society. Both *wen* and *li* found themselves at the center of republican and then Communist propaganda campaigns that intended to solidify control by managing even the smallest aspects of identity. Chiang Kai-shek's New Life Movement in the 1930s, for example, promoted personal hygiene and polite behavior in an effort to remold the population. It explicitly harked back to Confucian ideas of *li* even as it promoted the ideals of modernity, and all in the service of a very uncivil state. China echoed remarkably similar themes in the 1980s through campaigns to line up, not to spit, and to say "please" and "thank you." The long-held ethic of civility may have been important to the consolidation of democracy in Taiwan, but like any cultural value, it was no guarantee of any particular result.

Trust and Social Capital

The work of Robert Putnam, first in Italy and more recently in the United States, has brought increasing attention to the role of social capital in civil society. Putnam argues that horizontal ties of social trust create a sphere where individuals can influence the publicly shared understandings that govern collective life. These ties foster high levels of trust, which facilitate social coordination and decrease opportunities for corruption. An absence of such ties encourages an all-powerful state to step into the breach. Thus, he argues, northern Italy has fostered a thriving economy and civil society because of its long tradition of community association, while southern Italy has lagged behind because it relies instead on patron–client ties and other forms of vertical relationship.[10]

China does possess some of the resources that social capital theorists think are important. Certainly it was far better endowed than some recent observers have claimed. For example, Francis Fukuyama's assertion that "the lack of trust outside the family makes it hard for unrelated people to form groups or organizations" in China will not stand up to close scrutiny.[11] Chinese societies featured many kinds of organizations of related people, and they still do. Local elites organized into charitable groups to provide granaries for famine relief and schools for the children of the poor. They also constructed networks based simply on friendship, which was, after all, one of the five core Confucian social relationships.

Groups of unrelated people ran most temples dedicated to community deities. These were often organized as shareholding corporations, with local surname groups or neighborhood regions holding the shares. Sworn brotherhoods provided another cultural mechanism to unite a group of unrelated people through the metaphors of kinship. Various broader religious movements, from Buddhism to secret sects, brought people together as well. All of these mechanisms still exist. Even the kinship ties beyond the nuclear family that most people draw on are as much achieved as ascribed. Historically, the large lineages of southeastern China were not the automatic results of descent from a common ancestor, but were the creations of groups already on the ground, who left some kin out and included others. The kin ties that people actually mobilized in daily life also show their achieved nature, as people will draw selectively on certain kin.[12]

These networks are important in business, as I discussed briefly above, but also in politics. They played a major role in the organization of local elections in Taiwan during the authoritarian period, and have taken on similar roles in the People's Republic now that village elections take place there. Probably more important than those token elections in the long run is the way these traditions of horizontal connections have allowed people in Taiwan to adapt extraordinarily quickly to democracy once they finally had a chance. But simply changing institutional structures is not enough to guarantee the success of democracy, as we see from the failure or at least very stumbling beginning of democratic reforms in many places. The survival of these ties through decades of harsh authoritarian rule has allowed the Taiwanese to make a much easier transition to democracy than, for example, people in many Eastern European societies where communism had more successfully atomized local social ties.

But we must be cautious here. The concept of social capital runs the danger of fostering a naive and romantic communitarianism, a Toquevillian ideal type of local communities united through their voluntary organizations. In fact, of course, distinctions of power, age, and gender affect even village-level ties of trust. The situation is particularly complex in Chinese societies because the state often worked, or attempted to work, through just these ties. The Qing Dynasty attempted to mobilize village-level ties, for example, in the *bao-jia* system, which organized people into small groups to maintain security and help collect taxes.

The actual political legacies of such groups are thus mixed. Local temples could indeed act against an aggressive state, as when some temples in Taiwan organized against the Japanese takeover in 1895. But they could also organize hand-in-hand with the state, as when local elites organized militias against the Taiping Rebellion in the mid-nineteenth century, and based them in local temples. Modern Taiwan's environmental movement also shows some of the civil potential of temple-based ties. In one case the local temple successfully organized people in a three-year crusade opposing the construction of a light oil refinery. Elsewhere on the island, though, an identical refinery was built with little resistance after the investor made large donations to all the local temples. As with all the cultural resources I have discussed, these horizontal ties of trust have to be seen in a broader political and economic context. By themselves they are no guarantee of change.

One sign of Taiwan's successful transition to democracy was a sudden flowering of both social movements and civil organizations of all kinds after the long state of emergency was finally lifted in 1987. The previous decade had seen some organizations develop gradually in politically safe fields like environmental protection and consumers' rights, much as they are doing in China today. Immediately after 1987, though, full-blown movements emerged in labor, women's rights, indigenous people's rights, and nearly every other kind of social interest. Groups also suddenly thrived in areas well outside politics, from village-level amateur baseball teams (previously forbidden) to globalizing new Buddhist movements.

Most of these organizations came after democratization was well under way. They appear to be effects of democratic transition more than causes. Their rapid rise, however, was only possible because of the cultural and social resources that already existed. Ties like this appear to have played a crucial role in the successful consolidation of democracy more than in the transition itself.

The People's Republic of China, at least so far, shows instead the way such ties can be incorporated into hierarchy. For example, China has allowed a vast expansion in the number of nongovernmental organizations (NGOs) over the last few years. Most of them, however, are "nongovernmental" in name only. Much of their funding comes from government sources, and many of their officers are government officials who took early retirement or were appointed directly by supervising state offices. Legally, NGOs are part of a classic corporatist arrangement where only one group is permitted to represent each social sector; the state grants it a kind of monopoly in exchange for cooperation. In spite of this level of political incorporation, however, we still see significant mobilization of culturally sanctioned local ties to organize local demonstrations or to pull in votes at local elections. The potential exists for a development comparable to the consolidation of democracy in Taiwan.

Implications

One could easily expand this brief discussion of factors important to market development and democratic politics. The expansion would be unlikely, however, to alter this general overview of the relationship between culture and change. Chinese culture offers multiple possibilities, and its varied strands magnify or diminish as people draw on them differentially in particular social, political, and economic contexts. While culture alone is not the engine of change (or of stasis), it is an intimate part of how people perceive and respond to their broader environments.

Culture remains important even at the most mundane levels of policy. To give just one example, I was part of a research team looking at indoor air pollution issues in the rural hinterland of Anqing city, in southern Anhui Province. China has been increasingly concerned about its massive environmental problems over the last few years, and the central government has passed many new laws and policies to encourage positive change. They have, for instance, banned leaded gas from the largest cities, and moved many urban areas away from using coal for heat, even though coal is the one energy resource China has in abundance. In Anhui, by far the most important environmental campaign at the time of the research was to clean up the Huai River, in the northern part of the province, by closing approximately a thousand polluting paper mills. The government's propaganda machine actively promoted this and other environmental themes at the time. According to the *China Environmental Yearbook* for 1996, 240 government offices in Anhui mounted 1,921 programs through the mass media, conducted 350 other propaganda activities, and held 128 training courses.[13]

Still, our survey found people quite unconcerned about these issues. For example, they reported that burning their dried rice stalks in the fields (which provides some fertilization) did not pose an environmental or health hazard, even though the smoke from the burning had forced the closure of the local airport during our interview period. They have no concerns about the coal and dried stalks they burn for heat and cooking, although these fuels fill their homes with heavy particulates and other pollutants. In fact, 63 percent of them did not even recognize the term *environmental protection* (*huanjing baohu*).

Educational campaigns directed at broad environmental goals are clearly not enough to affect behavior. Part of the problem is that people are scarcely moved by broad arguments about the need to substitute less polluting fuels and technologies; why should they care about issues of global warming or acid rain that falls on people hundreds of miles away? Given that they also involve some added expense, these policies are hardly likely to foster change.

China does have its own indigenous environmental attitudes, but most of these concern local issues. Geomancy, for example, was a divining system intended to provide residents with the benefits of natural energy flows through the local environment. When gods intercede in environmental issues, as they sometimes do in Taiwan, they also argue for the protection of their local following and show no concern with the environment as a value in itself. People's behavior in China is thus far more likely to respond to local issues: to the financial value in local crops lost to tainted irrigation water rather than the abstract importance of clean rivers, or to the increased rates of asthma among their children from burning coal, rather than the distant dangers of global warming. Appeals to geomancy and related ideas could even be effective, although the government finds the idea distasteful.

Culture always affects how policies develop and work on the ground, but we cannot always easily read those effects off broad descriptions of tradition. The complex and changing currents that make up culture demand carefully acquired local knowledge, properly placed in context. While culture is both malleable and multiple, it is never simply an artifact of broader social forces. For all its messiness and change, culture has deeply influenced how Chinese societies have developed, and will continue to do so. For example, the uniquely Chinese cultural resources for things like trust or individualism grew out of traditions very different from the ones that fostered those ideas in the West. Even though the global spread of Western ideas has had a profound effect on all Chinese societies over the past century and longer, the existence of those indigenous traditions should lead us to expect that the Chinese will develop their own solutions to the problems of modernity. We can see the beginnings of this in the success of the kind of networked capital that I have discussed, or in the sorts of alternate civilities that helped Taiwan consolidate its democracy.

Notes

1. Max Weber, *The Religion of China: Confucianism and Taoism* (New York: Free Press, 1951).
2. William Theodore de Bary, "Confucian Education in Premodern East Asia," in *Confucian Traditions in East Asian Modernity*, ed. Wei-ming Tu (Cambridge, MA: Harvard University Press, 1996), 33.
3. Mark Granovetter, "Economic Action and Social Structure: The Problem of Embeddedness," *American Journal of Sociology* 91, no.3 (1985): 481–510.
4. Examples include S. Gordon Redding, *The Spirit of Chinese Capitalism* (Berlin: Walter de Gruyter, 1990); and Gary G. Hamilton, "Culture and Organization in Taiwan's Market Economy," in *Market Cultures: Society and Morality in the New Asian Capitalisms*, ed. Robert W. Hefner (Boulder, CO: Westview, 1998), 41–77.
5. Jiansheng Li, "Network Families: Kinship and Economic Change in Tianjin" (doctoral diss., Boston University, 1999).
6. Thomas A. Metzger, *Escape from Predicament: Neo-Confucianism and China's Evolving Political Culture* (New York: Columbia University Press, 1977).
7. Stevan Harrell, "Why Do the Chinese Work So Hard," *Modern China* 11, no.2 (1985): 203–26.
8. See Evelyn Sakakida Rawski, *Education and Popular Literacy in Ch'ing China* (Ann Arbor: University of Michigan Press, 1979); and Benjamin A. Elman and Alexander Woodside, eds., *Education and Society in Late Imperial China, 1600–1900* (Berkeley: University of California Press, 1994).
9. See Susan McEwen, "Markets, Modernization, and Individualism in Three Chinese Societies" (doctoral diss., Boston University,(1994).
10. Robert D. Putnam, *Making Democracy Work: Civic Traditions in Modern Italy.* (Princeton, NJ: Princeton University Press, 1993).
11. Francis Fukuyama, *Trust: Social Virtues and the Creation of Prosperity* (New York: Free Press, 1995), 75.
12. For a detailed example, see Li, "Network Families."
13. For this and other information on this case, see William P. Alford et al., "The Human Dimensions of Pollution Policy Implementation: Air Quality in Rural China," *Journal of Contemporary China* 11 (2002): 504.

13

Buddhist Economics in Asia

CHRISTAL WHELAN

Any discussion of "Buddhism" and its effects on economic, social, or political development in Asia is risky for a number of reasons. First of all, so-called Buddhist countries are often in reality multicultural and multireligious, and separating these streams is a most difficult task. Second, "Buddhism" comes in varieties—Theravada, Mahayana, Vajrayana—and an effervescence of newly arisen religious movements that are certainly "Buddhesque" if not Buddhist. The doctrinal and practical emphases of these diverse orientations lead in a number of directions. Third, after centuries of culture-specific elaboration, the original "Buddhism" may be so totally transformed that Buddhism begins to resemble its own iconography—a bodhisattva with a multitude of faces, a thousand arms. In short, Buddhism is no monolith; yet some common ground does exist to warrant a discussion.

How important is religious infrastructure in advancing development in Asia? Since the mid-1970s, Buddhists in various countries have begun earnestly to discuss alternatives to the dominant Western economic model of development. For instance, in Japan the late president of Miyazaki Bank, Inoue Shinichi, argued that if a modern consumerist way of life is reflected in a free-market economy, then a Buddhist way of life requires a "Buddhist economics." Others have drawn inspiration from E. F. Schumacher's proposal for a new basis of economics derived from his experience in Myanmar. A chapter titled "Buddhist Economics" in his *Small is Beautiful* found resonance with similar critiques among Buddhists worldwide. CEOs and academics alike began their own research into the potential for new Buddhist forms of management and economics. Such initiatives held in common the idea of combining commerce or work with spiritual practice. They focused on the fifth part of Buddhism's Noble Eightfold Path, "Right Livelihood," and how to achieve it in a context of late modernity.

As an advanced technoindustrial nation, Japan has long used Buddhism to justify development within the framework of a person's work, whatever it might be, as a legitimate pathway to Enlightenment. In this way, Enlightenment is both the goal and the impetus for increased economic activity. In the words of the seventeenth-century Zen monk Suzuki Shosan, "All commercial activity is the Buddha's activity."

In other words, Buddhism need not retard progress since it neither condemns nor advocates the acquisition of wealth, condemning only the attachment to wealth. This suggests a significant potential for philanthropic enterprise. Indeed, the expansion of a global network of "engaged Buddhists" is perhaps the most significant development within Buddhism in recent years. It has spawned fruitful exchanges such as that between Phra Phaisan Visalo, one of Thailand's leading development monks, and one of Japan's leading economists, Nishikawa Jun, who is interested in models of alternative development. Major Japanese NGOs such as the Buddhist Aid Center and the Shanti Volunteer Association have contributed money and technical expertise in various parts of Asia. These NGOs together with the many small ones launched by the Thai Buddhist activist Sulak Sivaraksa, have helped Buddhists understand more deeply the political, economic, and social roots of many of the ills that plague their countries.

Given the productive exchanges promoted by engaged Buddhists, it is not surprising that Buddhism should be playing a major role in Mongolia's current economic and cultural revival, which follows in the wake of more than seven decades of severe antireligious policies under both Chinese and Soviet Communist domination in which hundreds of lamaseries were looted and destroyed and their monks eliminated or "secularized." Beginning in 1990, Mongolia began to shift from its pro-Soviet orientation and opted for sweeping political and economic reform. The country's adoption of a new democratic constitution and promotion of free enterprise provided the foundation for a modern state, but Buddhism provides the spiritual impetus for restoring Mongolia's seriously degraded environment and cultural heritage.

Prime Minister Nambaryn Enkhbayar, a devout Buddhist, typifies this new movement. A Buddhist activist raised as a communist, Enkhbayar is a pioneer in Mongolia's environmental and development policies. Drawing upon Buddhist teachings and practices, he uses the terms *Buddhist ecology* and *Buddhist economics* in describing the many development projects currently underway in Mongolia. Funded by the World Bank and other international organizations, the national campaign to identify "sacred sites," restore the lamaseries, and build new ones is part of a larger vision to revitalize these traditional institutions, transforming them into models of a sustainable lifestyle and providing local information centers, spiritual repositories, and identity markers of what it means to be "Mongolian" in the modern world. This trend places the lamaseries and the lamas at the cutting edge in a country that nurtures entrepreneurship and a free enterprise system.

The mountainous Kingdom of Bhutan presents a variation on the theme of Buddhist economics. The kingdom has one of the smallest and least developed economies in the world. It is based on agriculture, forestry, and the sale of hydroelectric power to India. Bhutan's slow development may be attributed to the premium it places on conservation—environmental, cultural, and material. King Jigme Singye Wangchuk describes his country's distinctive approach to development as maximizing the "Gross National Happiness" (GNH). Whether as a result of rhetoric or reality, Bhutan has rejected Westernization and embarked on an alternative course of "planned modernization" where ecological and cultural integrity take precedence, and a "closed number" limits tourists in a potentially thriving industry. The government protects 20 percent of its total land in wildlife preserves.

Since 1961, Bhutan has established several kinds of industries, introduced a modern monetary system in place of traditional barter, and is now no longer a subsistence economy. Before 1961, the country had neither automobiles nor roads for motor vehicles and just fifty-nine schools. By 1990, it had seven thousand cars, 2,280 kilometers of roads, and 240 schools. In spite of these significant changes, Bhutan's slow and cautious development policy reveals that for this small Buddhist kingdom, economic achievement is no substitute for GNH.

Cambodia shares many of the problems that have plagued Mongolia and have severely hampered its development: brutal persecution of Buddhism, enforcement of a Communist economic system, and severe environmental degradation. The defoliants the United States used during the Vietnam War destroyed Cambodian forests and wetlands, resulting in the pollution of streams and lakes that rendered much of the country's fresh water unsafe. In addition to religious persecution, the Khmer Rouge closed schools and executed thousands of teachers in an attempt to create a socialist agrarian society. Between those who fled and those who lost their lives, Cambodia has suffered a serious brain drain. Throughout the 1970s, Cambodia endured a civil war, a terrorist regime, and the Cambodia-Vietnam War. This warfare virtually destroyed Cambodia's economy; since 1991 it has largely depended on foreign aid.

Buddhism has permeated Cambodian life for a thousand years. Traditional villages consist of a group of houses clustered around a Buddhist *wat* or monastery that acts as a center for education and community exchange. Organizations such as Buddhism for Development have introduced concepts of socially engaged Buddhism to Cambodian monks so that they can assume leadership positions in the villages that surround their *wat*. With more than 3,500 monasteries nationwide, Cambodia's approach to involving Buddhism in the national restoration resembles the strategy adopted by Mongolia. A leader in this movement is Maha Ghosananda, supreme patriarch of Cambodian Buddhism, sometimes referred to as "Cambodia's Gandhi" and a "Living Treasure." He advocates "people-centered" development in reconstructing his nation. Given the immediate threat to human health that environmental degradation presents, the recovery of the environment is top priority. With assistance from the Alliance of Religion and Conservation, the pagodas are managing active conservation projects, starting educational radio programs, coordinating water management, and actively promoting fuel-efficient energy production.

In Thailand, perhaps the best-known Buddhist activist is Sulak Sivaraksa, an outspoken critic of the free-market system, which he refers to as "free-market fundamentalism." He berates an ideology that permits but one paradigm of development in the "universal spread of modernity." For Sivaraksa, consumerism and capitalism are simply modern forms of greed that use seductive advertising to compel people toward ever-increasing consumption and accumulation. A more moderate Thai voice is that of Prayudh Payutto, a monk and renowned Buddhist scholar. Thailand's candidate for the Nobel Peace Prize several years ago, Payutto is author of *Buddhist Economics: A Middle Way for the Market Place*. He argues that an economics inspired by *dhamma* (*dharma* or "Buddhist teachings") must be concerned with how economic activities influence the entire process of cause and condition, and affect the three interconnected spheres of human existence: individual, society, and nature. He stresses that the purpose of Buddhist society is spiritual enlightenment, in contrast to capitalism's drive for an ever higher standard of living and accumulation of wealth.

Myanmar is a resource-rich nation, but it remains one of Asia's most impoverished and authoritarian. Buddhism is the center of individual life and the monastery the heart of the community. Forbidden to work, monks make their daily rounds to beg, and those who feed them gain religious merit. Typically, every adolescent boy enters a monastery as a novice for a period of time. When the country was under British colonial rule, however, the traditional link between government and Buddhism was broken, leading to a deterioration of the monastic orders and their schools. English became the language of upward mobility. The social disintegration that ensued eventually provoked a nationalist movement. Leaders in this movement used modern institutions such as the Young Men's Buddhist Association to initiate reforms.

Myanmar has been unable to achieve economic stability. The most significant Buddhist activity in recent years has been the prodemocracy movement led by Nobel laureate Aung San Suu Kyi. Committed to nonviolent political and social change, Aung San Suu Kyi exemplifies an engaged Buddhist stance in which modern democratic values and fundamental Buddhist values work together to promote human rights, ethnic conciliation, and social reform. To protest her continued house arrest, most foreign nations have cut their aid to Myanmar. The negative image of the military government has impeded foreign investment, exports, and the development of a potentially lucrative tourist industry.

Bordered by Myanmar, Thailand, and Cambodia lies a landlocked nation. Known as the "Lao People's Democratic Republic," Laos is one of the few official communist states in the world today. For most of its history, however, Buddhism has served as the state religion and permeated virtually every institution. The *wat* or pagoda, a unifying symbol of village identity, has long been the focal site of religious ceremonies, secular meetings, and until very recently, the only place to receive any formal education in the country. All this changed abruptly in the 1950s when Laotian Buddhism encountered the growing pressure of a communist regime that became the ruling party in 1975. Unlike the leaders of Cambodia and Mongolia whose policies led to horrific persecutions of Buddhism, the Lao People's Revolutionary Party adopted a strategy of co-optation as it confronted a Buddhism it recognized as possessing formidable roots in Laotian culture.

Instead of opting for a "total solution," government officials sought to use the clergy to gain the support of the Laotian people. To accomplish this, they tried to convince the monks of the fundamental unity of Marxism and Buddhism: Did not both embrace as a primary goal the cessation of suffering premised on the equality of all people? With the express intention of supplanting the traditional religious hierarchy, the new regime established its own religious organization: the Lao United Buddhist Association. Some monks fled to Thailand at this point, but some who remained joined the organization; those who resisted were sent to political reeducation centers. With the clergy forbidden to engage in village decision making or to give sermons, laity and clergy alike had sufficient reason to abandon the *wat*. The net effect of these oppressive measures was to badly compromise the moral authority of the monks in the eyes of the Laotian people. Perhaps most insidious was the sort of Marxist–Buddhist syncretism that eventually emerged. In the late 1980s, the government began to decentralize its control and encourage private enterprise. Party officials were then allowed to participate in Buddhist ceremonies and even to be ordained as monks in order to earn merit after the death of a close family member. These reforms also permitted something of a Buddhist revival: donations to the *wat* increased, and ceremonies and festivals resumed, more elaborate than before. Indeed, the boundaries had become very blurry between Buddhism and Marxist ideology.

It appears that in recent history, Buddhist economics has not had a chance to develop in Laos. Aside from this complicated religious situation of a Marxist–Buddhist syncretism, Laos still lacks even the most primitive infrastructure. It has no railroads and only a rudimentary road network, and nearly half of its population lives below poverty level in a subsistence economy. Its greatest resource is the mighty Mekong River along its border with Thailand. Thus far, the country has three operating hydropower plants which overwhelmingly export electricity to Thailand. The economy could benefit from aid and foreign investment. No further improvements seem feasible under the present political system.

Sri Lanka presents an exceptional case in terms of Buddhist economics because it is a multicultural and multireligious nation where Sinhala Buddhist nationalists are engaged in civil war with minority Hindu Tamils. In Sri Lanka, Buddhism has shown an alarming capacity for both racism and violence driven by Buddhist fundamentalism. In contrast, the Sarvodaya Shramadana Movement, a very active and successful Buddhist organization founded by A. T. Ariyaratne, demonstrates how Buddhist principles may be applied in pursuit of social transformation. Ariyaratne organized "work camps" for high school students in impoverished low-caste villages. The students meet with the villagers, discuss what improvements they need to create a better life, and then help implement these changes.

Sarvodaya later launched its Hundred Villages Development Scheme to establish a "reawakening" of a hundred selected communities, shifting at this point from an educational mission for students to a village economic development movement. Sarvodaya initially worked with the government's rural development departments, but now receives considerable funding from European organizations. Placing humans above all else, the object of Sarvodaya's program is human "awakening." Ariyaratne advocates an "economy of modest sufficiency" supported by low and middle levels of technology.

The Buddhist countries discussed above raise some important questions. If the sole intent of modern economics is the accumulation of wealth, what influence can Buddhism have on this process? In terms of long-term sustainability, is the current secular trajectory of economic development promoted by advanced nations the only viable model? Or might Buddhism offer some alternatives to evolve a more effective mechanism for survival? The Buddha's focus on the individual as the unit of enlightenment rather than the social sphere has often led Buddhists to focus on development of the "small is beautiful" variety. But this is not always the case. Japanese Buddhists have successfully applied Buddhist principles on a large scale in companies and businesses that generate both wealth and faith. Nobel laureate Aung San Suu Kyi combines a deep religious faith with a democracy movement that shows Buddhism's applicability to modern political struggle in forging a civil society. But in all of these cases, political, economic, and social progress are seen as instrumental in achieving the main goal, which is clearly spiritual advancement of the individual.

The data below shed some light on development as defined by the UN Universal Declaration of Human Rights: democratic freedoms, social justice, and prosperity, with prosperity perhaps better thought of as ending poverty.

With respect to democracy/freedom, the performance of the Buddhist countries is irregular. The Freedom House 2004 rankings, with a high score of 2 (free) and a low score of 14 (not free) are as follows:

Mongolia	4 (free)
Bhutan	11 (not free)
Cambodia	11 (not free)
Laos	13 (not free)
Thailand	5 (free)
Myanmar	14 (not free)
Sri Lanka	6 (partly free)

With respect to social justice, the following list is compiled from 2003 World Bank data on the Gini Index (Namibia is the worst at 70. The Scandinavian countries are at about 25).

Mongolia	44
Bhutan	not available
Cambodia	40
Laos	37
Thailand	43
Myanmar	not available
Sri Lanka	34

With respect to ending poverty, the 2003 UNDP data on the percent of population living on $2 per day or less are as follows:

Mongolia	50%
Bhutan	not available
Cambodia	not available
Laos	73%
Thailand	32%
Myanmar	not available
Sri Lanka	45%

It is difficult to generalize from these data. Mongolia is among the freest countries in the third world; Myanmar is among the least free. The Gini data on Mongolia, Cambodia, and Thailand are typical for third world countries, but Sri Lanka does much better: the United Kingdom is at 36, the United States at 41. The only Buddhist country to have experienced sustained high rates of economic development is Thailand; however, as in Indonesia, Malaysia, and the Philippines, the Chinese minority has made a vastly disproportionate contribution to that growth

It is still difficult to draw meaningful conclusions about Buddhism per se from such data. The diversity within Buddhism requires a careful case-by-case analysis in recognition of the major divisions of Buddhism, the numerous sects within those divisions, and the variations in each country in which each sect is functioning over time. The pluralism within the tradition derives partly from the fact that each Buddhist sect focuses on select sutras and may well ignore the remaining corpus. These sutras are the sermons of the Buddha that his disciples wrote down after his death. Like rolling stones, over time they have acquired vast accretions of commentaries that have also become a vital part of the tradition. Sometimes a sect may focus almost entirely on the writings of its own founder, in which his path to Enlightenment acquires supreme authority, while other sources are pushed to the margins. More crucial still, Buddhism is a religion of practice and has developed sophisticated psychological and corporeal techniques (meditation and yoga) that may in actuality loom larger than any text. Since such a great diversity of practices falls under the general rubric of "Buddhism," any thoughtful discussion on the subject must begin with the following question: Which Buddhism in what country and during what historical period is under discussion?

For example, the "Bloodbowl Sutra" arrived in Japan from China at the end of the medieval period. Originally directed at those who had committed sins involving blood (i.e., violent crimes), it relegated such people to the Blood Pool of Hell. However, in Japan the sutra underwent a peculiarly misogynist transformation and was used to legitimate the inferiority of women on the basis of biology. Viewing women as contaminated by the blood from childbirth and menses, this new interpretation placed women categorically in the Blood Pool of Hell. Permeated with the *bushi* or "warrior" ethos, Japan's Kamakura period positively supported a male-dominant society, and this sutra helped make the ideology more plausible.

Furthermore, one of the most important sutras in various Japanese sects, the Lotus Sutra, states that a woman must be reincarnated as a man in order to achieve Enlightenment at all. While it would be mistaken to conclude that this sutra has been the *cause* of women's oppression in Japan, it has certainly played a part in legitimating the status quo. In fact, until very recently, Japanese law did not allow women on any of its sacred mountains, which were reserved for training male Buddhist clergy. The law was only changed in 1872 after Japan embarked on its tumultuous program of modernization under the new Meiji leadership. But pockets of resistance still exist in Japan, as revealed by the recent controversy over UNESCO's declaration of Mount Omine in Nara as a World Heritage Site. The head priest of the Buddhist temple on the mountain's summit argued that he had the right to exclude women on the grounds of maintaining "tradition."

To return to the roots of Buddhism, the original *sangha* or Buddhist community in India in the Buddha's time certainly suggests a democratic ideal: everyone is equal in the search for Enlightenment. Since then, however, Buddhism has generated a multiplicity of complex and hierarchical institutions, both monastic and lay, wherever it has become indigenized. This fact supports one indisputable generality: religion is always inextricable from political, economic, and social factors.

14

Cultural Change in Islamic Civilization

BASSAM TIBI

For Islam, "culture matters" more with respect to social change than it does with any other civilization. Muslims share a belief that cultural values are revealed by God and are therefore immutable. However, I believe—and will argue in this essay—that Muslims must seek a value-change in their traditions if their societies are to develop economically, politically, and socially.

Muslims are typically reluctant to acknowledge the cultural obstacles in the way of development. The reordering of the Middle East after the liberation of Iraq from its Ba'th-Saddamian despotism is a case in point. The strategy of "regime change" was flawed not only because it was introduced from the outside but also because it ignored the fact that culture matters. It failed to take into account how Iraqi Muslims think and how they view political change. So American political and military decision makers were surprised to encounter a hostile Iraqi population. U.S. troops were promised a flowery reception by people hitherto oppressed by barbarian means, but found quite a different attitude. After the liberation, a Shi'i cleric stated this view: "We are grateful to Allah for freeing us from Saddam, not to America." This is an expression of a cultural world view.

How can a country or an entire region be democratized in the face of a popular culture that supports an Islamic shari'a state? Islamic shari'a contradicts democracy and individual human rights, and without a change in the values that underlie it, there will be no democracy or human rights. To be sure, only Muslims themselves can do the job, but even outsiders can see what will be necessary: a change in cultural values instead of insistence on the immutability of Islamic cultural values as directly revealed by Allah.

The Issue and the Inquiry

Islamic public opinion perceives the West as not only hostile to Islam, but also responsible for the condition of the Muslim world. Among the effects of the terrorist attacks of September 11, which al-Qaida legitimized as a jihad of the "oppressed Muslim people," is a debate over the state of Islamic civilization. It is intriguing to see Western scholars and orthodox Islamist propagandists sharing some of the same explanations and answers in this debate. Some Western scholars tell us that terrorism has structural causes stemming from underdevelopment and poverty. Anti-American Europeans trace these maladies of development to "U.S.-led globalization." And Islamic fundamentalists blame the "globalism of the West" for developmental deficits. Unlike the so-called "structural roots" analysis of Western Europeans, the Islamic accusations are combined with a culture of self-victimization. The Iranian scholar Daryush Shayegan diagnoses this attitude as a "cultural schizophrenia."[1]

I prefer the concept of "defensive culture" for analyzing Muslim responses and attitudes toward modernity. In my book on the contemporary crisis of Islam, I analyze the exposure of the mostly pre-industrial Islamic countries to the industrialized West which creates great pressure. But instead of cultural innovation, Islamic efforts to deal with modernity are restricted to defensive–cultural rhetoric or instrumental adaptation without value change, neither of which leads to cultural reform. Being hostile to the West and blaming it for one's own problems becomes a habit. But the problems are homemade, and the attitude itself is a part of the problem.

Cultural impediments to development are ignored by Western scholars committed to cultural relativism. They frequently label references to cultural constraints on development as a "constructed" Western perception, not a reality. These scholars repudiate the notion that culture matters, arguing that terrorism and underdevelopment are not an essential part of the political culture of contemporary Islam. Arab writers are bolder than their Western peers, identifying a "crusader-Western-Zionist conspiracy" directed against Arabs and Muslims.

In this inquiry I raise several questions. Are there any links between prevailing cultural values, attitudes, and worldviews on the one hand and social–structural realities on the other? Is the view that the world of Islam is truly underdeveloped only based on Western standards? Can some missing cultural dynamic explain Islamic stagnation? In addressing these and other questions, we must also ask whether progress-prone values and progress-resistant values exist in various societies, and if so, how the former can be promoted.

We might also ask why we lack answers for these questions. I have mentioned blaming others and the censorious attitude based on the accusation of "Orientalism." A tendency to reduce everything to economic factors and overlook the interplay between culture and social change also plays a role. The result is a downplaying of the importance of cultural values in social, economic, and political development. I challenge this view by illuminating the place that culture and values occupy in the present realities of the Islamic world. In this pursuit it is relevant to focus first on the Islamic debate itself.

The debate started in 1929, as the prominent Islamic revivalist Emir Shakib Arslan (1869–1945) devoted a series of very influential articles in the Islamic revivalist journal *al-Manar* to the question, "*Limatha ta'akhara al-Muslimun wa taqaddama ghairahum*" (Why are Muslims backward, while others have progressed?)[2] Though he looked to "culture" for answers, he based his view not on analysis but instead on primordial cultural beliefs.

Arslan's point of departure was the Muslim belief that their religion is their culture and their values come from God; no one is entitled to revise what God has revealed. According to Arslan, Muslims were backward because they deviated from the cultural values of "true Islam." This explains why they have not progressed. Some who have asked this question, he said, "have assumed that...the key to progress is to adopt the thoughts of Einstein...Pasteur...Thomas Edison...etc." But "no, they are mistaken...these scientific advancements are by-products, not origins." Instead, "the jihad is the highest ranking science from which all other sciences are derived." If Muslims follow the Koran, "they will equal the Europeans, Americans and Japanese in science and prosperity."[3]

In this statement we find a revival of the traditional Islamic world-view, even though Arslan was considered a modernist. Arslan gives a standard Islamic cultural explanation of underdevelopment in Islamic societies, one still held by educated Muslims. The difference now is that the traditional views include accusations that the Western states have been conspiring against Muslims. The basic argument remains the same: lack of progress stems from deviating from Islamic values, enticed by the West, which has thus been able to keep Muslims underdeveloped and maintain its dominance. Both Arslan's perspective and current views accept culture and values as key issues, and therefore both insist that the only culture that leads to progress is Islam.

The Islamic worldview is based on established perceptions of the scriptural doctrine that it inhibits material pursuits and propagates fatalism. The underpinning is cosmological knowledge, not verifiable knowledge. By "jihad," Arslan does not mean a resort to violence; he refers to the original Koranic understanding, Muslim self-exertion. Still, as a scriptural believer, Arslan does not question or rethink any Islamic values. He believes that Allah, not man, is the shaper of man's destiny. His values are theocentric and consequently fatalistic.

Contemporary Islamists, too, blame the West, not Muslims. *Salafi* (orthodox) and Islamist writers share the view that the West is to blame for the backwardness of the Islamic world, having invaded the abode of Islam in order to Westernize or Christianize it. In this view, *al-ghazu al-fikri* (intellectual invasion) and *taghrib* (Westernization) are considered to be the real source of the misery of Islamic societies. *Taghrib* is viewed as an evil, and the remedy is to de-Westernize contemporary Islamic civilization.

The Diagnosis: Contemporary Muslim Societies and Global Human Progress

To engage in a serious analysis, beyond accusations of Western conspiracies and the evils of globalization, we must examine Islamic civilization itself. The Arab world, the hub of Islamic civilization and its cultural core, is very underdeveloped. This is evident from the *Arab Human Development Report 2002*,[4] a significant document prepared by Arab experts and scholars on behalf of the United Nations. It suggests that underdevelopment is related to the fact that "the wave of democracy...has barely reached the Arab States."[5] Compared with similar regions, "the Arabs suffer from a freedom deficit." The "lack of genuine representative democracy and...restrictions on liberties" can explain the shortcomings of the Arab world.[6] Lack of democracy and human rights and low levels of education explain the gulf between most Muslim societies and the advanced democracies of the West and East Asia.

But why do Muslims accept these poor conditions? This progress-resistant culture is accepted because most Arabs are not educated. Tens of millions of adults are illiterate, two-thirds of them women. The Muslim human rights activist Abdullahi An-Na'im lists discrimination against women as among the Islamic values that contradict individual human rights.[7] In response, Islamist Muslims claim that they have their own conceptions of human rights values. But Islamic human rights are hardly compatible with individual rights.

Gender inequality is certainly a major factor in the underdevelopment of Muslim societies. But other factors must also be considered. In its early history, Islamic civilization was highly developed and was the world's most expansive civilization. Marshall Hodgson, the great historian of Islam, says of the early days of Islamic civilization, "A visitor from Mars might well have supposed that the human world was on the verge of becoming Muslim," considering "the strategic and political advantages of the Muslims," and "the vitality of their general culture."[8] When and why did this highly developed culture decline? Why did capitalism grow from Protestantism and not from Islam? Maxime Rodinson, the great French scholar of Islam, asks these same questions in his pivotal *Islam et capitalisme*.[9] But Rodinson's preoccupation with economic constraints—even though he partially honors culture—keeps him from seeing that "Islamic culture" might have played a role. Instead of focusing on economic factors, I will examine the cultural explanations for why Muslims have lagged behind.

Muslims have a common worldview based on a shared core of values. Their point of departure is that the Koran is the ultimate knowledge of God which he passes to humanity via his messenger, Mohammed, through verbal inspiration. No knowledge can stand above that provided by the Koran, which is the ultimate and absolute truth. All values are derived from this holy book.

Once Muslims debated the meaning of the Koran, arriving at different interpretations *(tafsir)*. But no Muslim is entitled to read the text of the Koran critically, as Christians do with the Bible. In Islam, questioning the text leads to *kufr*, or heresy. *Sultat al-nas* (the un-questioned authority of the text) is an essential part of the Islamic worldview, and a huge obstacle that keeps Muslims from accommo-dating to a changing world. There is a tension between the believed scriptural immutability and ever-changing reality.

These cultural values and attitudes are passed to later generations through child-rearing practices and education in Koranic schools, where Muslim children learn how to read and write with the text of the Koran. Though too young to grasp its complex meaning, they are still compelled to memorize the text. This rote learning approach transfers to other realms of knowledge, including science. Naturally this attitude is a major constraint on intellectual development, tend-ing to suppress curiosity and dissent, two keys to human progress. The "crisis in Muslim education"[10] is a cultural one. A culture that transmits knowledge through rote learning is not a progress-prone culture. It promotes not creativity but dependency and orthodoxy.

How, then, was Islamic civilization in a position to reach the zenith that it did in its early history? The answer is chiefly the Helleniza-tion of Islam between the ninth and twelfth centuries, as Muslims appropriated and further developed Greek philosophy and science. Hellenization facilitated a cultural change that allowed Islam to ac-cept the primacy of human reason and the rise of an Islamic variety of rationalism. A closer look at Islamic history during those medieval centuries reveals not only cultural innovation but also an intellectual and institutional battle between Islamic rationalists and scripturalists.

Their differences were framed as *bi al-aql aw bi al-wahi* (judging by reason on one hand or by the grounds of revelation on the other), that is, between the Hellenized rational disciplines (philosophy and science) and the Islamic scriptural sciences (the study of the text of Koran and the text of the Hadith of the prophet, i.e., the Sunna tra-dition). But Islamic orthodoxy was in control of the institutions of learning and could keep the rational sciences out of the curriculum. Thus it kept those sciences from being institutionalized and spread-ing in the Islamic world.

Rationalism in Islam declined, and so, in consequence, did Islamic civilization. Even educated Muslims are scarcely aware of this his-tory. Instead, in discussions of the decline of Islamic civilization, there is an obsession with the Crusades. From this perspective, the United States and Israel have replaced the traditional crusaders. No one talks about the internal factors that have contributed and still contribute to underdevelopment in the Islamic world.

Modern Islamic history includes many efforts to revive Islamic rationalism, but they have not been widely accepted. One contemporary Islamic philosopher who stands in this tradition, Mohammed Abed al-Jabiri, unequivocally states that "the revival of Averroes rationalism or progress is the bottom line for an Islamic civilization."[11] Averroes (1126–98 CE) studied Aristotle and developed the philosophy of *al-haqiqa al-muzdawaja* (double truth: religious and philosophical). Thus he finessed any conflict between *aql* (reason) and *wahi* (revelation) by establishing different realms for each. In his view, religious truth should be restricted to religious affairs while the more worldly philosophical truth should prevail in the nonreligious sphere. Averroes introduced the separation of the religious and the worldly in Islam. But his philosophy did not prevail.

New cultural values can only affect social change when they become institutionalized. The rational sciences were never institutionalized in Islam because the Ulema (priestly) orthodoxy prevented the application of rational analysis to Islamic learning. The glorious achievements of early Islamic civilization were the consequence of dedication to the rational sciences, not to the shari'a. They were the accomplishment of Islamic rationalists, not of Islamic orthodoxy. I find that this distinction and clarification is missing in most accounts of Islam's early positive impact on the West, especially in the writings of Edward Said and his followers.

Recent efforts to revive Averroes and Islamic rationalism have failed; the Moroccan Mohammed al-Jabiri is prominent among those who have tried. Al-Jabiri complains that contemporary Arabic thought has not been able to vault the obstacle of tradition. "The survival of our philosophical tradition…can only be Averroist…The Averroist spirit is adaptable to our era, because it agrees with it on more than one point: rationalism, realism, axiomatic method, and critical approach."[12] This is the vision of an enlightened Muslim, but it clashes with the conspiratorial obsession and a mindset focused on accusations rather than self-criticism.

Others have tried to deal with the gap between Islam and the West. Some saw education as the instrument for innovation, so students were sent to Europe to learn modern science and technology. The first imam sent to Europe in modern times was Rifa'a R. al-Tahtawi. He was assigned to supervise a group of Muslim students, but found the West fascinating and was given permission to become a student himself. In his Paris diary, Tahtawi acknowledges that Muslims need to adopt Western accomplishments: "Europeans, though Christians, are superior to Muslims in the sciences."[13] He was amazed that scholars of religion (*ulema*) were not also honored as scientists (also *ulema* in Arabic) and that Europeans distinguished between scientific knowledge and religious belief.

Tahtawi urged his fellow Muslims to learn from Europeans. But he was careful to stress that ideas and beliefs adopted from the West must be related to the rules of Shari'a law. Tahawi's way of thinking demonstrates the will to adopt selected items of modernity without becoming modern. I characterize his posture as an expression of "semimodernity."

Tahtawi reasoned that Muslims were the first to discover modern science, but that Islamic civilization declined while the West carried forward these Islamic accomplishments. Muslims should now claim these contributions back, adopting knowledge from the West in acts of repossession or retrieval. This sounds enlightened, but it reveals the all-too-frequent cultural attitude of Muslims who claim to have the ultimate knowledge revealed by Allah: they need not learn from others.

Tahtawi helps us understand Islam's predicament with modernity. He was clearly a Muslim liberal and a modern revivalist, not an Islamist. But passages in his Paris diary are very similar to some in contemporary Islamic fundamentalist writings that deal with science and technology in the context of their encounters with modernity. Fundamentalists split modernity into "culture" (values) and "instruments" (science and technology). They adopt the latter while vehemently rejecting the former. They never question their belief that they are morally superior to non-Muslims. The outcome is what I call "the Islamic dream of semimodernity." In this regard Islamists seem to be no different from the liberal Muslim Tahtawi. In fact, on the issue of precluding any learning from the West[14] that may lead to a conflict with the shari'a, Islamic modernists share the mindset of the Islamists. Learning from the West is allowed only in conjunction with a clear rejection of fundamental Western values. Only Islamic values are valid. Hence my diagnosis: This orthodox Islamist concept of knowledge is a characteristic of a progress-resistant culture.

Four different streams influence contemporary Islamic civilization, however unevenly. The first is political Islam or Islamism, which seems to provide at present the most powerful response to modernity. Its message is clear: Take the instruments and leave the worldview and the values. This has been the response to the UNDP report in the

Arab press.[15] The terrorists of September 11 are the best example of this mindset. Their worldview was medieval and the values they were committed to were progress-resistant, yet they were able to handle the complexity of modern technology, even navigating aircraft.

The second stream is Wahhabi Salafi orthodoxy, which rejects any innovation. Wahhabism in Saudi Arabia is one example; Bin Laden is another. His form is a synthesis of political and Wahhabi Islam that bridges orthodoxy and fundamentalism.

The third stream is the popular Islam of the religious *Tariqa* orders, based on oral traditions, not scripture. Given that popular Islam is strongest among illiterate rural people, it is not bound to the scriptural shari'a nor to its monolithic mindset. Therefore, popular Islam—with some exceptions—is rather tolerant and pluralistic, albeit not in a modernizing sense.

The fourth stream is reform Islam. For the topic at hand it is the most important, though it is the weakest. In the late nineteenth century, its leading exemplar, Muhammad Abduh, sought to accommodate to the modern culture of science and technology but failed because he sought accommodation without cultural change.[16]

The preceding rough diagnosis of the cultural constraints underlying the current backwardness of Islamic civilization shows why Muslims have failed to come to terms with modernity. The prevailing culture is progress-resistant, and it impedes all efforts to adopt standards of progress and cope with modernity. In my view, without cultural change, democratic institutions cannot be introduced successfully. "Rethinking Islam"[17] is indispensable. The Islamic dream of semimodernity—adopting items of modernity without adopting a culture of modernity (see note 15)—is a chimera.

We must take the cultural factor more seriously in order to understand the lack of democratization and flawed development. The impasse in post-Saddam Iraq illustrates this. Are breakthroughs possible in this progress-resistant culture? In the better days of Islamic civilization, Muslims were willing to learn from others and were therefore successful. Today we need to ask, what can be done to change contemporary Muslims' cultural resistance to learning from others?

The Prescription: Cultural and Religious Reforms

Muslims must open their minds and free themselves from medieval jihad theology, and free the sacral *fiqh* jurisprudence from thoughtless scripturalism and an obsession with proselytizing. This is easy to say. It is extremely difficult to realize.

In his *Philosophy of Islamic Law,* the Islamic apologist writer Mohammad Muslehuddin says Islam needs no reform and rejects any effort by a Muslim in this direction. Muslehuddin states the prevailing Islamic public choice:

> Divine law is to be preserved in its ideal...as commanded by God....The view . . . that the law should be determined by social needs [is mistaken]....God alone knows what is really good for mankind..... Islamic society is the product of [shari'a] law and has ideally to conform to its dictates. The law...does not change....Those who think of reforming Islam are misguided....Why should it be modernized when it is already perfect and pure, universal for all time?[18]

This is an anti-modernization based on a fatalistic worldview. Muslehuddin speaks for the many Muslims who unquestioningly accept the revealed scriptural truth. Any deviation can be condemned as *kufr* (heresy) and be followed by *takfir* (accusation of heresy and then excommunication). Those who deviate may even risk execution as "unbelievers." Therefore cultural change is a risky undertaking.

The orthodox Islamic worldview inhibits material pursuits and nurtures irrationality. The Arabic language is replete with religious rituals of fatalism and expressions of the minimal influence humankind has over its destiny. Muslims commonly use the phrase *insh'a Allah* (if Allah wills) when asked whether a job will be done. If a traditional Muslim faces a challenge or is expected to accomplish a task, the phrase is *tawakal 'ala Allah* (rely on God).

Of course, most Muslims do not live by the very tough religious rules of the shari'a, because that is simply not feasible. John Waterbury coined the term *behavioral lag*[19] for the difference between what people say and what they do. Articulated cultural/religious values may thus not really influence actual behavior. "Behavioral lag" evokes the "cultural schizophrenia" that Daryush Shayegan made the title of his book, mentioned earlier.

One hears in Western scholarship, above all in Edward Said's attack on "Orientalism," that the world of Islam, and particularly the Arab world, is backward because of Western prejudice and malice. The Muslim philosopher Sadik Jalal al-Azm pointed out that, in attacking the West, Said is pursuing an "Orientalism in reverse."[20] A democratic political culture cannot thrive if taboos forbid the re-thinking of Islam. Bu Ali-Yassin, a Syrian social scientist educated in Europe, argues that Islamic taboos exist in three basic areas: religion, politics, and gender issues.[21] One cannot publicly discuss any of these areas without exposing oneself to harsh criticism or even to physical punishment. In such a culture, no religious values can be reformed, no societies can undergo transformation, no politics can be democra-tized, and no gender relations can be remade.

What is needed are cultural and religious reforms that pave the way for a new, progress-prone Islamic worldview. We must listen to the Moroccan philosopher al-Jabiri's call to a return to rationality as the way out of Islamic/Arab backwardness. It is necessary to "rethink Islam" through the mindset of rationalism and disseminate the ideas and ideals of a new Islam in the mosques, in homes, in schools, in political discourse, in the media.

Reinhard Bendix coined the term *spiritual mobilization* as a re-quirement for social change. Clearly distinguishing between the adoption of modern items and a modern outlook, he points out that "modernization in some spheres of life may occur without result-ing in modernity."[22] He describes how the gap between culture and technology has "created advanced and follower societies, and the ef-forts to close it by...ad hoc adaptation of items of modernity" put "obstacles...in the way of successful modernization."[23]

Being a Muslim myself, I sincerely believe that the established Is-lamic worldview can be changed through reform. The rationalist phi-losophers in Islam (al-Farabi, Avicenna, Averroes) and the theological defenders of reason (al-Mutazilites) as well as contemporary radical-reform Muslim thinkers from Arkoun to al-Jabiri show us the way. We must follow it for accomplishing an embracing of modernity and change by Muslims.

Conclusions

The UNDP's *Arab Human Development Report 2002* is indispens-able for understanding both the current condition of Arab, and by implication many other Islamic countries, and the reasons why they are lagging behind. Without democracy, individual human rights, and full literacy, real development cannot occur. Nor can changes occur in these areas without an underlying cultural change underpinning the needed transformation. Values influence people's thoughts and actions. We must understand the key role that culture plays in the political, economic, and social evolution of societies. The report makes this point eloquently.

> Culture and values are the soul of development. They provide its impetus, facilitate the means needed to further it, and substantially define people's vision of its purposes and ends. Culture and values are instrumental in the sense that they help to shape people's hopes, fears, ambitions, attitudes and actions, but they are also formative because they mould people's ideals and inspire their dreams for a fulfilling life for themselves and future generations. There is some debate in Arab countries about whether culture and values promote or retard development. Ultimately, however, values are not the servants of development; they are its wellspring.
>
> Governments, Arab or otherwise, cannot decree their people's values; indeed, governments and their actions are partly formed by national cultures and values. Governments can, however, influence culture through leadership and example, and by shaping education and pedagogy, incentive structures in society, and use of the media. Moreover, by influencing values, they can affect the path of development.[24]

Some of the reaction to this report illuminates the difficulties facing those who would reform Islam. In the influential *al-Hayat,* Riyad Tabbarah attacked its "distortions" and "great scholarly gaps," which compel Muslims to use "great caution" in dealing with it, in particular with "the recommendations [about] how to push forward Arab development." Tabarrah argues that the Arab countries must look "for ways to import technology without importing Western ills."[25] By "ills" he means the values of progress-prone cultures.

In the late nineteenth and early twentieth century, cultural innovations were promoted mostly by Christian Arabs, including Salamah Musah, Nadrah al-Yazijih, Georges Hanna, and others now mostly forgotten.[26] Today we find no courageous thinkers like Salamah Musah, who asked for cultural change and radically criticized traditional Arab culture as not being prone to progress. We no longer find Syrian-Lebanese and Egyptian Christians giving shape to intellectual debates. Along with the cultural re-Islamization of Arab discourse, this process coincides with three other developments.

1. De-Christianization, a phenomenon also related to the de-Westernization of knowledge. Until its bloody conflict of 1976, Lebanon, with the many newspapers, journals, and publishing houses based in Beirut, was a major cultural window to the rest of the world. This is no longer the case: a process of de-Christianization and de-Westernization has occurred as middle-class Christians emigrated to the West. Among the indicators of this sad change are the low numbers of book translations from Western languages into Arabic. Western books have been substantially replaced by the growing body of literature that can be classified as "political Islam." The second UNDP report addresses this situation.

2. The disappearance of reform Islam. In Egypt we still find a few important reformers like Mohammed Ashmawi, who lives under protection and faces the threat of death. Others, like H. Abu-Zaid, have left the country. Most Muslim reformers live in asylum in Western Europe and North America.

3. A return to purist Islam, scriptural and selective as recommended by Muslehuddin. This is the orthodox variety. The other variety is political Islam/fundamentalism. Both are thriving in contemporary Islam and are part of the ongoing desecularization.

Against this somber background, the West should not be self-congratulatory. It has nurtured the taboos of political correctness and the presumptions of cultural relativism that undermine free debate of the issues most central to progress in the Arab/Islamic world. At stake is Western civilization as a source for universal standards of progress and development. David Gress describes the history of "the idea of the West":

Although multiculturalism might seem to contradict universalism, the two were compatible; indeed, multiculturalism was simply universalism applied to cultural politics…universalism…never solved its fundamental dilemma of being both a Western idea—the idea that Westernization was global and irresistible—and an anti-Western idea—the idea that Western identity had fortunately come to an end.…The dilemma of universalism derived from the ambiguities of the New West itself:…was it the fruit of a historic identity?…The dilemma posed the question of Western identity for the third millennium.[27]

In referring to the debate on multiculturalism, I do not digress from the subject at hand. Both Western and Islamic societies are touched by global migration. The politicization of Islam discussed here also affects the development of a progress-prone culture in the European Islamic Diaspora, which is becoming a gated community. In the West, particularly in Germany, scholars like Samuel Huntington are defamed for drawing attention to culture's relevance to the performance of societies and pointing to the conflict that arises from clashing worldviews. In the world of Islam, the cultural relativism of the West is used to establish legitimacy for a variety of neoabsolutist ideas.

I believe that a universal ethical code along the lines of the UN Universal Declaration of Human Rights is indispensable to world peace and progress. Such a code is possible only if contemporary Muslims agree to "rethink Islam" and do away with neoabsolutism. Europeans also need to stand by the civilizational identity of the West.

There will be no improvement in the world of Islam or its relations with the West without a major change in values and attitudes in the former. Any attempt to impose a solution from the outside, as in Iraq, will lead to defensive attitudes of rejection and self-assertion, mounting anti-Westernism and anti-Americanism, and the strengthening of the illusory belief that Muslims can de-Westernize and Islamize the world. What is needed in Iraq is an education in democracy as an introduction to progress-prone culture.[28]

Among the various explanations for the cultural rigidity of contemporary Islam, one is prominent: a cultural unwillingness to learn from others that also may have a psychological dimension, because learning from others can be seen as wounding one's ego, or sense of self-worth. The rejection of innovation is a second major factor, and in addition to the cultural/religious explanation, the same psychology may also be operative. The third explanation is political. "The Revolt against the West" is a term coined by Hedley Bull who argues that Islamic fundamentalism is directed not only against Western hegemony but also against Western values. As he puts it, Islamic fundamentalism is viewed as a "cultural liberation" that allows one to engage in "cultural re-assertion...of indigenous culture."[29] Bull goes on to wonder whether this "revolt against Western dominance...is not a revolt against Western values as such."[30]

The coincidence of globalization and cultural fragmentation is the fourth and final impediment.[31] By this I mean that the processes of globalization change worldwide economic and political structures but not culture, which is always local and persistent. People of different cultures may use the same technical and scientific tools (e.g., computers, the Internet) without sharing the same values. Cultural fragmentation is an obstacle to universalizing the values on which peace and progress depend.

Never has the gap between Islam and the West—and the intimacy between them—been as intense as it is now. Benjamin Barber describes our time as *Jihad versus McWorld*.[32] He is right about Islamic attitudes being anti-Western and anti-American. The prevailing view among the Islamists is that through jihad, *Pax Americana* should be replaced by *Pax Islamica*. This resistance to coming to terms with the Western (and one might now add, East Asian) values of progress and development is related not only to the cultural obstacles analyzed here but also to the anti-Western worldview that prevails in the world of Islam. We cannot reduce jihad to a protest against globalization. It extends, I am afraid, to a protest against progress and development themselves.

Notes

1. Daryush Shayegan, *Cultural Schizophrenia: Islamic Societies Confronting the West* (Syracuse, NY: Syracuse University Press, 1997).
2. Emir Shakib Arslan, "*Limatha ta'akhara al-Muslimun wa taqadamma qhaira-hum* (Why Are Muslims Backward, While Others Have Progressed) reprint (Beirut: Maktabat al-Hayat, 1965), (English translation Lahore 1944 and 1968). Extracts of this book are included in John Donhue and John Esposito, eds., *Islam in Transition* (New York: Oxford University Press, 1982), 60–64.
3. Ibid., 176 (my translation from Arabic).
4. UNDP, *Arab Human Development Report 2002. Creating Opportunities for Future Generations* (New York: United Nations, 2002).
5. Ibid., 2.
6. Ibid.
7. Abdullahi A. An-Na'im, *Toward Islamic Reformation* (Syracuse, NY: Syracuse University Press 1990), chap. 7, in particular. 170–81.
8. Marshall C. S. Hodgson, *Rethinking World History, Essays on Europe, Islam and World History* (Cambridge, UK: Cambridge University Press 1995), 97,
9. Maxime Rodinson, *Islam et Capitalisme* (Paris: Editions du Seuil, 1966).
10. See. S. S. Husain and S. A. Ashraf, *Crisis in Muslim Education* (Jeddah, Saudi Arabia: 1979) (distributed in the United Kingdom by Hodder and Stoughton), on Islamic education; see also B. Tibi, *Islam between Culture and Politics* (New York: Palgrave, 2004), chap. 8.
11. Mohammed al-Jabiri, *Arab Islamic Philosophy* (Austin, TX: University of Texas Press, 1999), 120.

12. Ibid., 124, 128.
13. This and the following quotes are from Rifa'a R. al-Tahtawi, *Takhlis al-Ibriz fi-talkhis Paris*, new edition in Arabic (Beirut: Dar Ibn Zaidun, n.d.). The German edition is: *Ein Muslim entdeckt Europa* (Munich: C. H. Beck, 1988).
14. B. Tibi, *Islam and the Cultural Accommodation of Social Change* (Boulder, CO: Westview Press, 1990), chap. 7 on education. See also note 10 above.
15. Riyad Tabbarah, Review of the UNDP-2002 Report (note4), *al-Hayat*, November 10, 2002, 10. For an analysis of this mindset see B. Tibi, "The Worldview of Sunni Arab Fundamentalists: Attitudes toward Modern Science and Technology", in: M. Marty and S. Appleby, eds., *Fundamentalisms and Society* (Chicago: The University of Chicago Press, 1993), 73-102.
16. Mohammed Abduh, *al-Islam wa al-Nasraniyya bain al-ilm wa al-madaniyya* (Islam and Christianity between Science and Civilization), new printing (Cairo: Dar al-Hadatha, 1983); see also,Malcolm Kerr, *Islamic Reform. The Political Theories* (Berkeley: University of California Press, 1966).
17. Mohammed Arkoun, *Rethinking Islam* (Boulder, CO: Westview Press, 1994).
18. Mohammad Muslehuddin, *Philosophy of Islamic Law and the Orientalists* (Lahore, Pakistan: Kazi Publications, 1985), 242, 247.
19. John Waterbury, *The Commander of the Faithful Morocco* (New York: Columbia University Press, 1970).
20. Sadik J. al-Azm, *Dhihniyyat al-Tahrim* (The Mentality of Taboos) (London: Riad El-Rayyes Publ., 1992); on Said see, 17–85.
21. Bu Ali Yassin, *al-Thaluth al-Muharram* (The Triple Taboo)(Beirut: al-Tari'a, 1973).
22. Reinhard Bendix, *Nation Building and Citizenship. Studies of Our Changing Social Order*, rev.ed. (Berkeley: University of California Press, 1977), 411.
23. Bendix, *Nation Building*, 416.
24. UNDP, 2002, 8.
25. Riyad Tabbarah, Review of the UNDP-2002-report, *al-Hayat*, November 10, 2002, 10.
26. See *Mukhtarat Salamah Musah* (Selected Writings of Salamah Musah) (Beirut: Maktabat al-Ma'arif, 1963); Nadrah al-Yazijih, *"Rasail fi hadarat al-bu's* (Essay on the Civilization of Misery")* (Damascus: al-Adib, 1963); Georges Hanna, *al-Insan al-Arabi* (Beirut: Dar al-Ilm, 1964).
27. David Gress, *From Plato to NATO. The Idea of the West* (New York: Free Press, 1999), 503ff.
28. See B. Tibi, "Education and Democratization in an Age of Islamism," in Alan Olson, David Steiner, and Irina Tuuli, eds., *Educating for Democracy: Paideia in an Age of Uncertainty* (Lanham, MD: Rowman & Littlefield, 2004), chap. 19, 203–19.
29. Hedley Bull, "The Revolt against the West," in H. Bull and A. Watson, eds., *The Expansion of International Society* (Oxford: Clarendon Press, 1984), 223.
30. Ibid.
31. For more on this see B. Tibi, *The Challenge of Fundamentalism*, rev. ed. (Berkeley: University of California Press, 2002), chap. 4 and 5.
32. Benjamin Barber, *Jihad vs. McWorld* (New York: Ballantine Books, 1995).

15

Islam Matters

Culture and Progress in the Muslim World

ROBERT W. HEFNER

However great its diversity, Islam still matters, and matters deeply, in the contemporary world. It is the way in which it matters for political participation and economic well-being that I wish to discuss in this chapter. In the broad-stroke discussion that follows, I want to touch on three issues: the values and tensions of Muslim politics; Muslim attitudes toward capitalism; and finally, the recent crisis of Muslim politics and religious authority. The evidence from my first two arguments suggests that the political–economic evolution of the Muslim world has been more decisively shaped by patrimonial politics and distinctive balances of power than by an unchanging religious disposition. My third point is that, while Muslim civilization still commands abundant resources for progressive development, social change in modern times has upset the delicate balance of power among political Islam's varied cultural streams. In so doing, it has given a disproportionate influence to a small number of believers committed to an ideologized and totalizing interpretation of the faith. Because these antipluralists wield an influence vastly out of proportion with their numbers in society, they threaten many of the resources Muslims bring to the modern age. Further progress toward economic improvement and equitable political participation, then, will depend on a political and cultural reformation led by Muslims *for* an Islam capable of defusing this threat to the Muslim majority. Hints of just such a reformation are already visible in parts of the Muslim world, but so too is the scale of the challenge.

The Cultural Contradictions of Muslim Politics

At their founding, Christianity and Islam differed profoundly in their attitude toward the political establishment, and this early disposition has influenced each religion's political culture to this day. In its first years, the Christian community's social base lay among Jews from the lower-middle and laboring classes of Roman Israel. After Paul's ascent to leadership in the Jesus movement around 48 CE, Christianity spread beyond its Jewish base to ethnically mixed populations around the Mediterranean. Notwithstanding its social success, until the conversion of the Emperor Constantine in 312 CE, Christianity retained the social ethos, so vividly expressed in its gospels, as a nonelite religion uneasy with any too-direct collaboration with Caesar. Inevitably, however, the church's subsequent development was deeply influenced by matters of this world. Under the influence of Constantinist proposals for an integrated church and state, Christianity developed a more cooperative relationship with state authorities; Constantine and later rulers were even asked to settle theological disputes. Church collaboration with state authorities remained the norm until the emergence of nonconformist Protestantism in the seventeenth and eighteenth centuries.

Despite this evolution, in one important respect the legacy of early Christianity remained distinctive, not least of all by comparison with Islam. Jesus's injunction to distinguish that which is God's from that which is Caesar's created a normative precedent for a significant separation of religious and state authority. Equally important, during its first three centuries the church developed entirely outside the state, often suffering at the hands of the latter institution. These influences left a lasting mark on church organization. The Christian Church differed from religious traditions like Islam by virtue of its centralized ecclesiastical institution and relative autonomy in matters of personnel recruitment and training, ritual and doctrine, and finance and infrastructure. Although in practice different churches enjoyed differing degrees of autonomy, the persistence of a centrally coordinated and significantly autonomous ecclesiastical institution gave Western Christianity a cultural and political dynamic different from Islam.

Early Islam showed little of early Christianity's hesitation about state power. The Prophet Muhammad was not merely the charismatic bearer of a new religious prophecy but also a lawgiver and the founder of a state that was to become one of the Old World's most successful empires. Nineteenth- and early twentieth-century Western scholars, including Max Weber,[1] viewed the close union of religion and state achieved under the Prophet's leadership as proof that Islam was at heart a "warrior religion," embodying the militaristic ethos and aggressive ambitions of nomadic Arab tribes. But Weber's analysis owed more to nineteenth-century European caricatures than it did to Muslim history itself. The early Muslim community recruited its leadership from among the urban commercial classes in caravan centers like Mecca and Medina, and only secondarily from among the tribal nomads of the Arabian peninsula. The evidence of the Koran and traditions of the Prophet confirms that, rather than tribal warrior values, early Islam "represents a partial triumph of urban norms over nomadic ones and city over desert power."[2]

Although Weber mischaracterized Islam's origins and early ethos, he was grappling with what is indeed a fundamental point of contrast between early Muslim and Christian political culture, a difference relevant for understanding Muslim politics today. The early Muslim community showed little of the conviction of St. Augustine or other early Christians that government is evil, even if a man-made necessity. In the classical Muslim view, the state is an instrument of unqualified good, facilitating the implementation of God's law as well as Muslim supremacy among nations. Muslim jurists express this same view today when they distinguish Islam from Christianity by saying that Islam is personal devotionalism and state politics. Conservative Islamists invoke this concept to insist that Islam allows no separation of religion and state.

Known in Arabic as shari'a or "the path," divine law too has a social place and authority in Muslim political theory different from anything seen in Christianity. Just as Muslims believe that revelation was sealed with the divine instructions given to the Prophet Muhammad, shari'a is seen by most religious scholars as all-encompassing and complete. The function of the religious jurist, then, is not to formulate law but to interpret it in accordance with strictly delimited interpretive procedures. Similarly, the proper role of the Muslim ruler is not to be a sovereign but to create an environment in which Muslims can prosper and implement God's law. Since God alone is the source of the law, God alone is sovereign. Neither the state nor the ruler make the law; the law, so to speak, makes them. Although formulated early on in Muslim history, these concepts of divine sovereignty and shari'a supremacy have in modern times become a mainstay of conservative Islamist critiques of democracy and secular law.

What looks at first sight like a principle entirely different from the Christian ideal, however, has in practice proved to be anything but simple. In an oft-cited work, Bernard Lewis echoes conservative Islamist claims in observing that "in classical Islam there was no distinction between Church and state."[3] Inasmuch as this was the case, however, it was so only in the idealized thought-worlds of religious commentaries, not actual social practice. In the real Muslim world, from early on a significant separation of religious and state authority existed for the simple reason that the relationship between scholars and rulers was mediated by meanings and interests more varied than the law itself.[4] No sooner had the Prophet Muhammad passed away than this tension between a unitarian ideal and a differentiated practice became glaringly apparent. The first four successors to Muhammad as leaders of the Islamic community, the so-called rightly guided caliphs, could not all agree on the proper order of succession, and a bitter dispute broke out between three of the caliphs and the Prophet's son-in-law, Ali. Supporters of Ali went on to form the Shi'i branch of Islam (about 14% of the world's Muslim population), while the former became the Sunni. This early conflict illustrated the difficulties of the Muslim community's transition from a charismatic movement to an institutionally differentiated organization. This dispute did not yet signal a full separation of religion from state, but it did indicate a *pluralization* of religious and political authority. Never again would the Muslim community enjoy the simple unity enjoyed under the charismatic leadership of the Prophet.

This incipient pluralization gave way to an even more systematic separation of religious and political authority following the establishment of Mu'awiya's caliphate in Jerusalem in 661 CE. Although he and later caliphs preserved the appearance of election by acclamation, Mu'awiya's ascension effectively marked the beginning of dynastic patrimonialism as the principle of state in the central Muslim lands. From this point on, dynastic rule was the norm in the Muslim Middle East until the abolition of the caliphate in the new Republic of Turkey in 1924. The decline of the earlier Islamic communitarianism was also signaled by the shift of the empire's capital in the eighth century away from the Arabian peninsula to the more hierarchical and populous territory of Syria.

Today Islamist activists regard the replacement of the original system of "elected" caliphs with dynastic rule as proof that Muslim politics had been corrupted by irreligious elites. Activists like Osama bin Laden and Abu Bakar Ba'asyir (of Southeast Asia's Jemaah Islamiyah) insist that the only way to restore Muslim greatness is to replace nation-states and secular constitutionalism with a caliphate modeled on Islam's predynastic heritage. This idealized prescription, however, ignores a complication: the very injunction that Muslims should not distinguish religious and political authority inevitably invites an outcome like that seen in the first centuries of the Muslim era. By concentrating religious and political power in one ruler, these modern, statist interpretations of shari'a politics do away with the checks and balances required to protect religion from corruption at the hands of the powerful. Ironically, early Muslim jurists sensed this danger and insisted that a ruler who violated the trust accorded him must be punished or replaced. But neither they nor the law offered any details on the mechanisms through which such a removal might take place.

This shortcoming illustrates a general tension at the heart of classical Muslim political theory, one still present in radical Islamic writings today. A formula designed to make God the sole sovereign by uniting religion and state inevitably invites the subordination of religious authority to the interests of those strong enough to get themselves in power. The formula invites this outcome because fusing religion and state eliminates the checks and balances needed to protect religion from abuse at the hands of self-interested elites.

Although jurists found it difficult to devise principles for addressing this problem, in practice they were aware of the dangers of subordinating themselves and the law to the state. In the eighth and ninth centuries, when most of the great schools of Islamic law were forming, jurists developed several doctrines to protect their authority from state meddling. For example, they insisted that the "gate" of authoritative interpretation or *ijtihad* was closed: no further interpretive innovations were needed or allowed. Although this claim is rejected by reformist Muslims today, the gesture served, among other things, to limit rulers' right to meddle in legal affairs. At the same time, the principle legitimated the role of the jurists as final arbiters in interpreting the tradition.

Seen from this latter perspective, the closure of *ijtihad* and the insistence on the finality of the law were partial functional equivalents to Western Christianity's separation of church and state, in that both

measures aimed to carve out a religious sphere safe from state interference. Other scholarly practices showed a similar wariness toward
the state. In their written commentaries, for example, jurists often
voiced sharp criticism of state-appointed religious judges. Not all
Muslim lands developed the institution of state-sponsored religious
courts and judges, but most did. Where states operated religious
courts, it was not uncommon for rulers to use them to advance their
own interests rather than to uphold the law, not least by appointing
ill-qualified relatives or political clients to serve as judges.

Actions like these only deepened independent scholars' resentment
of officialdom's involvement in religious affairs. Even when invited,
many prominent scholars refused to serve as judges for the state, on
the grounds that such cooperation was inevitably corrupting. "Of
three judges, two are in Hell," says one recorded tradition of the
Prophet, none-too-subtle in its opinion of judges.[5] (Stories of holy
men overcoming unjust rulers were a "classic theme in the Moroccan
moral imagination,"[6] as in most of the Muslim world. Not surprisingly, then, even where rulers appointed respected jurists to serve as
state legal experts, "they have no monopoly of giving *fatwas* [reli-
gious opinions], and the practice of consulting private scholars of
high reputation has never ceased."[7] In practice if not canonical principle, then, there were many efforts to achieve a separation of state
and religious authority.

We can draw three conclusions from this discussion, all relevant
for understanding the powers and perils of Muslim politics today.
The first is that, however much the shari'a seemed to prescribe otherwise, in practical fact there was a widespread separation of religious
and state authority. Another way of stating this point is that the real-
and-existing politics responded to much more than divine law.

The second point to note is that there were always several political–cultural streams flowing through Muslim civilization. The jurists
stewarded the canonical knowledge, but even they knew some tension between the unitarianism of high doctrine and the pluralism of
worldly practice. In addition to the juristic streams, an imperial culture was associated with the Muslim courts. Its main characteristic
was that, even when paying lip service to the law, it was oriented to
meanings and interests more varied than the law alone. Imperial Islam achieved its cultural efflorescence in the Indo-Persian world, the
second most important of Muslim world areas after the Arab and
one celebrated for its achievements in the arts and sciences. Before

the nineteenth century, Indo-Persian ideals of state prevailed not only in Persia and India but also in Central Asia and the Muslim states of the Indonesian archipelago. In all these regions one saw extensive restrictions on the public authority of religious scholars, and, conversely, greater discretion for rulers in matters of the law.

The third conclusion is the one most directly relevant for grasping the ambiguities of Muslim politics today. However much practical Muslim politics responded to more complex concerns, the conviction that the legal doctrines formalized in the eighth and ninth century were God's eternal and all-encompassing commands remained deep-rooted in jurist culture. This was so despite two important qualifications: first, that most believers knew little of the detail of the law; and, second, that in practice many scholars repeatedly showed that they were willing and able to bend legal rules to respond to new challenges. Notwithstanding this practical flexibility, the idea of an enduring and finished law remained central to the canonical tradition. Its cultural force was apparent in the fact that jurists found it impossible to assimilate the lessons of history in a way that directly altered the terms of the law. Interpretations could change; the law was for all time. For a scholar to think otherwise would invite the charge that he was asserting an authority reserved for God alone and, therefore, engaging in heretical "innovation." This cultural model of the jurist role combined with scholars' vulnerability to state authorities to insure that the majority of jurists were conservative in political affairs.

A second subpoint follows from this first. As the practice of classical Muslim politics illustrated, the ideal of a seamless fusion of religion and state was usually quarantined from political life. That is, the ideal was rarely drawn into real-and-existing political affairs, but was never eliminated entirely; it remained latent and accessible for those determined to seek it out. Those with a grievance toward the political establishment could always cite deviation from the law as grounds for rebellion. On a few occasions in Muslim history, then, the quarantine was lifted, so to speak, when dissident scholars and rebels invoked God's law to decry the corruption of the world and call for rebellion. Only in the late modern era, however, did this appeal to the law as an instrument of rebellion become a chronic refrain. As the Muslim world was upended by Western colonialism and modernity, a few Muslim thinkers saw the law as a weapon to beat back the disquieting pluralism of the modern world and return to the supposed simplicity of the Prophet's community. In the final section of this chapter, I discuss the implications of this dilemma for modern Muslim politics and culture.

Islam and Capitalism

Although it was the focus of great scholarly attention a generation ago, the question of Islam and capitalism has been overshadowed in recent years by discussions of Muslim politics. One question that has loomed large in Muslim commentaries on the market concerns the compatibility of Western or conventional banking with Islamic religious principles. The Koran prohibits *riba,* which is sometimes translated as "usury" and other times as "interest on capital" in any form. For many contemporary Muslim activists, the prohibition on *riba* has become a key symbol of the difference between Western capitalism and Islamic economics. In 1973 the Saudi government put its weight behind this concept as it founded the Islamic Development Bank, one purpose of which was to promote no-interest "Islamic" banking around the world. Shortly after it was established, the Islamic Republic of Iran did away with bank interest entirely. More generally, since the late 1970s governments in most Muslim-majority societies have either directly sponsored Islamic banks, or allowed their establishment, usually alongside a preexisting and much larger conventional banking sector.

Islamic banks employ a variety of accounting and contractual techniques to avoid paying direct interest on capital while still allowing banks to earn returns on their funds. The most common arrangements include joint-venture partnerships, equity partnerships, and leasing arrangements, all of which replace interest on principle with some kind of profit-sharing or rental agreement. One practical consequence of these arrangements is that management costs at Islamic banks tend to be slightly higher than at conventional banks, because profit-sharing requires banks to track borrower's business performance more closely than does conventional banking.

This small difference noted, the techniques of Islamic banking have been shown to be entirely compatible with modern capitalist markets. Not only are they compatible, in fact, but their broader social impact differs little from that of conventional banks. In particular, although many Muslim activists have hoped that Islamic banks might be more equity-enhancing than conventional banks, this has not proved to be the case. Less literalist Muslim thinkers, such as former president Abdurrahman Wahid of Indonesia, see this outcome as proof that the prohibition on *riba* was never really intended to ban all payment of interest on capital, but only to prohibit usury. Wahid and many other liberal-minded Muslim thinkers accuse proponents of Islamic banking of confusing the letter of the law with its spirit.

Other issues that have been cited to distinguish Islamic economics from modern Western capitalism include the obligation of all but the poor to pay a small share of their income (typically about 2.5% of net earnings) as alms. The funds accumulated are supposed to be distributed to the needy and to institutions such as schools and mosques involved in propagating the faith.

Notwithstanding prescriptions like these, it is clear that the letter of Islamic law presents few obstacles to market institutions, while providing many market-friendly injunctions. The Koran itself abounds with commercial imagery. It urges believers to engage in trade in a spirit of goodwill (4:29), stresses the importance of the faithful to fulfill all obligations in contracts (5:1; 16:91), and otherwise affirms the importance of private property, freedom of exchange, and security of contract. Two prominent Muslim writers on Islamic economics have recently summarized the Koranic perspective as affirming that "the market mechanism should be the basic co-coordinator of the Islamic economic system."[8] With its ethical appeals to care for the poor and avoid immodest displays of affluence, the spirit of Islamic economics includes a strong ethical element. But that makes it no more market-unfriendly than Christian democracy, social democracy, or welfare capitalism.

Notwithstanding their religion's compatibility with market institutions, modern Muslims have long expressed serious reservations about specific features of modern capitalism, including, most recently, the deleterious consequences of economic globalization. Their objections rarely focus on questions of inequality in the ownership of the means of production, as in Marxist critiques of capitalism. Thus in most Muslim commentaries, the class system is not the issue, although its excesses may be. Instead, Muslim critiques of the global economic order tend to highlight cultural and political matters on the margins of the formal marketplace. Many commentators, for example, object to the disproportionate cultural influence the West enjoys as a result of its hegemonic position in the global economic system. They point out, plausibly enough, that Western films, television programming, satellite broadcasts, advertising, and pornography reach more deeply into the Muslim world than anything the modern West has ever had to endure. Given the scale of this cultural onslaught, Muslim concerns are no more surprising than those heard in capitalist countries like France or even the United States, whenever the operations of global capitalism threaten some aspect of those countries' cultural heritage. Moreover, inasmuch as the sexual and lifestyle habits promoted by some Western media are as much at variance with traditional Christian values as they are Muslim, we should not be surprised to see that some Muslims have misgivings about what the marketplace has to offer. In the West, after all, Christian democrats, environmentalists, conservative Christian evangelicals, and communitarians have all decried the stimulation of consumer desires for the purpose of maximizing profits.

Perhaps the most striking difference between the Muslim and Western experience of modern capitalism, then, has less to do with questions of the law than with the simple fact that the modern capitalist market came to be localized or "embedded"[9] in the Muslim world in a way strikingly different from the pioneer capitalisms of the West. Markets and premodern capitalism had deep roots in Muslim civilization. In its early phases, the Muslim expansion was directly associated with a dramatic growth in long-distance trade. Vast commercial networks linked the Middle East and South Asia to West Africa, Central Asia, and Southeast Asia. In the sixteenth century, the greatest commercial center in the world lay not in the Christian Mediterranean but in the arc of commerce that linked Muslim-ruled India with Arabia and the Gulf to the west and Southeast Asia and southern China to the east.

Although the trading class was multiethnic and multireligious, its organization was largely a Muslim affair. Indeed, in the early modern period, the Southeast Asian portion of this trade emporium experienced an "age of commerce"[10] that achieved a cultural dynamism similar to that of Renaissance Europe. The period saw a growing urban trading class, political demands for formal limitations on rulers' power, and humanistic developments in religion and the arts.

These promising precedents were effectively destroyed when European colonialists arrived in the Indian Ocean region during the eighteenth and nineteenth centuries. Here and elsewhere in the Muslim world, the colonial interregnum guaranteed that modern capitalism came to be seen not as something rooted in Islam but as a foreign institution imposed by force. As if to reinforce this perception, the Europeans were not really free traders when it came to their colonies, but instead used state power to reserve the commanding heights of the economy for themselves.

In light of this bittersweet history, it is not surprising that real-and-existing capitalism is still seen by many Muslims as foreign and neocolonial. The conviction is reinforced by the fact that so many of the goods, services, and rules of the capitalist game are still today controlled by Western agents and respond to interests different from those seen as Muslim. Although Iran, Turkey, and Malaysia have seen the growth of a significant middle class, no Muslim society has developed a capitalist class with the gravitational pull of its Western counterpart. Nor has the capitalist tide raised enough boats to create the large middle-class and multisided (rather than bipolar) class structure that helps convince people of the advantages of power-sharing and pluralism. More than any deep-seated objection based on divine law, it is these "recent" social realities that underlie Muslim ambivalence toward the global marketplace.

The Struggle For Islam

If indigenous capitalism's gravitational force remains weak in the Muslim world, that of the neopatrimonial state is still strong. In the absence of powerful towns, an independent bourgeoisie, and a strong legal system, it was the state that spearheaded the drive for national development before and after the colonial era. In many countries, this state-centric pattern has recently only gotten worse, not better. In oil-rich countries, for example, easy control of petroleum revenues made ruling elites less willing to reach compromises with business and civil groupings. In Baathist Syria, Saddam's Iraq, and Suharto's Indonesia, authoritarian leaders used the state to prevent the growth of independent media, professional associations, labor unions, political parties, and other groupings that might check state power.

Mosques, religious schools (*madrasa*), and other Muslim institutions did not escape unscathed from this crippling of civil society. Nonetheless, in many countries, Islamic organizations fared better than their secular counterparts. In part this was so because the classical stewards of the tradition, the religious scholars (*ulama*), had long since learned how to get by in hard political times. Rulers were reassured that religious scholars represented no serious threat.

But there was a more subtle aspect to the situation. Before the 1960s, many Muslims, the majority in most countries, had been intellectually casual about their profession of faith. During the 1970s and 1980s, however, the Muslim world witnessed a dramatic increase in mosque construction, religious education, pilgrimage to Mecca, and Islamic publishing. The groundwork for some of these changes had been unwittingly laid in the 1950s and early 1960s, when secular nationalist governments set up programs of mass education. These initiatives created the first generation of Muslim youth with near-universal literacy skills (poor Muslim countries like Afghanistan and Pakistan were not part of this literacy revolution). Some among the newly educated applied their reading skills to economic and secular ends, but others used them to deepen their knowledge of Islam.

One striking indicator of this development was that, in just a few years, a new market in inexpensive Islamic books and magazines came into existence across the Muslim world. Reading this literature, people who had never had the opportunity to study in madrasas could now learn the fundamentals of their faith. Not surprisingly, then, within the newly literate public there soon emerged a new class of popular Muslim preachers, commentators, and intellectuals. Though most had little if any background in the abstruse learning of the scholarly establishment, they still asserted their right to interpret the faith on their own terms. Religious authority in the Muslim community, in other words, was being pluralized. The development was politically potent because it occurred at a time when the secular-nationalist ideology of the governing elite had begun to lose its luster, as people noticed its inability to deliver on its promises of prosperity, justice, and progress.

The religious resurgence also benefited from a basic demographic shift. Since the 1960s, the proportion of the population living in cities and towns has grown exponentially across the Muslim world. This urbanization converged with new forms of mass marketing and consumption to make the inequalities of mass society far more glaring. Meanwhile, the slums of Cairo, Lahore, Dacca, and Jakarta saw a remarkable expansion in the number of mosques and madrasas. Local centers of study and worship came to serve as a point of reference and association for the urban poor and lower-middle class. The resurgence created new networks and circles of trust, and a "social capital" aimed at investing in the business of piety.

A key point of disagreement among scholars writing on social capital, and the reason I touch on the concept here, is whether the values and networks created by religious associations can serve as a form of *democratic* social capital, in the sense that they strengthen democratic values and participation. Tocqueville's famous study of democracy in nineteenth-century America is often cited as evidence in the affirmative, since he viewed American churches as locally based institutions that nurture "habits of the heart" compatible with democratic life.[11] Other writers, however, are reluctant to extend this generalization to all religious associations. They argue that for an association to be truly civic, and to generate social capital for democratization, it must be open to all citizens. Associations premised on religious conviction may create networks and solidarities antithetical to a democratic public sphere.

The issues in this debate are important and provide several clues to the implications the Islamic resurgence will have for democratic progress in the Muslim world. Whether religious or otherwise, not all associations are alike in their social and political impact on public and political life. In particular, not all are democracy-friendly.

In the case of the Muslim world, these cautionary words help to clarify some of the issues surrounding the Islamic resurgence and democratization. The first point is that, measured in terms of its scope and density, the Islamic resurgence was a social event of historically unprecedented proportions, especially in the residential neighborhoods of the new urban poor and lower middle class. Mosques and madrasas went up in almost every corner of town, the call to prayer came to mark the rhythms of the day, and more and more women began to veil. By any measure, the resurgence represented a great transformation in civil society, marked by a vast increase in the networks and resources dedicated to religious expression.

The second observation is equally important, although often overlooked in post-September 11 discussions of Islam. It is that in its early years the resurgence was not particularly political. In most countries, the great majority of resurgents were interested in just what they claimed: heightening public devotion, affirming an identity as Muslim, and asserting the relevance of Islam for modern life. The key symbols and practices of the resurgence were not political but pietistic: learning to read Arabic, reciting the Koran, wearing the veil (for women), keeping the annual fast, and otherwise giving an Islamic hue to daily life. The Muslim world was not alone in witnessing the resurgence of religion in the public sphere. On the contrary, a similar "deprivatization" of religion took place in many parts of the world during the 1980s and 1990s, including Hindu India and parts of the Christian West.

The third observation one can make about the resurgence, however, raises more sobering questions for Islam and democratization. It is that, in light of the scale and energy of the resurgence, it was inevitable that at some point certain individuals and groups would attempt to exploit it for political ends. The resurgence created new solidarities and networks in societies with grievous political problems and few avenues for citizen participation. Just as Christian leaders played an important role in nineteenth-century American politics and Hindu revivalists are active in India today, some people jumped into the religious arena with the hope of channeling its energies toward political ends. In what was typically a later phase of the resurgence, then, one saw efforts to redirect its social capital into explicitly political projects.

One cannot stress too strongly, however, that the ambitions of this politicized Islam have been anything but uniform. Some among those resurgents responded to the crisis of state and civil society by calling for a seamless fusion of religion and state through state-sponsored enforcement of shari'a. The proponents of this unitarian Islam claim that their ambition is based on the model of the Prophet and early Muslim history. As I have suggested above, however, this religious memory forgets as much as it remembers. It overlooks the fact that a richly differentiated political landscape took shape as the Muslim community evolved from a small charismatic movement to a great world civilization. Rather than fidelity to Islam, the statist dream bespeaks a modern obsession, one familiar from modern Western history: the dream of using the state to coerce citizens toward cultural conformity.

Another cultural stream in Muslim politics, however, has spoken out against the obsession with state power and appealed for a pluralistic organization of Islam and state. Whether with Abdolkarim Soroush and the reformists in postrevolutionary Iran, Nurcholish Madjid and the "renewal" movement in Indonesia, or Rachid Ghannouchi in Tunisia, a central theme of this pluralist Islam has been the insistence that some degree of separation of state and religious authority is vital *so as to guard the sanctity and values of Islam itself.*

In other words, unlike Turkey's Mustafa Kemal and other Muslim secularists, these pluralist reformers advocate a desacralization of the political (or portions of it), not in order to privatize or push back the religious, but to protect and deepen its highest values.

"Religion forbids us from assuming a God-like character," writes the Iranian dissident (and former anti-American militant), Abdolkarim Soroush.[12] He continues: "This is especially true in politics and government where limiting the power of the state, division of powers, and the doctrine of checks and balances are established in order to prevent accumulation of power that might lead to such Godly claims." The separation that Soroush and others have in mind is not of the order preferred by French laicists or American secularists: it does not demand that religion be purely private or kept out of the public sphere. The arrangement envisioned builds instead on a precedent latent in the actions (if not the statements) of Islam's classical jurists. Namely, pluralist Muslims seek to protect what they regard as Islam's highest ideals by refusing to grant state officials a monopoly in religious affairs. Rather than a unitarian fusion, then, the pluralists propose to locate the center of gravity for public religion in the associations and dialogue of civil society, as well as in a system of government subject to effective checks and balances.

Whether this remarkable mutation in Muslim political culture will spread and become the model for a broader, pluralistic reformation of Muslim politics will depend upon more than the cogency of a few intellectuals' arguments. Already, however, in countries as varied as Turkey, Iran, Indonesia, and Malaysia, we have seen efforts to scale up this pluralist Islam into a mass movement for religious and political reform. In the Islamic republic of Iran, in particular, events since the election of the reformer President Khatami in May 1997 have demonstrated that the youth wing of this new middle class has grown deeply disaffected with the reigning conservative interpretation of Muslim politics. Soroush's evolution from Islamist militant—he was architect of the revolutionary purges at the University of Teheran in the mid-1980s—to bold democrat provides one of the many indices of this breathtaking, if troublingly uncertain, transformation.

At the same time, however, recent events have shown us that the antipluralist conservatives enjoy some tactical advantages over the moderates. The first is that the militants self-select into well-organized and ideologically motivated organizations, while the moderates tend to be less comprehensively organized, if organized at all. As recent political violence in Indonesia and Pakistan has shown, many moderate Muslims eschew activism of any sort, preferring the cool comfort of private devotion to heated political battles. As in contemporary Iran, the moderates may be forced into action by conservative attacks, but, lacking the ideological fervor of their rivals, many may prefer to wait out the storm rather than sacrifice their lives for all.

A second and even more disturbing advantage enjoyed by the conservatives became strikingly apparent in the aftermath of September 11, 2001, although its foundation was laid several years earlier. Terrorist groups like Al Qaeda and the Jemaah Islamiyah have taken advantage of the networks provided by globalization to link their finances and military resources to local conflicts to which Muslims are party. Before the Taliban were overthrown in late 2001, the arms, military training, and ideological motivation provided at Al Qaeda camps in Afghanistan served as a potent catalyst for some of the Muslim world's most volatile conflicts. In linking transnational networks to local conflicts in this way, international terrorists have been able to give local radicals an influence in their homelands vastly out of proportion to their actual numbers in society. This unintended by-product of globalization threatens to undercut moderates' efforts to reform Muslim politics and protect Islam.

If the hardliners enjoy certain tactical advantages, the moderates nonetheless have one crucial advantage: the pluralizing consequences of modernity. One little-remarked but deeply important feature of today's globalization is that by making societies more permeable to the flow of people and ideas, globalization has made it easier for people to make independent assessments of their own cultures and institutions. We need only recall the subtly subversive impact of West German television on East German communism to appreciate that the freer flow of information makes it easier for people to reach conclusions other than those sanctioned by ideological canon. The impact of such comparisons is not always Western-friendly, of course. Some people outside the United States may take a long look at the orations of American politicians on CNN and come away unimpressed. But that's what's so powerful about the new global media. The freer flow of images and information allows a late-modern *bricolage* (to use Lévi-Strauss's old term), whereby people pick and choose and reach conclusions more eclectic than before. Inasmuch as this is the case, we must take care *not* to assume that local culture is all that counts in actors' consciousness. The evidence from the Muslim world and elsewhere is that growing numbers of people engage in outside-the-box/ outside-the-culture comparisons. Many Muslims are concluding that the Islam they profess must be compatible with economic progress, higher education, women's dignity, and freedom from the intimidation of self-appointed thugs. We should not underestimate the power of this conviction in the Muslim world.

The long-term outcome of the struggle between these rival streams in Muslim political culture will depend on broader developments in society. A civic outcome will require, among other things, a more pluralist balance of power between state and society. This achievement will require in turn that religious scholars accept and legitimate the new social pluralism. If civility and pluralism prevail, however, they will do so not because of the triumph of secularist modernism but because a new generation of Muslims understands what their classical predecessors acknowledged in practice if not always in word: that a separation of powers and a desacralization of the state is in the deepest interest of Islam itself. Certainly the fate of the Muslim world in the twenty-first century is still far from clear. But there are grounds for cautious hope, because that future depends not just on age-old religious commentaries but on thoroughly contemporary cultural matters.

Notes

1. Max Weber, *The Sociology of Religion* (New York: Free Press, 1965).
2. Bryan Turner, *Weber and Islam* (London: Routledge & Kegan Paul, 1974), 35.
3. Bernard Lewis, *The Political Language of Islam* (Chicago: University of Chicago Press, 1988), 2.
4. Ira Lapidus, "The Separation of State and Religion in the Development of Early Islamic Society," *International Journal of Middle East Studies* 6, no. 4 (1975): 363–85.
5. Brinkley Messick, *The Calligraphic State: Textual Domination and History in a Muslim Society* (Berkeley: University of California Press, 1993), 143.
6. Henry Munson, *Religion and Power in Morocco* (New Haven, CT: Yale University Press, 1993), 27.
7. Joseph Schacht, *An Introduction to Islamic Law* (Oxford: Clarendon Press, 1964), 74.
8. Farhad Nomani and Ali Rahnema, *Islamic Economic Systems* (London: Zed, 1994), 55–56.
9. Mark Granovetter, "Economic Action and Social Structure: The Problem of Embeddedness" *American Journal of Sociology* 91 (1995): 481–510; Hefner, "On the History and Cross-Cultural Possibility of a Democratic Ideal," in *Democratic Civility: The History and Cross-Cultural Possibility of a Modern Political Ideal*, ed., Robert W. Hefner (New Brunswick, NJ: Transaction, 1998), 3–49.

10. Anthony Reid, *Southeast Asia in the Age of Commerce, 1450–1680*, vol. 2, *Expansion and Crisis* (New Haven, CT: Yale University Press, 1993).

11. Alexis de Tocqueville, *Democracy in America*, trans.George Lawrence. (Garden City, NY: Doubleday, 1969).

12. Abdolkarim Soroush, *Reason, Freedom, and Democracy in Islam* (Oxford: Oxford University Press, 2000), 64.

16

Hinduism and Modernity

PRATAP BHANU MEHTA

The relationship between Hinduism—or any religion—and modernity is methodologically difficult to delineate. Discussions of this relationship often begin with lists of modern values such as equality, liberty, toleration, individualism, self expression, and economic acquisitiveness. We then ask to what extent these values can find support within the tradition's teachings and how reformers have introduced them. While such exercises can be useful in saving a religion from caricature, they generally shed little light on the actual—and often paradoxical—dynamics that link the world's diverse array of religious traditions with the ideas and practices of modern democratic politics.

This is so for several reasons. First, a tradition's teachings—even if wonderfully rich and complex in themselves—may have a historically indeterminate relationship to questions of social organization. Hinduism's emphasis on the importance of coming to know and develop one's fullest potential, of realizing one's highest self, for example, would seem to be a promising resource for the democratic imagination. Yet the history of Hindus records few attempts to create a social structure that might favor such an endeavor. The real point in such matters is not what a tradition teaches, but how and what its adherents think. Humans are not merely passive products of culture or religious doctrine, but agents who constantly and actively imagine and re-imagine their beliefs and social worlds.

Second, the process of articulating a tradition will often involve contradictions and compromises. For example, many ideologies that attacked the caste system ended up accommodating themselves to its requirements. Or consider Catholics who practice contraception and accept abortion, or Muslims who engage in usury. Are they necessarily being insincere about their religious allegiance? In other words, are the tensions and compromises inherent in a religion an artifact of its ideological structure, or the infirmities of its adherents? Third, and perhaps most important for present purposes, to the extent that religious ideas matter, they do so in ways that are often unintended and paradoxical. As Max Weber argued, it was not Calvinism's teachings themselves but their unlooked-for side effects that powered the rise of capitalism in northwestern Europe. To neglect such complexities is to risk misrepresenting both how a given tradition works in practice and how its beliefs might be related causally to a political order such as democracy or a modern system such as capitalism.

In the case of Hinduism, these problems are further compounded because of three debates associated with it. First, is Hinduism—and by extension other Indic religions—a religion in the Western sense of the term? Is it held together by a set of beliefs or by a set of practices? What is the relationship between practices and beliefs? Second, what is the scope of Hinduism? Anthropology and other disciplines inspired by structuralism tend to see society as a unified whole, pervaded by a single ideological system. One unfortunate consequence of this assumption was that almost every practice in society came to be related to religion; from the start observers assumed that no domain lay outside of it. Hence it was easy to conclude that Hinduism was responsible for pretty much everything, good or bad, that went on in Indian society. One argument I will make in this chapter is that it is not religious teaching per se that determines a religion's fit with modernity. The more important question is whether, in certain domains of activity, religion simply cedes to other sources of ideological legitimacy. As part of the process of social reform, large domains of activity are pulled away from their religious moorings. As the disjuncture between economy, politics, and values grows, it becomes difficult to causally attribute behavior in any of these domains to some integrated system of values.

Finally, Hinduism presents an interesting challenge because it is a system that has historically been premised on a diverse and radical form of relativizing. Weber put it well: Indian tolerance rests upon this absolute relativizing of all ethical and soteriological command-ments. They are organically relativized not only according to caste membership, but also according to the goal or end the individual seeks. The issue is not negative tolerance but positive, relative, and graded appreciation of quite contrary maxims of action. And Hindus recognize that the various spheres of life operate in a lawful ethical autonomy and have equal and independent value. All this resulted from their equal devaluation as soon as ultimate questions of salva-tion were at stake.

This fact that everything is relative makes it very difficult to ar-ticulate an "integrated" conception of *dharma* within Hinduism. On the one hand, certain soteriological goals, like *moksha* or liberation from the cycle of birth and death, are granted hierarchical preference. *Dharma* also has certain features of a universal ethic. Virtues like for-bearance, patience, freedom from envy, tranquility, and freedom from desire are enjoined as being universal. It has maxims of conduct that apply to all castes: do no harm, tell the truth, do not steal, live purely, control your passions. But these very general connotations of *dharma* are rapidly qualified by a series of adjectives that make the *dharma* relative to caste, time (*yuga dharma*), place, context (*sadharana dhar-ma*), and even individual temperament, thus allowing for a good deal of flexibility. As Weber had noted, the caste system was premised on some differentiation of functions, implying that duties were specific to each caste. In an extreme instance, even a band of robbers could have its own dharma! Texts such as the *Arthshastra* argue that as a profession even the *vesyas* (courtesans or royal prostitutes) have their own dharma. Thus the entire social order is premised on the prolif-eration of specialized duties. It is difficult to imagine how a single moral economy could integrate into one single whole the obligations of householders and those of courtesans. Thus the question of what values are obligatory becomes a highly contingent one: the answer is, "it all depends." Therefore, at an ideological level, it has been easy for Hinduism to accommodate modernity.

Hinduism, Modernity, and Democracy

It has often been remarked that the word "Hindu"—which comes from the same root as the name India—is not a term of self-identification, but rather a catchall description used by visitors from the West who originally meant it as shorthand for "those who live east or south of the Indus River." Even at the time of Alexander the Great, such people were comparatively numerous and exhibited great and obvious diversity, so the question "Who is a Hindu?" is an old and valid one. Over the years, a congeries of movements have sought to explain and create a unified Hindu identity. In the modern period, most critically, a unified Hindu legal identity began to emerge as a product of state formation (first colonial and then sovereign) in the nineteenth and twentieth centuries.

Among the most remarkable chapters in the story of how the state has modified and defined Hindu identity was a case that the Indian Supreme Court resolved with a landmark 1966 ruling following almost two decades of litigation.[1] The court made the Swami Narayana sect of Bombay comply with a 1947 law that had opened Hindu temples to all worshipers, including members of "untouchable" hereditary castes. The ruling denied the sect members' claim that they were non-Hindus and hence exempt from having to admit the despised castes. The court worried that letting a Hindu sect evade the reach of progressive laws would stifle efforts to reform Hinduism at large. The court emphasized Hinduism's historic capacity for internal reform, its progressive outlook, its flexibility, its compatibility with social equality, and its extraordinary tolerance. Hinduism, the court taught, is not only consistent with democracy, progress, equality, and social reform, but also requires a commitment to these things.

The court not only focused on the issue of who counts as a Hindu, it also struggled with the task of defining Hinduism itself and came up with a seven-item list of Hindu essentials. The invidious caste distinction at the heart of the case was itself a reminder of the complicated transformations that Hinduism has had to undergo in order to become compatible with democracy. With all its interdictions, exclusions, and regulations, the caste system is one of the most elaborately and egregiously hierarchical social conceptions that humans have ever entertained. Dominant interpretations of Hinduism long legitimized it. A society preoccupied with caste would hardly seem to be a promising ground for democracy, individual freedom, or equality. While it is true that freedom and equality remain subject to political contestation in India, it is striking that this most hierarchically ordered of societies should have so readily embraced, in principle at first and then increasingly in practice, the principles and the procedures of liberal democracy.

The speed of the change in these millennia-old customs is also stunning. Universal suffrage first arose as a topic of discussion in the early 1890s. By the mid-1920s, the major movements representing Hinduism had accepted the principle. Since India's independence from Britain and partition from Pakistan in 1947, the overall direction of political change has been toward greater power for the numerically vast but long-downtrodden lower castes. They now occupy the political center of gravity in the world's largest democracy. All of this is even more remarkable when one reflects that in the first half of the twentieth century, no social theory extant anywhere would have advised the introduction of universal suffrage in a poverty-ridden, caste-bound, and largely illiterate society.

Crucial to such trailblazing writings was Hinduism's complex encounter with colonialism. The presence of the British Raj and all it signified put pressure on Hindu traditions and forced Hinduism to rearticulate its own principles. Such rethinkings are matters of active human choice, and the directions they take can be unpredictable. Colonial rule was legitimized by the ideas that subject peoples or societies were in some sense backward and that they were not *nations,* and hence had no claim to recognition as sovereign entities. This background is crucial to understanding how Hinduism has been rearticulating itself since the nineteenth century. In part the process has been defensive, with attempts to show that Hinduism is the source of all that modernity prizes, from democracy to science. Whatever one thinks of such hermeneutics, they have had the effect of legitimizing new values in Hindu terms. To claim, even on dubious grounds, that one's tradition is a source of democracy is to acknowledge democracy's stature and legitimacy. In its encounter with other traditions, including liberalism and enlightenment, Hinduism became aware that if it failed to claim as its own certain values identified with progressive modernity, it would always remain vulnerable both to criticism by outsiders and to defections by its own adherents. Reform may come from high principle, but it may also come from a tradition's sense of what it needs to do to survive external and internal challenges.

The imperative of creating a nation required new and more horizontal forms of mobilization. Nationalism, as Leah Greenfeld points out, is the crucible of modern democracy.[2] Any articulate anticolonial critique must assume that the colonized society can be a self-governing nation. Indians could demand self-determination only by appealing to the authority of a new entity in the social imaginary, "the Indian people." But doing so would require privileging their status as members of this people—as citizens of a nation struggling to be born, in other words—over older and more restrictive forms of identification such as sect, clan, or caste. It would also mean granting this people at least a modicum of participatory access. Thus did anti-colonial nationalism tend to bring secular and democratic ideas along in its logical train.

As important as the imperatives of social reform and nationalism were, however, they would not have been enough to make Indians feel an "elective affinity for democracy" had certain longstanding features of Hinduism not been present. The notion that democracy fits nicely into, or even can somehow be said to spring from, Hindu tradition may have begun as part of a defense against colonialist claims, but certain features of Hinduism bolster this line of thought. Hinduism does have a certain supple, plural, or open quality. In a recent ruling, the Indian Supreme Court confessed that they found it "difficult, if not impossible to define Hindu religion or even adequately describe it," and continued:

> Unlike other religions in the world, the Hindu religion does not claim any one prophet; it does not worship any one God. It does not subscribe to any one dogma; it does not believe in any one philosophic concept; it does not follow any one set of religious rites or performances; in fact, it does not appear to satisfy the narrow traditional features of any religion or creed.[3]

Moreover, Hinduism is a tradition whose source texts contain a great deal of what might be called skepticism. As the *Mahabharata* says: "There are many different Vedas, the law books are many, the advice of one sage is necessarily different from that given by others. The real rules of duty remain buried in a dark cave. The only path is the way in which great men [or in some readings, "a great many men"] have lived their lives." Within primal Hinduism, in short, the question of authority was open to a remarkable degree. Hinduism's complex encounter with colonialism—and with modernity more generally—both tested that openness and made it possible for Hindus who grasped the inner and outer challenges facing their tradition to leverage the tradition's openness in constructive ways.

Some of the opposition to British-led reform was simply reaction-ary. But another strain of feeling opposed less the substance of this or that reform than the British role in it. Partha Chaterjee, whose analy-sis of these episodes is the most impressive I have seen, argues that the emergent nationalist imagination was dividing society into two domains: the outer, material, public domain and the inner, spiritual, private one. The outer domain was conceived of as the realm of pub-lic institutions, economics, technology, and civil society. This domain was the social space where creative borrowing from the West could take place. The inner domain was supposed to remain the ambit of tradition and a distinct cultural identity. In this sphere, which was taken to include religion and family life, nationalists rejected emula-tion of the West and sought to preserve what they saw as venerable cultural traditions. Crucially, nationalists believed that the nation as a whole was entitled to claim sovereignty over this inner domain.[4] Opposition to British reforms such as the Age of Consent Act be-spoke this shift in the "agency of reform from the legal authority of the colonial state to the moral authority of the national community."[5] Nationalists felt that the task of authenticating, articulating, codify-ing, and reforming tradition should belong to the entire nation.

The nationalists had two goals: to throw off colonial subordina-tion and to take distinctively "national" traditions out of the realm of the unselfconscious and merely customary so that the nation itself might claim them to further its self-realization as an autonomous people deserving of sovereignty. Of course, who exactly might be said to constitute the nation and on what terms was and is deeply con-tested. The general expectation among Indian nationalists seems to have been that each of the subcontinent's various sub-communities would take charge of revivifying and reforming its own traditions and customs.

Such thinking helped to inspire a spate of Hindu and Muslim re-form movements that swept across early twentieth-century British India. The idea was to make substantive reforms, and to refashion communal identities in the process. Muslim reformers sought to replace the variegated array of customary practices that their core-ligionists followed in various parts of India with a common and re-formed Muslim personal law. This effort culminated in the passage of the Shariat Application Act of 1937. At about the same time, wide-ranging Hindu reform movements were paving the way to modernize

Hinduism. The precise agendas of such movements and the furious controversies they generated need not detain us here. What is crucial is that these movements were not merely challenging the authority of the colonial state to interpret native traditions but were opening up these religions to a far-reaching self-examination. This was a contest over doctrine, authority, and identity.

Authority and Ambivalence

But who did have authority to speak for indigenous traditions? That never became clear. Hindus in particular had unique issues of their own to wrestle with as they tried to answer this question. One issue was Hinduism's own ambivalence about politics. As one of the most astute analysts of Indian political thought puts it: "Kingship remains, even theoretically, suspended between sacrality and secularity, divinity and mortal humanity, legitimate authority and arbitrary power, dharma and adharma."[6] Political power and spiritual authority were firmly separated, as exemplified by the traditional distinction between the priestly Brahmins and the Kshatriya (warrior) caste. The king inhabited the realm of necessity, where politics had its own autonomy and an internal logic that brooked no outside interference. But the king drew his legitimacy from his service to the "spiritual order," just as the priests depended upon the king for physical protection. The upshot is that Hindu thought's version of the separation of church and state has never been quite stable. And yet politics, even when dependent upon religion for earthly legitimization, has never in Hindu thought taken on messianic or apocalyptic significance. The world of the political is significant, but it can never become an arena for what Eric Voegelin called "the immanentization of the eschaton."

In practice, this Hindu capacity to imagine the political without expecting it to give meaning to everything or comprehensively relieve the human estate has been of great service in defining the secular space that liberal democracy requires. A respect for the proper autonomy of different spheres of human action and a refusal to pine for a single moral order that can render the world whole are aspects of the Hindu moral imagination that not only reinforce democratic politics but also help to set healthy boundaries for it. When Hindus claim that democracy has been a "natural" outgrowth of Hinduism, they may be gesturing at something like this account of Hindu political prudence and moderation. The Hindu tendency to see politics as an autonomous but limited sphere obviates the need to impose a single doctrinal orthodoxy and permits a well-advised toleration of various forms of social existence. Indeed, Hindu intellectuals' discussions of democracy often seem to equate it with a kind of group pluralism: Sarvepalli Radhakrishnan's influential *Hindu View of Life* mostly sees democracy as a matter of ensuring that each group "should be allowed to develop the best in it without impeding the progress of others."[7]

Yet contrary to what Radhakrishnan and other neo-Hindu apologists have claimed, traditional Hindu intellectual pluralism long coexisted with the imposition of the most rigid social orthodoxy and hierarchy. Different groups were tolerated only so long as they stayed well within certain narrow boundaries and conventions. While the specific distribution of power and authority among castes could be fluid, and while various species of protest against caste hierarchies arose from time to time, pre-modern Hinduism on the whole remained bound up with the phenomenon of caste. Many Hindu reformers, such as Vivekanada, thought that political democratization might be the only sure means of improving the lot of historically marginalized groups, since their ranks were so large and democracy does so much by majority rule. The empowerment of India's lower castes continues, and still encounters resistance.

Hinduism may have been hierarchical, but it was at the same time so plural that Hindu society was nearly impervious to projects for imposing centralized uniformity. Even after colonialism and then statehood brought a measure of centralization, the pluralism of Hindu group life continued to spin such a complex web of cross-cutting cleavages that no single group could hope to dominate, a circumstance indirectly propitious for liberal democracy. To gain power required building alliances whose very formation would tend to rub the sharpest edges off a group's own claims. Hinduism's skeptical streak and sophisticated approach to ethical reflection, moreover, precluded dreams of reducing the complexity of Hindu society to an imposed conformity of allegedly "pure" thought or belief.

Another unique aspect of the Hindu situation was the impact of Islamic conquests in the subcontinent during the centuries before the British achieved dominance. Hindus had lived under a congeries of regional and local rulers, including the Muslim Mughal emperors, and had nothing like the Islamic caliphate, whose specter still haunts the imagination of the Muslim world. The absence of any historical model of a kingdom that represented Hindus as Hindus made it easier to experiment with new political forms and provided leeway for fresh thinking about political questions. This "do-it-yourself" quality of the Hindu experience may also help to explain why so many Hindus have been and continue to be fascinated by the idea that democracy is somehow a "Hindu" system that springs from Hindu sources and represents Hindus as such.

Hinduism has mostly known only local forms of authority, whether embodied by Brahmins in some areas or by other dominant castes elsewhere. Modern times brought all-Indian political forms (first the raj, then the republic) and an all-Indian consciousness to go with them. As state consolidation made strides, traditional forms of authority became ever more limited in their appeal. Appeals to such fading and fragmented sources of authority could no longer legitimize anyone's hope to rule the huge new entity being created across the vast reaches of land between the Himalayas and Sri Lanka. With traditional authority dropping out of the picture, in practice the sole recourse for all those hungering and thirsting after political legitimacy and credibility was popular mobilization in some guise or other. Only democracy, in other words, could fill the void left by the old authorities' unavoidable withdrawal.

As internal and external pressures for change mounted, Hindus had to face them without any institution that had *prima facie* authority to direct the reforms. There is no Hindu Vatican. What agency, then, could have the power and the legitimacy to undertake an overhaul of religious traditions? What would be a credible representative and institutional process through which to carry out these reforms? In India after independence, the answer turned out to be obvious. The modern state, with institutions legitimized by universal suffrage, could take upon itself the task of reforming Hinduism. The modern Indian state is secular: it favors no establishment of religion and accords equal citizenship to people of all religious descriptions. Only Indonesia and Pakistan have more Muslims than India, while Christianity has been present on the subcontinent for millennia. Yet the Indian Constitution has been rightly called a charter for the social reform of Hinduism: the secular, democratic government of this Hinduism-suffused society is the authoritative vehicle for the reform of Hinduism. Perhaps secularism, like cricket, is a quintessentially Indian game that just happens to have been invented elsewhere.

Thus the Indian state not only aims to reform Hindu practices, but also has been in some sense authorized to do so by Hindus. In the Indian context it is legitimate for state institutions such as the Supreme Court and the Lok Sabha (parliament) to concern themselves with reforming or eliminating such invidious socio-religious practices as second-class treatment of "untouchables." Faced with the question of who shall decide, Hindus in effect answered: "We all will, and the federal Republic of India will be our means." Democracy was an answer to the conundrum of authority, not a product of allegiance to values.

Hinduism and Economic Development

The value system of Hinduism and the social structure it sustained were widely held to explain South Asia's inability to attain decent economic performance after 1750.[8] Again, the locus classicus of this view was articulated by Max Weber, who suggested that the effects of Hinduism on economic progress were "essentially negative." Two principal mechanisms of Hinduism were thought to have negative consequences. First, acceptance of the doctrine of *karma* was said to lessen ambition and aspiration and encourage a fatalistic acceptance of one's condition rather than determination to ameliorate it. Second, caste made Indian society paradoxically versatile and immutable at the same time. Groups had considerable room for mobility within the caste system, since political power was not always confined to particular caste groups. It was even possible to renounce caste society as an individual.

Caste was stable because it was linked to two tendencies that at first seem opposed. On the one hand caste was traditionalist and anti-rational. It manifested itself through endogamy, rules of pollution and purity, and ritual observances and practices. On the other hand it was rationalized by karma theology, which explained why an individual was born in a particular social location. The theological underpinnings of caste produced an extraordinary traditionalism, where any deviations from the prescribed order would result in some kind of ritual degradation. Moreover, the fact of ritual seclusion produced a considerable social distance between various groups and made collective action difficult. On this basis Weber argued that because of their seclusion, the traders "remained in the shackles of the typical oriental merchant class which by itself has never created a modern capitalist organization of labor."[9]

This powerful and influential story has come to be seen as deeply flawed for several reasons. The first has to do with a different understanding of what gave the caste system its apparent stability. In this view the immutability of caste had little to do with the power of Hinduism's theological tenets. It was rather a product of a complex amalgam of forces: economic relations combined with the need to legitimize the political power of particular groups, resulting in extraordinarily stable social hierarchies. But these hierarchies were often disturbed and rendered more fluid with changes in political power. What anthropologists were identifying as the immutability of caste was simply a projection into the past of a state of affairs that obtained under colonial rule and its immediate aftermath. As evidence of this, caste relations have undergone an extraordinary transformation with the advent of democracy. Caste in urban settings has a very different function from caste in conditions of rural scarcity.

Second, there is very little evidence that Hindu "beliefs" produced something akin to a fatalistic acceptance of the world. There was no dearth of striving or ambition. But most importantly for the purposes of the development of capitalism, Weber was simply mistaken in his assumption that ritual seclusion would inhibit traders' activities. As the influential contemporary historian Chris Bayly has written: "Caste at the level of geographically extended kin groups had an important role in the organization of trading diasporas; at the level of the commensal *jati* group it was relevant to the social and economic organization of artisan groups." Bayly finds it "difficult to see how caste could have been the prime parameter of mercantile organization in complex cities," and points out that "forms of arbitration, market control, brokerage, neighborhood communities and above all conceptions of mercantile honor and credit *breached* caste boundaries and imposed wider social solidarities on mercantile people."[10] In other words, caste did not act as a barrier to wider economic rationality or the emergence of wider social solidarities.

Like most religions, Hinduism's core ideology was thought to be particularly detrimental to the status of women. The Hindi poet Maithlisharan Gupta summed it up: "They call us goddesses and treat us like slaves." Again, the relationship between gender discrimination and patriarchy on the one hand and Hindu religious beliefs on the other remains complicated. Most of the texts on the ritual side of Hinduism and the rights of women display streaks of misogyny, while the tradition's epic texts do recognize women's agency. But women were subordinated to an extraordinary degree, and many practices that secured this subordination—child marriage, secluded widowhood, preference for a male child—were enforced in the name of religion.

Equally striking is the fact that reform movements helped dislodge the ideological legitimacy of female subordination. Formally, the Indian state, through a series of legislative enactments and judicial decisions, has been extremely progressive and the last vestiges of discrimination are being removed. But women continue to live in appalling subordination. The signs of this are everywhere: family preferences in allocating nutrition, female infanticide, the distribution of property rights, harassment at workplaces. India is extremely progressive in statistical terms, for example male-female ratios in higher education; but the declining proportion of females to males in the population reminds us of the massive scale of discrimination and subordination. Patriarchy has proved stubborn. In many cases, for instance the decline in population sex ratios, religious leaders have taken the initiative on reforms. But the hard rocks of patriarchy have proven difficult to dislodge.

It is true that caste and the complex rituals, interdictions, and exclusions it generated have impeded one fundamental idea of modernity: that each person is the author of his or her own life. This radical conception of autonomy was found nowhere in traditional religions. Part of the contest over religion concerned the question of whether any authority external to the individual should exercise power over her. Hinduism had an easier time dealing with this question because of its internal diversity and the absence of a natural source of authority. It could not easily lend itself to underwriting any political order and hence left space for modern politics to flourish. Liberating the teleology of everyday life from (sometimes inhuman) ritual has proved to be an arduous task. But amazingly, the social reforms undertaken in the last century have at least delegitimized traditional sources of authority in this area. This does not mean that Hindus all accept modern values of liberty, equality and economic advancement. But it does at least mean that their religion offers few objections to their doing so. Nor does this mean a lessening of religiosity—far from it. But it does mean that modern Hinduism has become a protracted contest over what being a Hindu means. It is one of Hinduism's virtues that it has at least given many of its adherents a way of transcending the confines of their own tradition without making that tradition seem despicable.

Notes

1. *Shastri Yagna Purushdasji v Muldas Bhunadardas Vaisya.*
2. Leah Greenfeld, *Nationalism: Five Roads to Modernity* (Cambridge: Harvard University Press, 1992).
3. *Prabhoo vs. Kunte, SCC 1995.*
4. Partha Chatterjee, *The Nation and Its Fragments: Colonial and Postcolonial Histories* (Princeton: Princeton University Press, 1995).
5. Karuna Mantena has greatly clarified my understanding of this history.
6. J. C. Heesterman, *The Inner Conflict of Tradition* (Chicago: University of Chicago Press, 1985), 111.
7. Sarvepalli Radhakrishnan, *The Hindu View of Life* (London: Unwin, 1960), 70.
8. See, for representative views, Kusm Nair, *Blossoms in the Dust* (New York: Praeger, 1962); Abbe Dubois, *Hindu Manners Customs and Ceremonies* (Oxford: Clarendon Press, 1906).
9. Max Weber, *Religion of India*, 112. The religion of India; the sociology of Hinduism and Buddhism. Translated and edited by Hans H. Gerth and Don Martindale. Glencoe, Ill., Free Press (1958).
10. Chris Bayly, "Indian Merchants in a Traditional Setting: Benaras: 1780-1830 in *The Imperial Impact: Studies in the Economic History of Africa and Asia* (London: Athlone Press, 1988).

Part IV
The Media

17

Journalism and Values

CARLOS ALBERTO MONTANER
MARIANO GRONDONA
Translated by Marilu Del Toro

Can newspapers and magazines become the means for transmitting the values that lead to economic development and a deepening of democracy? And can that happen without manipulation or indoctrination? These questions drive the reflections that follow.

Some of the oldest dailies in the world are Latin American. Chile's *Mercurio* was founded in 1827; *La Nación,* one of the continent's great dailies, was established in Buenos Aires in 1870 by Bartolomé Mitre; Santo Domingo's *Listín Diario* was founded in 1889 and remains the flagship of the Dominican press, even though Rafael Leonidas Trujillo's dictatorship closed it down for more than two decades.

Latin American newspapers were an ideological battlefield even before the continent's republics were established in the first decades of the 1800s. In the 1700s, the Spanish colonial authorities sometimes grew neglectful of their zealous censorship, and the creoles dared to defend dangerous ideas in print. On the other hand, well into the twentieth century, hardly any books were being printed in Latin America; bookstores and independent writers were scarce; and universities were often sleepy institutions, seldom home to original proposals or vibrant debate. As a result, newspapers and magazines practically monopolized public debate in print, with more informal discussion taking place in Masonic lodges, cafes, and social clubs.

If we make the traditional journalistic distinction between "opinion" and "information," we will see that problems arise in both types of journalism when we try to promote the qualities that characterize a prosperous, democratic society.

Opinion Columns

As a general rule, we do not count too much on articles or opinion columns to change the political and economic cultures of our countries. For more than three decades one of us, Carlos Alberto Montaner, has written a column published throughout Latin America, Europe, and the United States. This broad readership forces a constant search for themes of equal interest to readers in San José, São Paulo, Miami, and Madrid. Local anecdotes can be developed into universally interesting columns, but they must illuminate broader issues; few readers are interested in faraway events. The other author, Mariano Grondona, has had a similar experience during several decades of writing for Hispanic America in the magazine *Visión* and for Argentina in the daily, *La Nación*.

We have both learned a sad lesson that has immunized us against any kind of triumphant temptation: columnists rarely "create" public opinion. Rather, they usually give elegant and logical form to what their readers already believe in a disorganized and fragmented way. Nor do editorial writers "make" readers. What they do is find them. They collect them and keep them interested in the newspaper that their readers habitually buy.

The reader does not look at every section of the newspaper with the same attitude. He approaches the news pages to find out what is going on in the world: what happened in Kosovo, on the New York Stock Exchange, or at the stadium of his favorite sport. The news may sadden or gladden him but it is unlikely to trouble him seriously. Perhaps he will learn of a new medicine for treating migraines or a prodigious new piece of software, but his reaction to this information is rarely visceral.

The opinion piece, however, is different. In the opinion pages the reader seeks agreement, complicity. The pleasure in reading lies in being able to say, "This is what I would have said or written about this topic." And he feels annoyance for the opposite reason: "How does this idiot dare come to these mistaken conclusions?" Hence the doubtful impact of columnists who are too eccentric. They may be so original in their arguments, interests, and reasoning that few readers get from them the comforts of easy understanding and ready agreement.

Still, even though we humbly accept the limitations of the opinion column and recognize that the horoscopes, comic strips, and sports pages tend to have more readers than in-depth articles, it is no less true that some faithful and impassioned readers follow their columnists day after day and are delighted when they find in print what they wish they had written, gradually establishing with their newspaper an emotional tie much like the esprit de corps seen in sports clubs. In fact some newspapers focus on opinion rather than information (especially now that radio and television often get the news to the public faster than the dailies can). Madrid's *ABC* and Paris's *Le Figaro*, two of the most successful European newspapers, grow more inclined each day to maintain their quota of readers with the bylines of famous columnists.

In a way, by this revitalization of opinion, journalism can return to the great tradition of the nineteenth century, when each newspaper was more of an ideological frontline than an informative medium, and readers followed the *mano a mano* discussions—the incendiary debates—of the columnists with the same sense of partisan commitment with which Spaniards followed the matches of the great bullfighters.

Biased Information

Let us now look at news journalism. Why is there not greater ideological balance in the press? Why are so many more journalists on the left than on the right (labels we admit are rather limited and unfair)?

The main reason is probably the psychology of many young people who enter university journalism departments or the media. These are not people who want above all to think objectively about reality, who feel a pressing need to devote their lives to the search for truth. On the contrary, they are idealistic young people, who see many things wrong with this vale of tears and think they know how to fix them. They want to change the world, not report on it. Low-intensity crusaders ("liberals" or "do-gooders" in American parlance) are predominant in Latin American journalism.

Liberalism is a real and legitimate political force in developed societies because it reaches out toward progressive, realizable goals beyond the substantial development that has already been achieved; unfortunately it is dysfunctional in underdeveloped countries, where basic needs are less widely satisfied. Those who look at underdevelopment with the liberal perspective of the developed world overlook this important fact.

Hence egalitarianism, an admirable value in developed countries, becomes in developing countries a kind of populism that can hinder the dissemination of other values and attitudes that are necessary but have not yet been acquired. These include order and respect for legality, respect for the market and property rights, a fiscal policy that does not undermine the formation of capital and that nurtures sensible budgets in tune with the real possibilities of raising funds for the national treasury. Because these have been the ruling values for so long in developed countries, they are considered "conservative." But because they do not yet prevail in developing countries, they are the truly "progressive" values that underdeveloped countries need—notwithstanding the scorn they sometimes incur from idealistic journalists who believe themselves to be in the vanguard of progress.

The Influence of Talk Shows

To speak only of one aspect of the immense influence that television has on society, and particularly on the young, let us say a word about talk shows. As Walter Cronkite noted in his memoirs, the problem with TV journalists is that they often compete not with each other, as happens in the press, but with highly popular situation comedies, law and order shows, sports events, and movies. Talk show journalists, particularly those who air on prime time, may risk low ratings or loss of identity.

But those who succeed—for example, Larry King in the United States—may become institutions with a powerful influence on an audience that is vastly larger than the audience of the press. To be sure, this larger audience is more diverse. When a columnist writes, he addresses himself to a well-known universe of readers who by and large agree with his views. In contrast, the TV audience offers the opportunity to reach people ideologically and culturally distant from those who address them, opening a wider scope for promoting the values of development—or whatever else the host may favor.

How Do Values Form and Change?

Recognizing the limited persuasive capacity of opinion journalism leads us to ask: how, then, do people acquire a coherent view of the problems that afflict society? The answer is obvious: in their families, among their friends and colleagues, and from those we consciously or unconsciously choose as role models. "Word-of-mouth" is how humans have formed and transmitted values for tens of thousands of years, while the printing press has only been around for five centuries and audiovisual communications media for less than one century.

Perhaps the most eloquent example is the failure of totalitarian propaganda in the twentieth century, for example in the Soviet Union. Print, radio, television, and cinema were incessantly and exclusively devoted to inculcating the official ideology. But this media monopoly often failed to change the deeply held beliefs that guided the behaviors of individuals. People would obey and repeat slogans but often without believing. In both open and totalitarian societies, when people begin reading newspapers in adulthood, their personalities and fundamental views have been formed and the official propaganda merely bounces off these beliefs.

Even though neither opinion journalism nor propaganda usually manages to change readers' closely held beliefs, informational bombardment in a biased direction may have this effect. For example, if a reader believes that euthanasia is never justified because it violates God's law, he will probably not change his opinion after reading a column by Dr. Kevorkian, the famous defender of assisted suicide in cases of terminal illness. But if a reader is exposed to a systematic campaign of biased information about, say, the mischief of "perfidious Albion" (as Spanish Anglophobes used to refer to Great Britain), he may well end up with a negative stereotype of the English, a prejudice that may persist for a long time.

The biased journalism of developing countries has a favorite target: capitalism. Though it has been the primary mechanism of economic development in the leading countries, capitalism is frequently

presented in underdeveloped countries as the villain, the agent that
carries the imperialist virus, the windmill converted quixotically into
a giant that must be assaulted. In these circumstances, how is it possible for capitalism to gain mass support?

Joseph Schumpeter identified a related paradox in *Capitalism, Socialism and Democracy*: though the only successful economic system
in the history of the world, capitalism has also reaped the worst image
among intellectuals. Even today, many artists, writers, theologians,
and journalists harbor a preference for socialism. By legitimizing the
wicked profit motive as the motor of economic life, capitalism made
itself repugnant to idealists, in contrast with the noble solidarity that
socialism claims for itself. Even before Schumpeter, Max Weber had
warned that while men of action were guided by an "ethics of responsibility," because they were in charge of companies or the state,
intellectuals were guided by an "ethics of conviction," in which the
efficacy of results did not matter so much as the sanctity of intentions. As Jean-Paul Sartre underscored in *Dirty Hands*, the intellectual cares less about changing society than saving his own soul.

Capitalism did not develop in the West *thanks* to intellectuals
but *in spite of* them. In developed countries, they have constituted
a welcome, benevolent opposition that modifies and humanizes the
trajectory of capitalist societies without significantly diverting their
capitalist economic mainstream. In underdeveloped countries, which
still live within a premodern culture, capitalism is, by contrast, pre-
carious, weak, and almost nonexistent. The anti-capitalist preaching
of intellectuals finds fertile ground, while the partisans of economic
development are at a disadvantage: it is difficult for them to communicate the collective experience of millions of people who live better
thanks to capitalism in the face of academic polemics or the "progressive" press.

If, as we have claimed, journalism tends, like political parties, to
identify itself with values that already exist in society; and if these
values, far from favoring capitalism, resist it; and if capitalism is the
only known path to economic development, the resulting vicious cycle appears to be insuperable. If people still harbor premodern values,
by definition resistant to the decisions that would lead to economic
development, and if both the media and the political parties, using
those beliefs in order to gain readers or voters, reinforce them with
the biased management of their messages, how can the values that
made developed countries prosperous take root in a democracy?

Democratic Learning

Given that most people in poor countries oppose development, a pro-development desperation sometimes arises, leading to the belief that authoritarianism is the only way out of this dilemma. Only an enlightened despotism, capable of imposing decisions from the top, can lead to economic development. Eventually capitalism will become a rooted reflex and the masses will come to support it, allowing the resumption of democracy, now in combination with capitalism.

This path was attempted more than once in the underdeveloped world: Spanish economic development took off in the last years of Franco's dictatorship; rapid economic development in East Asia was launched under the dictatorships of Park in Korea, Chiang in Taiwan, Lee in Singapore, and Deng in China; and the Chilean miracle was initiated under the Pinochet dictatorship. Democracy followed in Korea, Taiwan, and Chile, and the same transformation may well occur in Singapore and China.

But even though it was economically fruitful, the authoritarian path to economic development sometimes turned out to be bloody. In the real world, "enlightened" despots are hard to find. Latin America has experienced a generous share of unenlightened despots. If the path chosen to overcome economic underdevelopment is authoritarianism, the cure may prove worse than the illness.

Is there, then, another way? In countries where an anti-capitalist culture prevails, is it possible to aspire to economic development while remaining a democracy? The answer is yes—by making mistakes. As Max Weber observed, values favorable to economic development were born from the Calvinist/Puritan cultural revolution of the seventeenth century. As these values emerged at the dawning of the modern age, Anglo-Protestant countries gained an advantage over the rest of the world that persists today. For someone in the United States, England, or Australia, economic development requires little more than to multiply the original cultural seed.

But many countries did not benefit from that cultural seed. They arrived at democratic capitalism through a process of trial and error, sometimes centuries long. Faithful to the values of a premodern culture, they persistently pursued economic development without significant results. Then, through the enlightened despotism of Frederick the Great and Bismarck in Germany or the Meiji Restoration in Japan, or through a slow and painful process of democratization in Italy, Portugal, or Greece, they discarded the traditional formulas and adopted, although not without detours and blunders, the only formula that leads to economic progress.

The road of collective learning through trial and error is the only road that remains open to the poor democracies of the third world. It is a long and sinuous road, but it is also the only alternative to the risky shortcut of authoritarianism. While it may sometimes have functioned effectively in the past, the authoritarian path to democratic capitalism is unlikely to be acceptable in today's world, dominated as it is by a democratic consensus.

The Role of Journalism

Heirs to a traditional, paternalistic, and premodern culture, underdeveloped countries should persist in the trial-and-error path of democratic learning. What is democracy, after all, if not a collective experiment by an entire people, who evaluate it through free debate, periodically settling at the polls what it has learned through the process?

Democratic learning is taking place. In India, after decades of democratic socialism, capitalism has dawned. Is not Lula's Brazil leaving behind the anti-capitalist postulates that marked the earlier political career of its new president? Was not Fernando Henrique Cardoso the champion of dependency theory (that most powerful of anti-capitalist doctrines) in his youth before becoming Brazil's pragmatic democratic–capitalist chief of state?

What should journalists who favor economic development do while this laborious process of collective maturation takes place? On one hand, though they are in the minority, they should insist repeatedly on the values that lead to economic development. They should not contradict majority currents of thought with disdainful arrogance, but they should offer their views diligently and humbly to their fellow citizens. We must remember how the distinguished columnist Raymond Aron defended his principles as a voice in the wilderness of Marxist dogma that dominated the intellectual circles of postwar France.

But at some moment, perhaps sooner rather than later, popular receptivity will increase in the wake of catastrophic populist leadership. Have the presidencies of Alan García in Peru, João Goulart in Brazil, Juan Perón in Argentina, the Sandinistas in Nicaragua, and

Hugo Chávez in Venezuela taught their nations anything? At some point, the people have no choice but to look squarely at reality. This is the moment when pro-development journalism must take the offensive.

This historic turn in popular expectations may be imminent. Unlike Protestant culture, which strongly emphasizes integrity and sometimes lapses into self-satisfaction and arrogance, Catholic culture, the roots of which fed Latin America for centuries, emphasizes sin. The great saints in Catholicism were almost always great sinners. The light came to them only afterwards. Like the prodigal son, after having sinned against economic rationality for centuries, Latin Americans may be on the verge of modernity, thanks, precisely, to their failures.

Stages and Strategies

In developed countries, journalism is "liberal" but its power is limited: it can modify but not undermine the prevailing capitalist consensus. In underdeveloped countries, in Latin America and elsewhere, journalism is "populist" but powerful and reinforces the prevailing anti-capitalist consensus.

The inevitable failure of populism, however, pushes us toward the moment when all but the most fervent ideologues will see the inevitable link between capitalism and economic development. At that moment, the ideas of a pro-development journalistic minority, if it has managed to survive, will begin to be sought after. The ideas they have long been promoting will become the new orthodoxy, but this time an orthodoxy that helps fulfill the aspirations of the people.

This suggests a sequence—the word *dialectic* comes to mind—in Latin America and the Third World: a sequence that starts out as populist and quite possibly authoritarian, passes through a transitional stage in which the limits of populism become apparent, and concludes (at the end of history?) with a democratic capitalist consensus. This dialectic suggests a three-phase operational strategy for the champions of democratic capitalist development: first resist, then prepare, and finally deploy.

The recent *Latinobarometro* polls are unsettling with respect to Latin America's declining faith in democracy. But that decline is driven by the failure of democratic electoral processes to produce vibrant economies in most but not all countries. Before long, it will become apparent that the failure is not rooted in democratic processes and "neoliberal" economics but in the traditional cultural rejection of the capitalism and entrepreneurship that have driven the advanced democracies to prosperity. At that moment, our long years of minority dissent in the media will be vindicated. At that point, Latin America will be, like Spain before it, on the road to the first world.

18

The Global Battle
for Cultural Domination

REESE SCHONFELD

With the advent of the information age, we have reached a critical moment in human history: satellite communication and the Internet now permit a free flow of information that cannot be dammed. Civilizations, nations, penetrate each other, delivering messages that can affect and may even infect targeted cultures. Just as democracies can subvert dictatorships, so can dictatorships subvert democracies. Theocracies can be converted to rationalism; secular societies can be transformed into theocracies.

Since it is virtually impossible to block international satellite distribution, an increasing number of groups have begun using satellite television networks as propaganda engines intended to impose their values upon other cultures. Hezbollah funds al-Manar out of Lebanon; the Chinese religious cult Falun Gong produces its New Tang Dynasty Television out of New York. Propaganda may be delivered in news or documentaries, but it is far more powerful when delivered as entertainment.

During the twentieth century, much of the world relied on the West for entertainment programs, which naturally projected Western cultural values. Now emerging nations have begun to produce their own entertainment, reflecting their own cultural values. The Hispanic version of soap operas, *novelas*, are now the world's most widespread entertainment programming. Indian films are seen all over the world. Recently, I was asked if I could help an American venture capital company acquire Chinese film libraries. The battle for entertainment supremacy has already begun.

The concept of "entertainment supremacy" is based in large part on the Pentagon concept of "information supremacy," which was developed at the end of the first Gulf War. By 1991, the United States, through CNN, had achieved worldwide informational domination. After that war ended, Iraqi generals told debriefers that they had received most of their information about the conflict from CNN. From that experience, the Pentagon developed its theory that informational supremacy would be as valuable as military superiority in winning future wars.

By the time Gulf War II rolled around, the battle for information supremacy looked very different. The Arab world had developed its own cable news network, al-Jazeera, the Islamic equivalent of Fox News—respectable but slanted. Al-Jazeera covered the war just about as well as Western news networks and had the advantage of maintaining better sources in Iraq and the rest of the Arab world. Western networks were often forced to use al-Jazeera material. The new Iraqi government so resents al-Jazeera that it has shut down its Baghdad bureau indefinitely and expelled some of its journalists. Net result: during the siege of Najaf, Western networks were forced to use news video from the Hezbollah's more radical network, al-Manar.

Satellited entertainment programs cross all boundaries, carrying their own cultural messages intentionally in their text or incidentally in their subtext. Bernd Schiphorst, the former head of Bertelsmann television, once remarked that *Knight Rider*, an innocuous American police/adventure series, helped bring down the Berlin Wall. East German authorities had banned satellite reception, but East Germans demanded more varied, non-government-controlled television. They beat their trashcan covers into satellite dishes, built their own receivers, and spent hours watching Western entertainment brought to them by RTL, the newly launched Luxembourg satellite service. Most East Berliners paid little attention to RTL news or documentaries because they assumed all such programs were propaganda. They did, however, accept Western entertainment programs as accurate representations of life in the West. On the surface, the programs appeared mindless and trivial, but they carried a subtext: the standard of living enjoyed by most Americans and other Westerners was considerably higher than that of East Germans.

Knight Rider starred David Hasselhoff as a detective who drove a supercar. Equipped with artificial intelligence, it conversed with Hasselhoff, helping solve cases. When the Berlin Wall came down, Hasselhoff was so popular that he sang at the formal ceremonies commemorating the great event. The car, however, lost its status. To the great disappointment of the East Germans, it was a fiction—even the United States did not have cars that talked.

The Cold War adversaries, East and West, communist and capitalist, shared many values. Both were based on rationalism, seeking progress and material improvement in this life, not the afterworld. "Standard of living" was the criterion over which they battled. How did the East Germans come to know that Westerners lived better than they did? What made them resent their own standard of living? They learned of it innocently from *Knight Rider* and, according to Schiphorst, they resented it so much that it led to the overthrow of communism in East Germany—a prototypical example of the effect of entertainment supremacy.

Competition between capitalism and communism seems superficial when compared with the deep cultural divide between Western secular societies and fundamentalist Islam. Some fundamentalists reject all forms of entertainment. When the Taliban ruled Afghanistan, television, radio, videos, even audiocassettes, were banned, and movie theaters were closed. Other fundamentalists encourage entertainment but use it as a propaganda tool. Al-Manar preaches Shiite fundamentalism on behalf of Iran. Saudi Arabia satellites transmit several Wahabi channels, which have become popular in Sunni regions. On one network, a Saudi sheik advises viewers that although the Koran instructs husbands to beat their wives when they disobey, it does not say how hard to beat them. He suggests that a slap with a silk handkerchief might be sufficient.

Fundamentalist Arab networks are rigidly doctrinaire, but secular Arab networks, which have far more viewers, model their entertainment programming on American television. "Reality shows" are the battleground over which the culture war is raging. *The New York Times*'s Thomas Friedman takes great comfort in that trend: "Consider what was the most talked-about story in the Arab world in recent weeks. Iraq? No. Palestine? No. It was *Super-Star*, the Lebanese version of American Idol!" (September 3, 2003). Naturally, the Fundamentalist Islamic Action Front condemns *Super-Star*, claiming the show facilitates substitution of the culture of globalization, led by America, for the cultural identity of the Arab people.

As content, *Super-Star* seems innocuous: a talent contest produced by Future TV, in which viewers help choose the winner. The contestants are male and female, women do not wear veils, and, perhaps most importantly, viewers are encouraged to vote. In August, 4.5 million Middle-Easterners chose, as most talented, a Jordanian singer rather than a Syrian performer. The vote was 52 percent for the Jordanian, 48 percent for the Syrian. Rami Khouri, editor of the *Beirut Daily Star* told Friedman: "I do not recall in my happy adult life a national vote that resulted in a 52 to 48 percent victory."

Does the success of *Super-Star* indicate a small shift toward democracy? Friedman hopes so; he sees satellite TV as a key to cultural change. But in what political direction? In the *New Yorker*, David Remnick quotes an American University of Cairo student:

> The Islamist influence will grow and will dominate....I see people at A.U.C. tilted toward the Jihadist cause more and more. They're watching satellite television; they're watching Saudi-financed channels.... under Sadat and Nasser, Islamists were oriented towards moral issues in Egypt. Now the word is: "We are fighting for our lives...and the message is getting through." (July 7, 2004)

Following the success of *Super-Star* on Future TV, the Lebanon Broadcast Company (LBC) launched *Star Academy*, a similar reality/talent show. The contestants live in a dormitory atmosphere: men and women do not share quarters, but the women are not veiled and occasionally fraternize with their male rivals. Winners are determined by judges, e-mails, phone calls, and the studio audience. They are rewarded Western-style, become instant celebrities, get a show biz gig and a chance to make big money. In a culture with little upward mobility, *Star Academy* offers the possibility of moving up in the world.

The success of *Super-Star* and *Star Academy* prompted MBC, a secular Gulf satellite network, to launch *al-Rayes*, a tamer version of the Dutch reality show *Big Brother*. Fundamentalists killed it after only two episodes because on its debut program, a young Saudi kissed a Tunisian girl on the cheek and, according to *Gulf New*, "all hell broke loose...the kiss was perceived as a sign of moral depravity" among Muslims of every stripe. MBC TV bowed to the general uproar, canned the show, and apologized. *Gulf News* concluded that "A kiss on *al-Rayes* is so over the top that even moderate Arabs are appalled. It further indicates that the cultural evolutionary process requires time and tact, irrespective of conservative or liberal preferences" (*Gulf News*, May 2004).

Despite such setbacks, satellite television may be the only way to introduce Western cultural values to the Arab street. In a world of mullahs and imams, it is too dangerous to present foreign ideologies at ground level. The success of *Super-Star* and *Star Academy* demonstrates that young Arabs share a desire for democracy, fame, and fortune, desires that Islamic fundamentalists seem eager to suppress.

The Lebanese Broadcasting Company, the most successful network in the Middle East, is owned and programmed by Lebanese Christians who learned their television in the United States. It schedules American sitcoms and adventure shows, Mexican *novelas*, and BBC historical dramas. *The West Wing* provides an up-close look at democratic politics. The plot is full of conflict, but its subtext is that dissent and disagreement are tolerated in Western societies and that democracy works the better for it. What could pose a greater threat to the feudal, theocratic culture of the Middle East?

There is nothing subtextual about al-Manar, the fundamentalist Muslim network funded by Hezbollah and up-linked from Lebanon that features news, documentaries, historical dramas, kids' shows, and religious programs. It produces two different program schedules: a Shiite broadcast signal for consumption in Lebanon and Iran, and a pan-Islamic satellite network seen throughout the world. Both networks schedule news programs and documentaries that portray Americans in Iraq as murderers and terrorists. They claim that American soldiers violate Iraqi mosques and Iraqi women. The Israelis, too, are portrayed as murderers and terrorists, while Muslim suicide bombers are recruited openly and glorified as martyrs.

Al-Manar's most successful program, *al-Shattat,* is a Syrian dramatic series that pretends to present a full, "historical" view of Zionism including the classic anti-Semitic myth, *The Protocols of the Elders of Zion.* The Protocols, a Czarist forgery, accused Jews of killing babies and baking their blood into matzos as part of the Passover ritual. Al-Manar aired it in prime time during Ramadan 2003, when TV viewing is highest throughout the Muslim world. In *al-Shattat,* Jews are depicted as monsters; Muslims are victims who ultimately destroy their evil tormentors. Al-Manar shows Jews in skullcaps and prayer shawls plotting Passover murders. They seize an Arab, who may know of their plot, bring him in bound to a stretcher, slice off his ear, pour molten lead down his throat, and dispose of his body. They then drain the blood of an Arab child and bake it into matzos, which they distribute throughout the ghetto. All shown in full color.

After *al-Shattat* was aired, Israel lodged a protest with France, as a member of the Inter-Government Organization that regulates Eutelsat, the satellite which carries al-Manar. The Israelis reminded the French of the long and violent anti-Semitic history of *Protocols*. In response the French parliament passed a law authorizing French media regulators to drop any satellite channel that disseminated "anti-Semitic" messages. A year later al-Manar was banned there and in the United States, though it is still available on Eutelsat outside of France and on other American-owned or French-controlled satellites (except those serving the United States).

Israelis tolerated al-Manar's messages of hate for four years. They had been delivered only through news and documentary programs. It was *al-Shattat*, propaganda masquerading as entertainment, that forced Israel to act. TV news is like a newspaper; consumed one day, fish-wrap the next. Entertainment may become mythology, and myths are incontrovertible.

The Protocols of Zion still resonate in Eastern Europe and are now taking root in the Arab world. *Al-Shattat* was Hezbollah's follow-up to the Egyptian program, *A Knight Without a Horse*, a much less graphic version of the *Protocols* aired during Ramadan 2002. Within fundamentalist Islam, there is a keen propaganda war for the hearts and minds of the Muslim world. Will Iran's Hezbollah or Egyptian satellite television win that battle?

The Far East is in the midst of its own entertainment war: state-controlled Chinese broadcast (CCTV) and cable programming networks vs. New Tang Dynasty Television (NTDTV), a satellite service associated with the Falun Gong cult. China is officially areligious while the Falun Gong preaches a unique mixture of Buddhism and Taoism. According to David Rennie in the *London Telegraph*, its founder, Li Hong Zhi, "claims to have been sent to earth by a supreme being, who commissioned him to save humanity from its corrupted morals and the technological evils of science" (April 26, 1999). Speaking to Michael Forney of *Time Magazine*, Li offered his opinion that "humankind is degenerating and demons are everywhere"—as are extraterrestrials—and that Africa boasts a 2-billion-year-old nuclear reactor. "He also says he can fly" (July 2, 2001). Right now, he is flying his message into China via his own satellite network, NTDTV.

At first, in 2003, the network's signal was encrypted, which meant that most Chinese could not watch it. A year later, it arranged for unencrypted carriage on Eutelsat, the same satellite company that delivers al-Manar. The People's Republic of China (PRC) objected strenuously to the broadcast of a philosophy so antithetical to its own. Eutelsat ignored the PRC's protests and its threats to pull its commercial traffic from Eutelsat satellites everywhere. France's lack of response to the Chinese—not unlike its ignoring Israeli protests over al-Manar's airing of *al-Shattat*—proves that sovereign nations cannot protect themselves from inimical ideologies delivered through entertainment or factual programming originating outside their borders.

NTDTV executives deny affiliation with the Falun Gong, but the ones I talked to are members of the sect and affirm their spiritual connection to Buddhism and Taoism. The Falun Gong identifies the original Tang dynasty as "the most glorious era in Chinese history…with the rise of Buddhism, the people lived with deep respect for virtue and divine guidance" (New Tang Dynasty promotional material). Thus, the ideological clash of the Chinese government and Falun Gong is a battle for entertainment supremacy between a nation that denies there is a God and a man who proclaims he *is* God.

The Falun Gong is the most formidable opponent that the PRC has ever faced. In April 1999, ten thousand Falun Gong members suddenly turned up in front of the Chinese Leadership Compound in Beijing, squatted down, and demanded official recognition as a "sect," which would give the group official standing. The government refused. Following the refusal, five people identified by the Chinese Government as Falun Gong burned themselves to death in Tiananmen Square to protest the refusal. Then in June 2002 the Falun Gong engineered a communications triumph. It hijacked the state-controlled CCTV network's broadcast of the World Soccer Cup finals and replaced several hours of programming with Falun Gong spiritual messages.

NTDTV executives deny that the network has a political, social, or religious agenda. Nevertheless, its programming reflects the views of its founder. The morning children's cartoons contain no violence. The six daily news programs and the financial reports carry items that would not appear on CCTV, and other items are slanted in accordance with Falun Gong doctrine. NTDTV programs, like *Meet the Press*, or explorations of science, technology, and "social issues," its documentaries, and its costume dramas based on Buddhist history all reflect the founder's antiscientific and antimodernist views.

NTDTV Primetime features Hollywood movies from the 1930s through the 1950s. They are affordable but, more important, they conform to NTDTV's avowed intention to promote democratic cultural change so that "more people can enjoy peace and freedom and live harmoniously among different races and beliefs" (New Tang Dynasty promotional material). Hollywood films of the 1930s and 1940s promote a similar credo. They applaud democracy and treat religion with reverence; when good fights against evil it always prevails. The message could not be more simple: black and white, no grays, a trip back to what Li Hon Zhi sees as a glorious past.

Will the burgeoning NTDTV audience react as East Berliners did with *Knight Rider*? Will it take a leap from communism to capitalism, from atheism to faith? Not likely. State-controlled CCTV combats NTDTV with a wide variety of television and cable networks, among them entertainment channels, twenty-four-hour news, sports, and financial channels, and a children's network. Provincial and municipal governments operate local broadcast stations and control cable systems that already reach more than 100 million homes; the cable fee is only slightly more than a dollar per month.

Cable systems in populous metropolitan areas are adding capacity, and most now feed as many as sixty channels, among them Chinese versions of CNN, MTV, ESPN, Lifetime, and CNBC. There are art/culture channels and movie channels featuring recently released American features. Most Chinese seem to share the U.S. taste in films, and Chinese government movie standards are similar to those in the United States: violent action is virtually unedited, while sexually explicit scenes are censored.

Given the impressive range of subjects and networks offered to the public under government auspices, NTDTV faces stiff competition for viewer attention. But thanks to Eutelsat and despite PRC objections, it has managed to sneak in and stay on. The PRC reflects the values of a secular and progressive nation. The Falun Gong is a conservative spiritual sect, and the PRC sees it as a subversive cult. Its growing popularity amazes and alarms the Chinese government.

In the early 1970s, the Reverend Pat Robertson launched his Christian conservative program on television stations throughout the United States, and it has helped bring together disparate groups into a massive movement with serious influence on American political life. The PRC fears that the NTDTV broadcasts may have a similar impact on China. Interestingly, American conservatives and Christian fundamentalists now support the Falun Gong; see William Safire's *New York Times* column, "Go, Falun Gong!" (August 30, 2004).

Adding further variety to its programming, CCTV has given American programmers access to some of its prime time hours. Encore International, a subsidiary of the U.S. company Liberty Media, provides and sells the advertising for feature films and *novelas* on CCTV. The films must be approved by CCTV personnel, who are government officials, and taboos include anything controversial like the Nationalist government, Chiang Kai Shek, or Sun Yat Sen. The Taiwanese flag is never shown. But as China shifts from an agrarian to an industrial society, the PRC is gradually introducing issues of social progress via entertainment television.

Population Communications International (PCI), a nonprofit U.S. group affiliated with the United Nations, works with broadcasters in emerging nations to produce culturally relevant radio and TV dramas, particularly soap operas. Since 1999, PCI and CCTV's Channel 8 have developed a primetime serial, *Bai Xiang* (*Ordinary People*), set in rural China, about a strong woman named Luye who defies her husband and gives birth to a little girl. This is a brave decision, given China's "one child" policy (the government provides a stipend, free education, and free medical care, but only for one child). After her daughter is born, Luye divorces her husband, remarries, and then divorces her second husband when he too demands that she bear him a son. Eventually Luye launches a successful business, and she and her daughter gain the respect of their fellow villagers.

In its second year, *Ordinary People* introduced another issue: sexually transmitted diseases. Luye's first husband contracts AIDS through a bungled blood transfusion. (Over 1, million Chinese are now HIV positive and China has admitted to past inadequate blood screening procedures.) Next year's episodes will introduce environmental issues, notably industrial pollution. Luye and her daughter must deal with village authorities about pollution, politics, and profits as a rural society moves into the twenty-first century. *Ordinary People* has the highest ratings on CCTV in its time slot.

CCTV and the other state-owned networks are advertiser-supported and attempt to attract the largest possible audience. NTDTV, on the other hand, is message-driven, deriving its support from ideological backers, just as Pat Robinson did. If NTDTV ever gains entertainment supremacy and converts a mass audience to its beliefs, the face of the PRC will be far different from today. The long-term future of China may hinge on a satellite battle in the sky.

Epilogue

On March 15, 2005, the Associated Press reported that Eutelsat was terminating its contract with NTDTV on "commercial grounds. 'Eutelsat is not reacting to pressure from the Chinese authorities or any other authority,' the company said in a statement." The next day the International Federation of Journalists (IJF) claimed, according to the *Wall Street Journal*, that "the inexplicable decision to end the contract…appears to be a shocking act of censorship." The IFJ suggested that "Beijing has warned [Eutelsat] that business opportunities linked to broadcasting 2008 Olympics might be at risk." NTDTV has taken the matter to court, but as of now NTDTV is no longer available in China.

Soap operas and their Latin American cousins, *novelas*, were once thought of as light entertainment, of little cultural significance. At first, soaps dominated the foreign market; now *novelas* are much more popular. Why? Because soaps reflect American cultural attitudes while *novelas* are far more relevant to life in the developing world.

Western cultures offer women opportunities that other societies do not. Soap opera heroines are independent achievers with a wide variety of romantic and economic choices. *Novela* characters dream of improving their standard of living by marrying up or by forging a career based on primitive skills: sewing, cooking, opening a small shop. This lack of social mobility helps explain the success of *novelas*: American audiences think they can achieve the same success as soap opera heroines; third-world women know they don't have a chance.

Soaps and *novelas* both air daily, but *novelas* are seen in prime time, not in the afternoon. *Novelas* run for twenty to thirty weeks and have a beginning, middle, and an end, while soaps roll on forever. Family groups gather to watch *novelas*, which are constructed as family sagas with three generations of characters. HBO's *The Sopranos* resembles a *novela*.

Since the mid-1980s, three nonprofit organizations have recognized the propaganda potential of serial dramas and are working with broadcasters to modify cultural behavior through them. The

Johns Hopkins Center for Communication Programs (CCP), Population Communications International (PCI), and the BBC World Service Trust help create programs that promote democracy, women's rights, access to healthcare, and economic and environmental progress.

CCP's credo is "educating through entertainment with an emphasis on serial drama." Since its founding in 1982, CCP has established guidelines: the problems addressed must be highly dramatized; indigenous cultural values must be taken into account; storylines must be personally relevant to the viewer; and production quality must be equal to that of commercial programs. CCP programs are more direct than PCI or BBC productions. In its Bangladeshi series involving AIDS, a doctor tells his staff: "We must hate the disease, not the patient...people do not get infected by touching." Then he grasps the patient by the arm and the victim cries out, "At last someone has touched me. Now, I realize that I am not an animal." Because CCP receives government funds, it must make the government's message loud and clear.

PCI, funded by private foundations, deals for the most part with issues of gender, population control, and sexually transmitted diseases. It reaches out to some of the world's largest nations (e.g., China, with *Ordinary People*) and to some of the smallest, such as the tiny Caribbean island of St. Lucia. When a population explosion threatened St. Lucia, PCI stepped in. Radio is St. Lucia's only mass medium, so PCI and a local station created a fifteen-minute radio series full of love, romance, and safe sex. St. Lucia is predominantly Roman Catholic, and public discussion of birth control is taboo. Therefore, condoms were referred to as "catapults." Phrases from the series—"Do you have a catapult?" "Is your catapult on?"—became part of everyday life. Sales of condoms rose, population growth cooled, and an entrepreneur launched a new line of condoms called Catapults (now the number one brand on the island).

The BBC, which has a noble tradition of helping emerging countries, has established the privately funded BBC World Service Trust. Its brief calls for "reducing poverty" and "empowering citizens at grass-roots levels"—through entertainment. A BBC/Nigerian project, for example, dramatizes both democratic participation and the empowerment of women in a single radio series. *Voices* features a character named Mama Major, a load carrier in the central market. The market's streets are strewn with garbage and pitted with potholes, making it impossible for load carriers to navigate their routes. At first, the local council refuses to help, but Mama Major reminds the council chairman that he is up for reelection and threatens to organize all the load carriers against him. He gets her point and cleans up the market.

Like CCP and PCI, the World Trust addresses AIDS and birth control. BBC joined with the Doordashan National Network and India's National AIDS Control Organisation to produce a mystery series starring an HIV-positive detective, Vijay. The program is described as "an entertaining popular drama which also encourages people to change their sexual behavior." Targeted at a rural population, it has been the seventh highest-rated program in India, reaching more than 150 million people. Vijay solves cases involving quack doctors, superstition, rape, domestic violence, and dowries, among other matters. (Detective Vijay has AIDS, but as in *Ordinary People*, it was acquired through a bad blood transfusion. Sexual transmission is not for heroes.)

Novelas are produced for a mass audience, much of which has yet to join the middle class, and are aired on hundreds of television stations and networks throughout the Far East, Eastern Europe, and Africa. In the Middle East, they are featured on satellite networks like the Lebanese Broadcasting Company, which changes its *novela* schedule during Ramadan, when TV audiences change their viewing habits.

Encore, the US satellite network, has added dubbed Mexican and Peruvian *novelas* to its Chinese TV schedule. *Ugly Betty*, a classic Hollywood ugly-duckling tale, captivated the Chinese audience: "Take off your glasses, let down your hair and suddenly you're beautiful." *Ugly Betty* does not become beautiful, but her looks are considerably improved: she gets her man and succeeds in business. *Ugly Betty* was so popular that Televisa, the Mexican *novela* factory, produced a follow-up series with Betty as boss of her company, structured more like a Western soap. That series was canceled after twenty episodes due to poor ratings. It would appear that *novela* viewers are more interested in a woman's struggle to get to the top than in female characters who are already there.

Encore followed *Ugly Betty* with *Simplemente Maria*, the story of a Peruvian girl who falls in love with her employer's son, gets pregnant, and is fired. She then learns how to sew, saves money, buys a sewing machine, and eventually becomes a Paris fashion designer.

When *Simplemente Maria* aired in Latin America, sales of Singer sewing machines went through the roof. Ditto in China when Encore ran the program there.

There are four Spanish-language networks in the United States, all featuring *novelas*. Univision, the dominant network, carries Televisa's *Mi Gorda Bella*. It runs at 6 PM and is watched by 6 percent of all Hispanic households. The heroine is overweight and ridiculed for it. In the first act she cries a lot but slims down; in the second, she gets revenge on her tormentors; in the third, she marries the man she always wanted.

Univision boasts that its *novelas* are "mas sentimiento." Soaps are not sentimental. *Novelas* are the Harlequin novels of the second and third world. Plus, they offer the world's largest Victoria's Secret market: plenty of pictures of lingeried ladies cavorting with Latino hunks. As for racial attitudes, since black is not beautiful in Latin America, *novela* heroines are always light skinned and mostly blonde and/or blue eyed. Male leads, usually played by Argentineans, can pass for Spaniards, Italians, or Frenchmen. In Latin America upward mobility means marrying richer and whiter.

Globo, the Brazilian *novela* factory, is somewhat more progressive. It recently introduced a *novela* featuring a highly successful black family. But since Brazilians are not yet ready to accept the idea of white servants in a black household, the family retainers are also played by blacks. Globo does pay attention to other social issues, including drug use and AIDS (the latter, again, only from nonsexual transmission). Male homosexuality is taboo, but Globo frequently uses lesbian plot lines—two negligees are better than one.

Televisa *novelas* are paying increasing attention to their teenage audience. Safe sex and HIV are part of their plot lines, and condoms are openly advocated. In the midst of a population explosion throughout Latin America, Televisa, a responsible broadcaster, believes that the discussion of contraception cannot be avoided. There is no mention of male homosexuality, although Televisa occasionally uses stereotypical gays—hairdressers or fashion designers—as comic characters.

In the United States, Proctor & Gamble pioneered radio soap operas in the 1930s (P & G manufactured soap, hence the name "soap operas"). Their plots were just as sentimental as *novelas*, and American housewives responded just as enthusiastically as Latin Americans do now. But it all changed in the mid-1970s, when American audiences grew worldlier and the sentimental was replaced by the sensational. Soaps took on a harder edge.

Three significant events—two sociological, one technical—changed soaps forever. First, in the 1950s, America became far and away the world's richest country. As the country became solidly middle class, poor people almost disappeared from soap operas. Second, American housewives began pursuing careers, so the soap opera audience was no longer home. Third, Nielsen installed TV People Meters, which measure the sex, age, education, and income of television viewers. Advertisers now buy commercial time based on who is watching, not on how many. In particular, advertisers went after high school and college girls. As the networks programmed the soaps for younger viewers, family sagas and morality went out and thrills came in.

American soaps today are sensational, populated by vampires, voodoo, reincarnations, psychics, and miracles. Rich people seduce and back-stab their way to even greater fortunes. Pleasure is everything, sex is routine, and drug use rampant. Evil triumphs as often as not, crimes go unpunished, and there is no moral compass—all in an attempt to attract the largest, youngest audience. So far, it is working. The University of Texas rescheduled its most popular classes to the morning to avoid conflicts with afternoon soap operas.

On *General Hospital*, in 1981, the leading character, Laura, married Luke, a man with whom she had fallen in love although he had once raped her. It was the highest rated episode in the history of soap operas. Villains became stars. As for heroines, sweetness was out, bitchiness was in. Cynicism and sophistication dominated soap operas; *novelas* remained true to their shop girl audience. Innocence flourished abroad, but vanished at home.

Soaps have attempted to confront some social issues. As far back as 1987, NBC launched *Generations*, a soap opera with a successful black family at its core. The show lasted three years. Several soaps now include black families in subplots, and black characters are a permanent fixture in the soap opera landscape.

Soaps are conflicted about gender issues; as in Brazil, lesbians may be important characters, but gay men are not. Erica Kane, the central character in the long-running ABC soap *All My Children*, has a gay daughter, Bianca, who is raped and bears a daughter. The baby is kidnapped, thereby avoiding political controversy surrounding gays' fitness as parents. In December 2004 Bianca got her baby back, but within three months Bianca was written out of the show. The president of ABC Daytime told the *New York Times*: "For some people, minorities—of color, of sexuality—are road blocks to full viewer commitment." Since viewer commitment is a requirement for soap operas, Bianca finds a new job in Paris; but like the kidnapped baby, she can always be brought back if the audience misses her. Other American soaps deal peripherally with gay characters, but none has ever achieved the status of "tent pole"—that is, characters upon whom story lines are built.

After the Nobel Prize winner Colombian novelist Gabriel García Márquez wrote and produced several movies that failed, he went on television to proclaim that Latino writers who wanted to reach and affect a mass audience should turn to scripting *novelas*. CCP, PCI, and the BBC Trust explicitly exploit the power of serial dramas in an attempt to change cultures, but entertainment programming created for purely commercial reasons is far more effective. There's no doubt about it, entertainment programming changes minds. There has never been a more effective propaganda vehicle than a 24/7 satellite channel—but only if people watch it.

Twentieth-century America was shaped by entertainment. An agricultural nation suffused with Victorian morality was transformed into an industrial nation with a relativistic, almost-anything-goes attitude. Millions of immigrants learned English in movie theaters and from television sets. Movie subtexts included lessons in cultural behavior and, most importantly, inculcated American values in their audiences. Now, in the early twenty-first century, the counterculture has raised its head, and religious television and movies and gospel music are trying to reverse the trend.

The Federal Communications Commission (FCC) in the United States and public broadcasters in Western Europe generally reinforced democratic values and, particularly in entertainment shows, portrayed a traditional middle-class lifestyle that supported conventional social norms. An American growing up in the forties and fifties worried that his own family was the only one in the country that wasn't as perfect as *Father Knows Best*. Middle-brow television confirmed traditional attitudes and influenced viewers to conform to them. It was not until the late sixties that entertainment television began to transform racial attitudes, with programs like *Julia*, *The Jeffersons*, and *The Cosby Show*. Those three programs showed blacks making their way up in America. Julia was a nurse, a single mother battling to keep her family together. George Jefferson was a successful middle-class entrepreneur with attitude. Bill Cosby played a highly successful professional, surrounded by a strong and loving family, respected and loved by all who knew him.

At the same time, Gordon Parks, Jr. created *Superfly*, a movie that glorified drug dealers and the gangster life. There are no Cosby clones on television now, while the *Superfly* culture lives on through hip-hop with its "niggas" and "hos." Cosby disapproves, and he has provoked a bitter cultural war within the black community. The battle between middle-class values and hip-hop is as obvious a struggle for entertainment supremacy as one is likely ever to see. It will be decided by which programs get on television, which movies are made, and what music gets on the air.

The FCC began granting licenses to U.S. broadcasters in the 1920s. Europe and most of the rest of the world followed a different path. Governments kept for themselves a monopoly on the airwaves. They set up commercial-free public television networks supported by a tax on radios, later on television sets. Communist Europe, Asia, and Africa followed that model but frequently ran the networks as government agencies.

Commercial broadcasters in Europe do not want competition from public television stations. Their goal is to turn public broadcasting powerhouses, like the BBC, into foreign versions of PBS, America's feeble attempt at a middlebrow network. British television viewers pay an annual license fee to support the BBC. In return, the BBC broadcasts eight channels of programming to everyone in Britain at no further cost. It pays for kids' channels, a high-culture channel, a news channel, and a political channel, as well as three channels of general programming. And it carries no commercials.

I regard the BBC as the best broadcaster in the world. Its news coverage exceeds all others in breadth and depth: many more bureaus, many more documentaries, and more knowledgeable reporters and producers. It still maintains a symphony orchestra, still produces Shakespearean dramas and original television plays, and airs programs about museums, architecture, films, and jazz. The BBC also provides top-rated general entertainment programs, which compete with commercial television programs.

For most people in Britain, the popular entertainment programs make the BBC worth the license fee. The BBC produced shows like *Eastenders*, an evening soap opera with working-class characters, which has dominated its time slot for two generations. It also produced *Top of the Pops*, a British version of *Your Hit Parade*, and *Parkinson* (now defected to the commercial ITV), a more intelligent version of *Larry King Live*. It acquires popular programs like *The Simpsons, X Files, 24,* and *Lois and Clark* from American networks—which drives commercial broadcasters up the wall. When the BBC bids against them for hit programs, it drives the prices up and takes large audiences from them. The private networks make less money. End of story.

In September 2003, I spoke to Eastern European broadcasters in Bucharest on "How to Guarantee Independent Public Broadcasting." They were in the process of creating, or had just created, public broadcasting networks in former Soviet bloc countries. They will be dependent on government funding, but their countries are about to join the European Union. An EU lawyer, Herbert Ungerer, was present to offer information and answer questions about EU public broadcasting regulations. The EU is profoundly "free market." It does not allow subsidies for businesses that compete with private enterprise. There are certain exceptions, and public broadcasting is one of them. But the functions of the public broadcasting network must be clearly delineated in its charter in order to survive court challenges from private broadcasters.

The new Eastern European networks share a problem with PBS: private broadcasters have long since entered their markets. PBS, eternally underfunded, has yet to play a significant role in American television. Most of the Eastern European networks will meet the same fate unless they get license fees—and commercial broadcasters will fight tooth and nail against that. They will sue. Therefore, I suggested to the assembled broadcasters that they get the widest and clearest governmental remit they possibly could for their networks. I advised them to follow the BBC example and make sure that the remit includes popular entertainment programs, popular movies, sitcoms, quiz shows, even soap operas. I then cited the role that *Knight Rider* had played in Berlin in 1991.

All hell broke loose. Karol Jacubowicz, vice-chairman of the Steering Committee on the Mass Media, Council of Europe, rose in attack. He sneered at the possibility that Germans would take political action based on a mere entertainment show like *Knight Rider*. The Berlin Wall had come down because serious thinkers had proven to the people of East Germany that communism was wrong. "Who is this David Hasselhoff?" he thundered. "What kind of people do you think Germans are?" When I tried to reply, my mike was cut off. To Jacubowicz and the Eastern European broadcasters, their role was to present high culture: programs designed for intellectuals, artists, and their wannabes. Leave the popular stuff to someone else. It is unlikely that public broadcasters will ever reach mass audiences under that formula. Some attitudes never change.

A Media Plan for Emerging Nations

It should be clear by now that I prefer public television over private. Commercial television, even when regulated, selects program content only to reach the largest audience possible. Since advertising is its only source of revenue, it has no choice: it sells its audience to its advertisers by the pound and the mass audience weighs most. Therefore, commercial networks compete with each other by offering programs that appeal to even their dumbest viewers. In the world of commercial broadcasting, bad television drives out good.

If I were now designing a media plan for an emerging nation, I would not grant commercial licenses for at least twenty years. Public broadcasting, which is better suited to introduce cultural values, must have a head start or it will fail. I would fund programming through television license fees or from government tax revenue. I would do my best to keep out foreign satellite broadcasts, and, following the Chinese example, I would begin to build a national cable network that could deliver a wide variety of cable programs so long as their cultural messages coincided with our values. My media promulgation might read something like this:

Recognizing that media shapes cultures, and believing that the "values and attitudes on which democratic governance, prosperity, and social justice importantly depend" (Culture Matters Research Project credo) must be promoted and protected, we hereby declare:

- All broadcast media are to be owned and operated by government agencies.
- In order to provide variety in programming, government-owned cable systems will be built. Foreign satellite channels may be carried on cable, but only with government consent.
- News and discussion shows will not be censored.

- Government will participate actively in producing and acquiring entertainment programs.
- We will acquire Hollywood features of the late 1930s to 1950s, since they reflect the attitudes and values we promote.
- We will review more recent Hollywood and other foreign films and attempt to acquire those reflecting positive values.
- We will acquire foreign television programs that demonstrate the positive effects of values that we wish to encourage, such as *Law and Order*, the U.S. series, which illustrates the importance of a constitutionally governed system of justice.[1]
- We will review Brazilian and Mexican *novelas* and select those most relevant to our people. We will begin to produce our own films and series so that they may be more directly applicable to life here.
- We will work with Johns Hopkins, The BBC World Service Trust, and PCI, to obtain production expertise and financial support for programs that best deliver our message.
- Once we have developed the expertise, we will endeavor to build our own media center to produce our own entertainment programming. We will make every effort to block those international satellite entertainment programs that undermine our cultural values.

As evidence in support of the above, I offer Botswana, a thriving and vibrant democracy in the midst of southern Africa. According to the UN's Human Development Report, it has achieved the third highest per capita income growth of any country in the world since the mid-1960s. Botswana, wisely I think, did not introduce television until the mid-1990s. Instead it concentrated on public radio, which still dominates. The cost of homegrown television is so high that small, emerging nations cannot afford to produce much of it. Therefore, they depend on inexpensive, imported programs which carry cultural messages from different worlds which are often unsuitable for the local audiences. Moreover, they carry commercials which create an appetite for goods and services often unavailable or too costly for third world viewers, getting them to pay more for goods that are often unneeded, thereby draining the resources of undeveloped economies. People spend, rather than save. By sticking with radio, Botswana made sure that mass media consistently supported its democratic ideals and its economic framework. Of course, Botswana has been blessed with leaders who support those ideals. Perhaps, democracy only survives when leaders and mass media are on the same page.

The Culture Matters Research Project (CMRP) classifies cultures as progressive or retrograde on the basis of certain values. I judge the effects of entertainment programming on a similar basis. If I were certain that CMRP values would prevail in our emerging society, I would be less restrictive with our media. But I am more afraid of demagoguery than I am confident about rational persuasion. I am more fearful of invidious ideas planted by entertainment programming than comforted by the possibility that more benevolent messages might bring about positive cultural change. Therefore, with extreme reluctance, I would advise the leader of an emerging nation committed to the goals of the UN Universal Declaration of Human Rights to keep absolute control of the messages delivered within his country.

To put it bluntly, total freedom of satellite transmission and of the Internet is a lose/lose proposition for democracy. Totalitarian nations will ban messages of which they disapprove. Democratic nations who allow demagogues to preach to their citizens may soon find that their democracy has been destroyed. The greatest fear of democrats is the specter of one man, one vote, one time. Clever demagoguery with widespread distribution will make that fear a reality.

And of course the Internet permits total worldwide access with no intermediaries. Think of Hitler's voice over a Leni Riefenstahl video with a Wagnerian soundtrack delivered simultaneously to every computer in the world, and saved to be played over and over again, and consider the consequences. Internet censorship is currently scheduled to be debated in December 2005 in Tunis. Tunisia, Egypt, China, Russia and Iran are pressing for the right to regulate Internet messages within their boundaries. If I were a third world leader, I would line up with them. The International Freedom of Expression eXchange (IFEX) reports that Tunisia blocks news, information, and other websites and police surveil e-mails and Internet cafes. The IFEX threatens to move the meeting to another site. Nevertheless, if I were a third world leader, terrified of an Islamist takeover, I'd do the same.

I began by quoting Thomas Friedman and his hopes for cultural reform through satellite-delivered entertainment programs. Now Friedman is worried. Quoting CBS reporter Scott Pelley, he reports (October 24, 2004) that the Iraqi nickname for American troops is "Jews." They use "Jews" the way we used "Krauts" in the Second

World War or "Charlie" in Vietnam. This trend has been fanned by Arab satellite TV stations, which show split-screen images of Israelis bashing Palestinians and U.S. forces bashing the Iraqi insurgents.

I believe that educating to hate is all too easy. Educating to tolerate is a far more difficult process. All television is educational, and we must choose our textbooks very carefully.

Note

1. A Russian television network has acquired rights to the *Law & Order* format. It will be interesting to see how it treats questions of valid confessions and search and seizure, which are so important to the U.S. series.

Part V
Leadership

19

Public Policy and Culture

RICHARD D. LAMM

I.

I was elected governor of Colorado in 1974 and took my seat in 1975. My lieutenant governor, George Brown, was Colorado's first black official elected on a statewide basis and one of the first black lieutenant governors in the nation. Both of us had a passionate interest in the education of minority kids and particularly in the troubling drop-out rate of both blacks and Latinos. We would meet regularly with the black and Latino members of the legislature to discuss the problem.

Colorado has enjoyed good race relations for most of its history. We passed a public accommodations act in the late 1890s, shortly after *Plessy vs. Ferguson* said the nation could be "separate but equal." We passed a fair housing law early in 1957 and have enjoyed strong public support for civil rights legislation. We were the second state in the nation to give women the right to vote. Colorado was not perfect, but it certainly merited being labeled a progressive state.

Our administration took a number of initiatives in education. Some succeeded, some failed; but those dealing with black and Latino students were particularly frustrating. We initiated English as a Second Language (ESL) programs for Latino students and then passed one of the nation's first bilingual education programs. Little or no improvement followed. The legislators said that "Anglo teachers" were "tracking" Latino students, so we helped the Denver School District create an all-Latino school with a Latino principal and all Latino teachers. Same drop-out rate.

The only explanation that the black and Hispanic caucuses would consider was "racism and discrimination." Any failure on the part of a minority community must be the fault of society as a whole. As a former civil rights attorney, I tended at first to agree, but it soon became apparent that this explanation was inadequate. Yes, there was racism and discrimination in our society, but was that the sole cause for the education shortfalls that plagued these two communities?

Sometime during my twelve years as governor I read that the highest family incomes in America were achieved by minority groups that had been discriminated against. Studies showed that Japanese families had the highest incomes, followed by Jewish and Chinese families. I asked myself: Did any of these groups have an easy time in America? In my lifetime we had unjustly placed a large number of Japanese-Americans in camps and in many cases confiscated their assets. Jews had been denied access to "restricted" neighborhoods, hotels, and clubs. Chinese had been persecuted, even lynched; and in 1882 Congress passed the Chinese Exclusion Act, which was not repealed until 1943. These high-achieving groups had encountered racism and discrimination but had prevailed and prospered. What could we learn from their success?

A governor has to deal with myriad issues and has to turn his or her mind in a thousand directions every day. But I remained aware of the black and Latino underachievement issue, grew increasingly concerned about it, and kept asking questions. I observed how students from poor Russian-Jewish families and poor Asian families excelled while Latino children from the same neighborhood dropped out in large numbers or performed poorly. Latino students who were bright and curious in the fourth grade often lost interest and dropped out after ninth grade. Recent Census Bureau data show that only 14 percent of the nation's Latino males go on to higher education, compared with 43 percent of blacks and 72 percent of whites. And Latinos are the fastest growing minority group in America, having recently overtaken blacks.

Toward the end of my third term I had an epiphany. I came across a study that showed that Jewish and Asian students did twice as much homework as black and Latino students and got twice as good grades. Was this the answer—or part of the answer—to the difference in school performance? The successful groups had found discrimination a hurdle but not a barrier. Discrimination had delayed but not defeated them. But this insight raised its own set of problems. How do we instill the necessary attitudes, habits, skills, and focus in black and Latino students? We knew these students had the aptitude but lacked the motivation to succeed in school and beyond.

In 1963 my wife and I spent six months traveling in Latin America. We learned that the standard explanation for Latin America's poverty, social injustice, and authoritarianism was "Yankee imperialism." It sounded plausible. The same explanation was circulating in Africa, where both political and intellectual leaders identified "colonialism" as the root of underdevelopment, an explanation echoed in some European and North American circles. Were it not for European domination and the legacy of colonialism, many African and Latin American intellectuals argued, their countries would be prosperous and democratic. Moreover, the rich countries were rich because the poor countries were poor—the former had exploited and impoverished the latter. This "dependency theory" was widespread in third and first world universities and was of course axiomatic in the second world: the Soviet Empire, China, and Cuba.

In the mid-1980s I came across Lawrence Harrison's *Underdevelopment Is a State of Mind*, one of the most important books on public policy I have ever read. Harrison argued that culture—values, attitudes, and beliefs—explains much of the difference in the relative success of peoples and nations. I soon came across similar views. In *More Like Us*, James Fallows writes: "In the long run, habits, values and behavior of ordinary people determine national strength."[1] As Senator Patrick Moynihan put it: "The central conservative truth is that it is culture, not politics, that determines the success of a society. The central liberal truth is that politics can change a culture and save it from itself." These statements made sense to me then and make even more sense now.

While on a trip to Taiwan to promote economic relationships with Colorado, I was reminded that Taiwan, South Korea, Singapore, and Hong Kong—then the fastest growing economies in the world—had all been colonies. Taiwan was a Japanese colony from 1895 to 1945, Korea from 1910 to 1945. Singapore was a British colony from 1819 to 1959, Hong Kong from 1842 to 1997, when it was reincorporated into China. All experienced astonishing rates of economic growth after World War II, South Korea, Taiwan, and Singapore as independent countries, Hong Kong as a British colony. Moreover, South Korea and Taiwan are now full-fledged first world democracies, while Hong Kong has held on tenaciously to the democratic traditions it acquired as a British colony, in the face of pressures from the central Chinese government.

In passing, we should note that the recent history of the Korean peninsula suggests the limits of culture's influence. North Korea and South Korea share—or at least shared until the 1950s—a common, essentially Confucian culture. South Korea has since vaulted into the first world, while North Korea remains mired in totalitarian governance and intense poverty. Politics matters too.

Why have former colonies in East Asia succeeded while former colonies in Africa remain stuck in poverty? As Samuel Huntington notes in his foreword to *Culture Matters,* Ghana and South Korea were at essentially the same level of development in the early 1960s. Yet today, Ghana's gross national income per capita calculated on the basis of purchasing power parity is about $2,000, while South Korea's is about $15,000.

Colonialism was an unhappy chapter in the history of many countries, including the United States. European colonialism in Africa disrupted traditional African societies and divided tribes, and its consequences should not be minimized. But the abuses of colonialism cannot explain all the ills of Africa. As Daniel Etounga-Manguelle writes in *Culture Matters*: "Several decades have passed during which we have been in substantial control of our own destiny. Yet today Africa is more dependent than ever on rich countries."[2] In contrast, the former colonies in East Asia have exploited the advantages of colonialism and minimized the disadvantages.

On retiring from the governor's office, I returned to academic life. When I would raise culture as a cause of underachievement, I was astounded at the reluctance of my colleagues even to discuss it. Academic life in America is dominated by a liberal orthodoxy, in which cultural explanations of why some do better than others are taboo. But we do Africa no favor by supposing that the "legacy of colonialism" explains its disappointing performance since independence. As Etounga-Manguelle argues, African culture, including fatalism, sorcery, authoritarianism, and an excessive communitarianism, contributes powerfully to today's African reality. In Latin America too, as

Mariano Grondona and Carlos Alberto Montaner explain in *Culture Matters*, fatalism, authoritarianism, excessive individualism, and low levels of trust have powerfully influenced Latin America's evolution in almost two centuries since independence. Nations have to own up to their problems if they are to correct them. Portugal and Belgium were particularly abusive in their treatment of natives in their African colonies, but nowhere was colonialism without its abuses. On the other hand, colonialism left Africa with some important assets, like health facilities, schools, roads, ports, water and sewage systems, and electrical power. So what explains Africa's slow progress after independence while East Asia, now including China, has moved rapidly ahead? At home and as immigrants, the Chinese, Japanese, and Koreans emphasize education, merit, achievement, saving, and, in general, building for the future. These values, rooted in Confucianism, are not common in Africa.

Pursuing these ideas, I came across Thomas Sowell's great contribution, *Race and Culture*. Sowell argues that "racial, ethnic, and cultural differences among peoples play a major role in the events of our times, in countries around the world, and have played a major role in the long history of the human race....The history of cultural differences among peoples enables us to understand not only how particular peoples differ but also how cultural patterns in general affect the economic and social advancement of the human race."[3]

Don't back away from discussing culture, urges Sowell; it is central to understanding the different success rates among different nations. Why did uneducated and unskilled Chinese rubber plantation laborers in colonial Malaya produce more than double the output of the Malay workers? Why do the fewer than 5 percent of Indonesians who are Chinese account for 80 percent of the country's capital? A culture that stresses hard work, saving, and advancement clearly plays a role. Sowell points out that national comparisons tell much the same story as comparisons between groups within the same society. Development in poor countries can often be attributed to entrepreneurial foreigners: the British in Argentina and the Germans in Brazil come to mind. The Germans and Jews, Sowell writes, accounted for a good part of Russia's development.

Human beings are creatures whose behavior is molded by culture, including the customs and the institutions of their society. "We build our buildings," says Winston Churchill, "then they build us." We are all products of the culture into which we are born and whose values and attitudes we begin to acquire in the first days of life. This insight sent me into the second part of my odyssey.

II.

The ancient Greeks had a saying "To know is all; to ask is to know half." When I discovered that culture was an important determinant of how societies evolve, my focus of inquiry switched to the second half of Moynihan's aphorism: how can politics "change a culture and save it from itself"? What public policies can mold a culture? What tools are available to a leader to change a culture?

In a real sense, politics is about culture and cultural change, an assertion highly relevant to the 2004 presidential contest in the United States. Generally, conservative political parties like the Republicans wish to "conserve" traditional values and the policies and institutions that flow from them. Liberal parties like the Democrats tend to focus on the imperfections and injustices in a society and to seek to rectify them. In the United States, one hears frequent references to "the culture wars." These "wars" are, in essence, political.

History is rich with attempts to impose cultural change from the outside—Soviet Russia's imposition in Eastern Europe of the value system associated with Marxism-Leninism is a representative example. Those imposed upon resist the alien value system, but over time, they may adopt it—*absorb* may be a better word—at least in part. For example, the former East Germany, arguably the most economically advanced of the communist Eastern European countries, lags behind the rest of a reintegrated Germany, perhaps because it absorbed some communist attitudes and ways of working.

But my focus is not on efforts to impose cultural change. Rather it is with those options and tools available to leaders *within* societies who are committed to cultural change. Japan and Turkey provide two interesting examples of how this can work.

In 1853, Japan, under the 250-year-old Tokugawa Dynasty, was a traditional, isolated feudal society ruled from Kyoto by the Shogunate—the Shogun and his staff. That year Commodore Matthew Perry cruised into Tokyo Bay with a flotilla whose technology was so far ahead of Japan's defensive capabilities that Perry could have brought the country to its knees. Perry's mission was trade, not conquest, but the lesson of Japan's impotence was not lost on the

Japanese, particularly after they were forced to sign unequal treaties that granted Westerners economic and legal advantages.

The Shogunate was staggered. Its power began to erode, a process that would lead to its overthrow in 1868 by a group of mostly young feudal lords committed to change and modernization. The Emperor Mutsuhito (later given the imperial name Meiji) was restored to his symbolic leadership role, and centralized government replaced the Tokugawa feudal system. The seat of government moved from Kyoto to Tokyo. In the following decades, Japan transformed itself from a weak, traditional, isolated society into a world power. An external trauma had opened Japan to change, and the Japanese responded by looking carefully at the most advanced nations—Europe and the United States—and adopting their policies, institutions, technology, and, to some extent, their culture. I say "to some extent" because some elements of Japanese culture were worth preserving, many of them derived from the Confucian value system imported along with many other aspects of Chinese culture a millennium earlier.

Japan knew what it had to do to move into the modern world, borrowing from countries demonstrably more advanced. But the Japanese retained much of their traditional culture that was compatible with modernization, above all diligence, achievement, merit, and frugality. "Work much, earn much, and spend little," wrote the philosopher Ninomiya Sontoku, who elsewhere warned: "The wealth of our parents depends on the industry of their ancestry, and our wealth depends on the accumulated good deeds of our parents. Our descendants' wealth depends on us and on our faithful discharge of duty."[4] These sentiments are just as characteristic of Chinese and Koreans and have much to do with the success of those countries and of their peoples when they migrate.

Japan also had another advantage: a long tradition of what we today call "social capital." In *Trust: The Social Virtues and the Creation of Prosperity*,[5] Francis Fukuyama identifies three countries with long-standing traditions of "spontaneous association": the United States, Germany, and Japan. In the case of the Japanese "miracle" starting in 1868, it is difficult to sort out how much was attributable to a change in culture and how much to freeing an existing culture to do its magic.

In the case of Turkey, there is less ambiguity. Turkey, like Japan, was blessed with a natural leader, Ataturk, and experienced a breakdown of the old order which left a vacuum for that leader to fill.

Leveraging the chaos following World War I and the new nationalism arising out of the collapse of the Ottoman Empire, Kemal Ataturk shook Turkey to its core. Lord Kinross observes: "Ataturk's ambition was to create a new country and he wanted nothing less than to transform Turkish society, to sweep away a medieval social system based for centuries on Islam and replace it with a new one based on modern western civilization."[6]

Brilliant military victories and skillful diplomacy won Ataturk the prestige and power to bring Turkey into modernity. His accomplishments were breathtaking. He separated Islam from politics and closed the religious schools, moved to emancipate women, made the wearing of the fez a criminal offense, chose like-minded reformers for the new parliament, and founded his own political party. A new civil code, modeled on that of Switzerland, was adopted.

For decades, Ataturk and his party ran Turkey essentially without opposition, although his vision allowed for democratic politics. After his death Turkey moved gradually toward democratic pluralism and today has made more progress in that direction than any other Islamic country. It is the first non-Christian country to be a candidate for admission to the European Union. Its acceptance into the EU would be the crowning achievement for Ataturk's eighty-year-old vision.

The transformations of Japan and Turkey were of immense importance to the two countries and to the world. The leaders responsible for the transformations appreciated how far their countries had fallen behind, but rather than viewing themselves as victims of foreign devils, they perceived that what needed changing was not outside but inside. And in both cases, they looked to more advanced countries to learn how.

Great leadership in times of chaos and trauma can, in time, transform a country. But how does one change a society in the absence of chaos and trauma? Conscious efforts to change value systems are not uncommon, but they often are labeled as "political" or "ideological" rather than "cultural": one person's cultural change is another person's political change. Franklin Delano Roosevelt forever changed America and its political culture, in ways that reach to the essence of how Americans think about themselves individually and collectively. But the same national work ethic, desire for upward mobility, and propensity for freedom, cooperation, and wealth creation were present at both the beginning and end of his administration. The culture was modified but not transformed. "Transformation" is, however, the right word for the recent experience of a few other countries.

Most economic analysis begins with a country's resources, institutions, policies, political and economic climate, and basic structure of government and industry. Few economists look first to culture. Some go so far as to assert that culture doesn't matter, that people are essentially the same all over the world, and that the only thing that really matters is good policies that incorporate the right incentives.[7] But if that were true, why would some immigrant groups—the Chinese prominent among them—do better than others in societies where the same economic signals operate for all?

Singapore has vaulted from the third world to the first in only a few decades, a trajectory reminiscent of Japan's transformation during the Meiji Restoration. Singapore's saving and investment rates have been extraordinarily high, and it has been wide open to foreign investment. Education has had the highest priority: Singapore's goal has been a highly-educated labor force at all levels, from management to the lowest worker. The country has had an authoritarian but progressive leader in Lee Kuan Yew, who, as a graduate of Cambridge University, has had a deep exposure to western culture. As a predominantly Chinese nation, Singapore, like Japan, Korea, Taiwan, Hong Kong, and China, and the overseas Chinese, has been the beneficiary of the "Confucian" cultural tradition, with its emphasis on education, merit, achievement, and frugality. Singapore's inherited culture is thus an intrinsic part of its success story. But it is not the whole story. Singapore's leadership has deliberately and purposefully sought to develop the full array of traits, habits, values and skills that is necessary for success in the modern world. Lee Kuan Yew has observed: "The quality of a people determines the outcome of a nation. It is how you select your people, how you train them, how you organize them and ultimately how you manage them that makes the difference."[8]

Cultural change is difficult under the best of circumstances. People tend to be blind to their own areas of incompetence and need. Singapore was lucky to have the right leader in Lee, his authoritarianism notwithstanding. But the lessons of Singapore, though important, are limited. As Edgar H. Schein notes, "Singapore's small size made it possible to think of the entire nation as a community and demand of everyone in the nation a commitment to teamwork and a joint effort by articulating a vision of Singapore's future that everyone could identify with."[9]

Another example of the ability of strong leadership to modify cultural traits is Puerto Rico under Luis Muñoz Marín, who was governor from 1948 to 1964. Spain ruled Puerto Rico for nearly four hundred years, and until his administration Puerto Rico was a typical Latin American society: high levels of poverty, low levels of education, inequitable distribution of land, wealth, and power, authoritarian politics, and disdain for physical labor, moneymaking, technological skills, and nonhumanistic learning. Puerto Ricans seldom felt they could rise above their birth status. If one was born poor and friendless, the chances were overwhelmingly in favor of dying that way. It was God's will. One could, however, acquire merit in the eyes of God or one's master by leading a pious and good life, which among other things called for an acceptance of the social status quo. This was a vastly different culture from that of the United States, which acquired Puerto Rico after the Spanish-American War in 1898. As Henry Wells describes it: "Whereas the American view stresses individual rights, personal initiative, private enterprise, equality of opportunity, and the like, the Hispanic attitude is indifferent to all such considerations. Its focus is on the distinctive inner quality of the individual personality."[10]

The United States sought to Americanize Puerto Rico. Nowhere was Americanization more consciously promoted than in the public schools. As Puerto Rico's first commissioner of education, Martin G. Brumbaugh, put it in his first annual report, "The spirit of American institutions and the ideals of the American people, strange as they do seem to some in Puerto Rico, must be the only spirit and the only ideals incorporated in the school system of Puerto Rico." Yet most Puerto Ricans resisted the imposition of the alien culture.

Although elections for a bicameral legislature were instituted in 1917, it was not until 1948 that Puerto Ricans elected their own governor. Muñoz Marín, who had founded the Popular Democratic party in 1938, was the son of the prominent political leader Luis Muñoz Rivera, who served as Puerto Rico's resident commissioner in Washington from 1910 to 1916. Having lived most of his early life in the United States, Muñoz Marín was bicultural. As Puerto Rico's first elected governor, in 1948, he seized the opportunity to launch a cultural revolution aimed at modernizing the island. He promoted economic development through Operation Bootstrap, which encouraged new investment from the United States. He provoked a revolution in the education system: religious instruction was ended in public schools; public education was made available to females; and boys and girls shared the same classroom. Rote memorization gave way to education that called for experimentation and pragmatic solving of problems.

During Muñoz Marín's sixteen years as governor, Puerto Rico experienced transforming rates of economic growth. Today, it is the most affluent society in Latin America. Teodoro Moscoso, one of Muñoz Marín's principal aides and first U.S. Coordinator of the Alliance for Progress, wrote in 1988, "the most fundamental cause of our economic takeoff was the political leadership of Muñoz Marín. He changed the state of mind of the Puerto Rican people. He changed the culture."[11]

Yet Puerto Rico's transformation is far from complete. Per capita income on the island is half that of the poorest U.S. state. Unemployment rates and welfare usage are substantially above U.S. averages. And Puerto Ricans who migrate to the mainland do very poorly in education, income, and upward mobility. We do not appreciate how powerful the momentum of traditional values can be.

III.

As governor of Colorado, I encountered the frustrating reality of minority underachievement, above all in schools. I became convinced that I knew the principal cause of the problem: inculcation from a child's earliest days of cultures that do not value education and upward mobility. But I felt helpless to do anything about it. One reason for this was the unwillingness of many citizens, public officials, and educators to countenance the idea that culture matters, much preferring an explanation that blames racism, discrimination, and intolerance. Yet the United States is today a transformed society with respect to race and ethnicity, from what it was in the mid-1960s. Racism, discrimination, and intolerance still exist, but the vast majority of Americans reject them.

An equally important source of my frustration was not knowing what to do to change the values that stand in the way of blacks and Latinos. We tried several innovations and failed. That is why I attach so much importance to the findings of the Culture Matters Research Project.

It is now clear to me that political leaders can bring about cultural change at the national level through a vision of a better society, a vision glimpsed in the cases above. Respect for and a willingness to learn from other, more advanced societies is a thread common to the cases of Meiji Japan, Turkey, Singapore, and Puerto Rico. But introspection and self-analysis were also common to the transformations. Bernard Lewis's wise observation is highly relevant: "When people realize that things are going wrong, there are two questions they can ask. One is, 'What did we do wrong?' and the other is, 'Who did this to us?' The latter leads to conspiracy theories and paranoia. The first question leads to another line of thinking: 'How do we put it right?'"

"Who did this to us?" is still widely heard in the third world and among underachieving minorities in the United States. Increasingly, though, voices from these same groups are heard asking the first question. One of these is the black linguist John McWhorter, a participant in the Culture Matters Research Project, who points to the currents of separatism, "victimology," and anti-intellectualism in contemporary African-American culture as massive obstacles to advancement.[12] Another is Lionel Sosa, a Mexican-American who sees several elements of traditional Latino culture as the chief impediment to upward mobility for Latino immigrants.[13]

Finally, it is indispensable that we get rid of the taboo of talking about culture. In Orlando Patterson's words: "Culture as explanation languishes in intellectual exile partly because of guilt by association [with reactionary analysts]...only the worst of some very bad reasons for the rejection of cultural explanations. Another of these is the liberal mantra, still frequently chanted, that cultural explanations amount to blaming the victim. This is sheer nonsense..."[14]

Without addressing culture, we will not find solutions for the problems of poverty and underachievement.

Notes

1. James Fallows, *More Like Us* (Boston: Houghton Mifflin, 1989), 14.
2. *Culture Matters* (New York: Basic Books, 2000), 66.
3. Thomas Sowell, *Race and Culture* (New York: Basic Books, 1995), 1.
4. Peter Duus, *The Rise of Modern Japan* (1976).
5. Francis Fukuyama, *Trust: The Social Virtues and the Creation of Prosperity* (New York: Free Press, 1995).
6. Lord Kinross, *Ataturk* (New York: HarperCollins, 1964).

7. See, for example, William Easterly, *The Elusive Quest for Growth* (Cambridge MA: MIT Press, 2002).

8. Lee Kuan Yew, *From Third World to First, the Singapore Story 1965–2000* (New York: HarperCollins, 2000).

9. Edgar H. Schein, *Strategic Pragmatism: the Culture of Singapore's Economic Development Board* (Cambridge, MA: MIT Press 1996).

10. Henry Wells, *The Modernization of Puerto Rico: A Political Study of Changing Values and Institutions* (Cambridge, MA:Harvard University Press, 1969).

11. Teodoro Moscoso, "The Will to Economic Development," in L. Ronald Scheman, ed., *The Alliance for Progress: A Retrospective* (New York: Praeger, 1988), 83.

12. John McWhorter, *Losing the Race* (New York: Free Press, 2000).

13. Lionel Sosa, *The Americano Dream* (New York: Dutton, 1998).

14. Orlando Patterson, "Taking Culture Seriously," in Lawrence Harrison and Samuel Huntington, eds., *Culture Matters* (New York: Basic Books, 2000), 206.

Part VI
Development Projects

20

Donor Projects and Culture Change

The Case of Costa Rica

JAMES W. FOX

In the broadest sense, most promoters of development believe in Marx's conception of culture: a person's, or a society's, cultural worldview is determined by the conditions of production. Serfs living in a world of arbitrary weather and arbitrary temporal power will be fatalistic and nonentrepreneurial. A society where most people work for small businesses, where technological change is common, and where the rewards for efficiency and productivity are obvious, will be one with progress-prone cultural values.

In general, donors have sought to push developing-country societies in the progress-prone direction. Indeed, the behavior patterns of donor agents resident in developing countries, or of Peace Corps volunteers, or even of religious proselytizers, have typically embodied most of the progress-prone cultural patterns of the Culture Matters Research Project typology (see appendix 20.1). Their example has surely had some influence on the people with whom they interact during their careers. This influence, though probably real, is likely too small to have a significant impact on the recipient country.

Donors have also sought to change culture through their development projects. In this chapter I analyze the mechanisms at work in six different types of donor interventions that lend themselves directly to changes in culture, and then examine a concrete case of cultural change over time.

Mechanisms

I examine the mechanisms that operate in programs focusing on agriculture, education, family planning, women, microfinance, and democracy and governance.

Agriculture

From the beginning of foreign aid, donor projects have sought to identify and transfer productivity-increasing technology in agriculture. The rural sector everywhere is the repository of traditional values, and early donors saw such values—passivity, reliance on tradition, suspicion of education—as a major obstacle to development. Donors have tried to transfer an attitude toward technology that addresses the Culture Matters factors of entrepreneurship and innovation, and also influence some of the worldview factors—notably those on destiny, wealth, and knowledge. (The factors are all listed in the matrix in appendix 20.1).

Most development theorists would have expected the mechanism for cultural change here to have been economic. Better technology would demonstrate the value of knowledge in raising incomes, thereby discrediting traditional approaches and fatalism. This would lead to increased investment, greater emphasis on learning and knowledge, and more entrepreneurship. In the wake of these changes, other progress-friendly values would follow gradually.

Has this happened? The level of technology in agriculture has increased dramatically in the last half century. This has led to increased valuation of knowledge and technology and increased understanding that education and investment are key to material success. Has anyone systematically analyzed the process of cultural change that has resulted? Not so far.

Education

Education was second only to agriculture in early thinking about cultural change. In 1950 literacy was the province of the elite in developing countries, with, on average, 65 percent of the population unable to read. With enormous donor help in building schools, training teachers, writing textbooks, and developing curricula, this share had fallen to 25 percent by 2000.

The Republic of Korea was one of the most remarkable examples of this process. In 1945 fewer than half of primary-age students were in school; a generation later, the nation had virtually 100 percent primary enrollment. And it did so while losing half its teachers (Japanese nationals), changing the language of instruction from Japanese to Korean, and fighting a war in which it twice lost its capital to the enemy. Thus, it was done against almost overwhelming odds—with the need for a massive program of teacher training, curriculum design, and textbook writing and distribution. It was done in the early years with classes as large as a hundred students, in schools with double shifts. At first USAID proposed Western ideas: local control of schools, emphasis on cognitive rather than rote teaching methods. These were rejected by the Korean government, which sent the American experts packing in 1948 and adopted a very centralized system, a national curriculum that gave heavy play to memorization and rote learning and featured heavy ideological content. Korea has since been held up as a successful development case because of its emphasis on mass education.

The particulars of the Korean case are enough to discourage easy generalizations about the prospects of improving culture by reforming education. Nevertheless, the power of literacy as a vehicle for individual empowerment—for connection to world culture and values and for going beyond village or tribal values—is enormous. Literacy may not result in "development-friendly" cultural values, but it certainly opens the door to such values. Some in every culture will surely walk through.

On the other hand, sub-Saharan Africa has been the region with the most dramatic increase in school enrollments and literacy over the last half century. The outcome of this experiment with education as a vehicle for positive cultural change and for economic development has been, to say the least, disappointing. Why did mass education succeed in Korea and fail in Africa?

Family Planning

USAID has been promoting family planning for more than three decades. For many in developing countries, the shift from having as many children as God sends to a conscious decision about how many children to have and when, is surely as fundamental as any in family life. Acceptance of family planning would seem to be a total rejection of a passive worldview in favor of one where an empowered individual or family choice is central.

Fertility has declined dramatically in developing countries since the mid-1950s: from 6.2 children per woman between 1950 and 1955, to 2.9 between 2000 and 2005. In most countries, with the notable exception of some African countries like Niger, families have embraced the idea of fewer children. What caused this change in culture? Family planning advocates have claimed success from direct efforts to change cultural values, but there is only very weak evidence to support this view. The predominant explanation that econometric studies offer for fertility decline largely involves changes in circumstances rather than in culture per se. Families in urban areas choose to have fewer children than rural families, a fact usually attributed to a changed balance between the costs and benefits of children. Higher-income families have fewer children than poorer ones. Recent research has suggested that family income is a less reliable predictor of fertility control than family possession of consumer durables like televisions and refrigerators. In effect, it is a family's embrace of modern conveniences and the values they imply, rather than its income, that most reliably predicts its willingness to have few children.

The enormity of the change in cultural outlook implied by even the concept of fertility control is captured by Tolstoy in *Anna Karenina*, when Anna explains to her sister the existence of this possibility:

> "Impossible!" said Dolly, opening her eyes wide.
>
> For her this was one of those discoveries the consequences and deductions from which are so immense that all that one feels for the first instant is that it is impossible to take it all in, and that one will have to reflect a great, great deal on it.
>
> This discovery, suddenly throwing light on all those families of one or two children, which had hitherto been so incomprehensible to her, aroused so many ideas, reflections, and contradictory emotions, that she had nothing to say, and simply gazed with wide-open eyes of wonder at Anna. This was the very thing she had been dreaming of, but now learning that it was possible, she was horrified. She felt that it was too simple a solution of too complicated a problem.
>
> "*N'est-ce pas immoral?*" was all she said, after a brief pause.

Women in Development

After family planning, promotion of an increased role for women has been a constant theme for donors, led by USAID, for more than two decades. In some traditional cultures, efforts to change the status of women attack fundamental values in the society. Seeking such changes might be compared to efforts to promote desegregation in Alabama and Mississippi in the 1950s. The mainstream dominant culture saw such changes as a fundamental attack on basic community values, and resisted change by all possible means. Direct assault with federal troops was possible in the U.S. South; it is not possible in many developing countries. More indirect methods are needed. The education of women is an obvious tool, and has produced substantial results. In most countries, female literacy, while still lagging behind that of males, has been growing more quickly, with the trend lines suggesting convergence with male literacy within a decade or two.

These efforts to empower women have unleashed forces for cultural change that are very powerful but are still working their way through society in developing countries. Conclusions on the impact of these efforts are being sought, and some interesting insights may emerge. So far, however, the results have been disappointing. The vast literature on women's issues in developing countries has largely focused on the extent to which women have been denied equality, together with demands for their equal treatment. For example, a World Bank document encouragingly titled *Evaluating the Gender Impact of Bank Assistance* does not include among its twenty-eight papers a single clear example that offers useful empirical evidence on the relative effectiveness of alternative approaches to promoting equality for women.

Microfinance

Microfinance has been seen by proponents as a key tool for empowering poor people by providing access to capital. The most ambitious microfinance approach has gone much further, into direct cultural change. This is Grameen Bank in Bangladesh, founded by Mohammed Yunus. Considering value change to be central to changing the status of women in Bangladesh, Yunus designed his programs as both an economic and cultural tool for improving their status. To borrow

from Grameen Bank, women were required to organize groups (usually composed of five people) with joint liability for loans. If any
member did not repay loans, they had to be assumed by the others.
More fundamentally, before qualifying for a loan, each woman had
to make sixteen "decisions" about her conduct. These are included as
appendix 20.2. At their core, they represent a program to change cultural values in a much more "developmentally friendly" direction.

Since this innovation, microfinance has been adopted in many
other countries, often as an instrument for empowering women. In
others, it is simply a tool for offering access to capital to a sector of
the economy that has traditionally lacked it, and, therefore, is the sector where capital is likely to be most productive. What has been the
result of these efforts?

In Bangladesh, Grameen Bank has been an enormous success, attracting more than two million clients. Two other microfinance institutions there—BRAC and ASA—have been even more successful,
attracting even larger numbers of clients and achieving higher repay-
ment rates on loans. The two imitators both used individual, rather
than group, liability, and gave less attention than Grameen to the
culture-change aspect. Indeed, many believe that Grameen's cultural-
change activities have been of only marginal significance; the issue
is still being researched. The mainstream thinkers on microfinance
today appear to believe that it is indeed a tool for cultural change and
empowerment of women. But, they argue, the key tool is cash in the
hand and not commitments to live better or joint borrowing.

Democracy and Governance

In recent years, donor agencies have begun to pay considerable attention to democracy and governance, even examining the extent of corruption, in developing countries. In terms of the typology in appendix
20.1, this mainly concerns values sixteen through twenty-one: rule of
law, radius of identification and trust, association (social capital), the
individual and group, authority, and the role of elites. Whether or not
democracy is the best form of government is still debated. Churchill's
dictum that it is the worst, except for all the others, suggests that any
conceivable form of government will be far from perfect.

In recent years donors have been more outspoken in denying assistance to nondemocratic or corrupt governments and raising assis-

tance levels to countries with more democratic governance and less corruption. At the same time, this is only one among many influences on donor assistance. Moreover, distinguishing between democratic and nondemocratic governments is far from easy, as is judging the level of corruption in a society.

From the perspective of this study, an interesting question would be the extent of support for democratic values before the donor intervention (or withholding), compared with the extent of such support later. So far, I know of no studies that offer convincing evidence on this matter. A 2003 report by the General Accounting Office (GAO) on USAID democracy programs in Latin America laments the lack of baseline data on attitudes and values at the outset of the intervention.

Cultural Change Processes in Microcosm

In a few cases social scientists have looked at a specific geographical location in a manner that provides detailed information on both economic processes and cultural behavior patterns over an extended period. I have found case studies on three countries. Comparative studies exist for Panajachel, Guatemala, for 1945 and 1973, by Tax[1] and Hinshaw;[2] for Palanpur, India, over five decades, summarized by Lanjouw and Stern;[3] and for two Costa Rican villages between 1950 and 1995, described in Loomis[4] and Romagosa and Castañeda.[5]

The value of such case studies is that they provide documentation on the cultural change process that has occurred over the period studied, as well as on the economic, social and political forces at work, including donor-supported interventions. With luck, such documentation may generate productive thinking about the importance of the various factors in play.

The case analyzed here is Costa Rica, as reported by Romagosa and Castañeda. Two villages, San Juan Sur and Aquiares, located in eastern Costa Rica, were studied extensively by a group of social scientists from Michigan State University (then Michigan State College) around 1950, headed by Charles Loomis. San Juan Sur was a village populated by small farmers, while Aquiares was an estate, or hacienda, where the workers lived in estate housing and were paid wages. The effort included considerable data collection on political, social, and cultural attitudes as well as other aspects of behavior. The two villages were resurveyed in 1995, using a similar instrument.

Comparison of the two surveys provides a basis for thinking about cultural change dynamics.

Economic Changes

Both communities prospered over the period, with both incomes and population rising. San Juan Sur was the more dynamic, with population rising 167 percent, compared with 34 percent growth in Aquiares. Potential for gainful employment in coffee production probably explains most of the difference. Aquiares was already largely planted in coffee in 1950, so the area planted increased only slightly. In San Juan Sur, coffee acreage increased sixfold as farmers planted land previously in pasture, forest, or other crops. Part of this change reflects increased specialization in coffee: farmers stopped growing vegetables for their own consumption, instead purchasing such products from others with part of the income they earned from coffee. While the increased area planted with coffee provided more employment, the determining factor in increased incomes was higher productivity in coffee. Yields quadrupled over the period. Coffee prices declined in real terms over the period, offsetting some of the yield gains, but a hectare of coffee produced about 2.5 times more in purchasing power terms in 1995 than it did in 1950. This is about the average increase in real wages and incomes of the people in the two villages.

Both villages also benefited from the extension of water and electricity to their communities and from improvements in health and education facilities. Much of the health improvement came from better treatment of human waste, which eliminated a major source of diarrhea. While water and sewerage services played an important role in improving health, education was critical. People were healthier in 1995 because they knew more about the causes of disease.

Changes in Living Conditions

The 1950 data show relatively primitive living conditions. Most people lived in simple one- or two-room houses of wood or "rancho" construction. In San Juan Sur 84 percent of the people had no toilet, even outdoors; the same was true of 97 percent of people in Aquiares. One-third of the houses in each village had dirt floors; fewer than one household in twenty had a radio. All of the radio-owners were in Aquiares: foremen or other technical personnel living in houses close enough to the hacienda's generator to have access to electricity. Transistor radios had not yet been invented. Running water and electricity were almost totally lacking in the two communities. Fewer than half of the houses contained any books, and wall decorations were few and simple—pictures of saints or interesting scenes, often cut from a newspaper or magazine.

Although the San Juan Sur/Aquiares study did not include health data, a broader health survey of the region in 1953 by some of the same researchers found infant mortality to be 170 per 1000 births, with miscarriages and stillbirths accounting for another 14 percent percent of pregnancies—in total, 31 percent of all pregnancies ended badly. Trichocephalus infections were found in 96 percent of the researchers' sample and hookworm in 62 percent. Doctors assisted at 2 percent of childbirths, with midwives (66%) the most common attendants.

Long before 1995 rancho houses had disappeared. Most houses in both communities were now made of concrete, with concrete or tile floors. All had electricity, and nearly all had piped water and indoor plumbing. Health conditions also had improved dramatically, as both villages were brought into modern medical-care networks. Nearly all births now take place in hospitals, mainly through the social security system, with which more than 70 percent of households are affiliated.

Communication with the outside world has been revolutionized. While fewer than 5 percent of the households had radios in 1950, more than 80 percent in each village owned color televisions in 1995. Residents of the two villages have been integrated into a wider world; they are in touch with events elsewhere in Costa Rica and aware of events, trends, and norms around the world. Their most ambitious offspring migrate to San José, returning home for visits with different cultural values from those they learned in the village.

Value Changes

Some social values within the communities have been constant—notably, respect for hard work and for collaboration within the community—while others have changed. The most striking change is a dramatic increase in tolerance of people who deviate from community norms. For example, Protestants, unmarried couples living together, and homosexuals are stigmatized far less than they were in 1950. The local priest has declined dramatically in prestige over the period, while a variety of other occupations have gained in prestige. Schoolteachers also declined in prestige. In 1950, before the road was built, teachers had no choice but to live in the village, and they saw themselves as progressive leaders bringing modernization to the community. Now they live in Turrialba, a larger city nearby, and only arrive for school hours to do a job.

The status and freedom of women increased dramatically over the period. Women only gained the vote in Costa Rica in 1948. In 1950, women typically needed permission to leave their houses. By 1995, this had changed dramatically, and both villages fielded women's soccer teams. Women in 1995 were also more likely to attain leadership positions in the community than in 1950, though they have yet to achieve social equality with men.

Some customs have changed because of encroaching values from outside the village. But changing conditions have spurred other changes. For example, the rituals of a procession through the village with religious symbols and a tiny casket, associated with the death of an infant in the village—a weekly occurrence in 1950—has disappeared, as improved health conditions have transformed this from a normal part of village life to a rare event.

Increased access to the outside world clearly weakened the commitment of people to the community as a social network and repository of values. Young people acquired foreign ideas from television and movies that made them less willing to accept the traditional norms and customs of their own community.

Environmental Impacts

Though similar in many ways, the two villages provide an interesting contrast that highlights the multidimensional character of development. Contrary to standard assumptions about the exploitative nature of plantation life, the hacienda workers in Aquiares were in some respects consistently better off than small farmers in San Juan Sur. Aquiares children had six years of school when the latter had only three; they also had water, electricity, and health care earlier. Even today, water availability is better in Aquiares, and all have health care coverage under the social security system, while some in San Juan Sur do not. On the other hand, incomes are higher in San Juan Sur, and long traditions of community self-help and political activism have created a more self-reliant social pattern.

In sum, both communities have provided paths to better economic and social conditions for their residents. But those paths meander over different portions of the steep hillside of development. Even progress in the organization of the household can be attained in substantially different ways. In Aquiares, the woman of the household manages family finances alone in 44 percent of households, while the man alone does so in only 19 percent; in San Juan Sur, the man does it alone in 48 percent of the households, and the woman in 29 percent. This could be related to the fact that in San Juan Sur, household finances are closely tied to farm management and investment decisions. Or it may indicate that farm ownership reinforces patriarchal traditions in a way that the wage system of employment at Aquiares does not.

The Role of Foreign Aid in Aquiares and San Juan Sur

When it comes to ultimate beneficiaries of development assistance, such as the residents of Aquiares and San Juan Sur, the role of foreign aid cannot be separated from other factors. Nevertheless, some activities left discernable "footprints." In coffee, the quadrupling of yields surely owes a significant amount to donor-promoted initiatives. First, U.S. agronomists introduced scientific approaches to coffee production by identifying nutrients lacking in the soil. This knowledge apparently led to significant and rapid increases in yields. Second, USAID and other U.S. government assistance to coffee research helped develop and disseminate new coffee varieties that produced higher yields and required less care. These improvements were probably introduced into the communities through a variety of channels: extension agents, 4-S clubs (the local equivalent of 4-H clubs), fertilizer salesmen, and word of mouth between farmers. San Juan Sur has long had a 4-S club, the product of an early effort by U.S. agricultural advisers who organized 158 clubs in Costa Rica in the 1950s.

Collaborative efforts by USAID, the World Bank, the Inter-American Development Bank, and the Costa Rican government to improve rural roads, public health, education, electricity, telephones, and water and sewerage also touched the communities, at least indirectly. In more recent years, the restoration of macroeconomic stability to the country has provided a more favorable environment for people in the villages. A seriously overvalued exchange rate prior to U.S.-assisted stabilization between 1982 and 1984 heavily penalized coffee producers and was probably a factor in the bankruptcy of the Aquiares hacienda during that period. The overvalued exchange rate probably also contributed to the consequent temporary decline in the number of people living and working there. The creation of alternative sources of employment, such as the baseball factory in Turrialba which employs a dozen women from both villages, is a legacy of donor-assisted export and investment promotion efforts.

Drawing Conclusions About Donor Project Impact

The above discussion raises a number of important questions about the possibility of linking donor projects to cultural change. First, can one measure whether or not culture has changed? For most of the measures in appendix 20.1, baseline studies of cultural values prior to a donor intervention are virtually nonexistent. This makes it impossible to track the cultural changes that result from any donor project. This is true even if one could find end-of-project measures of cultural values, itself a rare commodity. At the same time, there can be little doubt that much has changed in the worldview of most people in developing countries.

Second, to what degree can any cultural change (however measured) be attributed to donor involvement? The discussion above, particularly of the Costa Rican case, shows clearly that multiple forces are at work in cultural change processes, even if information to address the previous point is available. In the Costa Rican villages, both the entry of mass communication and the exit of young people for the capital city were likely to have been factors of great importance in cultural change for the people remaining in the villages. Mass education and the obvious success of public health measures in reducing mortality would surely have affected the extent to which "the will of God" was seen as directing everything. In this dynamic environment, any specific donor intervention would be only one of various forces at work that were attacking the traditional values that people held in this society. With so much happening simultaneously, attribution of change to any specific intervention would be speculative.

Given these considerations, the general direction of research in this area might be redirected toward a different target: trying to identify whether donor projects are pushing in the right direction (i.e., toward more progress-prone values) or the wrong one (i.e., away from them). In the United States since the welfare system was overhauled in 1994, compelling evidence shows that the system indeed pushed in the wrong direction for several decades by encouraging dependence on government largesse. Donor agencies sometimes view the poor in developing countries as so helpless and uncalculating that they see possible incentive effects as not worth considering. Two books prepared for the World Bank's recent massive study of poverty, by teams headed by Narayan[6] and Chambers,[7] both titled *Voices of the Poor,* offer specimens of this genre.

It is possible that some fruitful conclusions will come from analyzing donor projects on the basis of the incentives they put into play. Evaluation reports may find some evidence that some projects have perverse consequences. On the other hand, evaluators may self-censor reports of such unintended outcomes, limiting the usefulness of this approach.

If some useful material from studies could be gathered, it might provide the basis for new guidelines for donor programs that would heighten donor concern about adverse incentives resulting from donor projects, or of donor-induced cultural changes that encourage views in column 3 rather than column 2 in appendix 20.1.

Notes

1. Sol Tax, *Penny Capitalism: A Guatemalan Indian Economy* (Washington, D.C.: U.S. Government Printing Office, 1953).
2. Robert Hinshaw, *Panajachel: A Guatemalan Town in Thirty-Year Perspective.* (Pittsburgh: University of Pittsburgh Press, 1975).
3. Peter Lanjouw and Nicholas Stern, *Economic Development in Palanpur Over Five Decades* (Oxford: Clarendon Press, 1998).
4. Charles Price Loomis, ed., *Turrialba: Social Systems and the Introduction of Change,* (Glenco, IL: Free Press, 1953).
5. Ivelina Romagosa and Amilcar Castañeda, "Life in Two Costa Rican Villages, 1950 and 1995," USAID, 1996.
6. Deepa Narayan, Raj Patel, Kai Schafft, Anne Rademacher, and Sara Koch-Schultev, *Voices of the Poor: Can Anyone Hear Us?* (New York: Oxford University Press for the World Bank, Washington, D.C., 2000).
7. Robert Chambers, Deepa Narayan, Meera Shah, and Patt Petesch, *Voices of the Poor: Crying Out for Change* (New York: Oxford University Press for the World Bank, Washington, D.C., 2000).

Appendix 20.1

Typology of Progress-Prone and Progress-Resistant Cultures

Based on the original structure of Mariano Grodona with inputs from Irakli Chkonia, Lawrence Harrison, Matteo Marini, and Ronald Inglehart

Factor	Progress-Prone Culture	Progress-Resistant Culture
WORLDVIEW		
1. Religion	Nurtures rationality, achievement; promotes material pursuits; focus on this world; pragmatism	Nurtures irrationality; inhibits material pursuits; focus on the other world; utopianism
2. Destiny	I can influence my destiny for the better.	Fatalism, resignation, sorcery
3. Time orientation	Future focus promotes planning, punctuality, deferred gratification	Present or past focus discourages planning, punctuality, saving
4. Wealth	Product of human creativity expandible (positive sum)	What exists (zero-sum), not expandible
5. Knowledge	Practical, verifiable; facts matter	Abstract, theoretical, cosmological, not verifiable
VALUES, VIRTUES		
6. Ethical code	Rigorous within realistic norms; feeds trust	Elastic, wide gap twixt utopian norms and behavior=mistrust
7. The lesser virtues	A job well done, tidiness, courtesy, punctuality matter	Lesser virtues unimportant
8. Education	Indispensable; promotes autonomy, heterodoxy, dissent, creativity	Less priority; promotes dependency, orthodoxy
ECONOMIC BEHAVIOR		
9. Work/ achievement	Live to work: work leads to wealth	Work to live: work doesn't lead to wealth; work is for the poor
10. Frugality	The mother of investment and prosperity	A threat to equality because those who save will get rich, provoking envy

Factor	Progress-Prone Culture	Progress-Resistant Culture
11. Entrepreneurship	Investment and creativity	Rent-seeking: income derives from government connections
12. Risk propensity	Moderate	Low
13. Competition	Leads to excellence	Is a sign of aggression, and a threat to equality— and privilege
14. Innovation	Open; rapid adaptation of innovation	Suspicious; slow adaptation of innovation
15. Advancement	Based on merit	Based on family and/or patron, connections

SOCIAL BEHAVIOR

Factor	Progress-Prone Culture	Progress-Resistant Culture
16. Rule of law/ corruption	Reasonably law abiding; corruption is prosecuted	Money, connections matter, corruption is tolerated
17. Radius of identification trust	Stronger identification with the broader society	Stronger identification with the narrow community
18. Family	The idea of "family" extends to the broader society	The family is a fortress against the broader society
19. Association (social capital)	Trust, identification breed cooperation, affiliation, participation	Mistrust breeds extreme individualism, anomie
20. The individual/ the group	Emphasizes the individual but not excessively	Emphasizes the collectivity
21. Authority	Dispersed: checks and balances, consensus	Centralized: unfettered, often arbitrary
22. Role of elites	Responsibility to society	Power and rent seeking; exploitative
23. Church-state relations	Secularized; wall between church and state	Religion plays major role in civic sphere
24. Gender relationships	If gender equality not a reality, at least not inconsistent with value system	Women subordinated to men in most dimensions of life
25. Fertility	The number of children should depend on the family's capacity to raise and educate them	Children are the gifts of God, they are an economic asset

Appendix 20.2

Grameen Bank: The Sixteen Decisions Required of Participants in Grameen Groups

1. We shall follow and advance the four principles of Grameen Bank—discipline, unity, courage, and hard work —in all walks of our lives.

2. We shall bring prosperity to our families.

3. We shall not live in dilapidated houses. We shall repair our houses and work toward constructing new houses at the earliest opportunity.

4. We shall grow vegetables all the year round. We shall eat plenty of them and sell the surplus.

5. During the planting seasons, we shall plant as many seedlings as possible.

6. We shall plan to keep our families small. We shall minimize our expenditures. We shall look after our health.

7. We shall educate our children and ensure that they can earn what is necessary to pay for their education.

8. We shall always keep our children and the environment clean.

9. We shall build and use pit-latrines.

10. We shall drink water from tube wells. If it is not available, we shall boil water or use alum.

11. We shall not take any dowry at our sons' weddings, neither shall we give any dowry at our daughters' weddings. We shall keep our center free from the curse of dowry. We shall not practice child marriage.

12. We shall not inflict any injustice on anyone, neither shall we allow anyone to do so.

13. We shall collectively undertake bigger investments for higher incomes.

14. We shall always be ready to help each other. If anyone is in difficulty, we shall all help him or her.

15. If we come to know of any breach of discipline in any center, we shall all go there and help restore discipline.

16. We shall introduce physical exercise in all our centers. We shall take part in all social activities collectively.

21

Can Social Capital Be Constructed?

Decentralization and Social Capital Formation in Latin America[1]

MITCHELL A. SELIGSON

Ever since the Marshall Plan, development economists have been increasingly successful at writing prescriptions to stimulate economic growth in developing nations. They tell us, for example, that countries must avoid rent-seeking, control corruption, and harness inflation; they must also invest in physical and human capital to stimulate investment, and thus the growth of financial capital. Immediately after World War II, political scientists also developed a strong interest in stimulating growth, not of the economy but of democracy, and the rapid transformations of fascist Germany, Italy, and Japan into strong democracies made it appear that democratic development was going to be a "cake walk." It seemed that all they would have to do was impose democratic constitutions and have occupying GIs teach some civics lessons for democracy to take hold and prosper.

But they soon confronted a far more difficult reality. While economies in war-torn Europe recovered quickly and democracies flourished there and in Japan, the geographical spread and strengthening of democracy was far less impressive than the dramatic economic growth experienced, for example, by the Asian "miracle" countries. Good constitutions matter, as became clear in Japan, but the world soon learned that they were hardly all it took for democracy to emerge and flourish. When the Cold War ended and democracies suddenly emerged worldwide, political scientists had not yet conducted the decades of research they would need to develop the checklist that economists already had.

Among the most intriguing theories is that, as Harrison and Huntington put it, "culture matters": that for democracies to emerge and survive, societies require both good institutions and good political cultures.[2] The "typology of progress-prone and progress resistant cultures" that is being developed by Harrison and other contributors to the Culture Matters research project, including Mariano Grondona, Matteo Marini, and Irakli Chkonia, states that social behavior must involve cooperation, affiliation, and participation rather than individualism and anomie. No element in this theory has been more central than the hypothesized role of social capital in democratic development, popularized by Robert Putnam's now classic work on Italy.[3] He found strong evidence that political culture matters by demonstrating that newly created regional governments in Italy were stronger, more responsive, and more effective in regions with high levels of *preexisting* social capital.

Since the publication of that research, a veritable cottage industry has developed on social capital and its impacts. Researchers have found different types of social capital; those called "bridging social capital" seem to be positive for democracy, while other kinds, such as "bonding social capital" can sometimes hamstring democratic development.[4] Putnam's research, however, suggests that the formation of social capital extends over centuries, implying that it will be extremely difficult to change such deeply embedded patterns. Indeed, this was Banfield's conclusion to his classic work on "Montegrano," Italy decades earlier; he believed that village's political incapacity resulted from cultural patterns formed over many centuries. He argued, pessimistically, that "cultures do not remake themselves in fundamental ways by deliberate intention any more than villages."[5]

Other researchers, including Putnam himself, suggest that levels of social capital can change and that it can be built or lost in relatively short periods of time; for example, he has found that TV viewing can have a pernicious impact on social capital.[6] The broader theory rests on the premise that cultures themselves can change, with authoritarian, antidemocratic cultures giving way to democratic ones. Certainly that seemed to be the lesson from postwar Germany and

Japan. The argument has been that these were deeply authoritarian cultures, which, in the case of Germany, could not sustain democracy under Weimar, resulting in the emergence of fanatical fascism, genocide, and a war that took over 46 million lives.[7] But German values today seem to be deeply democratic, having evolved rapidly since the end of the war.

That assertion is hard to sustain because we really do not know what the Germans and Japanese were like before World War II, as modern survey research had not yet been invented. Right after the war, the U.S. army gleaned important evidence through surveys in Germany, and while that data is fascinating, it is data from after the war, gathered by an occupying army.[8] Inglehart, reviewing data from the 1950s and beyond, sees clearly that values in Germany and Italy have indeed changed.[9] Using that data, however, it is difficult if not impossible to sort out the causal element in what Inglehart aptly terms the "culture shift." We could make a good case that prosperity changed values, but that does not help practitioners who are attempting to promote democracy: the lesson of Germany, Italy, and Japan could well be that in order to foster democratic values, one need only sit by and watch the economy grow.[10]

While many have studied the nature, levels, and impacts of social capital, fewer have focused on how to stimulate its formation and expansion. Such research requires an experimental before-and-after design, which social scientists rarely have the opportunity to implement. The experimental part of Putnam's Italian study in the early 1970s emerged as Italy created regional governmental institutions for the first time in its history. Thus, Putnam could focus on the efficacy of those institutions in different regions, comparing those where social capital had been high before the installation of the new governments with those where it had been low. What Putnam found is that in the regions of high social capital, the new institutions were far more effective than in the regions of low social capital.

To move beyond Putnam's research we need situations where we can measure the increase (or decrease) of social capital that might emerge from programs designed to stimulate its growth. That area of inquiry has seen far less research, but it is the key to the chapters collected here. Landmark work at Cornell University, conducted in Asia by Avirudh Krishna and his associates, has shown that even though levels of social capital may be less than optimal, people find creative ways to harness what does exist and even create more of it.[11]

But other evidence that social capital can be created is mixed and limited.[12]

In general, democracy programs have limited impact.[13] This view is shared in a recent U.S. General Accounting Office (GAO) study of USAID democracy-promotion programs in Latin America,[14] which found that many projects do not incorporate evaluation methodologies that would allow the impact to be documented. A major recommendation of the GAO study was that U.S. foreign assistance should "establish a strategy for periodically evaluating" such projects "that is consistent across agencies, countries, and types of programs."[15]

In this chapter I describe one study that carefully measured the impact of a program to build social capital by expanding citizen participation in local government. The project operated in the context of a decentralization process that transformed the structure and resources of local government in Bolivia. In many ways this project resembled Putnam's study in Italy, which compared the effectiveness of regional governments. In both Italy and Bolivia, institutional changes were introduced, transforming local or regional government. In Italy, the independent variable Putnam studied was political culture in the form of social capital. In Bolivia, I used an experimental design to examine a program that helped empower citizens to exploit the resources made available by a nationwide program to decentralize national government and strengthen local government. This program was applied to some areas, in effect making them a treatment group, and not to others, making them a control group. Using survey data collected from individuals in both groups, we were able to measure the program's impact. The results, as I show below, have been positive, suggesting that social capital can be built in relatively short order, and giving us grounds for optimism that democracy can be built.

Decentralization and Popular Participation in Bolivia

In 1994, Sánchez de Lozada, president of Bolivia, ushered in a set of reforms designed to attack corruption and strengthen accountability by decentralizing many government responsibilities.[16] The Popular Participation Law (PPL) began what many observers see as "Latin America's most significant and innovative effort ever to extend and complement the institutions of representative democracy through decentralization."[17] Designed with the help of international development agencies, the PPL was intended to create a newly empowered local level of government; several provisions explicitly aimed to make local government officials more accountable to citizens.

Several features of the PPL and the later constitutional reforms associated with it were notable. It redrew municipal borders to incorporate rural communities previously excluded from local government, and institutionalized citizen oversight committees and grassroots organizations designed to have an ongoing role in local government. It dramatically increased the development responsibilities of municipal governments, transferred significant fiscal resources to municipal governments, and aimed to make municipal government more accountable by allowing a town council to remove a mayor with a three-fifths majority vote in case of misconduct. At the end of the process, local government in Bolivia was reorganized into 311 municipalities incorporating the entire national territory.

The DDPC Program

Much as in Putnam's Italy, in Bolivia a nationwide reform granted formal powers to a subnational government never before experienced in a country with a very long tradition of extreme centralization.[18] In Bolivia, a special program was established to improve local government by encouraging citizen participation and accountability. At the time of this study, however, that program was not national in scope. That situation provided us with the conditions of a natural experiment: some municipalities received the "treatment" of the special program while others did not. Thus, while the new laws transformed all the local governments structurally, only a subset of them received full access to the DDPC program. This fact makes it possible to hold institutional reform constant and look exclusively at the impact of the DDPC program, giving us an advantage that Putnam did not have in Italy. That is, we can separate out the program's impact from the structural reforms (i.e., decentralization and popular participation) themselves.

The objective of this analysis is to examine the impact that this effort had on social capital formation in Bolivia. The program, Democratic Development, Citizen Participation, has been supported by USAID since its inception. In this chapter I refer to the program by its Spanish acronym, DDPC. Since 1998 the Latin American Public

Opinion Project, now supported by Vanderbilt University, has been conducting surveys of democratic values and behaviors in Bolivia. Each survey has involved collecting data from a national probability sample of about three thousand respondents. Each sample has covered virtually the entire population of the country, including monolingual speakers of Quechua and Aymara, and people in remote rural zones, not an easy task in a highly mountainous country with a very low population density. The only adults excluded from the survey were monolingual speakers of other languages (e.g., Portuguese), who represent only a fraction of a percent of the population. Those studies have resulted in a series of monographs and articles.[19]

In our 2002 study we decided to select a special sample of municipalities or commonwealth associations of municipalities, called *mancomunidades* in Bolivia, and to compare the results for that sample with the nationwide results. We drew the sample of DDPC municipalities at random from the list of municipalities which had by that time experienced the full package of program inputs. This allowed us to make comparisons between those municipalities and *mancomunidades* and the rest of the country. Other municipalities, including some from which we drew our nationwide sample, received only some of the elements of the DDPC program.[20] To avoid confusion, we eliminated the data from those areas, so we could directly compare just the areas that experienced the "full-package" DDPC program and the sample from the rest of the country. As I note below, we also introduced controls to compensate for demographic and socioeconomic differences between the national sample and the DDPC sample.

The DDPC program began by selecting a small number of municipalities in which to engage in pilot projects. This effort was then scaled up under the "replicability strategy": DDCP provided small institutional strengthening grants to selected *mancomunidades* and departmental municipal associations, which they used to hire three to five technical staff members with expertise or training in such elements as municipal budgeting, participatory planning, municipal legislation, and meeting facilitation. The DDCP, in turn, trained these staff in its *Modelo de Gestión Municipal Participativa*, which, as a starting point, sought to increase citizen participation in defining the annual operating plan and budget. The efforts also focused on strengthening the capacity of the municipal executive and council to organize itself, properly prepare accounts, and respond publicly to the increasing demands of citizens.

A central goal of the project was to help citizens become more active in the municipality. The expectation was that citizens would take advantage of the new laws: participate more frequently in municipal meetings, feel that the municipal government was becoming more transparent and responsive than the national norm, and believe that they could exercise effective social control over the municipal government. Eventually, it was hoped, these two elements would increase citizen satisfaction with the performance of municipal government and, by extension, with the democratic system of governance.

Control Variables

Before we compared the special DDPC sample and sample for the rest of Bolivia, we had to determine whether the DDPC sample differed demographically or socioeconomically from the rest of the country. Since the DDPC program focused heavily on rural areas and smaller cities and towns, it is likely that the sample we drew on to represent the areas that received the full DDPC package of inputs would be more rural, and thus poorer and less well educated than the national population. We found no significant differences between the national and DDPC samples in terms of gender or age, thus reducing concerns over selection bias. We did, however, find significant differences in urbanization, education, and income. The DDPC sample is more rural and less well educated and has a lower average income than the sample from the national population. We controlled for these factors by treating them as covariates in the analysis of variance that I describe here.

Results

As we compared the data from the DDPC municipalities to those for the nation as a whole, we looked especially at three issues: participation, in the form of attendance at meetings; willingness to make demands of the authorities; and sense of satisfaction after complaining. We found that the more people participated, the more they felt their municipality was responsive. By using appropriate statistical tests, we were also able to see how these factors interacted.

Bolivians living in the regions where the DDPC carried out its full program attended meetings at significantly higher levels (24.6%)

than those in the rest of the country (19.3%), representing a difference of 27 percent even after we controlled for urbanization, income,
and education. These results are meaningful from an international
perspective, as they approach the highest level reported in the Vanderbilt University Latin American Public Opinion Project database,
where no country has participation levels above 29 percent.

Because making demands of one's local government is a more active form of participation than attending meetings, we speculated
that it could tell us more about popular involvement. As was true
for participation at meetings, we found that a significantly higher
percentage of people in the DDPC areas (26.1%) were willing to
make demands compared to 20.5 percent nationwide. As with meeting attendance, this represents a difference of 27 percent between the
two groups. And again the DDPC areas came close to matching those
countries at the top of the Vanderbilt list.

We also looked at the satisfaction level among those who made
such demands of their municipality: were they happy with the response they got? We found that DDPC area residents who made demands were significantly more satisfied, at 48.6 percent, compared to
39.8 percent for those who made demands in the nationwide sample.
We interpret this as meaning that municipios included in the DDPC
program have learned how to respond to citizen demands far better
than other municipios in Bolivia. This clearly indicates the program's
efficacy. But merely living in a project area does not make people satisfied: those in the overall DDPC sample had virtually the same level
of general satisfaction with municipal government as those in the rest
of the country. The key is making a demand: those who both live in
DDPC areas and make demands on their system are more satisfied.

Next, how does meeting attendance interact with satisfaction with
municipal services? Those in the DDPC sample, at 44.6 percent, did
not seem to be significantly more satisfied than those in the national
sample, at 45.6 percent. The picture changed, however, when we selected out those who had attended a municipal meeting within the
past year. Meeting attendees who live in a DDPC area were more
satisfied with municipal services (49.3%) than attendees nationwide
(45.2%). We interpret this as meaning that when citizens live in a municipality that has undergone major reforms and have contact with
their municipal government in the form of attending a meeting, they
are more satisfied with the services they get. This finding echoes the
one reported above. It seems that either making a demand or attend-

ing a meeting will raise the satisfaction level of DDPC area residents more than it will for their non-DDPC fellow citizens.

Overall, we found that residents of DDPC areas were more satisfied with municipal services, and with treatment by municipal officials. They also see their municipalities as more responsive, especially if they have attended a meeting in the past year. In combination, then, these results show that the DDPC program is changing the way municipalities are doing business, making them more responsive to their "customers." Of course, the resources to satisfy demands remain very constrained in Bolivia, given the overall low level of national income, but the DDPC project has found a way to increase citizen participation and satisfaction.

One particular area concerns, us, however: the gender gap. Earlier studies by the Vanderbilt project have highlighted the gender gap in participation in Bolivia. Has this gap narrowed in the general public, and within the DDPC sample? In terms of attending municipal meetings, DDPC participation is higher for both men and women. But the gap remains quite wide in both samples: nationwide, 14 percent of women and 23 percent of men had attended a meeting, compared to 20 percent of women and 39 percent of men in DDPC areas. Female participation is 60 percent that of males in the national sample, but only 51 percent that of males in the DDPC areas. This suggests that the program must do far more to narrow the gender gap.

We found a similar pattern for making demands. Nationally, 17 percent of women and 25 percent of men had made a demand in the past year, compared to 17 percent of women and 28 percent of men in DDPC areas. The gap between males and females is large in both groups, but larger in the DDPC sample. In the national sample, females make 68 percent as many demands as males, but only 45 percent as many in DDPC areas. In other words, females in the DDPC program exhibit no more social capital than women in the rest of the nation, which suggests that virtually all of the program's impact has been on males. This is a disturbing finding, one that calls for a reexamination of the program's methods and the degree to which it is gender sensitive.

Beyond Bolivia: Social Capital in Latin America

The program to build social capital in Bolivia that I describe here cannot be studied easily elsewhere in the region because there are no comparable "before-and-after" studies. Therefore, we have little quantitative evidence to draw on to generalize about building social capital in Latin America. The General Accounting Office (GAO) report cited earlier states that little such evidence is available in the six countries it covers.[21] Moreover, the Bolivian project is quite new; the gains we have carefully measured and documented may or may not persist. In this context, I describe one historical case that shows the long-term impact of local government strengthening in building social capital.

This example is from Costa Rica, an especially interesting case. It is far poorer than advanced industrial nations or even more advanced Latin American nations like Argentina, but it is widely recognized as having the longest and deepest tradition of democratic governance of any nation in Latin America. Civil liberties, including freedom of the press, speech, and assembly, are widely respected and protected. For over fifty years, free and open elections have been the hallmark of Costa Rica's politics, with observers worldwide seeking to copy elements of an electoral system that faithfully guarantees against voting fraud and corruption. Human rights, so often brutally abused in other Central American nations, are carefully respected, and one rarely hears even allegations of their violation.

Many researchers have attempted to explain why Costa Rica is such a strong democracy. They point out that for over fifty years Costa Rica has not had a standing army,[22] that significant elite agreements emerged in the 1930s,[23] and that nineteenth-century liberalism and agricultural policies had an impact.[24] Lawrence Harrison traces Costa Rica's cultural roots back even further, to the regions of Spain from which the early Costa Rican immigrants were thought to have come.[25] Few studies, however, have looked explicitly at the long-term impact of local government. For example, Nickson refers to the importance of local government in nineteenth-century Costa Rica, but does not link it to the emergence of social capital.[26] Other detailed studies focus largely on developments in the second half of the twentieth century.[27]

What is less well known is that throughout the 1800s and early 1900s, local government in Costa Rica was de jure and de facto responsible for the health, education, and welfare of its citizens. Thus, while other countries in the region developed a strongly centralist tradition—in which central government rapidly took over local autonomy and responsibility—Costa Rica had a strong localist tradition throughout its formative period. As a result, citizens regularly sought out their local governments and had contact with them on a wide variety of issues. This tradition had been eroding as the state centralized education, health and, eventually, welfare functions, but the tradition of strong, responsive local governments had been well established by then, and continued to predominate, especially in rural areas where central government presence was more limited. Even as late as the 1970s most citizens in rural Costa Rica looked to strong local governments.[28] Sadly, by the late 1900s, local governments were on the decline and interest in them had dropped as citizens shifted their attention to the growing central government.

Several recent attempts to resuscitate local government, such as the direct election of mayors and the separation of municipal elections from national elections, have thus far not helped rekindle interest in local government. In the first mayoral election 77 percent of the registered voters failed to vote, compared with an average of 30 percent at the national level. Still the historical illustration sketched below seems to show, descriptively at least, that social capital can be constructed. Despite some erosion, municipal government still plays a very important role in the lives of many Costa Ricans. This is illustrated by the results of a recent national survey[29] in which citizens of four countries in Central America were asked, "Should more responsibility and funding be given to municipal government, or should we let the central government assume more municipal services?" Costa Rica topped the list, with 73 percent responding yes, ahead of Nicaragua (70%), Guatemala (58%), and El Salvador (52%).

My own experience as a Peace Corps volunteer in rural Costa Rica illustrates the importance and impact that local government can have in building social capital. Coto Brus, where my wife and I were assigned, had only a few years earlier been established as a stand-alone cantón, the Costa Rican equivalent of a county, with its own municipal government. Earlier it had been incorporated into Golfito Canton.[30] Before World War II this region had a tiny population, mostly indigenous people who had long migrated between Costa Rica and Panama, but the wartime construction of the Pan American Highway brought a significant population influx. By the early 1960s it had attracted a large enough population to form its own local government.

In the 1960s Coto Brus was remote and inaccessible by vehicle from the rest of Costa Rica during much of the rainy season, when even large four-wheel-drive trucks could not cross the rain-swollen rivers. No bridges existed then. The region had very few public services other than primary schools in the settled areas, and one high school in the county seat of San Vito de Java. Medical services were virtually nonexistent; there was not a single physician in a region with over twenty thousand residents. The only medical assistance came from British volunteer nurses who ran a maternity clinic in San Vito.

The isolation, poverty, and lack of public services that Coto Brus experienced in the 1960s and 1970s were typical of many Central American regions. But Costa Rica was different because of the local government's role. Local governments in Costa Rica were, and remain to this day, very poor in material resources. The overwhelming majority of public tax income flows to the central government in San José. In spite of this limitation, as soon as the municipal government in Coto Brus was founded it began solving problems. Very few roads were paved, and electricity was available only in the largest settlements, and then only sporadically. With no telephone service, all communication with the outside world occurred via telegrams, and public transportation was a feeder bus line to San Jose, using an aging U.S. school bus that ran only twice a day, and then only to the county seat and villages along the way.

In short, citizens needed almost everything, but almost no capital was available. The municipal government, constrained though it was by limited resources, served as a focal point for all civil society groups seeking to overcome local problems. When hamlets evolved into villages, people formed school committees and contacted the municipal government for materials to construct a schoolroom. Normally villagers donated both the land and the labor for such projects, but the local government contributed the roofing material and perhaps some cement for the floors. When parents sought to build a soccer field so that their children would have a place to play, they asked the municipal government to loan its only tractor to level the land. Countless small-scale projects were completed this way, in a partnership between village organizations and the local government.

Beyond providing resources for local projects, municipal government became a conduit to the central government for requests to improve county services. One good illustration of the local government's key role in Coto Brus occurred in the late 1960s. At that time USAID was promoting a program to provide medical services in remote rural areas. It granted jeeps to the Costa Rican government, which in turn provided a health team —physician, public health worker, and nurse—to offer rural medical services. Based in San Vito, the team traveled each day to the villages, providing basic medical attention and public health education.

The key social capital-building component of this medical project was that no community could receive medical attention until and unless it had organized a local community development committee which was responsible for finding a place for the doctor to examine people and for the educator to give her lectures. The committee also had to collect a small fee from each prospective patient, to purchase a *ficha* that entitled them to a place in the waiting line to see the doctor. The funds collected were not handed over to the doctor but were designated to be used in the village for community development purposes.

The results were impressive. Community welfare committees sprang up in even the most remote villages, and many citizens became deeply involved in them. As a result, local leaders emerged in these committees, which began to extend their reach beyond the narrow task of preparing for the health team's regular visits. Some villages built community centers or soccer fields. Within a few years, these committees had become the central focus of community development in many villages. At the same time, whenever a new community project was being attempted, people would invariably decide to seek assistance, even if only token, from the municipal government. An important dynamic developed around this interaction between civil society and local government, one that helped strengthen them both and build social capital within the village and the cantón.

One vignette will illustrate how central this interaction was to community life. In 1968 the Ministry of Health announced that it was inefficient for the doctor—and the entire team—to travel from village to village, so the mobile teams were to be dismantled and medical service would be concentrated in the county seat. Evaluated purely in terms of efficiency, this was a good decision: as the doctor's time was the scarcest resource, he should not spend it traveling to see patients. But the villagers of Coto Brus saw it as a major blow to their communities, making them less desirable places to live and less likely to attract other settlers, an important local goal in this sparsely settled region. And, without regular physician visits, the community welfare association would lose its raison d'etre: it could no longer collect fees for the privilege of seeing the doctor or have either the funding or the motivation to build a community center to host the visiting medical team. In short, the social capital that had been built via the mobile doctor arrangement was being threatened. But, as the ministry would soon learn, it would not be easy to eradicate it.

In response to the ministry's decision to eliminate the mobile medical service, the welfare committees, working with the municipal government of Coto Brus, began to organize a protest. The community radio station, run by the Franciscan priests assigned to the county, was used to send messages to the various village welfare committees. They, in turn, sent protest telegrams to the ministry, but also to their legislative deputies in the province of Puntarenas, urging a change in policy. When those efforts failed, the municipal government and the community leaders organized a protest, sealing off the only road connecting the county to the rest of Costa Rica and demanding that the minister visit the region to respond to the local plea to restore the mobile medical service. At that time, the other countries of Central America were all authoritarian regimes, and such actions would no doubt have been met with force; Costa Rica, however, had long-established traditions both of democracy and of using dialog rather than repression to respond to citizen demands. So the minister and his assistants agreed to fly to Coto Brus and meet the citizens.

In preparation for the minister's arrival, the county welfare committees, along with the municipal government, planned extensively and carefully. They not only organized the citizens to show up en masse in San Vito on the day of the visit; they also selected the most articulate local spokespersons to present their case. Their efforts paid off. On the day of the visit, the crowd was so large that the entire event had to be held outdoors. The officials listened to the presentations and, after several hours of dialog, agreed to restore the service. The communities shared an enormous feeling of triumph in the weeks that followed.

This story contains some important lessons. First, local government had historically been central in Costa Rica, so it provided a natural locus for organizing when coordinated action was needed. The residents were far more effective because they could present a united front to the minister. Second, the municipal government worked in concert with civil society organizations from the villages to meet the health care challenge, a way of operating that had become institutionalized in Coto Brus long before the mobile health unit crisis. Third, the community could resist and eventually triumph over central government power largely because it had built social capital by institutionalizing the welfare committees in each village. The committees were used to meeting and organizing and also to working with their municipal government to address public issues.

In conclusion, I believe both the mobile health unit program in Costa Rica and the DDPC program in Bolivia are good illustrations of public policies that helped build social capital. The survey data support the view that social capital can be increased, as we found the DDPC program had a significant impact on raising it. But we also found that a wide gender gap still exists in Bolivia, and has not been narrowed in the DDPC municipalities. The descriptive illustration from Costa Rica shows how good public policies, those that stress local participation, can help build the kind of unusually strong social capital that allowed poor people in remote villages to confront their central government and win.

Several implications for social capital research can be drawn from this research. Social capital is not merely a given, an inherent inalterable characteristic of a population. Programs can be designed to increase social capital, just as they can be designed to reduce it (consider the impact of Stalinist terror on social capital). Most development programs, however, focus almost exclusively on the dependent variable of economic growth, without considering growth in social capital as an important additional or even primary goal. Development practitioners must think carefully about these implications.

Notes

1. This is a revised version of a paper presented at the Culture Matters Conference, Tufts University, March 26–28, 2004. I thank Eduardo Gamarra, José Garzón, and Maggy Morales for helpful comments.
2. Lawrence E. Harrison and Samuel P. Huntington, *Culture Matters: How Values Shape Human Progress* (New York: Basic Books, 2002).
3. Robert D. Putnam, *Making Democracy Work: Civic Traditions in Modern Italy*. Princeton, NJ.: Princeton University Press, 1993.
4. Robert D. Putnam, *Democracies in Flux: The Evolution of Social Capital in Contemporary Society* (Oxford, New York: Oxford University Press, 2002), 9–12.
5. Edward Banfield, *The Moral Basis of a Backward Society* (Chicago: Free Press, 1958), 166.
6. Putnam, *Bowling Alone: The Collapse and Revival of American Community* (New York: Simon & Schuster, 2000); Putnam, "Tuning In, Tuning Out: The Strange Disappearance of Social Capital in America," *PS: Political Science and Politics* 28, no. 4 (1995): 664–83.

7. Martin Gilbert, *The Second World War:*

8. Anna J. Merritt and Richard L. Merritt. *Public Opinion in Occupied Germany: The OMGUS Surveys, 1945–49* (Urbana: University of Illinois Press, 1970); Merritt and Merritt, *Public Opinion in Semisovereign Germany: The HICOG Surveys, 1949–55* (Urbana: University of Illinois Press: Office of International Programs and Studies Office of West European Studies, 1980); Richard L. Merritt, *Democracy Imposed: U.S. Occupation Policy and the German Public, 1945–49* (New Haven, CT: Yale University Press, 1995).

9. Ronald Inglehart, *Culture Shift in Advanced Industrial Society* (Princeton, NJ: Princeton University Press, 1990).

10. Michael Lewis-Beck and Ross E. Burkhart, "Comparative Democracy: The Economic Development Thesis," *American Political Science Review* 88 (1994): 903–10.

11. Anirudh Krishna, *Active Social Capital: Tracing the Roots of Development and Democracy* (New York: Columbia University Press, 2002); Anirudh Krishna, Norman Thomas Uphoff, and Milton J. Esman, *Reasons for Hope: Instructive Experiences in Rural Development* (West Hartford, CT: Kumarian Press, 1997).

12. Partha Dasgupta and Ismail Serageldin, eds., *Social Capital: A Multifaceted Perspective* (Washington, D.C.: The World Bank, 2000); Bob Edwards and Michael W. Foley, "Social Capital, Civil Society, and Contemporary Democracy," *American Behavioral Scientist* 40 (1997); Jeffrey J. Mondak, "Psychological Approaches to Social Capital," Special issue, *Political Psychology* 19, no. 3 (1998).

13. Thomas Carothers, *In the Name of Democracy: U.S. Policy Toward Latin America in the Reagan Years* (Berkeley: University of California Press, 1991); Carothers, *Aiding Democracy Abroad: The Learning Curve* (Washington, D.C.: Carnegie Endowment for International Peace, 1999); Marina Ottaway and Thomas Carothers, *Funding Virtue: Civil Society Aid and Democracy Promotion* (Washington, D.C.: Carnegie Endowment for International Peace, 2000).

14. U.S. General Accounting Office, *Foreign Assistance: U.S. Democracy Programs in Six Latin American Countries Have Yielded Modest Results: Report to Congressional requesters* (Washington, D.C.: GAO, 2003).

15. Ibid., 86.

16. This paragraph and the next are based on Jon Hiskey and Mitchell A. Seligson. "Pitfalls of Power to the People: Decentralization, Local Government Performance, and System Support in Bolivia," *Studies in Comparative International Development* 37, no. 4 (2003): 64–88.

17. Rene Antonio Mayorga, "Bolivia's Silent Revolution," *Journal of Democracy* 8, no. 1 (1997): 142–56, 152–53; quote from 152–53 .

18. R. Andrew Nickson, *Local Government in Latin America* (Boulder, CO: Lynne Reinner Publishers, 1995).

19. Hiskey and Seligson; Mitchell A. Seligson, *La cultura política de la democracia boliviana, Así piensan los bolivianos, #60* (La Paz, Bolivia: Encuestas y Estudios, 1999); Seligson, "El reto de la tolerancia política en Bolivia." *Reto, Revista especializada de análisis político* 8, no. Mayo (2001): 5–15; Seligson, *La cultura política de la democracia en Bolivia: 2000* (La Paz, Bolivia: Universidad Católica

Boliviana, 2001); Seligson, *Auditoria de la democracia: Bolivia, 2002* (La Paz, Bolivia: Universidad Católica Boliviana, 2003).

20. Specifically, it operated in 17 out of the 132 municipalities from which the sample was drawn, affecting 404 of the 3,017 respondents in the 2002 study.

21. U.S. GAO, 2003.

22. Kirk S. Bowman, *Militarization, Democracy, and Development: The Perils of Praetorianism in Latin America* (University Park, PA: Pennsylvania State University Press, 2002).

23. Deborah J. Yashar, *Demanding Democracy: Reform and Reaction in Costa Rica and Guatemala, 1870s–1950s* (Stanford, CA: Stanford University Press, 1997).

24. James Mahoney, *The Legacies of Liberalism: Path Dependence and Political Regimes in Central America* (Baltimore: Johns Hopkins University Press, 2001).

25. Lawrence E. Harrison, *Underdevelopment Is a State of Mind: The Latin American Case* (Boston, MA: Center for International Affairs, Harvard University and University Press of America, 1985).

26. Nickson, 155.

27. Christopher E. Baker, Ronald Fernández, and Samuel Z. Stone, *El gobierno municipal en Costa Rica: Sus características y funciones* (San José, Costa Rica: Associated Colleges of the Midwest Central American Field Program and La Escuela de Ciencias Políticas, Universidad de Costa Rica, 1972); Oscar Marín, *Régimen municipal*, vol. 1(San José, Costa Rica: Universidad Estatal a Distancia (UNED), 1987).

28. John A. Booth, "Costa Rica: The Roots of Democratic Stability," in *Democracy in Developing Countries: Latin America*, eds. Larry Diamond, Juan Linz, and Seymour Martin Lipset (Boulder, CO: Lynne Rienner, 1989); John A. Booth, Miguel Mondol, and Alvaro C. Hernández, *Tipología de communidades* (San José: Comunidad-Acción Técnica, 1973).

29. Ricardo M. Córdova and Mitchell A. Seligson, *Cultura política, gobierno local y descentralización: I. Centroamérica* (San Salvador: FLACSO, 2001).

30. Marc Edelman and Mitchell A. Seligson, "Land Inequality: A Comparison of Census Data and Property Records in Twentieth-Century Southern Costa Rica," *Hispanic American Historical Review* 73, no. 3 (1994): 445–91.

Contributors

Luis Diego Herrera Amighetti is a Costa Rican psychiatrist specializing in children and adolescents. He has served as Chief of the Department of Psychology and Psychiatry at the National Children's Hospital in San José, Costa Rica, also as the Chief of the Department of Adolescents at the Gaebler Center for Children in Waltham, Massachusetts. He is President of the Paniamor Foundation for the Promotion of Children's Rights.

Steven E. Finkel is Professor and *Daniel Wallace* Chair in Political Science, University of Pittsburgh, and jointly from 2005-2008, Professor of Quantitative and Qualitative Methods at the Hertie School of Governance, Berlin, Germany. His research interests are in the areas of political participation, voting behavior, the development of democratic attitudes and values, and research methodology.

James W. Fox is a former chief economist for the Latin American region for USAID and former head of USAID's evaluation unit for economic growth activities. He has also worked as an economist for the State and Treasury Departments and the Senate Foreign Relations Committee.

Mariano Grondona is the host of the weekly public affairs television program *Hora Clave* in Argentina. He is Professor of Government at the National University of Buenos Aires and a columnist for the newspaper *La Nación*. A contributor to *Culture Matters*, his most recent book is *The Cultural Conditions of Economic Development*.

Nikolas Gvosdev, Senior Fellow in Strategic Studies at the Nixon Center and editor of *The National Interest*, is a specialist in Eurasian and Balkan affairs with emphasis on how the historical, cultural, and religious inheritance of the region affects current developments. His most recent book is *Receding Shadow of the Prophet: The Rise and Fall of Radical Political Islam*.

Lawrence Harrison (co-editor) is a senior research fellow and adjunct lecturer at the Fletcher School at Tufts University. He is the author of "Underdevelopment Is a State of Mind," "Who Prospers?," and "The Pan-American Dream," and is co-editor, with Samuel Huntington, of "Culture Matters." Between 1965 and 1981, he directed five USAID missions in Latin America.

Robert W. Hefner is Professor of Anthropology and Associate Director of the Institute on Culture, Religion and World Affairs at Boston University. The author of many books on Islam, he recently completed a multi-country, collaborative project on civil democratic Islam and is completing a book, *Muslim Politics and the Quandary of Modernity*.

Samuel Huntington is Albert J. Weatherhead III University Professor at Harvard University, where he was also director of the Center for International Affairs for eleven years and Chairman of the Academy for International and Area Studies for eight years.. He is the author, most recently, of *Who Are We? The Challenges to America's National Identity* and is the co-editor, with Lawrence Harrison, of *Culture Matters*.

Jerome Kagan (co-editor) is the Daniel and Amy Starch Research Professor of Psychology at Harvard University, where his work has focused on child development. He has long been interested in the contribution of cultural variation to the character and personality of children. His most recent book, with Nancy Snidman, is *The Long Shadow of Temperament*.

Sharon L. Kagan is the Virginia and Leonard Marx Professor of Early Childhood and Family Policy at Teachers College, Columbia University, where she is Associate Dean for Policy. She is also Professor Adjunct at Yale University's Child Study Center. She is past president of the National Association for the Education of Young Children. Her most recent book is *Children, Families, and Government: Preparing for the Twenty-First Century*.

Richard D. Lamm is Co-Director of the Institute for Public Policy Studies of the University of Denver. He was Governor of Colorado from 1975 to 1987 and also served in the Colorado legislature. His most recent book is *The Brave New World of Health Care*.

Jim Lederman is a Canadian journalist who resides in Israel. He is the author of *Battle Lines: The American Media and the Intifada*.

Thomas Lickona is a developmental psychologist and professor of education at the State University of New York at Cortland, where he directs the Center for the 4th and 5th Rs (http://www.cortland.edu/character). A member of the board of directors of the Character Education Partnership, he is the author, most recently, of the book *Character Matters* and, with Matthew Davidson, the report *Smart & Good High Schools*.

Amy E. Lowenstein is pursuing a joint Ph.D. in developmental psychology and master's in public policy at Georgetown University. Her main research interests are early childhood development and programs and policies to support low-income children and families.

David Martin is an English sociologist and theologian. He is the author of *Tongues of Fire: The Explosion of Protestantism in Latin America* and *Pentecostalism: The World Their Parish*, and most recently, *On Secularization*.

Pratap Bhanu Mehta is President, Center for Policy Research, Delhi. He has also been a visiting professor at Harvard. His most recent book is *The Burden of Democracy*.

Carlos Alberto Montaner is the most widely read columnist in the Spanish language. A contributor to *Culture Matters*, he is the co-author, with Plinio Apuleyo Mendoza and Álvaro Vargas Llosa, of *Guide to the Perfect Latin American Idiot*. His most recent books are *Latin America and the West* and *La Libertad y Sus Enemigos*.

Richard G. Niemi is Don Alonzo Watson Professor of Political Science at the University of Rochester, where he has also served as Department Chair, Associate Dean, and Interim Dean. Among his fields of concentration are political socialization and civic education. He is recently the co-author, with Jane Junn, of *Civic Education—What Makes Students Learn*.

Michael Novak holds the George Frederick Jewett Chair in Religion and Public Policy at the American Enterprise Institute. He has written 29 books on the philosophy and theology of culture, among them *The Catholic Ethic and the Spirit of Capitalism* and *The Spirit of Democratic Capitalism*.

Georges Prevelakis is Professor of Human and Regional Geography at the Sorbonne. He is the author, among others, of *Athènes: Urbanisme, Culture et Politique* (L'Harmattan), *Géopolitique de la Grèce* (Complexe) and *Les Balkans, cultures et géopolitique* (Nathan). He has edited *The Networks of Diasporas* (L'Harmattan).

Fernando Reimers is the Ford Foundation Professor of International Education at the Harvard Graduate School of Education, where he directs the Global Education Office and the International Education Policy Program. He specializes in the study of the contributions of education to social and political development and is currently studying the contributions of civic education to democratic citizenship. He is the author of several books and articles and is an advisor to governments, universities and development agencies.

Reese Schonfeld was the founding president and chief executive officer of the Cable News Network. He also founded the Television Food Network.

He is the author of *Me and Ted Against the World; The Unauthorized Story of the Founding of CNN*.

Mitchell A. Seligson is Centennial Professor of Political Science and Fellow, Center for the Americas, at Vanderbilt University. He is the Director of the Latin American Public Opinion Project (LAPOP) and is co-editor, with John Booth, of *Elections and Democracy in Central America, Revisited*.

Bassam Tibi is Professor of International Relations at the University of Göttingen, Germany. He is also the A.D. White Professor-at-Large at Cornell University. He has been Visiting Professor at Bilkent University in Ankara, Turkey, the University of California (Berkeley), Harvard University, and the National University of Singapore. Among his recent publications are *The Challenge of Fundamentalism: Political Islam and the New World Disorder* and *Islam between Culture and Politics*, both recently republished in updated editions.

Eleonora Villegas-Reimers is Associate Professor of Human Development and Acting Dean of the Division of Child and Family Studies at Wheelock College. She specializes in moral and civic education. She has published a book and several articles on civic education and teacher professional development and consults for a number of development organizations on issues of teacher professional development, curriculum development and civic education.

Robert P. Weller is Professor of Anthropology and Research Associate at the Institute on Culture, Religion, and World Affairs at Boston University. He works on the relations among culture, society, and political change in China and Taiwan. His most recent books include *Civil Life, Globalization, and Political Change in Asia: Organizing Between Family and State* (editor), and *Discovering Nature: Globalization and Environmental Culture in China and Taiwan*.

Christal Whelan is an Earhart fellow at the Institute on Culture, Religion, and World Affairs at Boston University. She specializes in Japanese religion, cultural change, and visual anthropology. Her book *The Beginning of Heaven and Earth*,and companion film *Otaiya* deal with the cultural history of Christianity in Japan. Her current research is on Buddhist-oriented new religious movements.

Index